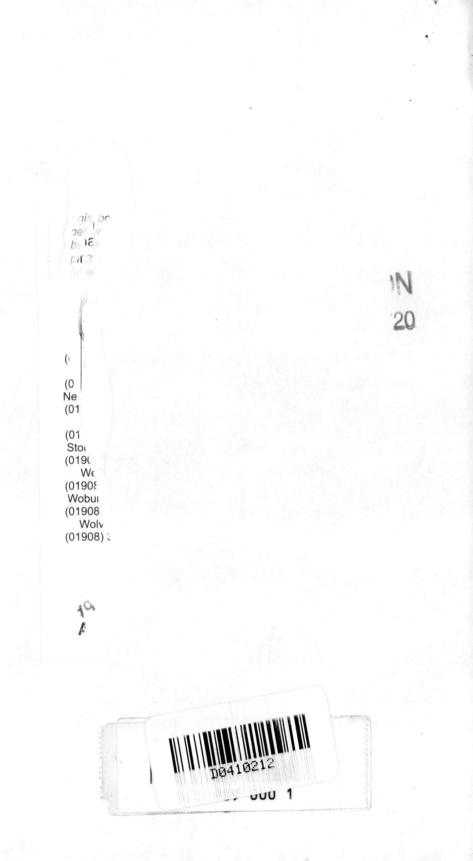

GERONIMO

The Man, His Time, His Place

ANGIE DEBO

PIMLICO

PIMLICO
An imprint of Random House
20 Vauxhall Bridge Road, London SW1V 2SA

Random House Australia (Pty) Ltd
20 Alfred Street, Milsons Point Sydney
New South Wales 2061, Australia

Random House New Zealand Ltd
18 Poland Road, Glenfield
Auckland 10, New Zealand

Random House South Africa (Pty) Ltd
PO Box 337, Bergvlei, South Africa

Random House UK Ltd Reg. No. 954009

First published in the United States of America by the
University of Oklahoma Press 1976
First published in Great Britain by Pimlico 1993

5 7 9 10 8 6

Printed and bound in Great Britain by
Clays Ltd, St Ives plc

ISBN 0–7126–5899–8

To the memory of *MARGUERITE HOWLAND*

whose competence with documents was equaled

by her ready helpfulness

The earliest known photograph of Geronimo, at about age sixty, taken by A. Frank Randall at San Carlos in the spring of 1884. "You never have caught me shooting." Courtesy National Archives and Records Service, Washington, D.C.

PREFACE TO THE FOURTH PRINTING

In my original preface I expressed regret over blank spaces in the record of Geronimo's life. Now I am glad to state that one small blank space has been filled by Dan L. Thrapp (ed.) in *Dateline Fort Bowie*, published by the University of Oklahoma Press in 1979, presenting the newspaper dispatches sent by the able Charles Fletcher Lummis from the Apache war zone in 1886. It gives me great satisfaction to rewrite my page 245 to include this detail regarding a previously unknown son of Geronimo.

ANGIE DEBO

Marshall, Oklahoma
August 17, 1986

PREFACE TO THE FIRST PRINTING

All my life I had heard about Geronimo. As a small child in northern Kansas I was told of the blanket of human scalps he was wearing when he was "captured" after his last "outbreak." (Scalping was not an Apache practice.) We children even gave his name to an especially cross-grained turkey gobbler. In Oklahoma, where I finished my growing up, incidents of his life as a prisoner of war at Fort Sill and of his appearance at various celebrations constantly filled the news. As late as 1916, seven years after his death, the Geronimo Motor Company was incorporated with great fanfare in nearby Enid. (The automobiles and trucks it turned out might have made the big time, except for a fire that burned down the plant and wiped out the investors.)

The supposedly factual story behind this sensationalism was that Geronimo, at the head of four or five hundred hostiles, had been captured after a successful military campaign and that the band had thereafter been held in captivity. The true account had appeared in a few specialized books, but these had not changed the accepted version. I myself assumed it was true and incorporated it briefly in two of my books, allowing it to stand in one I edited, repeating it in one I wrote.

Finally, in the 1950's I began to explore the life of Geronimo. After some reading and preliminary research in Apache history, I interviewed elderly members of the band who had known him and remembered the hiding, the raids, and the violent deaths of a hunted people's life-way. But my study was interrupted by other duties and other writing tasks, and my notes were filed away. Now in these last years I have returned to the subject, reinforcing these earlier insights by additional research.

The historical background at this time has been accurately established. Frank C. Lockwood's comprehensive account was published in 1938; Ralph Hedrick Ogle, after the most intensive research ever made in the field, published his study of government policy toward the related Apache tribes in 1940; and more recently Dan L. Thrapp's scholarly books and articles have presented special phases of the subject. All this work furnished the setting of Geronimo's life. There was no need for me to duplicate the research that has produced these findings. My task was to explore Geronimo's individual experiences, his motivations, his personal life and character. And he did not live in solitude against this background. He had a family and family ties extending to distant relatives. He had comrades and followers, friends and enemies, and among his associates were chiefs and leaders well known in Southwestern history. As far as possible I have presented all these people as actual human beings with their distinctive characteristics.

I wish I could believe that I have written a definitive biography. But too many times I have had to resort to "probably," "It seems that—," and "It is fairly certain that—," conjectures based on the best evidence obtainable, but still conjectures. Some of these may be wrong, but I doubt that evidence will ever be uncovered to establish all the facts beyond question. These Apaches were wild people, as wild as the deer that fleeted across the rocks and hid in the thickets of their mountains. The hunter might glimpse them, but that was all.

Still, even these glimpses of Geronimo are revealing. At a few conferences his words were recorded. Incidents of his life and impressions of his personality lingered in the memory of aged Apaches. Finally, during the twenty-three years of his captivity, his outward actions and his responses, though often misinterpreted, were observed and chronicled. He even dictated his reminiscences to a sympathetic listener. Thus he is seen not as a lay figure or a Wild West character but as an individual.

His energy, his determination, and his sturdy independence can be perceived as traits that distinguished him throughout his life. His strong economic sense is apparent, whether in supporting his family and providing for his band by hunting and raiding as a wild Apache or in setting up a profitable business of selling souvenirs and banking the money he acquired in his later days as a Wild West exhibit. He had an active intellectual curiosity and a capacity for original thought. He was hard-headed and practical-minded, ruthless in competition, stern and unbending in his judgments, unrelenting in his hatreds. But he was kind and affectionate to his family and constant in his friendships, and his love for his mountain homeland was the unchanging sentiment of his life. He and his white adversaries never arrived at the same definition of truth: to them he was simply a liar whose word could never be trusted; but if one can follow his reasoning, he is seen as a man of essential integrity. He was deeply religious, and when a promise was made with oath and ceremony—mere poetic trimmings to the white man—he kept his pledge. His suspicions were real, the instinctive distrust of any wild creature. And they were even well founded, based on acts of treachery he had seen. A lesser man could not have written his name so boldly on the history of the Southwest.

I have had much help in uncovering his story. When I visited the Mescalero Reservation in 1957 to interview Geronimo's son and granddaughter, I stopped at the nearby trading post of Mrs. Eve Ball. She willingly shared with me, a stranger, her unique knowledge of Apache personalities, and she has continued this assistance to the present day. Mr. Benedict Jozhe, long-time tribal chairman of the Fort Sill Apaches, has answered my questions and several times made the long drive to my home with Moses Loco, grandson of Chief Loco, to furnish needed information. In 1959 he brought the aged James Kaywaykla, thus giving me an opportunity to hear the story of the only surviving witness of the disaster that ended the career of the great Victorio.

Mr. John A. Shapard, Jr., of the Bureau of Indian Affairs, whose wife is a great-granddaughter of Chief Loco, has freely given me assistance and advice valuable beyond calculation. The late Colonel Ora E. Musgrove, who learned the true story of Geronimo's surrender when he was a young enlisted man at Fort Sill and followed it in his maturity by extensive research in the National Archives, made me a free gift of his findings. Mr. Dan L. Thrapp took much trouble going into his files to answer my questions. Dr. Berlin Basil Chapman, author of many scholarly books and articles about Oklahoma Indian history, loaned me his notes and some documents he had acquired during his research on a related project.

Mr. John M. Brown, stationed at the Naval Aviation Schools Command at Pensacola, put me on the track of material regarding Geronimo's imprisonment at Fort Pickens. Miss Jean Pitts of the Historic Pensacola Preservation Board conducted me on a tour of the area, and Mr. George D. Berndt, historian of the Gulf Islands National Seashore of the National Park Service, gave me specific identification of the sites and furnished me with contemporary newspaper accounts regarding the prisoners. Mr. Luis R. Arana, staff historian of the National Park Service's national monuments at Saint Augustine, first called my attention to Lenna Geronimo's meeting with her father at Saint Louis.

There are also the ever dependable archivists and curators in whose collections I worked. The late Marguerite Howland and her assistants in the documents department of the Oklahoma State University library guided me through many days of exploration. I could not have untangled Geronimo's family and tribal relationships except for the help of Mr. Gillett Griswold, curator of the

Army Artillery and Missile Center Museum at Fort Sill. Miss Jane F. Smith and Mr. Robert M. Kvasnicka of the National Archives and Records Service helped me solve many puzzling problems. And always I had the assistance of Mr. Jack D. Haley of the Western History Collections and Mrs. Alice Timmons of the Phillips Collection of the University of Oklahoma Library and of Mrs. Rella Looney, since retired, and of her successor, Mrs. Martha R. Blaine, Indian archivists of the Oklahoma Historical Society. Finally, in this age of electrostatic copies I am indebted to the archivists of collections I have not visited for making material available through the mail. I am also under obligation to owners of copyrights, who have given me permission to quote from published sources.

Most of all, I am grateful to my friends and neighbors, Hugh and Ramona O'Neill, who furnished transportation to places beyond my present driving radius. And when I employed Ramona to type the final copy of my manuscript, she carried on the work with a perceptive understanding that amounted to collaboration.

ANGIE DEBO

Marshall, Oklahoma

CONTENTS

ILLUSTRATIONS

MAPS

GERONIMO

INTRODUCTION

On September 5, 1886, the great news from Fort Bowie, Arizona, flashed across the nation. The day before, in Skeleton Canyon near the Mexican border, the Apache warrior Geronimo and the chief Naiche, son of the great Cochise, had surrendered to Brigadier General Nelson A. Miles. With them were sixteen warriors, fourteen women, and six children.

"APACHE WAR ENDED!" "GERONIMO CAPTURED!" Never were so many headlines owed by so many to so few. From the time these Indians had broken away, five thousand men of the regular army, a network of heliograph stations flashing mirror messages from mountain to mountain, and false promises at the end were required to effect their "capture." The paper work flowed in rivers of telegrams from army posts to Washington; since then it has burgeoned into many books. The word *apache* has become the designation of underworld characters in Paris, and during World War II American paratroopers shouted the name "Geronimo" as they stepped off into the sky. What manner of man was this Geronimo?

He was a red-handed murderer who "ought to be hung," screamed the western newspapers. He was cruel, selfish, treacher-

ous, and mendacious, with no virtues but courage and determination, said the best of the army men and Indian agents who tried to
cope with him. He was "only a medicine man," was hated by all
but a small faction of his own people, and owed his reputation to
sensational advertising, said the scholars and historians.[1]

In Geronimo's old age when he was a prisoner of war at Fort
Sill, Oklahoma Territory, in 1905, Stephen Melvil Barrett, superintendent of schools in nearby Lawton, tried to get permission
from the military to let him tell *his* side of the story. But Lieutenant
George A. Purington, the army officer in charge, bluntly refused—
the old Apache deserved to be hanged, he said, instead of being
spoiled by so much attention from civilians—and Barrett had to
appeal directly to President Theodore Roosevelt. A series of communications through channels (five pages of fine print, ten endorsements, six weeks of time) finally gave the required permission
with the condition that the manuscript be submitted to the army
chief of staff before publication.[2]

Barrett then secured the services of Geronimo's "nephew"
(actually his second cousin) Asa Daklugie, who had been trained
in the famous Indian school at Carlisle, Pennsylvania, and the
three worked together on the story. When it was finished, Barrett
first submitted it to the president, who read it and pronounced it
"very interesting" but suggested that Barrett "disclaim responsibility where the reputation of an individual is assailed." The army
chief of staff also found it "interesting," but indicated "a number
of passages which, from the departmental point of view, are decidedly objectionable." Barrett refused to back down on one
incident—the event that drove Cochise to hostility—but tempered
the other passages by footnotes stating that this was Geronimo's
opinion, not his.[3]

As a factual account the book suffers from the old warrior's

---

[1] See, for example, Frederick Webb Hodge, *Handbook of American Indians North
of Mexico*, s.v. "Geronimo," and Ross Santee, *Apache Land*, p. 176.

[2] S[tephen] M[elvil] Barrett, *Geronimo's Story of His Life*, pp. xiii–xx.

[3] *Ibid.*, pp. xxiii–xxvii, 115n. 2, 116n. 3, 138n. 3, 139n. 1, 147n. 7, 179n. 1, 181n. 4.
By a curious slip of the pen Barrett attributed the Cochise incident to Mangas Coloradas.

4

failing memory, especially in chronology, and also, perhaps, from his natural tendency to magnify his youthful exploits. Some imaginative editing is also apparent; one conspicuous example is the inclusion of scalping, which was not an Apache practice. But the book's spirit is unmistakably Indian, and it is the first account of the Apache wars from the inside looking out.

Two other such first-hand narratives have appeared in recent years. Jason Betzinez, whose mother was Geronimo's first cousin, had been out with the hostiles during 1882–83. During the long imprisonment following 1886 he had been sent to Carlisle, where he accepted its teachings and became a white man in all but blood. In his old age he wrote down his reminiscences in his careful penmanship, and Wilbur Sturtevant Nye, formerly stationed at Fort Sill, contributed some maps and helped with the organization. The resulting book, *I Fought with Geronimo,* was published in 1959. James Kaywaykla, who lived until 1963, retained his vivid childhood memory of flights and battles: "Until I was ten years old I did not know that people died except by violence." Eve Ball of Ruidoso, New Mexico, who has been closely associated with the band since 1949, took his story down in shorthand and published it in 1970 under the title *In the Days of Victorio.* It gives an intimate story of a closely knit group of individuals in their relations with each other and their reaction to tragedy. Like Geronimo's reminiscences, these two accounts reveal some confusion regarding details and sequence of events, but they show what it meant to be a hunted Apache.[4]

Other insights were gained from the studies of Morris Edward Opler, the ethnologist, who recorded the life-way of the people as

4 Incidentally, both these books refute Barrett's accounts of scalping. See *I Fought with Geronimo,* especially p. 86, where Betzinez says he never knew Geronimo to bring in a scalp, and *In the Days of Victorio,* pp. 13, 46, where Kaywaykla states, "I have seen hundreds of people killed but not one scalped." Scalping, however, did occur on rare occasions. In an interview (Apache, Okla., Jan. 26, 1955) Jason Betzinez told me he had heard of one incident when a woman took a Mexican's scalp in revenge for the killing of her son. And Asa Daklugie told Eve Ball that his band, the wildest of all Apaches, did occasionally take one scalp for use in the victory dance, but the man who performed the act had to undergo a four-day purification ceremony, during which he remained in isolation (Eve Ball to Angie Debo, December 20, 1960).

he worked among them during the 1930's. His informants not only described the primitive culture, but in some cases gave their recollections of events occurring during the wars. Finally, an immensely important unpublished compilation of the biographies of these Apaches has been made by Gillett Griswold, the civilian director of the United States Army Artillery and Missile Center Museum at Fort Sill. With the assistance of the aged survivors and their descendants and the examination of army records, he has collected statistical information—births, deaths, marriages, family relationships, and other data—as far as it can be determined, regarding 728 members of the band during the wars and the years of captivity.[5]

Thus, it is now possible to view the life of Geronimo in its native setting.

[5] This collection is hereafter cited as Griswold, "The Fort Sill Apaches."

CHAPTER 1

GOYAHKLA, THE CHILD

Geronimo placed his birth date in June, 1829, but he was almost certainly born a few years earlier. As the old warrior tried to organize the sequence of events, Barrett apparently attempted to arrange them according to the white man's calendar. Now, by matching his experiences with known historical dates, it is possible to construct a more accurate chronology. Jason Betzinez said that his mother and Geronimo grew up together as children. Her birth date can be fixed at approximately 1823 by her memory of Halley's Comet and "The Night the Stars Fell." It can also be established by contemporary evidence that Geronimo had a wife and three children in 1850 or earlier.[1]

To his birthplace Geronimo gave the Apache name of No-doyon Canyon and located it near the headwaters of the Gila River in what is now southeastern Arizona, then a part of Mexico.[2] At other times he stated simply that he was born in Arizona. But by modern nomenclature the Gila does not head in Arizona, for of the branches that unite near the present-day town of Clifton to form the main stream, one now carries the name into New Mexico.

1 See Betzinez, *I Fought with Geronimo*, pp. 14, 15, 18; *infra*, pp. 34–35.
2 Barrett, *Geronimo's Story of His Life*, p. 17. See also Betzinez, *op. cit.*, p. 14.

Daklugie accordingly moved the location upstream to the three forks of the river near the present Cliff Dwellings National Monument in southwestern New Mexico.[3] Geronimo could not have been mistaken about the site. Apaches regarded their birthplace with special attachment. The child was always told of the location, and whenever in its roving the family happened by, he was rolled on the ground there to the four directions. This observance took place throughout the growing years, and even adults sometimes rolled in this manner when returning to the spot where they were born.[4] But Geronimo or his editor could have been mistaken about the state. Even that seems improbable, however, for the Apaches soon became aware of such political subdivisions in dodging military forces. One can only say that Geronimo was born in the early 1820's near the upper Gila in the mountains crossed by the present state boundary, probably on the Arizona side near the present Clifton.

His father was Taklishim ("The Gray One"), the son of Chief Mahko of the Bedonkohe Apache tribe. His mother, although a full-blood Apache, had the Spanish name Juana.[5] Possibly she had been captured and enslaved by the Spanish. For centuries there had been a pattern of Apache raids on Spanish settlements and Spanish capture and enslavement and occasional escape of Apache women and children. As an adult, Geronimo spoke Spanish, which he might have acquired from his mother or which he might have picked up from his contacts with the Mexicans.

Geronimo never saw his grandfather, Mahko, who died when Taklishim was a young warrior. The chief had two wives, and after his death the principal one, whose name is not now remembered, continued to exert a strong influence within the tribe. She was the mother of five of his six children who grew to adulthood. One of these was Taklishim and another was a daughter whose daughter, Nah-thle-tla, became the mother of Jason Betzinez. Mahko's other

---

3 Eve Ball interview, July 26, 1971.
4 Morris Edward Opler, *An Apache Life-Way*, p. 10.
5 Griswold, "The Fort Sill Apaches," s.v. "Geronimo."

wife had one daughter, the mother of a notable woman named Ishton, the mother of Asa Daklugie.[6]

The grandchildren and great-grandchildren of Mahko were taught to revere his memory. Geronimo grew up listening to his father's tales of the chief's great size, strength, and sagacity, and of his wars with the Mexicans, at that time under Spanish rule.[7] Betzinez described another aspect of Mahko's life. He was peace loving and generous, raising much corn and owning many horses, which he traded with the Mexicans, and storing corn and dried beef and venison in caves, which he shared with the needy of his tribe.[8] Probably both characterizations are true. The Bedonkohes were relatively undisturbed in their mountain fastness during Mahko's lifetime, and at such periods trading relations might be established with the Mexicans, but there were traditions of old wars and raids. The young Geronimo thrilled to the stories of these exploits, while the gentle Betzinez listened to his mother's accounts of the chief's kindness and peaceable pursuits. Daklugie struck a fair balance. As he heard it, Mahko, although a great warrior, fought only when attacked, but there was one story of an epic battle with another Apache tribe.[9]

It is impossible to untangle completely the tribal divisions of the Apaches with whom the Bedonkohes were associated. Ethnologists have evaded the problem by classifying them all as Chiricahuas,[10] and this generalization has often been used in official records. In

6 *Ibid.*, s.v. "Mahko." I have accepted the statements of Geronimo, Betzinez, and Daklugie and the genealogy worked out by Griswold. It should be noted, however, that some of the older Fort Sill Apaches believe that Geronimo was born in Old Mexico. They remember that he spoke with an accent different from that of their own people. It is possibly significant that Barrett identified Mahko as chief of the Nednai Apaches, who in later historic times lived in Old Mexico. See *Geronimo's Story of His Life*, p. 35n. But even if this is correct, it seems well established that in Mahko's time the band lived in the area designated as Geronimo's birthplace.

7 Barrett, *op. cit.*, p. 15.

8 Betzinez, *op. cit.*, pp. 2, 14–15, 39.

9 Eve Ball to Angie Debo, June 25, 1973.

10 One earnest attempt has been made by a student of ethnology to distinguish these tribes and their component bands. See the thesis by William Grosvenor Pollard III, "Structure and Stress: Social Change among the Fort Sill Apaches and Their Ancestors, 1870–1960," M.A. thesis, University of Oklahoma, Norman, 1965. Pollard is convinced that the Bedonkohes were identical with the Mogollon Apaches sometimes mentioned in official reports and by travelers.

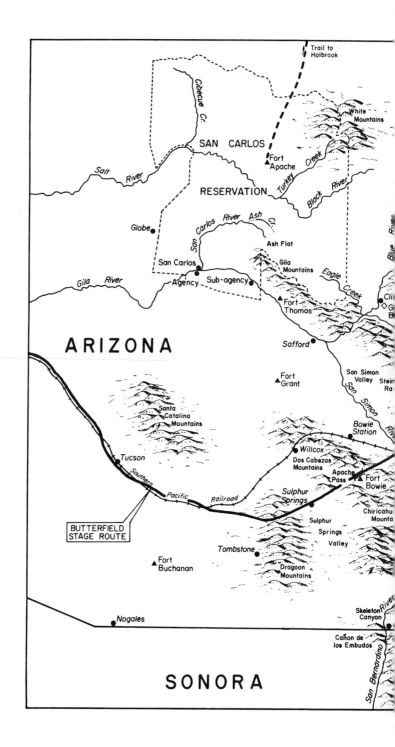

Geronimo's home range

earlier times all who lived in the jumbled mountains of south-eastern Arizona and southwestern New Mexico had been called the Gilas, with no differentiation of tribes and bands.[11] But to Geronimo's people the Bedonkohe tribe was a well-defined unit, though apparently there was no successor to Mahko. Its members always kept their tribal affiliation distinct but made temporary connections with related tribes and intermarried freely with them so that only nine or ten full-blood Bedonkohes were living when Geronimo dictated his memoirs in 1905.

At least four tribes can be recognized among the Bedonkohes' close associates. East of them in southwestern New Mexico were two that often merged. The Mimbrenos (sometimes called the Coppermines) lived in the Santa Rita and Silver City region and the mountains to the southwest. The Warm Springs (Ojo Caliente) tribe, known as the Chihenne or Red People because of a band of red clay drawn across their faces, ranged between the Mimbrenos and the Rio Grande, but their heartland centered around the pleasant bathing pool and the clear stream that issued from San Mateo Peak on the canyon of the Alamosa River above the Mexican town of Cañada Alamosa, later known as Monticello.[12] South of the Bedonkohes in the fastnesses of the Chiricahua, Dos Cabezas, and Dragoon mountains were the Chokonens or true Chiricahuas, and south of the Chiricahuas in the Sierra Madre of Old Mexico were the Nednais, wildest of all Apaches.

These related tribes had occasional contacts with other Apaches of New Mexico and Arizona. East of the Rio Grande were the Mescaleros, with whom the Mimbrenos and Warm Springs people were acquainted. To the north were the Coyotero and White Mountain Apaches, with whom their relations were never very close and sometimes hostile; and joining the White Mountains and Coyoteros were the Navahos, a kindred people no longer regarded

[11] Hereafter, to avoid repetition of the expressions "what is now Arizona" or "the present New Mexico" I shall follow the present state boundaries in identifying locations.

[12] Dan L. Thrapp treats the Mimbrenos and the Warm Springs tribe as one tribe, which he designates as the Mimbres (Mimbrenos); see *Victorio and the Mimbres Apaches*. It is true that the two bands were always closely associated and eventually became united, but I have followed Apache custom in distinguishing them.

as Apaches, with whom they sometimes visited and traded. To their west were many tribes of Apaches, some of whom they knew but whom they regarded as inferiors. Their name for them was Bi-ni-e-dine, meaning "Brainless People." One of these with whom Government policy was to bring them into unhappy proximity was a small nomadic tribe known as the San Carlos, which lived in the area between the Gila and San Carlos rivers.[13]

Into this setting Geronimo was born. He was given the name Goyahkla, with the generally accepted meaning "One Who Yawns," why or under what circumstances is not known. One can guess that yawning was the habit of a sleepy baby, but no characterization could have been more inappropriate to the energetic spirit that marked his personality. Some aged Fort Sill Apaches suggest a name slightly different in pronunciation, with the meaning "intelligent, shrewd, clever." As an adult, he became known by the Mexicans as Geronimo, and this name was adopted even by his own people. The Spanish-Apache feud had been inherited by the Mexicans after their independence; and according to one story, in a battle with them he was fighting like a fiend, charging out repeatedly from cover, killing an enemy with every sally and returning with the dead man's rifle. Each time he emerged, the Mexicans began to cry out in terror, "Cuidado! Watch out! Geronimo!" (Perhaps this was as close as they could come to the choking sounds that composed his name, or perhaps they were calling on St. Jerome.) The Apaches took it up as their battle cry, and Goyahkla became Geronimo.[14]

Of his babyhood, he said, "I rolled on the dirt floor of my father's tepee, hung in my tsoch (Apache name for cradle) at my mother's back, or suspended from the bough of a tree."[15] Although one always thinks of the slight, brush-covered wickiup as the Apache dwelling, his mention of a tipi is probably correct. George Catlin

---

[13] Barrett, *op. cit.*, pp. 12–15; Ball, *In the Days of Victorio*, pp. xiv, 29–30; Betzinez, *op. cit.*, pp. 2, 4, 9, 14–16, 43; Griswold, *op. cit.*, s.v. "Mahko," and "Coloradas, Mangus"; Eve Ball to Angie Debo, June 26, 1973.

[14] Woodworth Clum, *Apache Agent*, p. 29. Geronimo's own account of this battle is in Barrett, *op. cit.*, pp. 51–54.

[15] Barrett, *op. cit.*, p. 10.

An Apache woman and child. "I hung in my tsoch at my mother's back, or suspended from the bough of a tree." Courtesy Mrs. Eve Ball.

An Apache village in the region of Geronimo's birthplace, painted by George Catlin about 1856. "As a child I rolled on the dirt floor of my father's tepee." Courtesy American Museum of Natural History, New York City.

painted tipis when he visited the Gila Apaches about 1856.[16] According to Daklugie, it was only when his people were closely pursued during the wars that they adopted the wickiup, which could be easily set up and abandoned. He said they used deer and antelope hides with the hair left on for the tipi covering. It was placed hair side out and so cut with the natural direction of the animal's coat that the hair lay downward—a device that must have added much to the waterproofing of the lodge.[17] Even at the

[16] *Episodes from Life among the Indians and Last Rambles*, plates 138, 139, and 141. These paintings also show skin-covered A-frame structures interspersed among the tipis, but the type apparently did not survive. Catlin gave the date 1855, but he found war raging against the Apaches in New Mexico and the war did not begin until 1856. Catlin was notoriously inaccurate about dates.

[17] Eve Ball interview, July 26, 1971. See also Ball, *op. cit.*, p. 17.

present time a tipi is ceremonially used in the girls' puberty rites, a strong indication of its former importance in Apache culture. But the wickiup also has a long history. In its best form in time of peace it was a substantial, comfortable, dome-shaped dwelling built on a framework of poles.[18] Even in its brush and straw form the Apaches stretched a skin covering over it when their location was relatively permanent.

In spite of their precarious existence, these Indians had a rich and complex ceremonial life. Geronimo's parents certainly must have employed a medicine man or perhaps a midwife to fashion his *tsoch* with prayers and ritual, placing amulets on it to guard him against early death. When he was four days old, or possibly a little later, he must have been placed in it with much ceremony in the presence of relatives and neighbors, after which all participated in a feast. The Apache child did not actually stay in his cradle until his neck became strong enough to support his head when he was a month or more old. Then he spent most of his time there until he became old enough to crawl around the camp. When the age of walking approached, perhaps after he was already walking, came the ceremony of putting on his first moccasins, again with a medicine man in charge, which was celebrated by songs, prayers, and dancing and feasting for relatives and friends. In the spring, usually the spring following this ritual, came the ceremonial cutting of his hair. All this Geronimo inherited as the child of a people who cherished their children.[19]

As soon as he was old enough to understand, he also inherited Apache traditions. His father related exploits of war and hunting and events of recent history. His mother told him the origin myths of his people. She taught him to pray to Usen, a nebulous and remote Supreme Being often called Life Giver. But "We never prayed against any other person, . . . we ourselves took vengeance. We were taught that Usen does not care for the petty quarrels of men." She told him the legends and exploits of supernatural beings,

18 Oliver La Farge, *A Pictorial History of the American Indians*, p. 137. See also Opler, *op. cit.*, pp. 385–86.
19 Opler, *op. cit.*, pp. 10–18.

especially of White Painted Woman and Child of the Water, all connected with the emergence of the Apaches as sentient persons, and of the beneficent Mountain Spirits, who lived in hidden caverns and whose ceremonials and customs the Apaches duplicated. He must have learned also of witches, men and women whose malevolent Power brought calamity to individuals or the group.[20]

. His group comprised an extended family. He said he had three brothers and four sisters, but as far as is known only one of these was an actual sister, all the others being cousins. There was no word in the Apache language to distinguish cousins from siblings.[21] Indeed, a family of eight children was almost unheard of among the Apaches. Ideally, they spaced their children about four years apart by refraining from sexual intercourse until the previous baby was weaned at about age three (the same prohibition was observed to protect the unborn child during pregnancy). The man, of course, could have sex relations with another wife, but only the leaders could afford plural marriages. In the words of Opler's informants, he might "sneak around" and find "easy women," but throughout Apache society undue preoccupation with sex was regarded as a weakness.[22] It is apparent, however, from the Fort Sill birth records, that this family planning was frequently disregarded. Still, whether from conscious spacing or from the deaths of children weaned before they were ready for adult food, Apache families were small. Thus, it is typical that Mahko, with two wives, had, as far as is known, only eight grandchildren. All seven of these "brothers" and "sisters" of Geronimo can be traced, and among his "nephews," who in their turn were sometimes called his "brothers," were his most trusted warriors.[23] Throughout his life his family ties were very close.

"With my brothers and sisters I played about my father's home,"

20 *Ibid.*, pp. 196–200, 242–54, 267–72, 306–309; Morris Edward Opler, "Mountain Spirits of the Chiricahua Apache," *The Masterkey*, Vol. XX, No. 4 (July, 1946); Barrett, *op. cit.*, pp. 3–11, 18–19; Ball, *op. cit.*, pp. 68–70.
21 Opler, *An Apache Life-Way*, pp. 58–62.
22 *Ibid.*, pp. 5–6, 13, 141–42, 415; Ball, *op. cit.*, p. 8.
23 Griswold, *op. cit.*, s.v. "Mahko."

he said. This home was a cluster of dwellings. Usually when a man married he became a member of his wife's family, obligated to contribute to their economic support, but—since he was usually young with few possessions—he was entitled to use their property in time of need. The lodges of the daughters were built close to the parental abode, and intercourse was restricted only by the inconvenient courtesy of mother-in-law avoidance, which the Apaches, like many other Indians, were careful to observe. Sons, since they joined the families of their wives, might live at some distance, although their children shared in the affection of the paternal grandparents. But circumstances sometimes altered this residence pattern, and it seems fairly certain that all the sons and daughters of Mahko lived in close proximity.[24] Their children grew up in a time of peace, a condition rare in Apache history. As Geronimo recalled it, "During my minority we had never seen a missionary or a priest. We had never seen a white man. Thus quietly lived the Be-don-ko-he Apaches."[25]

In this undisturbed security the small boys and girls played together, imitating adult occupations, engaging in war games, hiding among the rocks and pines, making toys with great ingenuity or using those made by their parents, and hunting wild fruit and nuts. Geronimo seemed to remember with the greatest pleasure their excursions through the surrounding country.[26] Then, in accordance with Apache prudery, the sexes began to separate at the age of five or six, and the fathers began to train the boys, and the women the girls, in their specialized occupations.

The little girls began to assist in carrying water, bringing in wood, gathering and storing wild food plants, and cooking the meals; and they learned to dress the skins and make clothing, build the lodges, and weave the baskets. They were trained to be strong and vigorous, rising early and practicing the swift and tireless running upon which their lives might depend. The boys helped care for the horses, practiced much with the bow and arrow, and

---

[24] Opler, *An Apache Life-Way*, pp. 18–19, 24–25, 55–58, 62–65, 163–69; Barrett, *op. cit.*, pp. 19–20; Betzinez, *op. cit.*, pp. 14–15.

[25] Barrett, *op. cit.*, p. 34.

[26] *Ibid.*, pp. 19–20, 22, 25; Opler, *An Apache Life-Way*, pp. 45–49.

learned to make weapons and tools. They were subjected to even more rigorous physical training than the girls, rising before sunrise and bathing in the creek even when ice had formed on the surface. They were required to race up the side of the mountain carrying water in their mouths and were made to spit it out on their return to show that they had breathed properly through the nose. They shot small game as soon as they could handle their weapons; by the time they were fourteen they hunted with the men. They were systematically trained for war—shooting, dodging, hiding, tracking, learning to map the terrain and find their way back to camp.[27]

The Apaches had many contests in which these skills were used —arrow shooting, racing, wrestling—and there were also games of chance. There were other games with complex rules in which teams played against each other. The most important game was the hoop-and-pole game, in which each contestant tried to slide a pole toward a rolling hoop so that when the hoop toppled over it would rest on the end of his pole. This game was sacred, having been handed down from the animals before the emergence of the human race. The hoop and poles were prepared with great ceremony, and only men could play; women were not even permitted to come near the ground. All these games, whether of skill or chance, were accompanied by excited betting, for the Apaches were inveterate gamblers.

They also spent much time in feasting and dancing. Some of these social gatherings were connected with a ceremonial or religious observance such as the womanhood rites for a girl attaining puberty. More were purely recreational. "I was always glad when the dances and the feasts were announced," Geronimo remembered. "So were all the other young people." Men and women danced as partners in these social dances, which thus furnished some discreet courting opportunities in a society where the girls were closely supervised in their relations with youths of the opposite sex.[28] Geronimo did not refer to the fierce intensity of the war

27 Opler, *An Apache Life-Way*, pp. 49–51, 65–76; Betzinez, *op. cit.*, pp. 30, 55.
28 Barrett, *op. cit.*, pp. 26–28; Opler, *An Apache Life-Way*, pp. 339–40, 444–48, 454–56.

The hoop-and-pole game. Note the rolling hoop and the two contestants with their poles. The photograph may have been taken at the San Carlos Reservation in 1884. *This game was sacred, having been handed down from the animals before the emergence of the human race.* Courtesy Smithsonian Institution, National Anthropological Archives, Washington, D.C.

dance preparatory to a war party or a raid. Apparently he had few such experiences in his sheltered youth. He would have many thereafter.

These isolated Apaches were a happy and self-sufficient people. They loved the wild jumble of canyons and mountains that was their homeland. They knew the use of every plant, the habits of every animal, the storing of every item of food—perfect adaptation to environment, by white man's reasoning. They viewed it differently. As Geronimo explained it in his old age: "For each tribe of men Usen created, He also made a home. In the land created for any particular tribe He placed whatever would be best for the welfare of that tribe.

"When Usen created the Apaches He also created their homes in the West. He gave to them such grain, fruits, and game as they needed to eat. To restore their health when disease attacked them He made many different herbs to grow. . . . He gave them a pleasant climate and all they needed for clothing and shelter was at hand."[29]

But the Apaches did not depend entirely on natural products. Whenever they were relatively undisturbed they practiced an extensive agriculture. As soon as Geronimo and his "brothers" and "sisters" were old enough, they helped their parents in the fields. In his tribe both men and women joined in the work. Each family had its own plot—his family had about two acres—in an extensive field in a valley. They broke the ground with crude wooden implements and planted their crops, the corn in rows, the beans among the corn, and the pumpkins in irregular order over the plot. They cultivated them as needed, and the whole group shared the burden of protecting the field against their ponies and the deer and other wild animals. In the autumn they gathered the pumpkins and beans in the large woven baskets made by the women, tied the ears of corn together by the husks, and carried the harvest on the backs of their ponies to their dwellings, where the corn was shelled. Then the entire store was placed in the caves frequently found in their mountains. They laid down a layer of rock and oak branches on the cave floor, put the containers with the food on top of that, and closed the entrance with rocks sealed with mud.[30]

[29] Barrett, *op. cit.*, p. 15.
[30] *Ibid.*, pp. 20–21; Opler, *An Apache Life-Way*, pp. 371–75. Geronimo included melons among the crops grown, but possibly his memory tricked him, recalling the melons he raised later at Fort Sill. For the extent of Apache planting, see Secretary of the Interior, *Annual Report*, 1869, pp. 102–103, in which an army officer describes a field of at least one hundred acres of fine corn that had been planted and tended with

The Apaches also made from their corn a fermented drink known as *tizwin*, prepared by the women with the help of the children. They may have learned the technique from the Indians in Old Mexico or from the Spanish-speaking Mexicans. First they soaked the corn overnight in water. They dug a long trench and lined it with grass, placed the soaked corn in the trench, and covered it with another layer of grass. Sometimes they covered the whole with earth or with a blanket. After sprinkling the corn with water morning and evening for ten days, during which it sprouted, they took it out, ground it with their grinding stones (mano and metate), and then boiled it for four or five hours. Finally, they strained off the liquid and set it aside. After about twenty-four hours, when it stopped bubbling, it was ready to drink.[31]

It had a relatively low alcoholic content, but the Apaches were efficient drinkers; after a preliminary fast they achieved a calculated debauch that threw the whole band into disorder. There were quarrels, fights, even killings, as all the latent violence of a primitive people came to the surface. Certainly such disturbances must have occurred in Geronimo's childhood, but he said only that the beverage "was very highly prized by the Indians." In this sheltered time, secure in the affection of an extended family, he may have been relatively untouched by these occurrences. It is also possible that during this undisturbed period in the history of his people some moderation was observed in the use of the intoxicant.

Thus, the child Geronimo labored in the fields with his parents and no doubt helped in storing the food and making the *tizwin*.

---

the crudest of implements and irrigated by *acequias* constructed with almost unbelievable industry. The Apaches concerned were of the White Mountain tribe. For the techniques of constructing the *acequias*, see Grenville Goodwin, "Experiences of an Indian Scout," *Arizona Historical Review*, Vol. VII, No. 1 (part 1, Jan., 1936), pp. 32–33. This narrative by an old Apache has recently been published in Keith H. Basso (ed.), *Western Apache Raiding and Warfare: From the Notes of Grenville Goodwin*, pp. 93–185, from the field notes left by Goodwin at the time of his death, but I have used his own published version except where his notes give additional information.

31 Barrett, *op. cit.*, p. 22; Opler, *An Apache Life-Way*, pp. 369–70, 436.

Also, he began to hunt with the men—at the early age of eight or ten, he thought, looking back—but to him "this was never work." On the prairies that surrounded their mountains they found herds of deer, antelope, elk, and buffalo, which furnished much of their food supply. The buffalo were not plentiful, and the hunters had to travel some distance to find them. There is one record of a successful hunt northeast of Albuquerque.[32] The Apaches chased the big animals on horseback, riding close and killing them with arrows or spears. Their skins were used for tipi coverings and bedding. Geronimo said that it required more skill to hunt deer than any other animal. The hunters had to approach from downwind; sometimes if the animals were grazing in the open they had to spend many hours crawling long distances on the ground, keeping a weed or a bush before them to hide their approach. Deerskin, with the hair removed and tanned into softness by the women, was used to make their clothing. In the mountains were many eagles, which were hunted for their feathers. "It required great skill to steal upon an eagle," said Geronimo, "for besides having sharp eyes, he is wise and never stops at any place where he does not have a good view of the surrounding country." Fish abounded in the mountain streams, but although small boys sometimes threw stones at them or shot at them for practice with their bows and arrows, the Apaches had a strong taboo against eating them. "Usen did not intend snakes, frogs, or fishes to be eaten," said Geronimo.[33]

An equal revulsion existed against eating the bear, which, in a way not entirely clear, was supposed to be a sort of ancestor of the people. Or, as some Apaches said, a bear was like a person, could walk erect like a person, and might be the reincarnation of some evil individual. Grizzlies and black and brown bears were numerous in the mountains, and instances of ferocious attacks by them occurred often in Apache experience. The Indians defended them-

32 Opler, *An Apache Life-Way*, p. 327. Jason Betzinez, who belonged to the Warm Springs tribe, remembered a hunting trip on the High Plains beyond the Pecos River; see Betzinez, *op. cit.*, pp. 33–35. But it is doubtful that the Bedonkohes traveled as far east as that.
33 Barrett, *op. cit.*, pp. 31–34.

23

selves in these encounters, but if they were forced to kill the bear they let the carcass lie without eating any part of it.[34]

Geronimo came close to one such experience when in his early childhood he accompanied the women on a berry gathering expedition. One woman became separated from the others, and as she made her way on her pony through the thick undergrowth and pine trees with her small dog following, a grizzly bear rose in her path and attacked the pony. She jumped off, and the pony escaped. The bear then attacked her. She tried to fight him off with the long knife every Apache carried, and the dog distracted his attention by snapping at his heels. Finally he struck her over the head, tearing off almost the whole scalp. She fell but did not lose consciousness. As she lay on the ground, she struck him four good thrusts with her knife, and he left her. She bound back her scalp as best she could, then became so deathly sick she had to lie down. That night the pony came in with its loaded baskets. The Indians went out to hunt her but did not find her until the second day. They carried her home, and with the herbs and prayers of the medicine man she recovered.[35]

The Apaches, in fact, were very successful in treating wounds, for the Power of the medicine man (or woman), expressed through special songs and incantations, was reinforced by skillful treatment and a knowledge of the healing properties of native plants.[36] As Geronimo saw it, "The Indians knew what herbs to use for medi-

[34] Betzinez, *op. cit.*, pp. 32–33; John Russell Bartlett, *Personal Narratives of Explorations and Incidents in Texas, New Mexico, California, Sonora, and Chihuahua Connected with the United States and Mexican Boundary Commission during the Years 1850, '51, '52, and '53*, I, p. 321; Ball, op. cit., pp. 55–56. Once Mrs. Ball unwittingly served bear to Kaywaykla when in his old age he was a guest in her home. When he discovered what he was eating, his eyes became sharp points of fury, and he stalked out of the house. The next morning, his anger gone, he apologized. "I've been a member of the Reformed Church for sixty years," he explained, "but I've been an Apache much longer than that." Barrett apparently misquoted Geronimo as saying that bears were good for food and valuable for their skin. It is possible, however, that some of the western Apache tribes did not observe this taboo against bear meat. See, for example, Basso, *Western Apache Raiding and Warfare*, p. 187.

[35] Barrett, *op. cit.*, pp. 22–24.

[36] For an example of the healing of a badly shattered arm that the army surgeon wanted to amputate, see Britton Davis, *The Truth about Geronimo*, p. 168; for the practice of a woman with healing Power see Ball, *op. cit.*, pp. 16, 169–70.

cine, how to prepare them, and how to give the medicine. This they had been taught by Usen from the beginning. . . . In gathering the herbs, in preparing them, and in administering the medicine, as much faith was held in prayer as in the actual effect of the medicine." And he went on to say that some of the Indians were skilled in cutting out bullets and arrowheads from wounded warriors and that he himself had done much of that.[37]

The Apaches were also attacked at times by cougars, but they had no taboo against hunting the big cats. During his lifetime Geronimo killed several of them with arrows and one with a spear. The men carried them home on their horses, ate the meat, and used the skins. They valued the hide for making quivers for their arrows. "These were very pretty and very durable," said Geronimo.[38]

When Geronimo was still a young boy, a party of Nednai Apaches who had relatives in the band came up from Mexico to visit them. Among them was a youth named Juh,[39] the son of a chief or prominent leader. He was a stockily built boy who spoke with a stutter, strong-willed and at that age somewhat of a bully. When the Bedonkohe girls went into the woods to gather acorns, he, with some followers, would wait until they had completed their task and then snatch their filled baskets. Among the victims was Geronimo's favorite "sister," his cousin Ishton. One can perhaps recognize the tendency of a half-grown boy to make life miserable for a girl he admires (cf. Whittier, "the snowball's compliments."), but Mahko's widow did not make this allowance. She told Geronimo and some of his friends to waylay Juh and his companions and give them a good whipping. The one who told the story failed to follow up on the outcome, but knowing Apache obedience to elders, one can be sure that the matriarch's orders were carried out.

Later, after Juh had grown up and established himself as a war leader among the Nednais, he returned and married Ishton. Fol-

[37] Barrett, *op. cit.*, pp. 23–24.
[38] *Ibid.*, pp. 33–34.
[39] The explosive Apache syllable is pronounced more nearly like Ho or Who, and it is often spelled Whoa or Hoo.

lowing Apache custom, he became a member of her family, and he and Geronimo formed a friendship that was to endure throughout their lives—Juh "was as a brother to me," said Geronimo in his old age, looking back. But customs varied with circumstances, and after living for some time among the Bedonkohes, Juh took his wife and went back to join his people in the Sierra Madre.[40]

Some time after Juh's departure, Geronimo's father died, following a long illness. The relatives and friends dressed him in his best clothes, painted his face, wrapped a rich blanket around him, placed him on his favorite horse, loaded up all his belongings, and with crying and wailing bore him to a cave in the mountain. There they placed the body on the floor, with his possessions beside him, and sealed the entrance with rocks coated with mud so that it would be hidden. Only the close friends who performed an Apache burial knew the location, and they avoided the place thereafter. Even the name of the deceased was not spoken,[41] though strangely enough this taboo did not apply to Spanish nicknames.

Geronimo was not yet grown, but this was the end of his childhood.

[40] Betzinez, *op. cit.*, p. 15; Ball, *op. cit.*, pp. 123–26; Griswold, *op. cit.*, s.v. "Juh"; Barrett, *op. cit.*, p. 101. Pollard states that among the Mimbrenos and Warm Springs Apaches, as distinguished from the Chiricahuas, a married couple joined the husband's family after the birth of the first child, but he cites no authority, and his assumption that the same custom was observed among the Bedonkohes is not convincing. If he is correct, however, such a practice may explain the residence patterns of Geronimo and his associates; see Pollard, "Structure and Stress," p. 42.

[41] Barrett, *op. cit.*, p. 36; Betzinez, *op. cit.*, pp. 8n., 16; Opler, *An Apache Life-Way*, pp. 235–37, 472–76. In the account of Juh's visits and the death of Geronimo's father I have followed the order of events given by Betzinez and accepted by present-day Apaches. Barrett has Geronimo say that he was "a small child" when his father died, an obvious error in translation. He was a well-grown youth, old enough to assume the support of his mother.

CHAPTER 2

ADULT RESPONSIBILITIES

Juana never remarried after Taklishim's death, and young Geronimo assumed her support. Apparently by this time his sister, Nahdos-te, had married. (Her husband was a prominent Warm Springs leader named Nana, who was to figure largely in Apache history.) In their grief and loneliness Juana and Geronimo decided to visit Juh and Ishton and other relatives among the Nednais. It was a difficult journey, for they were unfamiliar with the terrain and the location of the water holes. More baffling was the absence of trails or any sign of camps and places where horses had been tethered. They were soon to understand that these wild Indians had learned to obliterate their tracks, conceal their camps, and keep their horses at a distance. But they finally reached Juh's stronghold in the Sierra Madre and were warmly welcomed by his people.[1]

Up to this time Geronimo had apparently not experienced the hostility between the Apaches and the Mexicans, but he had certainly been told of it. It went far back in Southwestern history. The Spanish conquistadores, who had reduced the settled Indians to

---

[1] Barrett, *Geronimo's Story of His Life*, pp. 36–37; Betzinez, *I Fought with Geronimo*, p. 16.

vassalage, had sent out slave-catching expeditions against the ranging Apaches. The Apaches retaliated, and the Spaniards incited the other tribes against them.[2] When the Comanches arrived in the Southwest, the Spaniards enlisted them also. Thus, the Apaches were driven into the mountains, and raiding the settled communities became a way of life for them, an economic enterprise as legitimate in their culture as gathering berries or hunting deer; and first the Spanish and then, after achieving independence, the Mexican government responded by systematic attempts to exterminate them by paying bounties for their scalps.[3]

This pattern had existed so long that even historians believed that the Apaches had always been a predatory race. And long experience had taught them all the tricks of survival. They knew the location of every water hole and hidden canyon. Men, women, and children could travel with incredible speed and secrecy, striking their enemies here today, a hundred miles away on the other side of the mountains tomorrow. If they had horses, they rode; if the going became too rough, they killed and ate their mounts and continued on foot. If attacked, they could scatter and fade into the surrounding rocks, traveling separately in order to leave no trail and collecting again in some predetermined place.[4] Incidents growing out of this age-old pattern formed the immediate background of Geronimo's career as a warrior and raider.

In 1835 the Mexican state of Sonora passed a law offering one hundred pesos (a peso was roughly equivalent to a dollar) for every scalp of an Apache warrior. Two years later the state of Chihuahua set a scale of one hundred pesos for a warrior's scalp, fifty for a woman's, and twenty-five for a child's. These offers even

---

2 These facts, as revealed in Spanish archives, have been presented by Jack D. Forbes in *Apache, Navaho, and Spaniard*. See especially pp. 24, 28, 120–21, 160–61, 207–208, 244–45, 281–85.

3 See Alfred Barnaby Thomas, *Forgotten Frontiers: A Study of the Spanish Indian Policy of Don Juan Bautista de Anza, Governor of New Mexico, 1777–1787*, especially pp. 187–94, 216–20, 253, 257–91, 312–38, for Spanish attempts to incite Comanches and Navahos against the Apaches and the payment of bounties for Apache scalps, ears, and heads.

4 Betzinez, *op. cit.*, pp. 6, 65.

attracted roving Americans who had wandered into Mexican territory, and they, too, took up the business of scalp-hunting.[5] Among these was one James Johnson, and his biggest haul was made in 1837 from the Mimbrenos.

In the heart of that tribe's territory were valuable copper deposits. (They are still being worked and may even have been worked in prehistoric times by Indians.) In 1804 a Mexican capitalist began extensive operations there. He brought in workmen; built a settlement, Santa Rita del Cobra (now Santa Rita), with a triangular fort and fifty or more adobe houses; and operated mule trains going out with packloads of ore to the city of Chihuahua and bringing back supplies. Some gold was also produced in the area—not in any spectacular quantity but enough to add to the profit from the copper mines. All the time he maintained an uneasy peace with the Mimbrenos.

Johnson had been operating a trading post in Sonora, and the Mimbreno chief, Juan José Compa, believed him to be his friend. Then Johnson came to Santa Rita with an accomplice and some relatively innocent mule buyers from Missouri, whom he had tricked into accompanying him. He laid out a generous supply of pinole and invited the Indians to help themselves. As they were eating, he fired into the crowd with a concealed blunderbuss (or perhaps a six-pounder) while his companion made sure of the chief. The surviving Indians counterattacked, killing some of the Missourians, but the archconspirators escaped. Estimates of the scalps they took vary from about twenty to four hundred, in either case a profitable day's hunting.

According to one story, the enraged Indians annihilated the mule train coming in with supplies and killed all the people in the settlement. Another account says that they overpowered the supply train, taking everything except one mule for each man to ride back to Mexico, and at the same time ensured the evacuation of the settlers by warning them that no more supplies would be permitted

5 Dan L. Thrapp, *The Conquest of Apacheria*, pp. 8–9 and notes.

to reach them. It is certain that the mines and the settlement were abandoned in 1838.[6]

As far as is known, the Santa Rita massacre and its aftermath did not involve the Bedonkohes. Probably they knew of it, since they were closely related to the Mimbrenos. And Geronimo was certainly involved in the Apache-Mexican hostility that followed. When as a youth he joined the Nednais, he must have gone out with Juh on raids of Mexican ranches and pack trains, killing the men and carrying off the horses and loads of freight, for he said that he was admitted to the council of warriors at the precocious age of seventeen,[7] and this admission was granted only after rigorous training and apprenticeship.

First the youth was taught the rules of survival. Have the women pound enough meat and fat for a week's food, and take along a supply of water. Cross open flats by night, and reach a mountain and hide in the brush by day. Locate water holes by climbing to a high place and looking for green spots; but do not go to them by day, only at night. Do not sleep under a tree—that is the first place where an Indian, a Mexican, or an animal will look. Find a place in the open under a bush or grass, but where you can reach cover quickly. If you become lost and want to call for help, make a fire and send up a smoke signal, but put it out and run away to a place where you can watch and see if anyone comes.

After the youth had mastered these techniques, he might volunteer to join a hostile expedition. As an apprentice warrior, he conformed to certain ceremonies and was known as Child of the Water. "War is a solemn religious matter," said Geronimo. The older men watched out for him, but he and his fellow apprentices were required to perform all the work about the camp—caring for the horses, getting the water and wood, doing the cooking, serving on guard duty. If he showed courage and dependability on four

[6] *Ibid.*, pp. 10–12; Ball, *In the Days of Victorio*, p. 46; John Carey Cremony, *Life among the Apaches*, pp. 30–32; Frank C. Lockwood, *The Apache Indians*, pp. 67–79; Bartlett, *Personal Narratives*, I, pp. 322–23.

[7] Barrett, *op. cit.*, pp. 37–38. Geronimo, of course, could only guess his approximate age.

such expeditions (the Apaches, like other Indians, regarded four as a sacred number) he was accepted as a warrior, a man among men.[8]

Perhaps the greatest joy that Geronimo felt in thus attaining his majority was the privilege of marrying a slender, delicate girl of the Nednai tribe named Alope.[9] The two had long been in love. In spite of the barriers that Apache custom interposed, youths of the opposite sex were aware of each other's preferences, and their feelings were usually considered in the marriage arrangements made by their families. The proper formality was for the parents or other representatives of the young man to call on the parents of the girl to make the agreement and the economic settlement while he waited outside the lodge and she sat sedately within behind her mother, with neither permitted to speak.[10]

But according to Geronimo, he made the arrangements himself. It was the accepted practice for a mature man to carry on the negotiations, and even as a youth Geronimo showed an independent spirit. Perhaps he felt that he had carried enough responsibility to be on his own. By his account, "as soon as the council granted me these privileges [of manhood] I went to see her father concerning our marriage." He asked "many ponies for her. I made no reply, but in a few days appeared before his [lodge] with the herd of ponies and took with me Alope. This was all the marriage ceremony necessary in our tribe."[11] In his reminiscences he did not find it relevant to explain how he acquired the horses or how many Mexicans he had to kill in obtaining them.

It is evident that he soon left the Nednais and returned with his wife and his mother to his native mountains. Betzinez, who was not born until 1860, believed that he remained with Juh, but his own account clearly indicates that he established his home with his

---

8 *Ibid.*, pp. 187–90; Opler, *An Apache Life-Way*, pp. 134–39.

9 This is the name given in Barrett, *op. cit.*, p. 38, and according to Eve Ball it was used by Asa Daklugie (Ball interview, July 26, 1971). Its liquid syllables have none of the harsh consonants that usually characterize Apache names, but the name, Gee-esh-kizn, given in Griswold, "The Fort Sill Apaches," s.v. "Geronimo," seems to be a variant spelling of the name of Geronimo's second wife.

10 Opler, *op. cit.*, pp. 77–81, 142–48; Betzinez, *op. cit.*, p. 18.

11 Barrett, *op. cit.*, p. 38.

Bedonkohe kindred.[12] As he described his domestic arrangements: "Not far from my mother's tepee I had made for us a new home. The tepee was made of buffalo hides and in it were many bear robes [sic], lion [that is, cougar] hides, and other trophies of the chase, as well as my spears, bows, and arrows. Alope had made many decorations of beads and drawn work on buckskin, which she placed in our tepee. She also drew many pictures on the walls of our home. She was a good wife, but she was never strong. We followed the traditions of our fathers and were happy. Three children came to us—children that played, loitered, and worked as I had done."[13]

Meanwhile, in 1846 war broke out between the United States and Mexico. Apparently Geronimo was not affected by it in his remote mountains, but his Mimbreno relatives learned of it and heartily approved. The historian will remember that in the early summer of that year Brigadier General Stephen Watts Kearny set out from Fort Leavenworth, near Independence, Missouri, to take New Mexico and California. He occupied Santa Fe and then traveled south. On the Rio Grande near Valverde before he turned southwest he met his first Apaches. They came to his camp in a friendly spirit and furnished him with four young warriors as guides, and he made an appointment to meet their leaders near the copper mines. When he reached that place, he found it deserted, with adobe houses falling into ruins and ten or fifteen shafts of the unworked mines. He continued on west to Mangas Creek, a tributary of the Gila heading between the Big and Little Burro Mountains.

There, on October 20, he met the Mimbrenos. Their leader was Mangas Coloradas (Roan Shirt, Red Sleeves), a chief of immense physical stature and corresponding courage and ability whose influence extended to many of the Apache tribes of the area. His people were dressed in motley garb, mainly Mexican, an indication of their success in raiding. They were mounted on good

---

12 *Ibid.*, pp. 43, 46–48; Betzinez, *op. cit.*, pp. 16–17.
13 Barrett, *op. cit.*, pp. 38–39.

horses, and the soldiers noted their superb horsemanship, even the children being accustomed to riding from infancy. One of the chiefs—probably Mangas—offered to help the Americans if they would invade Chihuahua, Sonora, and Durango. He said the Mimbrenos hated the Mexicans and would kill them all, but any Americans could pass safely through their country. Kearny continued west to California, but later Colonel Alexander W. Doniphan passed through on his way to join Zachary Taylor at Monterrey, and he received—and declined—the same offer. The Americans' accounts of these contacts show their disdain for the Apaches. Even so, friendly relations were established.[14]

But although the Apaches approved of the war, they were less approving of the peace that ended it. The Treaty of Guadelupe Hidalgo, ratified in 1848, which conveyed the Spanish Southwest to the United States, contained a pledge that the American government would restrain the Indians in its newly acquired territory from raiding in Mexico and would repatriate any captives they might take on such raids.[15] The next year an Indian agent was sent to Santa Fe to establish relations with these tribes, and in 1850 Congress established a rudimentary government for a Territory of New Mexico, which included the present New Mexico, Arizona, and southern Colorado. The Mexicans, of course, were left to cope with the Nednais in the Sierra Madre.

Following the peace, a joint commission was appointed to run the new international boundary, with John Russell Bartlett to head the American commission and General Pedro Garcia Condé to head the Mexican. John Carey Cremony, a young Boston newspaperman who spoke fluent Spanish, was employed as Bartlett's interpreter, and Colonel Lewis S. Craig was in command of his military escort. The joint commission set up the initial monument with appropriate ceremonies on the Rio Grande near El Paso on April 24, 1851. Bartlett had decided to use the Santa Rita copper mines as his headquarters while the survey worked west. He had the

14 Thrapp, *Victorio*, pp. 20–21; Lockwood, *op. cit.*, pp. 75–79.
15 William M. Malloy, *Treaties, Conventions, International Acts, Protocols and Agreements between the United States of America and Other Powers*, pp. 1112–13.

triangular fort repaired for the use of the military and the crumbling adobe houses made livable for the officers of the commission.

He reached the place himself in early May and soon set off to northern Mexico for supplies, passing through the state of Chihuahua to Fronteras in Sonora and finally reaching Arispe on the Sonora River. He was a careful observer, and as he traveled through this Mexican frontier region he noted the devastation wrought by the Apaches—towns empty of inhabitants and a vacant countryside with dilapidated houses and abandoned fields and orchards.[16] At Fronteras Bartlett was told of an event that was the greatest personal tragedy of Geronimo's life and the dominant influence of his future career. The story came straight from General Carrasco, who commanded the frontier troops of Sonora.

The state of Chihuahua had decided to try peace with the Apaches. It invited them to trade in the towns, even furnishing them rations. Such trade had frequently taken place between the Indians and Mexican settlements with which they had established amicable relations. They exchanged animal hides and furs and other wild products for brightly colored cloth, knives, ornaments, and other articles. Often they raided one Mexican settlement and traded the plunder with another that was willing to connive in their depredations. Now they had a market in Chihuahua for the horses and mules they took in Sonora. But "lately"—this word fixes the date at 1850 or possibly a little earlier—Carrasco disregarded the state boundary and came suddenly upon a band of Apaches trading at Janos, killed about twenty-five, and captured about fifty or sixty women and children, whom he took into the interior and distributed as slaves. The military commander of Chihuahua was greatly incensed at this invasion, but when he reported it to the central government, it supported Carrasco.[17]

Geronimo and Betzinez later told the story from the Apache side. Betzinez fixed the date as the summer of 1850. Geronimo's

[16] Bartlett, *op. cit.*, I, 206–207, 220–81.

[17] *Ibid.*, I, 267–68; Thrapp, *Conquest of Apacheria*, p. 8; Betzinez, *op. cit.*, p. 2. Cremony heard the same story from Carrasco and related it with an exaggerated number of Apache casualties in *Life among the Apaches*, p. 39.

date, the summer of 1858, is clearly in error, for he said it occurred at about the time of the boundary survey. By this time Geronimo and his Bedonkohe adherents had come under the leadership of Mangas Coloradas. In that fatal summer, with the great chief leading, they started on a trading trip to Casas Grandes. On the way they stopped at a town they knew as Kas-ki-yeh. Betzinez identified the place as Ramos, but since he was not born until 1860 and heard the story from his elders, Carrasco's designation of Janos may be accepted as correct.[18] As Geronimo told it:

Since it was a peaceable expedition they had taken their women and children along. They made their camp just outside the town, and every day the men went in to trade, leaving their families, horses, weapons, and supplies in camp under a small guard. But in spite of the supposed good will of the Mexicans, they took the precaution of deciding on a place of rendezvous in a thicket by the river that passed the town.

Late one afternoon, as the men were returning to camp, they were met by a few distracted women and children with the news that "Mexican troops from some other town" had killed the guard, captured the ponies and supplies, and massacred many of their people. At this news they all quickly scattered, fading into the landscape in the Apache way. Then at nightfall they began to gather at the appointed meeting place:

Silently we stole in one by one: sentinels were placed, and, when all were counted, I found that my aged mother, my young wife, and my three small children were among the slain. There were no lights in camp, so without being noticed I silently turned away and stood by the river. How long I stood there I do not know, but when I saw the warriors arranging for a council I took my place.

That night I did not give my vote for or against any measure; but it was decided that as there were only eighty warriors left, and as we were without arms or supplies, and were furthermore sur-

18 Betzinez, *op. cit.*, p. 3; Barrett, *op. cit.*, pp. 43, 113.

rounded by the Mexicans far inside their own territory, we could not hope to fight successfully. So our chief, Mangus-Colorado, gave the order to start at once in perfect silence for our homes in Arizona,[19] leaving the dead upon the field.

I stood until all had passed, hardly knowing what I would do. . . . I did not pray, nor did I resolve to do anything in particular, for I had no purpose left. I finally followed the tribe silently, keeping just within hearing distance of the soft noise of the feet of the retreating Apaches.[20]

~~~~~~~~~~~~~~~~~~~~~~

This account does not indicate how Geronimo knew that the members of his family had been killed instead of captured. He could have learned it from survivors who saw them die, but it seems that he managed to steal back to the scene of the massacre. Years later at Fort Sill he told the artist, Elbridge Ayer Burbank, that he found them all dead, lying in a pool of blood.[21]

Jason Betzinez's secondhand version of the disaster varies in many particulars from Geronimo's. He said that during the trading the Mexicans had treated the Apaches to their fiery mescal (*aguardiente*), made by distilling the fermented juice of the agave (century plant), and that the Indians were sleeping off the effects in their camp when the soldiers came killing and scalping.[22] In view of a statement made in 1852 by Mangas Coloradas,[23] it is probably true that some of the people in camp were intoxicated when the enemy struck. At all events, the survivors had a sorrowful homecoming. As Geronimo told it:

~~~~~~~~~~~~~~~~~~~~~~

For two days and three nights we were on forced marches, stopping only for meals, then we made a camp near the Mexican

19 That is, the Bedonkohes, according to Geronimo, lived in Arizona; other members of the party lived in New Mexico.

20 Barrett, *op. cit.*, pp. 43–45.

21 E. A. Burbank and Ernest Royce, *Burbank among the Indians*, p. 33.

22 Betzinez, *op. cit.*, p. 3. Apparently Betzinez had read Barrett's book; thus, he told Geronimo's story briefly as a separate incident, p. 16.

23 See *infra*, p. 47.

border,[24] where we rested two days. Here I took some food and talked with the other Indians who had lost in the massacre, but none had lost as I had, for I had lost all.

Within a few days we arrived at our own settlement. There were the decorations that Alope had made—and there were the playthings of our little ones. I burned them all, even our tepee. I also burned my mother's tepee and destroyed all her property.

I was never again contented in our quiet home. I had vowed vengeance upon the Mexican troopers who had wronged me, and whenever I . . . saw anything to remind me of former happy days my heart would ache for revenge upon Mexico.

This hatred of the Mexicans continued throughout Geronimo's life. Ev᾽n at Fort Sill he said, "I am old now and shall never go on the warpath again, but if I were young, and followed the warpath, it would lead into Old Mexico."[25]

Through this experience Geronimo received a gift of the Power that was to figure prominently throughout the rest of his life. Unlike Indians of some other tribes, the Apache did not go off alone on a conscious spiritual quest. Power came suddenly and unexpectedly. It was the life force of the universe, and it sought individuals through which to work. Its nature and the manner of its coming varied from person to person. In many cases it is easy for the skeptic to identify the experience as a dream. For example, an Apache telling of his father's vision said: "This happened towards morning, and he was sound asleep. Something touched him and told him to awake for it had good things to tell him. He pushed the cover off his head, and there beside him sat a silver-tip bear." The one to whom it came might be given a special song and ceremony to bring it into action, but no man could aspire to leadership and no woman could exert influence without it.[26] To say, as

---

24 It should be noted that the Mexican border before the Gadsden Purchase was farther north than at present; hence, the long journey to reach it.

25 Barrett, *op. cit.*, pp. 46, 110. Barrett inserted a touch of pathos by mentioning Geronimo's visits to his father's grave, an action forbidden by Apache taboos.

26 Morris E. Opler, *Apache Odyssey: A Journey between Two Worlds*, p. 42; Opler, *An Apache Life-Way*, pp. 186–216, 255–57, 261–64, 280–81, 306–309.

37

some of Geronimo's detractors have said, that he was "only" a medicine man is to ignore a fundamental tenet of Apache faith. As the years passed, he acquired many kinds of Power, but as far as is known the one he received at the time of his bitter loss was his first endowment.

He had gone out alone and was sitting with his head bowed weeping when he heard a voice calling his name, "Goyahkla!" Four times—the magical Apache number—it called. Then it spoke. "No gun can ever kill you. I will take the bullets from the guns of the Mexicans, so they will have nothing but powder. And I will guide your arrows."[27] The fact that he was often wounded, but never fatally, strengthened his belief. As late as 1897 he told Burbank that no bullet could kill him.[28]

He needed all the assurance his Power could give him. As soon as the warriors had collected weapons and supplies, Mangas Coloradas called a council and found that all were willing to take the warpath against the Mexicans. Geronimo was sent to enlist the help of their relatives. He went first to the Chiricahuas, whose chief was the great Cochise. There he was sure of a sympathetic hearing, for Dos-teh-seh, a daughter of Mangas, was Cochise's principal wife. The chief called a council at early dawn. Geronimo told his story, and the warriors agreed to join the campaign. He went next to Juh and the Nednais, with the same success.

According to Geronimo, it was not until the following summer that the war party set out. (Betzinez said it was in late fall of the same year.) They traveled in three divisions: the Bedonkohes [and certainly their Mimbreno relatives] under Mangas Coloradas, the Chiricahuas under Cochise, and the Nednais under Juh. According to Betzinez, the Warm Springs contingent was led by their chief, Baishan, whose name, meaning "knife," was translated by the Mexicans as Cuchillo or—because of the Apache practice of blackening their weapons to make them less conspicuous—Cuchillo Negro. But no doubt the Bedonkohe, Mimbreno, and

27 Sam Haozous interview, January 27, 1955.
28 Burbank and Royce, *op. cit.*, pp. 30–31.

Warm Springs warriors traveled together and were dominated by Mangas Coloradas.

They went south through Sonora, following hidden ways along river courses and through mountains, to Arispe. (They seemed to know that the military force that had ravaged their camp was stationed there.) Troops from the city came out to meet them, and there was some skirmishing. The following day the whole Mexican force—two companies of cavalry and two of infantry—came out to attack. A pitched battle followed, a departure from the usual Apache ambush from a hidden position. Geronimo, because he had suffered so much from these same soldiers, was allowed to direct the fighting. (This is his story, and it may well be true.) He arranged his warriors in a crescent in the timber near the river, and the Mexican infantry advanced towards them and opened fire. Geronimo led a charge against them, at the same time extending his crescent to outflank and encircle them and attack from the rear. (At least, that seems to be his meaning.) The battle lasted about two hours, the Apaches fighting with bows and arrows and in close quarters with their spears. Many of them were killed, but when the fight ended they were in complete possession of a field strewn with Mexican dead.[29] It was here, according to tradition, that Goyahkla received the name Geronimo.

Barrett added some trimmings, not only about a scalping orgy that followed, but also about a battlefield promotion of Geronimo to "war chief of all the Apaches." The word *chief*, as used by the Apaches, was a term as technical as the rank of an army officer or the title of a government official in white society, and all the Apaches, including Daklugie, have insisted that Geronimo never held that position. Eve Ball once reminded Daklugie of the statement in the story he had interpreted. "He laughed and said that neither he nor Geronimo told Barrett that Geronimo was a chief, but that Barrett made one of his uncle."[30]

Betzinez gave an account similar to Geronimo's of the extensive

29 Barrett, *op. cit.*, pp. 47–54.
30 Eve Ball to Angie Debo, February 27, 1972.

preparation, the war party and its leaders, and the fierce fighting, but he located the battle in Chihuahua inside the city of Ramos. He also said that Baishan was killed by the first volley of the Mexican guns—an obvious error, for Cuchillo Negro appeared very much alive in subsequent Apache history. But Betzinez's impressions are true. He heard the story told and retold for years thereafter, always with pride in what his people regarded as the greatest of Apache victories. And they never relaxed their hatred of the Mexicans.[31]

It remained now for the Apaches to cope with the ancient enemy and to enter into relations with the new invaders.

[31] Betzinez, *op. cit.*, pp. 4–9.

CHAPTER 3

MEXICANS AND AMERICANS

Bartlett returned from Sonora and arrived once more at the copper mines on June 17, 1851. On that very day he was visited by Mangas Coloradas and some of his people, who had been strangely absent throughout the spring. Mangas said that he had followed Bartlett several days and had been near his camp several times. This presents the intriguing possibility that the avenging Apache war party and Bartlett's wagon train had gone into Sonora at about the same time, that the battle before Arispe had been fought shortly after Bartlett's departure, and that the fast-moving Apaches had caught up with him towards the end of his journey.

In any event, Mangas warned Bartlett of the risk he had run in traveling without adequate protection when so many bad Indians were about. He said that he was a friend of the Americans and spoke of his meeting with Kearny. Bartlett told him of the war and the peace and explained that he had come to mark the boundary. He assured the Indians that the Americans would protect them if they behaved, but he said that the treaty bound them to protect the Mexicans against depredations across the border. The chief strongly disapproved of this provision. He said that his people had always stolen mules and taken prisoners from the Mexicans, but he promised not to molest the boundary commission.[1]

Bartlett was fair-minded and humane, and he believed that if the Indians were treated justly they would respond. Cremony regarded them with contempt and was sure they plotted treachery.[2] But Mangas Coloradas loyally observed his promise, and the Warm Springs Indians, who camped that summer on the Mimbres River below the copper mines, were equally friendly. Survey parties scattered fifty miles along the line were not molested. Wagons with stores for the camps went out safely, unprotected. Members of the commission traveled in small parties or alone unharmed. The mules and horses and a herd of cattle brought for food grazed undisturbed.[3]

This idyllic relationship was soon endangered by the unresolved issue of Apache-Mexican hostility. Late that same June two half-grown Mexican boys, captives of the Apaches, sought refuge in Cremony's tent. Bartlett turned them over to General Condé, who subsequently restored them to their families, but the Indians were greatly aroused. Finally, a council was arranged, and Mangas Coloradas and several other leaders of the two tribes—Cuchillo Negro, of the Warm Springs, Delgadito, probably of the same tribe, and Ponce and Coletto Amarillo, whose tribal affiliations are unknown—came with about two hundred warriors to confer with the American officials. Mangas began by asking, "Why did you take our captives from us?" And he went on to state his position: "You came to our country. You were well received. Your lives, your property, your animals were safe. You passed by ones, by twos by threes through our country; you went and came in peace. Your strayed animals were always brought home to you again. Our wives, our children and women came here and visited your houses. We were friends. We were brothers! Believing this, we came among you and brought our captives. . . . We believed your assurances of

1 Bartlett, *Personal Narratives*, I, pp. 297–302.
2 For his final evaluation, see *Life among the Apaches*, p. 320.
3 Bartlett, *op. cit.*, I, pp. 320–22.

friendship, and we trusted them." And again he demanded, "Why did you take our captives from us?"

Bartlett tried to explain the relationship contemplated by the peace treaty: "I have no doubt but that you have suffered much by the Mexicans. This is a question in which it is impossible for us to tell who is right, or who is wrong. You and the Mexicans accuse each other of being the aggressors. Our duty is to fulfil our promise to both . . . to show to Mexico that we mean what we say; and when the time comes . . . to prove the good faith of our promises to you."

Ponce became very angry. Delgadito was more conciliatory, but he defended the rights of his tribesman: "He cannot lose his prisoners, who were obtained at the risk of his life and purchased by the blood of his relatives. He justly demands his captives . . . and as justice we demand it."

Bartlett realized that the Indians could make things difficult for the commission. The Mimbrenos were camped on one side above the copper mines, and the Warm Springs band was on the other side in the broad valley of the Mimbres where the commission's livestock were grazing. He accordingly found a way to circumvent regulations against ransoming captives and offered to pay for the boys. The Apache leaders then held a short consultation, after which Delgadito announced: "The brave who owns these captives does not want to sell. He has had one of those two boys six years. . . . He is as a son to his old age. He speaks our language, and he cannot sell him. Money cannot buy affection. His heart cannot be sold. He taught him to string and shoot the bow, and to wield the lance. He loves the boy and cannot sell him."

It was true that the Apaches took captured children into their families and loved them as their own,[4] but Bartlett was bound by the treaty, and besides this, there was the appeal of the boys, who chose their own people in preference to the Apaches. He finally persuaded the council to adjourn to the commissary's stores, where calicoes, blankets, and sheetings worth $250 were laid out and

4 See, for example, Ball, *In the Days of Victorio*, pp. 113–14, 134, 167.

43

accepted. Bartlett thought that ended the matter, but it is clear that the Indians were not satisfied with the settlement.[5]

A few days later a Mexican teamster in the employ of the American commission deliberately shot and fatally wounded an Apache.[6] The Indians were mollified to see him brought in chains to a hearing, but Bartlett, mindful of proper legal procedures, wanted to send him to Santa Fe for trial. Ponce demanded his immediate execution so they could see it. Bartlett promised to turn the murderer's wages over to the victim's mother. She said she wanted blood, not money. The affair was finally settled by giving her thirty dollars, then due the prisoner, and promising to pay her his wages, twenty dollars a month, thereafter while he worked in chains. Bartlett thought that this settlement pleased the Indians, but it is apparent that they accepted it reluctantly.[7]

Their good relations with the commission quickly deteriorated. Several of Colonel Craig's mules disappeared. He blamed the Apaches and set off with thirty soldiers to their camp to recover the animals. They said they would hunt the mules—as apparently they did, and brought them back—but their friendly attitude changed after this encounter. Meanwhile, about four hundred Navahos arrived and camped on the Gila. It was probably they who made two separate raids on Craig's herd in August, making off with about seventy-five mules and some horses. Bartlett sent back to Doña Ana on the Rio Grande for more soldiers, and forty dragoons arrived. The Indians then ran off all of Craig's remaining mules and horses and the eighteen mules that had hauled the wagons of the dragoons. This time the Mimbrenos or their Warm Springs friends, possibly both, were almost certainly guilty.

During this time a small party of American miners had come in and started working the gold diggings the Mexicans had abandoned thirteen years before. The reopening of the mines was an

[5] Bartlett, *op. cit.*, I, pp. 311–17. Cremony also recorded the minutes of the conference in *Life among the Apaches*, pp. 58–66.

[6] The Mexicans living in the ceded territory, of course, became American citizens, but it will be necessary to continue referring to them as Mexicans to distinguish them from the incoming Anglos.

[7] Bartlett, *op. cit.*, I, pp. 228–29; Cremony, *op. cit.*, pp. 80–81.

ominous circumstance that was to dominate the future of the Mimbrenos. Then a party, in which Delgadito was seen and recognized, ran off all the intruders' cattle. The miners and some volunteers from the commission overtook the raiders and recovered the herd. "Our place was now in a state of siege," as Bartlett expressed it. The surveying parties were called in, and guards were stationed around the camp. Altogether, the commission and its military escort had lost about 150 horses and mules.[8]

This whole experience of the first official contact between an Apache band and a United States government agency reveals the tangled threads that were to form the future pattern. It shows how difficult it was even for men of good will like Mangas Coloradas and Bartlett to understand each other. Cremony had his own theory to explain it: lacking enough men to attack the commission, the treacherous chief pretended peace until he could bring in Navaho reinforcements (as though Apaches ever needed help in raiding!); when they arrived, he joined them. The high-minded Bartlett eventually came to the same conclusion.[9]

Geronimo was not present at Santa Rita that summer of 1851, but the conflicts that emerged there were to form the setting of his life. His own contact with members of the survey was uneventful. The commission left the Santa Rita camp on August 24 and continued westward. On September 5 the party went through Apache Pass in Cochise's mountains and came out in the valley beyond.[10] Somewhere along this line Geronimo saw his first white Americans. As he related it:

. . . we heard that some white men were measuring land to the south of us. In company with a number of other warriors I went to visit them. We could not understand them very well, for we had no interpreter, but we made a treaty with them by shaking hands and promising to be brothers. Then we made our camp near their

---

8 Bartlett, *op. cit.*, I, pp. 228–29, 317–18, 330, 343–53; Cremony, *op. cit.*, pp. 80–85.
9 Bartlett, *op. cit.*, I, pp. 326–29, 353–54; Cremony, *op. cit.*, pp. 48–51.
10 Bartlett, *op. cit.*, I, pp. 358, 373.

45

camp, and they came to trade with us. We gave them buckskin, blankets, and ponies in exchange for shirts and provisions. We also brought them game, for which they gave us some money. We did not know the value of this money, but we kept it and later learned from the Navajo Indians that it was very valuable.

Every day they measured land with curious instruments and put down marks which we could not understand. They were good men, and we were sorry when they had gone on into the west. They were not soldiers. These were the first white men I ever saw.[11]

᚛᚛᚛᚛᚛᚛᚛᚛᚛᚛᚛᚛᚛᚛᚛

The historian will remember that the boundary survey was never completed. Probably Bartlett had conceded too much to Condé in fixing the initial point, and American leaders committed to Manifest Destiny argued that it was not far enough south to include a level route for a transcontinental railroad. The dispute ended with the acquisition of another piece of Mexico by the United States through the Gadsden Purchase of 1853.[12] Incidentally, the treaty of purchase abrogated the pledge that bound the United States to restrain its Apaches from raiding in Mexico;[13] but of course each country had an international obligation to prevent hostiles from crossing the border—if it could.

Meanwhile, after the departure of the boundary commission in 1851, more prospectors were coming into the area around the Santa Rita copper mines, often denying all rights to the Apaches. The Apaches retaliated by numerous depredations and the killing of travelers. In July, 1852, John Greiner, then serving as Indian superintendent of New Mexico, called Mangas Coloradas and other leaders to Santa Fe and made a treaty with them. It committed the United States to give presents to the Indians and treat them well, to punish its citizens who wronged them, and to fix the tribal boundaries. Military posts and trading posts were to

11 Barrett, *Geronimo's Story of His Life*, pp. 113–14.
12 The whole story is told by Odie B. Faulk in *Too Far North; Too Far South*. It is clear that the survey of this new boundary was not the one that Geronimo encountered; see pp. 147–49.
13 Malloy, *Treaties, Conventions*, p. 1122.

be established in their territory. The Indians promised peace to the United States, with free passage of its citizens through their country, and committed themselves to make no more raids in Mexico.[14] They objected to this last provision. Greiner asked the reason, and Mangas Coloradas told of the recent massacre at "Kas-ki-yeh," and the one in 1837 at the copper mines.

"Some time ago," he said, "my people were invited to a feast; aguardiente, or whiskey, was there; my people drank and became intoxicated, when a party of Mexicans came in and beat out their brains with clubs. At another time a trader was sent among us from Chihuahua. While innocently engaged in trading ... a cannon concealed behind the goods was fired upon my people, and quite a number were killed. ... How can we make peace with such people?"[15]

Greiner concluded that "if half their statements are true, the Indians would be justified in seeking revenge."[16] Clearly they never intended to stop raiding in Mexico. Indianlike, they based the binding force of their commitments on their oral protests and not on the text of the final document. Geronimo gave Barrett a detailed account of his raids through the 1850's.[17] True, he was not a signatory to the treaty, but Mangas Coloradas was the leader in one of these raids and at other times shared in the spoils.

By this time the Bedonkohes seem to have become merged with the Mimbrenos, though they still retained their tribal distinction. Geronimo soon married a Bedonkohe girl named Chee-hash-kish. Jason Betzinez, who knew her well in later years, always characterized her as "a very handsome woman." She became the mother of a son, Chappo, and a daughter, Dohn-say (Tozey), afterwards known as Lulu, both of whom were to grow up to share in their father's wars and his captivity. Soon he took a second wife, also a Bedonkohe, named Nana-tha-thtith, who became the mother of

14 Charles J. Kappler, *Indian Affairs, Laws and Treaties,* II, 598–600.
15 Quoted by Thrapp in *Conquest of Apacheria,* p. 13.
16 Thrapp, *Victorio,* pp. 27–28.
17 This account gives the dates 1859 to 1868, but they do not fit known facts. For example, it had Mangas Coloradas leading a raid in 1867. Mangas was killed early in 1863.

one child.[18] This marriage indicates his rising importance in the tribe. Only a superior hunter and raider could support two wives.

Barrett must have recorded Geronimo's raids almost exactly as he reported them. There is little scalping, no sentimentality, no confusion of events and places, but a straightforward account in orderly sequence. In a culture in which a warrior's exploits were like so many academic honors, subject to check by his associates, they had to be accurately presented. Here one may see the logical working of Geronimo's mind and his essential integrity as he frankly admitted his failures and avoided self-glorification in his successes.

"All the other Apaches were satisfied after the battle of [that is, avenging] 'Kaskiyeh,' " he said, "but I still desired more revenge." He finally persuaded two other warriors—he carefully stated their names—to join him on a raid. They went on foot and carried three days' rations. He traced their route through the country to a small village—"I do not know the name of this village." There they found five horses tied, and they were attempting to steal them when the Mexicans opened fire from the town and killed his companions. Then they swarmed out and surrounded him. He ran and dodged and hid, sometimes shooting a Mexican from concealment, finally eluded them, and reached his home "without booty, without my companions, exhausted, but not discouraged." Some of the Apaches blamed him for the loss of the two men, "but I said nothing. Having failed, it was only proper that I should remain silent."[19]

A few months later he managed to persuade two other warriors to join him on another raid. Again, the account presents the same accuracy of detail. They selected a village which they planned to attack at daylight, but the Mexicans discovered their camp and fired into it, killing one warrior. In the morning the two survivors encountered a company of Mexican soldiers coming from the south, well mounted and carrying supplies for a long journey.

18 Griswold, "The Fort Sill Apaches," s.v. "Geronimo."
19 Barrett, *op. cit.*, pp. 55–57.

Geronimo and his companion followed them until they were certain that the Mexicans were on their way to invade the Apache range north of the border; then they hurried ahead and warned their people. The Mexicans arrived immediately afterward. The Apaches drove them back, killing eight, but they lost another warrior and three small boys.

Geronimo, with twenty-five men, followed the trail of the invaders into Mexico and ambushed a cavalry company in a mountain defile. The troopers dismounted and placed their horses on the outside for a breastwork; thus Geronimo had to lead a hand-to-hand charge. A soldier struck him over the head with the butt of his gun, knocking him senseless. The warriors succeeded in killing all the Mexicans, but a number of their own men were killed. They bathed Geronimo's head in cold water and restored him to consciousness, and he was able to walk back on his return, though his wound was long in healing and he carried the scar the rest of his life. His final summation: "In this fight we had lost so heavily that there really was no glory in our victory, and we returned to Arizona. No one seemed to want to go on the warpath again that year."[20]

The following summer, with twelve warriors, Geronimo made another raid into Mexico. They sighted a mule train loaded with provisions and attacked. The drivers fled, and the Apaches started back with the booty, but unknown to them, Mexican troops were in pursuit. As they were eating their breakfast one morning, careless of the usual precautions, the soldiers fired on them. Geronimo was struck near the eye by a glancing bullet, and as the raiders all scattered for cover he received a slight flesh wound in the side. They "returned home empty-handed" with "not even a partial victory to report. I again returned wounded, but I was not yet discouraged. Again I was blamed by our people, and again I had no reply."[21]

Geronimo remained at the home *rancheria* while his wounds

20 *Ibid.*, pp. 57–61.
21 *Ibid.*, pp. 61–63.

were healing. Many of the men went out on a hunt, and some of them went north to trade with the Navahos for blankets, leaving only about twenty in camp. One night three companies of invading Mexican troops surrounded the settlement. In the morning, as the women were lighting the fires (they used the primitive drill, twirling a stick in a notch in a flat piece of wood[22]), ready to prepare breakfast, the soldiers opened fire. Many women and children and a few warriors were killed, and four women were captured. Among the dead were Geronimo's wife, Nana-tha-thtith, and her child. There was no chance for defense. Geronimo managed to snatch his bow and arrows, and although his eye was still swollen shut he hit one of the officers. But all the survivors fled for safety in the rocks while the troopers burned their lodges and carried off their ponies, weapons, provisions, and blankets. A few warriors who had been able to secure their weapons followed the invaders back to Mexico but were unable to attack them.

The captive women were taken to Sonora as slaves. Some years later they managed to escape and were finding their way back through the mountains. One night when they were sleeping inside a brush wickiup they had built as a temporary shelter, they heard growling outside. Their campfire had burned low, and one of them, a girl of about seventeen, started to replenish it when a mountain lion crashed through the wall, sprang upon her, and dragged her some distance. She fought him as best she could, and the others came to her assistance, finally killing him with their knives. Then they stayed in the mountains for about a month and nursed the girl until she was able to walk. They finally rejoined their people, but she carried the scars throughout her life.[23]

During this same period, there was another invasion of American territory by Mexican troops, this time from Chihuahua. They struck the *rancheria* of Geronimo's cousin Nah-thle-tla, who was to become the mother of Jason Betzinez. She was married to a Bedonkohe warrior and was living with her husband and her two

---

[22] For a description of the method, see Opler, *An Apache Life-Way*, pp. 393–94.
[23] Barrett, *op. cit.*, pp. 63–67, 68n.

children in the mountains south of the present Lordsburg, New Mexico. Her husband had gone on a war expedition to Mexico, where they were joined by Juh. Near Namiquipa, in Chihuahua, the combined force attacked the Mexicans and, through Juh's brilliant generalship, defeated them, but Nah-thle-tla's husband was killed.

The women and children felt safe on the American side of the border, but the avenging Mexican force overran the defenseless camp, killing many of the people and capturing others, including Nah-thle-tla and her children. The captives were taken to the city of Chihuahua and distributed as slaves. Nah-thle-tla's children were taken from her, and she never saw them again. After several months of servitude there, she and another young woman were sold to a wealthy Mexican from Santa Fe. They were loaded into an ox cart, caged in with webbed rope and guarded by a vicious dog tied in front, and taken on the long journey, traveling past the familiar landmarks of their country on the way. In Santa Fe Nah-thle-tla worked at household tasks for her owners until she finally managed to escape and find her way home. She had traveled at least two hundred fifty miles through unknown mountains, eating piñon nuts, seeds, and berries and going on foot until she managed to steal a pony near the end of her journey.[24] Such epics of stamina and resourcefulness were repeated many times in Apache experience.[25]

Geronimo spoke bitterly of the fate of captives. Not many escaped, he said, and "Those who did not escape were slaves to the Mexicans, or perhaps even more degraded." But it appears from the stories of the women who managed to escape that most of them had not been unkindly treated in their servitude. Working with typical Apache energy and resourcefulness, they must have made valuable house servants. Geronimo contrasted their slavery with the Apache custom of adopting captive Mexican women and children as members of their tribes.[26] This was indeed true, but he

24 Betzinez, *I Fought with Geronimo*, pp. 19–24.
25 See, for example, *ibid.*, pp. 10–14.
26 Barrett, *op. cit.*, pp. 67–68.

failed to add that captive men were sometimes fiendishly tortured by the Apaches.

In the summer following the Mexican attack on his *rancheria*, Geronimo, with the death of another wife and child to avenge, enlisted eight men for a raid. They captured a long pack train loaded with blankets, calico, saddles, tinware, and loaf sugar. On their journey home, in the Santa Catalina Mountains of Arizona, northeast of the little adobe village of Tucson, they met an American driving a mule train. He fled, and they took his train. It was loaded with cheese, no doubt to supply the new boom towns of gold-rush California. At that time Americans traveling on the California Trail were comparatively safe from raids, but on this occasion the temptation had been too great for the Apaches to resist.

When the raiders returned home, Mangas Coloradas assembled the tribe, and there was feasting on mule meat, all night dancing, and distribution of the spoils. Mexican cavalry followed, reaching the place three days later, but this time the Apaches were prepared. The warriors went out in two divisions, one under Mangas and the other under Geronimo, hoping to surround and destroy the whole company and take their horses. But the Mexicans avoided the trap, although ten of their men were killed with the loss of only one Apache. They then retreated, and thirty Apache warriors followed them far into Mexico. "No more troops came that winter," said Geronimo. And for a long time the Apaches reveled in their supply of blankets, clothing, sugar, and cheese.[27]

The following summer Geronimo "selected three warriors" for his raid. They hid near a town and watched. At midday no one seemed to be stirring; thus, they chose the siesta hour for their attack. The people fled, and they looked through the houses, where they found many "curious things. These Mexicans kept many more kinds of property than the Apaches did." The raiders drove in a herd of horses and mules, loaded them, and returned safely to Arizona. There was more feasting and dancing and distribution of

27 *Ibid.*, pp. 69–71.

52

presents—enough supplies "to last our whole tribe for a year or more." Geronimo considered this "perhaps the most successful raid ever made by us into Mexican territory."[28]

The next year Geronimo went out with a larger party—twenty men. Before they left, they provided for the safety of their families. The whole band scattered, to reassemble about forty miles away. Thus "it would be hard for the Mexicans to trail them and we would know where to find [them] when we returned." In Sonora the raiders captured a pack train that proved to be loaded with mescal. At camp that night they "began to get drunk and fight each other. I, too, drank enough mescal to feel the effects of it, but I was not drunk." He tried to stop the fighting, but failed. He tried to put out a guard, but nobody would serve. He expected an attack from Mexican troops at any moment. Finally, the warriors stopped fighting, and sank into a stupor. Then he poured out the remaining mescal—this must have been a heart-breaking experience for an Apache—put out the fire, and removed the pack mules to a distance from camp. Next, he attended to those who had been wounded in the brawl, cutting an arrowhead from the leg of one, pulling a spear point from the shoulder of another, and guarded the camp through the night. The following day they loaded their wounded on the mules and started for Arizona. On the way they captured a herd of cattle and started to drive them home. This proved to be difficult—driving cattle on foot and caring for the wounded—but they arrived home safely and gave another feast on mule meat. Then they killed all the cattle, dried the beef, and dressed the hides. "These were the first cattle we ever had." They decided to capture more.[29]

During the next summer Geronimo went out with four warriors. All their previous raids had been on foot because of the necessity for concealment, but now they rode, for this time they were after cattle. They went down into Sonora as far south as the mouth of the Yaqui River and looked out on the Gulf of California—"a

28 *Ibid.*, pp. 71–73.
29 *Ibid.*, pp. 73–77.

great lake extending beyond the reach of sight," this mountain people's first view of the sea. They captured about sixty cattle and started home, grazing them in valleys on the way. They returned to more dancing, feasting, and butchering, drying, and storing of the meat.[30]

On the next year's raid, Geronimo, with nine warriors, collected "many" horses and mules, but Mexican troops followed and recovered the whole herd. The Apaches returned to Arizona with no booty. The following summer he went out with thirty mounted warriors, "collected all the horses, mules, and cattle we wanted," killing "about fifty Mexicans" in the process, and returned home with presents and feasting. The next year Mangas Coloradas led the raid with eight mounted warriors, including Geronimo. They found a herd of cattle, fought the *vaqueros*, killing two, and made off with the herd, but Mexican troops armed with rifles came upon them, recovered the cattle, and took out after the raiders. The Apaches, unable to reach them with only bows and arrows, left their ponies and sought cover in the timber. The Mexicans then abandoned the pursuit, collected the Indians' ponies, and drove the cattle back across the plains. The raiders returned home with no victory to report, with no spoils to divide, and without their own horses. "This expedition was considered disgraceful," said Geronimo. The members of the party "felt keenly the taunts of the other warriors" and wanted to return. Mangas would not lead them, but Geronimo set out with them and raided several settlements, returning with horses and mules loaded with provisions, saddles, and blankets. Again there was feasting, dancing, and dividing of the booty, but Mangas would not accept any of it.[31]

"About a year after this" Mexican troops again crossed the border and made away with all the horses and mules of the band. Geronimo took twenty warriors and trailed them. They found the stock at a cattle ranch in Sonora. They fought with the *vaqueros*, again killing two, and made off with their own animals and the

---

30 *Ibid.*, pp. 77–78.
31 *Ibid.*, pp. 79–83.

Mexicans' herd. Nine *vaqueros* followed their trail. Geronimo sent the stock ahead while he and three other warriors guarded the rear. One night near the Arizona line they saw the *vaqueros* camp for the night and picket their mounts. They stole into the camp, cut the horses loose, and silently led them away, leaving the *vaqueros* asleep. "What these nine cowboys did next morning I do not know. . . . I know they did not follow us, for we were not molested. When we arrived in camp at home there was great rejoicing in the tribe. It was considered a good trick to get the Mexicans' horses and leave them asleep in the mountains. It was a long time before we again went into Mexico or were disturbed by the Mexicans."[32]

Strangely enough, the American officials were apparently unaware of these frequent invasions of United States territory by Mexican troops, but they knew that the Apaches were raiding in Mexico. The relations of the Mimbreno and Warm Springs tribes with the Americans had improved dramatically since the treaty made in 1852. The Indians tried to observe the peace, even sometimes in the face of great provocation. Among several incidents was one leading to the death of Cuchillo Negro. Some Indians living to the north had killed the agent to the Navahos. In the spring of 1857 a military expedition sent out to punish them found it easier to attack the chief's *rancheria* near the upper Mimbres. Six or seven Apaches, including Cuchillo Negro, were killed, and nine women and children were captured. As far as can be determined, Cuchillo Negro was succeeded as chief of the Warm Springs tribe by Delgadito.[33]

In 1855 these Apaches were subjected to another pressure familiar in United States–Indian relations. Dr. Michael Steck had been appointed as agent to all the southern tribes from the Mescaleros to the Chiricahuas. He induced the Mescaleros and all the Warm Springs and Mimbreno leaders except Mangas Coloradas, who adroitly evaded him, to come to Fort Thorn on the Rio

32 *Ibid.*, pp. 83–85.
33 Thrapp, *Victorio*, pp. 51–52, 54–55; Betzinez, *op. cit.*, p. 9 and n.; Davis, *The Truth about Geronimo*, p. 111.

Grande and sign a land cession treaty. The Warm Springs tribe and the Mimbrenos ceded about twelve thousand to fifteen thousand square miles, retaining a reservation of about two thousand to twenty-five hundred square miles comprising their heartland. Steck was honest and hard working and sincerely interested in the welfare of the Indians, but his real sympathy was with the expanding white frontier. This reservation, he reported, contained the copper mines and the gold mine and deposits of iron, silver, and lead. He favored removing these Indians and the Mescaleros to the Gila; they would be better off living with the tribes of that region [these would include Geronimo and the Bedonkohes] far from white communities and travel routes, and at the same time "you throw open for settlement the finest and most desirable portion of New Mexico." The Senate, no doubt with this in mind, failed to approve the treaty,[34] leaving the Indians with no title to their homeland.

Meanwhile, traffic was increasing on the California Trail to the south, threading Doubtful Canyon southwest of the Mimbrenos' main settlements and Apache Pass in the country of the Chiricahuas, and small parties were constantly traveling it in safety. On September 16, 1858, the Butterfield Stage Line, carrying mail and passengers from Saint Louis to San Francisco, began its twice-weekly service on the route, with a station at each of those strategic places. On Christmas Day that year Steck set out on this trail for Apache Pass, where he held his first conference with the Chiricahuas. They had committed no depredations on the trail for the past two years, he said, but they raided regularly in Mexico. He held a friendly council with them and gave them some presents. By this time he had plans to remove them also to the Gila with the Mimbrenos, Mogollons (Warm Springs tribe), and Mescaleros.[35] This lightly expressed policy of uprooting tribes and crowding them together in one place was to have monstrous consequences in future years.

34 Thrapp, *Victorio*, pp. 42–46.
35 *Ibid.*, pp. 61–64; Secretary of the Interior, *Annual Report*, 1859, pp. 713–14.

Geronimo seems to have been present at this conference. As he told it, "One day during the time that the soldiers were stationed at Apache Pass I made a treaty with the post. This was done by shaking hands and promising to be brothers. Cochise and Mangus-Colorado did likewise. I do not know the name of the officer in command, but this was the first regiment that ever came to Apache Pass." There were no soldiers stationed at Apache Pass and no military post there until after a subsequent hostile encounter. His "soldiers" may have been a military escort with Steck, and the "post" may have been the Overland Mail station. And if his account does refer to the meeting with Steck, he was probably mistaken about the presence of Mangas Coloradas. But he placed the date with approximate accuracy, "about a year" before an event that occurred early in 1861, a very slight discrepancy in the memories of a long life remote from calendars and written records.[36]

An account showing the relative safety of travel through the Chiricahua and Mimbreno country at that time was written by Hank Smith, who later became a pioneer settler on the High Plains (the Llano Estacado) of West Texas. It seems to have been in the spring of 1859 that he was employed to drive twelve hundred head of cattle from Fort Buchanan, west of the Chiricahuas' range, to Fort Bliss at El Paso. He had twelve Mexican *vaqueros* to assist him, and a military escort of a sergeant and ten troopers accompanied him as far as Apache Pass. Large bands of Indians—fifty or a hundred warriors—met him, but always in a friendly spirit, making no attempt to scatter or steal the cattle. On two occasions they requested (and received) a beef to butcher and eat; at other times they conducted the drovers to water holes and assisted in watering the herd, asking a beef or two in payment. At the Mimbres River Mangas Coloradas' band was friendly and helpful. There the men rested the herd for two days, engaging in racing contests with the Indians. At Fort Bliss they turned the cattle over

---

36 Barrett, *op. cit.*, p. 116.

to the commissary department, short only twenty head for the entire journey.[37]

The following October, Steck, with no military escort, set out again to the west. He met about eight hundred of the Gila bands and distributed presents to them. Geronimo may have been present at this meeting, though he did not mention it in his reminiscences. Steck continued on his way to the broad San Simon Valley east of Cochise's mountains, where he met that chief with about four hundred Chiricahuas and distributed more presents. Cochise delivered to him three stolen animals and promised to watch over the mail coaches and travelers on the California Trail.[38]

But such peaceable relations were not to last.

[37] Hattie M. Anderson, "Mining and Indian Fighting in Arizona and New Mexico—Memoirs of Hank Smith," *Panhandle-Plains Historical Review*, Vol. I, pp. 81–86.
[38] Thrapp, *Victorio*, p. 65.

CHAPTER 4

TOO MANY WHITE MEN

The trouble began with mining development and settlements around Santa Rita in the heart of the Mimbrenos' country. With Steck's encouragement and some assistance in breaking up the land and repairing their *acequias*, they and their Warm Springs friends were farming industriously in the Mimbres Valley and along the Alamosa River below the springs, but it was evident that they would soon be crowded out. In the summer of 1858 work was resumed on the abandoned copper mines. The next year thirty settlers started Mowry City in the wide valley of the Mimbres River below the mines, all on tribal land. Also in 1859 a rich gold strike was made in the mountains northwest of Santa Rita, and the mushroom town of Pinos Altos sprang up there.

The miners were lawless and violent, with no respect for the Indians whose lands they were invading. They also encouraged Mexicans to come in and grow food for their mining camps and feed for their horses. This policy was, of course, a direct affront to the Indians, who had never accepted peace with that hated people, and in the inevitable conflicts the miners supported their protégés. In 1860 the army established Fort McLane a few miles to the south, but the miners openly defied the military authorities when they attempted to protect the Indians.[1]

Steck's report for 1860 gave a gloomy picture of the Mimbrenos. They had become destitute through the loss of game in the area and along the California Trail and demoralized by the whiskey that flowed freely near the settlements. They had been accused of killing some of the settlers' cattle, but considering their destitution and the fact that these unwelcome immigrants were operating in the heart of their country, the complaints were surprisingly few. Anglo and Mexican horse thieves were active in the area, and the Indians were blamed for their depredations also.[2]

Steck was sincerely concerned at the prospect that they would soon be dispossessed and homeless. By this time he had their reservation on the Gila selected, a fifteen-mile-square area including Mangas Creek (then called Santa Lucia Creek) and Springs and the rolling grasslands surrounding it, a few miles northwest of the mining area. He encouraged the Indians to farm there, and in 1859 he reported a well-tended tract about three miles long extending down the valley. But he was not satisfied merely to find a home for the harassed Mimbrenos. He wanted to include in the settlement the Mescaleros from their country east of the Rio Grande, the Mimbrenos' Warm Springs relatives, and the untouched Chiricahuas secure in their mountains to the southwest.

The following year New Mexico Superintendent James L. Collins recommended that the unrelated Jicarilla Apaches from the distant mountains of northern New Mexico should also be concentrated there. "The proposed change," he said, "would bring the whole Apache tribe together. . . . When thus united they would form a nation of eight or nine thousand souls. . . . All cultivating more or less, they could in a short time, if favorably located, be made self-supporting. . . . They are certainly more inclined to labor

---

1 Hank Smith was in the party that made the gold discovery. His account of the strike, the ensuing gold rush, and the riotous life of the settlement may be found in Anderson, "Mining and Indian Fighting," pp. 87–93, 101, 114. For the date, see p. 88n. See also Secretary of the Interior, *Annual Report*, 1858, pp. 548–49.

2 Thrapp, *Victorio*, pp. 65–66.

than many of the other tribes." Nobody wondered how they could all support themselves on this tiny acreage. Commissioner of Indian Affairs A. B. Greenwood gave Washington's blessing to the plan, and the land was set aside that year. As for Geronimo, he did not know that he was included in this policy. It was never carried out, and the Gila reservation was restored to the public domain in 1867.[3] Apache history at this period was dominated not by Washington but by swiftly moving events in the Southwest. In them Geronimo was deeply involved.

Characteristically, it was the miners who sparked the smouldering hostility into open war. It was almost certainly in the spring or summer of 1860 that Mangas Coloradas, always trying to keep the peace, went alone on a friendly visit to the Pinos Altos camp.[4] As James Kaywaykla heard the story later, Geronimo and two Warm Springs leaders, Victorio and Loco, whose names would soon be household words in the Southwest, pleaded with him not to trust the miners. Their warnings were justified; the miners tied him to a tree and lashed him unmercifully with their bullwhips. This action was not only cruel but also stupid. Mangas Coloradas was the acknowledged leader of all the Apaches of southwestern New Mexico and the father-in-law of Cochise. Understandably he went on the warpath, and naturally he went to enlist Cochise.[5]

Cochise had observed his pledge to protect travelers on the trail, and he maintained friendly relations with the employees and drivers he met at the Butterfield station at Apache Pass. He even had a contract to supply the station with wood during the winter of 1860/61. But apparently he joined Mangas Coloradas in the war against the white intruders in the latter's country. The fight-

3 Secretary of the Interior, *Annual Report*, 1859, pp. 713–14; 1860, pp. 243, 385. See also Thrapp, *op. cit.*, pp. 63–66 and n. 16.
4 Hank Smith told of a visit the chief made to the mines in the spring; Anderson, *op. cit.*, p. 91 and n. The Indians went to war in September. The atrocity referred to above might have taken place on this spring visit or on a somewhat later one. It would have taken some time for the chief's wounds to heal and for him to collect his warriors. Clum gives the year 1858, which clearly places the event too early; the Apaches at that time were still keeping the peace. See Woodworth Clum, *Apache Agent: The Story of John P. Clum*, pp. 29–32.
5 Ball, *In the Days of Victorio*, pp. 46–47.

ing began on September 27, and a bloody war it was. The Apaches gathered the Mexicans' corn, drove off the Mexicans' sheep and the miners' horses, and attacked the settlements and supply trains. They overwhelmed an emigrant train on the California Road, killing sixteen men, burning the wagons, and making off with four hundred cattle and nine hundred sheep, with only the women and children escaping in a wagon drawn by a swift team. The miners retaliated with attacks on the Apaches' *rancherias*, and pitched battles were fought between miners and Mexicans on the one hand and Indians on the other.[6] Apparently Geronimo was engaged in this fighting. He may have been referring to it when he said, "I had not been wronged, but some of my people had been, and I fought with my tribe."[7]

Soon an arbitrary act of the military brought the war to the country of the Chiricahuas. An eleven- or twelve-year-old boy of uncertain antecedents, probably half Irish and half Mexican, disappeared with some cattle from a squalid ranch home west of the Chiricahuas' range. It is now known that he was taken by a tribe living on the Gila and given to the White Mountain Apaches.[8] Later, as an adult under the name of Mickey Free, he would become an army interpreter in dealing with the Chiricahuas and their associates. Now, in late January, 1861, Second Lieutenant George Nicholas Bascom was sent from Fort Buchanan with fifty-four men to Apache Pass to recover him. Cochise, unsuspecting, came with his wife and young son, a brother, and two nephews to deliver some wood. At a parley inside the army tent, Bascom demanded the stolen boy. Cochise truthfully protested his innocence of the kidnaping but promised to find him if possible. Bascom did not believe the chief and said he would hold him hostage until the boy should be recovered. Cochise then whipped out his knife, slashed the tent wall, and escaped, but Bascom held the other Indians as prisoners. Cochise then captured three men

6 Anderson, *op. cit.*, pp. 94–105, 111–15.
7 Barrett, *Geronimo's Story of His Life*, p. 114; Clum, *op. cit.*, pp. 29–32.
8 Goodwin, "Experiences of an Indian Scout" (part 2), p. 38. Goodwin's informant was the boy's Apache foster brother.

from the stage station and a passing wagon train and offered to exchange. Bascom refused unless Cochise would produce the boy. As February dragged by, there was some fighting and maneuvering which can be only glimpsed. Bascom sent to Fort Buchanan for reinforcements and for medical assistance apparently to treat his wounded; seventy more soldiers arrived under First Lieutenant Isaiah N. Moore. The affair ended with Cochise killing his hostages and the two officers hanging theirs.[9] Cochise's wife and child were afterwards taken to Fort Buchanan and released. According to James Kaywaykla, the child was Naiche, destined to be Geronimo's closest associate in his wars and his imprisonment.[10] If this story is correct, the woman was Dos-teh-seh, the daughter of Mangas Coloradas.

At this time Geronimo and other Bedonkohes under his leadership were living among the Chiricahuas. It was probably at this period that he married a close relative of the Cochise family, a Chiricahua-Nednai woman named She-gha. Her brother, Yahnozha, was to become one of his most dependable warriors. Then at some undetermined date he took a third wife, a woman of his own Bedonkohe band named Shtsha-she.[11] Throughout Geronimo's life as a warrior he held to this pattern of two or sometimes three wives at once—"overlapping," as Daklugie expressed it— and Nana-tha-thtith had been killed some time before.

Geronimo was apparently not present when Cochise cut his way out of the tent, for his account is very confused, but he participated in the ensuing events and related them clearly. "In a few days

9 This story has been told many times. Good accounts with critical evaluation of all the sources may be found in Lockwood, *The Apache Indians*, pp. 100–107, and Thrapp, *Conquest of Apacheria*, pp. 15–18.
10 Ball, *op. cit.*, p. 155. Kaywaykla called the child an "infant," but Naiche was probably about five years old in 1861.
11 Griswold, "The Fort Sill Apaches," s.v. "Geronimo." The Apaches do not remember the name of the wife related to Cochise, but I found a wife named She-gha, who was probably she and who lived until 1887. It is possible that "She-gha" is simply another spelling for "Shtsha-she," but Miss Elaine Clark, a careful student of the Apache language, believes them to be different names; letter to Angie Debo, June 5, 1973. She concedes the possibility, however, that they may be identical, in which case I have confused the two throughout my narrative, for it would have been Shtsha-she who remained with Geronimo until 1887 while the sister of Yahnozha dropped out of sight before that time and is still nameless.

[after the tent episode]," he said, "we organized in the mountains and returned to fight the soldiers. There were two tribes—the Bedonkohe and the Chokonen [Chiricahua] Apaches, both commanded by Cochise. After a few days' skirmishing we attacked a freight train that was coming in with supplies for the Fort. We killed some of the men and captured the others. These prisoners our chief offered to trade for the Indians whom the soldiers had captured at the massacre in the tent. This the officers refused, so we killed our prisoners, disbanded, and went into hiding in the mountains. Of those who took part in this affair I am the only one now living."[12]

According to Jason Betzinez, the occurrence, which the Apaches characterized as the "Cut through the Tent" affair, aroused much indignation and interest even among bands distant from the Chiricahua country. "I have heard my parents as well as others discuss it many a time," he said.[13] Geronimo, to whom raiding was a way of life, described its effect with typical understatement: "After this trouble all of the Indians agreed not to be friendly with the white men any more. There was no general engagement, but a long struggle followed. Sometimes we attacked the white men—sometimes they attacked us. First a few Indians would be killed and then a few soldiers. I think the killing was about equal on each side. The number killed in these troubles did not amount to much, but this treachery on the part of the soldiers had angered the Indians and revived memories of other wrongs, so that we never again trusted the United States troops." But he put in a good word for Steck: "I do not think that the agent had anything to do with planning this, for he had always treated us well."[14]

At this very time events in the Southwest were controlled by the white man's Civil War. On February 8, while Cochise and the army officers were engaged in diplomatic and arrow-and-rifle

---

[12] Barrett, *op. cit.*, pp. 115, 117. It was certainly Barrett's error to attribute the tent incident to Mangas Coloradas instead of Cochise. Geronimo could not have made that mistake.

[13] Betzinez, *I Fought with Geronimo*, p. 41.

[14] Barrett, *op. cit.*, pp. 116, 118.

skirmishing around Apache Pass, a government for the Confederate States of America was established at Montgomery, Alabama. With much of the Butterfield Stage route in Confederate or disputed territory, it was decided in late March to abandon the service. The transcontinental mail and stage traffic was shifted to the great Overland Trail through Nebraska and over the mountains by the South Pass in Wyoming. Butterfield employees began to dismantle the stations and move the equipment from New Mexico and Arizona. One party under General Manager McNees, bringing in this property from the west, was ambushed and wiped out near the Doubtful Pass station by Indians believed to be led by Cochise.[15]

During July the federal military posts in New Mexico and Arizona were being rapidly evacuated as an invading Confederate force of Texans under Indian-hating Colonel John Robert Baylor advanced up the Rio Grande from El Paso; and Steck found it necessary to abandon his agency. At the same time, the Indians swept away all the livestock from the area around the copper mines, and the mines were deserted. On September 27, according to a newspaper published at Mesilla on the Rio Grande, Mangas Coloradas' warriors even attacked the town of Pinos Altos and fought an all-day battle with its defenders. The gold miners abandoned the place, and the settlers in the Mimbres Valley fled, leaving their houses and growing crops. The triumphant Indians believed they had driven out the soldiers and cleared their country of white intruders.[16] Geronimo's name does not appear in reports of these events, for he had not yet risen to prominence on the American side of the border, but there is no doubt that he was an active participant.

On August 1 Baylor proclaimed himself the military governor of a "Territory of Arizona" comprising the southern half of the two present states, with his headquarters at Mesilla. He organized

15 Hattie M. Anderson, "With the Confederates in New Mexico during the Civil War —Memoirs of Hank Smith," *Panhandle-Plains Historical Review*, Vol. II, pp. 80–82.
16 *Ibid.*, pp. 65–69; Secretary of the Interior, *Annual Report*, 1861, pp. 732–33; Thrapp, *Victorio*, p. 75.

two volunteer companies, the Arizona Rangers and the Arizona Guards, to reopen the road from the Rio Grande to Tucson. On March 20, 1862, he sent the following instructions to the captain of the Guards at Tucson: "I learn from Lieut. J. J. Jackson that the Indians have been in to your post for the purpose of making a treaty. The Congress of the Confederate States has passed a law declaring extermination to all hostile Indians. You will therefore use all means to persuade the Apaches or any tribe to come in for the purpose of making peace, and when you get them together kill all the grown Indians and take the children prisoners and sell them to defray the expense of killing the Indians. Buy whisky and such other goods as may be necessary for the Indians and I will order vouchers given to cover the amount expended. . . . Say nothing of your orders until the time arrives. . . ."

This order was disavowed by President Jefferson Davis and Secretary of War George Wythe Randolph. Later Baylor wrote a letter defending it. He had learned of this "law," he said, from a newspaper article, supposed it to be authentic, "and feeling convinced (as I do still) that such a policy was the only one suitable to the hostile and treacherous tribes, I acted on it."[17]

The Apaches continued raiding and killing at will throughout Confederate "Arizona," but the Texans were soon driven out by the Colorado Volunteers. At the same time, the summer of 1862, a "California Column" of eighteen hundred Union men under Brigadier General James Henry Carleton was advancing from the west. The Apaches under Cochise and Mangas Coloradas prepared an ambush high in the rocks above Apache Pass. They selected a strategic site overlooking the abandoned stage station and the nearby spring that meant life or death to men and animals on the trail.

They allowed a reconnaissance detail to go through on June 25 without open resistance, professing friendship but killing 3 men who had strayed from the command. Perhaps they were not yet

17 George Wythe Baylor, *John Robert Baylor, Confederate Governor of Arizona,* pp. 12–15.

in position. Then on July 14 an advance party under Captain Thomas L. Roberts, with 122 men and two mountain howitzers, entered the pass. When the soldiers approached the ambush, the Indians from their hidden positions, began picking them off, killing one and wounding others. Then the troops set up the howitzers and trained them on the heights, and when the shells began bursting among the Indians they withdrew. Cremony said that one of them told him later, "We were getting along well enough until you began firing wagons at us."

Cremony, who had been living in San Diego, had enlisted in the California Column and was in command of the supply train that was slowly advancing toward the pass. Roberts sent six men back to warn him, and some mounted Apaches pursued them. They all escaped but a private, who was cut off and surrounded. As the Indians were circling him for the kill, he managed to wound the impressive looking warrior who was in command. It is now known that the man wounded was Mangas Coloradas. The Apaches then abandoned the pursuit and concentrated on helping their stricken chief. Roberts went back to protect the train, and although the Apaches attacked it from the heights, the howitzers were again brought into play and the loaded wagons came through. The main column under Carleton followed without incident. The Apaches had failed. Carleton then left a detail to build a fort commanding the spring. This was the beginning of Fort Bowie, destined to a prominent place in the life of Geronimo and the history of his people. The date was July 28, 1862.[18]

It is significant that in this engagement the Indians, or at least many of them, were armed with rifles, which came mainly from white men they had killed—an indication of the extent of their depredations on the American side of the border during the two

---

[18] Thrapp, *Victorio*, pp. 79–81; Lockwood, *op. cit.*, pp. 135–41; Martin F. Schmitt (ed.), *General George Crook: His Autobiography*, pp. 163–64 and n. 5; Ball, *op. cit.*, p. 47. Cremony told an exciting story of this fight in *Life among the Apaches*, pp. 144, 155–67, but his account is unreliable. For example, he said the howitzers killed sixty-three Apaches. Roberts, an army officer, no doubt inclined to overestimate enemy losses, reported only ten killed for the entire engagement; the Indians said that none of their warriors was killed, but that several were wounded.

years since they began their war.[19] The use of these weapons also brought a new dimension to their raids.

Strangely enough, the account of this fight at Apache Pass does not appear in Geronimo's dictated memoirs. Tradition says that he was there, and it is incredible that he would have failed to participate in an attack so carefully planned and involving his closest associates. Perhaps he simply forgot to mention it. He was intimately connected with the next incident.

After the battle in the pass, Carleton proceeded without difficulty to the Rio Grande, and on September 18 he assumed command of the Department of New Mexico. He at once began to issue orders to his subordinates to kill all Indian men wherever found. If they should attempt to treat for peace they were to be told that "you have been sent to punish them for their treachery and their crimes; that you have no power to make peace."[20] (The historian Dan L. Thrapp characterizes Carleton as "the Union Baylor.") Within the next few months he rounded up the Mescaleros, and within a year, the Navahos, and he placed them on a small tract on the Pecos River named the Bosque Redondo. There the two tribes fought each other and starved and suffered. He tried to do the same to the related tribes he classed as "Gilas." Their subjugation was entrusted to Brigadier General Joseph Rodman West, who fully shared his views.

West proceeded to the Gila and made his camp near Mangas Springs, on the short-lived Santa Lucia Reservation, in preparation for a campaign against Mangas Coloradas and his adherents.[21] But these Apaches, like other Indians, were unable to grasp the concept of an overall government entity. Every military command was a separate unit. Geronimo innocently described the establishment of this base in the heart of his mountains under orders of the enemy of Apache Pass: "About ten years [after the boundary survey of 1851] some more white men came. These were all

19 For these depredations, see Secretary of the Interior, *Annual Report*, 1863, pp. 503–504.
20 C. L. Sonnichsen, *The Mescalero Apaches*, pp. 98–99.
21 Thrapp, *Victorio*, p. 83.

warriors. They made their camp on the Gila River south [actually southwest] of Hot Springs. At first they were friendly and we did not dislike them, but they were not as good as those who came first."[22]

Then he went on with his characteristic understatement, "After about a year some trouble arose between them and the Indians." Trouble indeed! It was the murder of Mangas Coloradas on January 18, 1863. There are several versions, but all agree that he was lured to his fate by a profession of peace. A party of gold seekers under the mountain man Joseph Reddeford Walker were traveling through the area on their way west and had camped at abandoned Fort McLane. It occurred to them that by capturing Mangas Coloradas and holding him as a hostage they would be ensured a safe journey; then if all went well, they would release him. Men from this party and a unit of the California Column accordingly got possession of the chief under a flag of truce at the abandoned Pinos Altos settlement. Then West appeared and took the prisoner. He placed him under guard with a strong indication of his wishes, and during the night the chief was shot by the guards "while attempting to escape." The army surgeon cut off his head, "boiled it in a great black pot," according to James Kaywaykla, and sent the skull to a phrenologist, who reported that it was larger than Daniel Webster's. It was afterwards used as a lecture exhibit.[23]

Geronimo characterized the murder of Mangas Coloradas as "perhaps the greatest wrong ever done to the Indians." His account shows the serious consideration they gave to what they thought was an opportunity to make peace. Apparently the chief and his followers had not left the Chiricahua country after the fight in the pass. There they received a report, perhaps as part of the plot, of the friendliness of Apache Tejo, a tiny settlement in the vicinity of their old home, now cleared of the miners and settlers who had

22 Barrett, op. cit., p. 114.
23 Daniel Ellis Conner, Joseph Reddeford Walker and the Arizona Adventure, pp. 32–42; Thrapp, Conquest of Apacheria, pp. 20–23; Thrapp, Victorio, pp. 82–83; Ball, op. cit., p. 48. Conner's eyewitness account seems to be the correct one.

driven them to war. The chief and three warriors "went to Apache Tejo and held a council with these citizens and soldiers. They told him that if he would come with his tribe and live near them, they would issue to him from the Government, blankets, flour, provisions, beef, and all manner of supplies." This sounded like the days of the absent Steck. The chief promised to return with his answer within two weeks.

"When he came back to our settlement he assembled the whole tribe in council." This, of course, included the Bedonkohes. "I did not believe that the people at Apache Tejo would do as they said and therefore I opposed the plan," said Geronimo, "but it was decided that with part of the tribe Mangus-Colorado would return to Apache Tejo and receive an issue of rations and supplies." If all turned out as represented, "the remainder of the tribe would join him and we would make our permanent home at Apache Tejo. . . . We gave almost all of our arms and ammunition to the party going to Apache Tejo, so that in case there should be treachery they would be prepared for any surprise." About half the tribe accompanied the chief, while the remainder remained in Arizona under the charge of Geronimo.[24]

But the arms and ammunition did not help the Apaches who went with Mangas Coloradas. Trustingly, he put himself in the power of the conspirators, thus forfeiting his life against any attempt at rescue. The next day, while his family and friends anxiously waited for word of his release, the soldiers attacked their camp, killing eleven or twelve, and, it is said, decorating the bridles of their horses with the scalps. Several fights followed, and two Apache camps were destroyed.[25]

Meanwhile, in Arizona the rest of the band with Geronimo was waiting for news of the chief and his party. "No word ever came to us from them. From other sources, however, we heard that they had been treacherously captured and slain. In this dilemma we

[24] Barrett, *op. cit.*, pp. 119–20.
[25] Conner, *op. cit.*, pp. 41–42; Lockwood, *op. cit.*, pp. 145–47; Thrapp, *Victorio*, p. 83.

did not know just exactly what to do, but fearing that the troops who had captured them would attack us, we retreated into the mountains near Apache Pass. . . . On this retreat, while passing through the mountains, we discovered four men with a herd of cattle. Two of the men were in front in a buggy and two were behind on horseback. We killed all four, . . . drove the cattle back into the mountains, made a camp, and began to kill the cattle and pack the meat." So much for the army's efforts to bring peace and order to the Southwest.

Before they finished their butchering, the Indians were attacked by cavalry, and one warrior, three women, and three children were killed. They had to fight with bows and arrows because most of their guns and ammunition were with the ill-fated band that had gone with Mangas Coloradas. They scattered, then reassembled at an appointed rendezvous about fifty miles away. Ten days later the same troops attacked again. The Indians retreated four miles back into the mountains, where they were joined by Cochise and some of his Chiricahua warriors, and he assumed command. A few days later more troopers attacked, and again they disbanded. This time the Bedonkohes "reassembled near their old camp vainly waiting for the return of Mangus-Colorado and our kinsmen. . . . Then a council was held, and it was believed that Mangus-Colorado was dead. I was elected Tribal Chief."[26]

One wonders whether this "election," like the previous one, was made up by Barrett. This time it might have occurred. The Bedonkohes had long followed the leadership of their great Mimbreno neighbor, Mangas Coloradas. Soon they were to become permanently merged with the Chiricahuas. If they did elect Geronimo as chief, his office ended with the separate existence of his tribe.

There was no successor to Mangas Coloradas. His son, Mangus, was young and lacked the drive required to establish authority over a people so strongly individualistic as the Apaches. The Mimbrenos united with their close relatives, the more numerous Warm

---

[26] Barrett, *op. cit.*, pp. 121–24.

Springs tribe. Delgadito was soon killed in a battle with Mexicans,[27] and Victorio and Loco became the Warm Springs chiefs.[28] Victorio was to rise to a place of greatness in Apache history similar to that of Mangas Coloradas. He also was physically impressive—Kaywaykla, a Warm Springs child, always remembered his "majesty of form and bearing"—"I think he was the most nearly perfect human being I have ever seen"[29]—and he was to show military strategy approaching genius. His entire "foreign" policy revolved around his love for the secluded basin on the Alamosa River that enclosed the healing waters that gave the tribe its name. When allowed to remain in that area, he observed the peace; any attempt to relocate him brought war.

Loco, though a brave and able warrior, sought peace throughout his life. It was even said by the war party that his Spanish name Loco indicated that he was "crazy" enough to trust the white men.[30] A pleasanter explanation is that once, in a battle with Mexicans, he risked his life by running through a hail of bullets to rescue a wounded warrior; the Mexicans called him "that loco Apache," and the name stuck.[31] There was never any question of his courage and skill. Once he killed a grizzly bear singlehandedly, armed only with a knife. And Betzinez remembered seeing him send an arrow entirely through a beef on issue days during his later reservation experience.[32]

Another prominent Warm Springs leader was Geronimo's brother-in-law, the aged Nana. Although he appeared feeble and limped perceptibly from a "broken foot," he seemed indestructible. He was to become the most uncompromising of all Apaches in

[27] Davis, *The Truth about Geronimo*, p. 111. Davis was greatly confused about tribes and leaders, but he made this statement on the authority of Mangus and Loco.

[28] Modern Apaches are in disagreement about which of the two was the chief. Jason Betzinez, who grew up as a member of the Warm Springs tribe and knew both of them well stated that they were elected as dual chiefs (*op. cit.*, pp. 24–25, 49). This duality seems to fit the position they took in negotiating with government officials during the 1860's. Later the tribe became divided over war and peace, and it seems apparent that the war faction recognized Victorio and the peace party, Loco.

[29] Ball, *op. cit.*, p. 41.

[30] *Ibid.*, p. 28; but for tributes to his courage and integrity, see pp. 138–39.

[31] Ball interview, July 23, 1971.

[32] Betzinez, *op. cit.*, pp. 6, 33.

their wars against the white man, but to his people he was a wise, kind, grandfatherly figure. He was the granduncle of Kaywaykla, and the child revered him for his tenderness to the young, his consideration of the women, his courtesy to his fellow warriors, and his complete devotion to his tribe.[33]

Also in the band was Nonithian, who was probably the son of Delgadito but too young to succeed to leadership. He married Geronimo's widowed cousin Nah-thle-tla and was to become the father of Betzinez and a daughter later known as Ellen. Soon he was killed trying to separate two drunken, fighting relatives.[34] All these members of the Warm Springs band were to be closely associated with Geronimo in the troubled times following the murder of Mangas Coloradas.

The federal government now began to make plans for administering the area. A month after the chief's death—on February 24, 1863—Congress cut off the western half of New Mexico to form the Territory of Arizona, thus establishing the boundaries of the present states. Later that year Steck came back with elaborate plans for his Apache charges. Their reservation should be protected by a patent, military posts should be established nearby to control them and keep off white encroachment, and ample rations should be furnished for their subsistence. Military conquest was impossible, he believed, but even if it were accomplished, it would cost three million dollars annually, and the tribes could be fed for one-twentieth of that sum. They should be encouraged to accumulate property, and he warned against allowing them to perpetuate such "absurd" customs as destroying the property of the deceased. (The white people had not yet adopted the extravagant burial customs of a later century.) He also would curtail their numerous celebrations, especially the elaborate puberty ceremony for the girls, in which the parents impoverished themselves to feast the tribe and "make night hideous with their songs."[35]

33 *Ibid.*, pp. 50–51; Ball, *op. cit.*, *passim*.
34 Betzinez, *op. cit.*, pp. 9n., 24, 26, 38.
35 Thrapp, *Victorio*, pp. 84–86.

This "womanhood" rite was, in fact, a beautiful celebration, free from the sadism that marks the puberty rites of many primitive people. The girl wore an elaborately trimmed buckskin dress and performed various rituals in and around an especially constructed tipi. She was advised of the duties and privileges of womanhood and was honored as the temporary embodiment of White Painted Woman. As one of the songs expressed it,

〰〰〰〰〰〰〰〰〰〰〰〰〰

You have started out on the good earth;
You have started out with good moccasins;
With moccasin strings of the rainbow,
     you have started out;
With moccasin strings of the sun's rays,
     you have started out;
In the midst of plenty you have started out.

〰〰〰〰〰〰〰〰〰〰〰〰〰

Special dances were performed for her, especially the Dance of the Mountain Spirits by masked performers wearing fantastic pronged headdresses—a deeply moving spectacle. There was much use of *hoddentin*, the pollen of the tule rush or sometimes of corn, always sacred to the Apaches. Every detail of the complicated ritual was carried out with prayer and ceremonial exactness, and the girl's extended family shared in the preparations and the expenses.[36] Certainly it *was* expensive—as expensive as a daughter's wedding in modern white society.

The Apaches, of course, were unaware of Steck's well-meant designs against their culture. Victorio, Nana, Loco, and the sons and even the widow of Mangas Coloradas began to make cautious peace overtures to him. But he was unable to make any headway with them in view of Carleton's insistence that they should be caged up with the other prisoners on the Bosque Redondo.[37]

---

[36] Opler, *An Apache Life-Way*, pp. 82–134. I personally have been more stirred by the Dance of the Mountain Spirits than by any other performance I have ever seen.
[37] Thrapp, *Victorio*, pp. 88–91.

Masked dancers impersonating the Mountain Spirits, with the accompanying clown. The photograph may have been taken at San Carlos by A. Frank Randall in the spring of 1884. Note the wickiups in the background. *In spite of their precarious existence, the Apaches had a rich and complex ceremonial life.* Courtesy Smithsonian Institution, National Anthropological Archives.

Finally, the Mescaleros suddenly left one night in the fall of 1865; then, Apachelike, they vanished, not only from Carleton's searching, but also from the ken of present-day historians.[38] Even this disappearance did not change Carleton's determination to round up the Warm Springs band.

Such differences between the civilian agents and the military were to continue throughout the Apache wars. But as at other times, this disagreement lay more in a conflict of authority than in fundamental philosophy. Steck and his superiors had consolidation plans similar to Carleton's except that they lacked the power to carry them out.

[38] Sonnichsen, *op. cit.*, pp. 118–22.

Probably even more than the Indians, the white citizens were the victims of Carleton's intransigence. With the Civil War ended, settlers were returning to New Mexico. Gold miners were back at Pinos Altos; about three hundred were working the mines by 1868. That year silver was discovered a few miles southwest, and Silver City soon sprang up there. The Indians seemed to have everything their own way, raiding and killing at will. They even swept the horses away from the military posts, putting the troopers on foot. Citizens' complaints joined Steck's protests at Washington, and Carleton was finally transferred to another assignment in the fall of 1866.[39] Two years later a treaty with the Navahos permitted them to return to their homeland, but the Warm Springs Apaches vainly pleaded for a reservation that would allow them to live in their country at peace.[40] Their efforts finally enlisted Cochise.

That formidable Chiricahua had killed and raided unchecked, especially on the California Trail. Then came his strange pact with Thomas J. Jeffords. In the mid-sixties Jeffords had served for eighteen months as superintendent of mails on the route between Fort Bowie and Tucson, where he himself was wounded by arrows and fourteen of his drivers were killed. Then he went alone into Cochise's stronghold. It was the first time since that redoubtable chief became a hostile that a white man had seen him and lived. Somehow the chief was impressed, and the two became fast friends. He never violated his bond with Jeffords, but he continued his war against all other white men.[41]

These relations certainly involved Geronimo, although his name had not yet come into public notice. One incident of these hidden years touched him very closely. Juh was living, as he frequently did, with the Chiricahuas. In the winter of 1869/70, as nearly as Apaches can reckon dates, he had left his pregnant wife, the wise and capable Ishton, there in his camp while he raided in Mexico. When her time came, her labor was so painful and prolonged that

---

39 Thrapp, *Victorio*, pp. 91–93.
40 *Ibid.*, pp. 98–100.
41 Lockwood, *op. cit.*, pp. 110–12.

death seemed imminent. The Apaches had none of the taboos observed by the men of some Indian tribes against events in the female cycle. Geronimo hastened to the camp of his favorite "sister" and climbed a mountain to pray alone. Later Apache memories stretched the time of her labor to the mystical four days. On the fifth day at sunrise, as he lifted his hands and eyes towards the east, his Power spoke: "The child will be born and your sister will live; and you will never be killed with weapons, but live to old age." The infant was born that day and received the name Daklugie, meaning "Forced-his-way-through" or "One-who-grabs."[42]

Meanwhile, in the summer of 1869 Loco and Victorio, from their *rancherias* on the Alamosa and the parallel arroyo of the Cuchillo Negro, had begun to make tentative peace offers to the military at the posts on the Rio Grande. The superintendent of Indian affairs for New Mexico suggested that they be settled with the recently repatriated Navahos. The Mescalero agent, unable to contact his invisible tribe, wanted them sent across the Rio Grande to his vicinity. Their historian, Dan L. Thrapp, says that one may search through the thousands upon thousands of documents in the government records without finding a valid reason given for uprooting them. All they ever asked was to remain at peace in their homeland.[43]

By that time, able and conscientious First Lieutenant Charles E. Drew had been appointed as agent to them and their relatives. (There was a brief period of appointing army officers to serve in this capacity, but the practice was soon forbidden by Congress because it removed an important area of patronage.) He managed to lure Loco, Victorio, and some other leaders to a council at Cañada Alamosa. The tribe maintained permanent peace with this Mexican town, trading stolen horses, mules, and cattle for whiskey, guns, ammunition, and food. At the council there they were vigilant and suspicious, bringing along forty fully armed warriors,

---

42 Ball interview, July 26, 1971; Eve Ball to Angie Debo, November 13, 1972.
43 Thrapp, *Victorio*, pp. 98–99.

maintaining lookouts on every hill, and keeping a guard over their horse herd.[44] Loco told Drew that not only the Warm Springs tribe, but Cochise and the Chiricahuas as well were willing to come in. But Washington took no action while the Indians patiently waited. Drew died the following summer. At the same time, Cochise visited the new military post soon to be known as Fort Apache in the White Mountain area of east central Arizona and conferred with the commanding officer there. Finally, in October of that year (1870) the Indian Office sent Special Agent William Arny to study the situation. He and Drew's successor finally induced the Indians to meet them at their Warm Springs retreat. Present were twenty-two chiefs and leaders with 790 of their people, including Cochise with his family and 96 of his Chiricahuas. Cochise was coming to realize the attrition of his tribe; his losses, though smaller than those of the enemy, could not be recouped as easily by his small band. He said that he and his people had killed many white men, but if the government would furnish them with food and clothing he would bring in the whole tribe in peace. He did not like the White Mountain area, but was willing to consider the Alamosa.[45] Victorio said that within a month there would be 1,000 to 1,200 Indians collected there.

In his report Arny urged the establishment of a reservation for all of these related tribes. He suggested six different locations, but he did include in his list the Alamosa Valley and the Warm Springs. There were fifty-two families of white squatters living there, he said, referring to the Mexican settlement of Cañada Alamosa, but since they had no title to the land they could be removed by paying them eleven thousand dollars for their improvements. His own choice of the six locations was the Tularosa Valley, an uninhabited place in the mountains of western New Mexico east of Fort Apache. Meanwhile, he would allow them to remain in

44 Secretary of the Interior, *Annual Report*, 1869, pp. 104–10. For the amicable relations between Cañada Alamosa (Monticello) and the Warm Springs Indians, see Betzinez, *op. cit.*, pp. 24, 26; Ball, *op. cit.*, p. 57; and Thrapp, *Victorio*, pp. 126–28.

45 Thrapp, *Victorio*, pp. 104, 125–26, 129 and note 50. As far as I know, only Thrapp has uncovered these overtures by the supposedly unapproachable Cochise.

their Alamosa homeland until they could be persuaded or forced to remove.[46]

Geronimo mentioned this Warm Springs council only incidentally, as a preliminary to a visit he made to the area. Soldiers had attacked his camp, killed sixteen of his people, captured all their horses and supplies, and destroyed their lodges. "We had nothing left; winter was beginning, and it was the coldest winter I ever knew." Game was scarce, his people were suffering, and he decided to seek help.

"We had heard that Chief Victoria of the Chihenne (Oje Caliente) Apaches was holding a council with the white men near Hot Springs in New Mexico, and that he had plenty of provisions. We had always been on friendly terms with this tribe, and Victoria was especially kind to my people. . . . We easily found [him] and his band, and they gave us supplies for the winter. We stayed with them for about a year, and during this stay we had perfect peace. We had not the least trouble with Mexicans, white men, or Indians. . . . No one ever treated our tribe more kindly than Victoria and his band. We are still proud to say that he and his people were our friends."[47]

Contemporary accounts confirm his story of about a year of comparative peace on the Alamosa. Then the United States government finally came up with an Indian policy. It was to involve Geronimo and all the related tribes.

46 *Ibid.*, pp. 130–31.
47 Barrett, *op. cit.*, pp. 124–28.

CHAPTER 5

WASHINGTON HAS A POLICY

Something had to be done about the hostile Indians. Prospectors, miners, ranchers, adventurers of all types were coming in increasing numbers to New Mexico and Arizona. Towns were springing up—wild, lawless, stirring with ambition. And there was always the traffic on the trails. Thus, the area was becoming more and more vulnerable to Apache raids and more vocal in its outcries.

Nobody on the frontier admitted that the Indians also had their experience of wrongs and suffering, but the federal government was torn between benevolence and severity. President Grant had proclaimed his celebrated Peace Policy, and a Board of Indian Commissioners, made up of distinguished philanthropists, had been created to influence and evaluate Indian administration. The Department of the Interior, with its Indian Office, and the War Department fought each other from the cabinet level in Washington to the agencies and armies in the field. All this in its most intense form came to the Apaches, beginning in 1871.

Clearly, these Indians had to be assured of a place to live and some livelihood besides raiding. That year Congress appropriated seventy thousand dollars for "collecting the Apaches of Arizona and New Mexico upon reservations, furnishing them with subsis-

settle with their Warm Springs relatives. But their mission failed because of their accidental meeting with Crook. He told them they had no business in Arizona and rudely ordered them home.[9]

By this time more than one thousand Indians had collected on the Alamosa, but they still had no title to their homeland. Every lawless act perpetrated by Indians, Anglos, or Mexicans was laid to their charge, and a large party of citizens of Silver City had recently made ready to wipe them out. Governor William A. Pile learned of the contemplated massacre and stopped it by "peremptory orders" backed up by troops. But the Indians learned of it and fled. Colyer reached Fort Craig on the Rio Grande on August 16 and went on up the Alamosa. He found hundreds of wickiups still standing, but no Indians. Finally, up the canyon in the vicinity of their springs he met Agent Piper, Loco, and Trujillo, but he decided that this area was too small and that it would be "preposterous" to buy out the three hundred or so Mexicans settled down the river. Looking around, he decided on the Tularosa Valley, formerly recommended by Arny.

Word was relayed to Washington, and on November 20 an order was issued setting the area aside. Then shortly after Colyer left, Cochise, even though he had failed to receive the messengers, came of his own accord with about thirty warriors and their families and settled on the Cuchillo Negro. Pope and Piper conferred with him, finding him anxious for peace but unwilling to go to the Tularosa. Victorio and Loco positively refused to go. The region was too cold, they said. Although the Apaches were mountain people, they required low valleys for their planting, and the altitude of the Tularosa was too high for comfortable winter dwelling or the maturing of their corn. It was finally decided to leave them undisturbed for the present.[10] Colyer did not subscribe to the plan of moving the Mescaleros across the Rio Grande to join them; instead, he recommended the establishment of a reservation for

---

[9] Thrapp, *Conquest of Apacheria*, pp. 99–100; Thrapp, *Victorio*, pp. 137–38.
[10] Thrapp, *Victorio*, pp. 133, 136–43.

them in their own mountains. This, their present reservation (with some changes in area), was set aside for them in 1873.[11]

Meanwhile, Colyer went on into Arizona, where he and his mission were subjected by press and citizens to all the strident vilification of a crude, new society. (Some of the epithets were "cold-blooded scoundrel," "red-handed assassin," and "treacherous black-hearted dog.") By this time Crook had his careful plans all made for a campaign against the Apaches. Then, as he expressed it, "I discovered from the newspapers that a Mr. Vincent Colyer had been sent out by the 'Indian ring' to interfere with my operations . . . and was going to make peace with the Apaches by the grace of God." He accordingly countermanded his orders and directed his subordinates to cooperate with the "peace policy." Colyer met with leaders of the different tribes—Apaches and other hostiles—and established reservations for them near the military posts in the vicinities of their various homelands. One of these areas, although subsequently pared down to satisfy miners and settlers, is still in existence—the Fort Apache Reservation for the White Mountain band and the Coyoteros, a large tract surrounding the military post of that name.

Thus, according to Crook, "Vincent the Good" traveled through the country "making peace as he went, and the Indians just immediately behind him left a trail of blood behind them from the murdered citizens." It was not quite as bad as that, but it was apparent that peace and good will would have to be supplemented by more drastic action. On November 5 in western Arizona a raiding party of Yavapais (known as Apache-Mohaves, but unrelated to the Apaches) Colyer had just settled on a reservation attacked and robbed a stagecoach, killing the driver and six of its eight passengers. Crook delayed his retribution for a time until their guilt was established,[12] meanwhile continuing his preparations for an intensive campaign against hostiles in general. He was supremely confident—"if this entire Indian question be left to

[11] Sonnichsen, *Mescalero Apaches*, p. 139.
[12] For the raid and the ensuing punishment of the raiders, during which Crook almost lost his life, see Thrapp, *Al Sieber*, pp. 90–103.

me . . . I have not the slightest doubt of my ability to conquer a peace with this Apache race in a comparatively short space of time."[13] Able as he was, he underestimated the fighting qualities of the Apaches.

In December he sent word to the bands that they must be on their reservations by mid-February to escape punishment; on February 7 he warned them that only nine more days remained. Then just as he was ready to start, he was notified, to his disgust, that Brigadier General Oliver Otis Howard was being sent out on another peace mission. Howard had a good Civil War combat record but an ostentatious piety that repelled fellow officers and westerners.[14] Indians, less reticent than white men in expressing religious feelings, liked and trusted him.

In late April, 1872, he arrived in Arizona, where he conferred effectively with the Indians and made some rearrangement of the reservations. Of these, the San Carlos Reservation, across the Salt River south of the Fort Apache Reservation, is still in existence, though with a reduced acreage. Both of these areas were formally set apart by executive order that year on December 14. Some of the Indians gladly settled down on these places of refuge, but Howard agreed with Crook that military force would be required to bring in the raiders.[15]

In July he met with the Warm Springs Apaches in New Mexico. The removal plans for that unhappy tribe had finally been carried out in the late spring of that year. An agency and a military post had been established on the Tularosa, and they had been ordered to settle there. By persuasion and threats Loco and Victorio had finally been induced to go, but only about three hundred of their people had joined them. The others, forced from their homeland, were widely scattered—and no doubt they raided. Howard visited the ones on the reservation, and they complained of the cold climate, impure water, much sickness, the death of their children, and a season too short for growing crops. Howard inspected their

13 Thrapp, *Conquest of Apacheria*, pp. 102–106; Schmitt, *op. cit.*, pp. 167–68.
14 Thrapp, *Conquest of Apacheria*, p. 106.
15 *Ibid.*, p. 111.

beloved Alamosa and frankly admitted that it was a more suitable location. He promised to have it set apart for them by corn planting time the following year. The relieved Indians failed to notice that this settlement was conditioned upon the consent of Cochise to join them there. For the present he advised the chiefs to remain where they were.[16]

Meanwhile, they assisted him to contact Cochise. Crook had been "intending to iron all the wrinkles out of Cochise's band ... I already had my spies in his camp and intended moving on him with my whole force after night, and surrounding him by daylight in the morning and give them such a clearing out that it would end him for all time to come, as his band was recognized as the worst of all the Apaches." But to the general's chagrin, Howard arrived first.[17]

Since his return from New Mexico and his meeting with the federal officials there, Cochise had committed no hostile acts, although some of his people had done so. But Howard considered it necessary as well as prudent to obtain help in approaching him. Victorio arranged for the general to meet Thomas Jeffords and a young warrior named Chee (Chie), who was a nephew of Cochise and one of his most trusted men; they consented to accompany Howard. The general also enlisted Ponce, probably a son of Mangas Coloradas and thus Cochise's brother-in-law.[18] Ponce spoke Spanish fluently and therefore could act as interpreter. He was believed to be the head of a band of raiders and would be heard from thereafter. Howard found them innocently gathering corn, possibly planted by Mexicans, in the canyon of the Cuchillo Negro.

With these assistants, Howard and his party set out on their 350-mile journey. At Silver City, where they spent one night, they

---

[16] Thrapp, *Victorio*, pp. 144–48, 151. See also Ball, *In the Days of Victorio*, p. 49.
[17] Schmitt, *op. cit.*, pp. 176–77.
[18] This identification of Chee and Ponce was given to Eve Ball by Asa Daklugie. Chee's descendants now live on the Mescalero Reservation. Regarding Ponce's relationship to Mangas Coloradas, Daklugie cited his father, Juh—"I think that is true. He was my father's *segundo* [second in command, or assistant, with the implication of the succession], and Juh should have known" (Ball to Angie Debo, June 25, 1973). Howard mistakenly attributed this relationship to Chee. There is no evidence that Ponce was related to the Ponce encountered by Bartlett.

were almost mobbed by its turbulent, Indian-hating citizens, but—as Howard expressed it— "fortunately there were present several sensible men" who protected them. Even so, he took the precaution of setting out the next morning before the town awoke. A few miles beyond they met a party of prospectors. One of them raised his rifle to kill the two Indians, but Howard rode his horse in between, and the bad man backed off from becoming embroiled with official Washington. When the party reached Cochise's domain, there were smoke signals, the bark of a coyote, and cautious reconnaissance by Chee before they were guided to the sheltered valley enclosed by towering crags which was the chief's stronghold in the Dragoons. Cochise finally rode in with his wife, his sister, and his young son Naiche, who appeared to be about fourteen years old. (His older son, Taza, was not present.) He greeted Jeffords affectionately and cordially shook hands with Howard. Howard described him as fully six feet tall and well proportioned, with large, dark eyes and a pleasant expression.

He told how the trouble started with the capture and subsequent hanging of his relatives at Apache Pass. "You Americans began the fight," he said, "and now Americans and Mexicans kill an Apache on sight. I have retaliated with all my might. I have killed ten white men for every Indian slain." But he was now ready to make peace, and he sent out messengers to call in his scattered lieutenants. These must have included Geronimo, for the latter participated in the negotiations and was a party to the settlement.

Howard remained there eleven days while the leaders were gathering for the council. (He made friends with the Indian children, even teaching young Naiche to write his name.) The final agreement was made on October 13. Cochise would have accepted Howard's suggestion that his people join their Warm Springs relatives on the Alamosa, but he was not able to persuade all of the leaders to consent to the removal. He therefore decided against going. It would break up his band, he said; the ones who remained would commit depredations in Arizona, while if he stayed he could collect and control them all, protect the roads, and observe the peace. He also laid down the condition that Jeffords serve as agent.

Howard accordingly agreed to set aside the Chiricahuas' homeland as their reservation. It lay on the Mexican border, extending fifty-six miles west of the New Mexico–Arizona line, and included the Chiricahua and Dragoon mountains and the intervening Sulphur Springs Valley. It was confirmed by executive order on December 14. Jeffords, busy with projects of his own, was reluctant to take the position of agent but was persuaded to accept.

Geronimo showed his pleasure with the agreement but was still suspicious. He went out of the mountains with Howard and Cochise to report to the military on the success of the meeting, he and Howard riding double on the general's horse. With true Apache agility he mounted by springing over the horse's tail, then reaching his place behind Howard with another spring. The two became friendly during the ride, but when they approached the soldiers Howard felt him tremble. At the same time Cochise put his warriors into skirmish order, ready for defense or flight. No doubt the Indians were remembering Mangas Coloradas and others lured to their death by a promise of protection. But the meeting passed off well. The agency, with Jeffords in charge, was established near Fort Bowie, and Geronimo entered into the peace that followed.[19] All his life he remembered Howard with affection and gratitude and expressed satisfaction with the agreement: "This treaty lasted until long after General Howard had left our country. He always kept his word with us and treated us as brothers. . . . We could have lived forever at peace with him. If there is any pure, honest white man in the United States army, that man is General Howard. All the Indians respect him, and even to this day frequently talk of the happy times when General Howard was in command of our Post.[20] After he went away he placed an agent

[19] Thrapp, *Victorio*, pp. 153–54, 350 n. 42; Lockwood, *The Apache Indians*, pp. 112–22; O. O. Howard, *My Life and Experiences among Our Hostile Indians*, pp. 186–225. Howard gave some additional details in a book he wrote for children, *Famous Indian Chiefs I Have Known*, pp. 112–36, 357. He made many errors in recording historical events, but his account of his own experiences appears to be accurate.

[20] By "our Post," Geronimo referred to the agency. Of course Howard was not in

at Apache Pass who issued to us from the Government clothing, rations, and supplies, as General Howard directed. When beef was issued to the Indians I got twelve steers for my tribe, and Cochise got twelve steers for his tribe."[21]

Geronimo may have exaggerated his own importance in saying that he and Cochise received equal portions for distribution, but his statement may well be true. He probably represented Juh and his band (because of his speech defect Juh usually let Geronimo speak for him) as well as all the homeless stragglers from the Warm Springs tribe. And one of Geronimo's outstanding traits in the later, better-known period of his life was his hard economic sense. Thus, it was typical that he should manage the distribution for these unrecognized participants.

As soon as Howard's conference with Cochise and his lieutenants in the Dragoons was over, Chee and Ponce reported back to the Warm Springs leaders on the Tularosa. Cochise's success in securing title to his homeland made them more dissatisfied than ever, and this dissatisfaction was increased when Howard's recommendation that they be permitted to return to *their* homeland was disallowed. Counting the three hundred unwilling transients on the Tularosa, and ignoring the exiled wanderers scattered—and no doubt raiding—from New Mexico to Sonora, the authorities reasoned that since Cochise had not consented to remove to the Alamosa the tribe was not numerous enough to warrant a reservation there. Early in 1873 Howard wrote from Washington to break the news to the disappointed leaders Ponce, Victorio, and Loco. "I am not the President or Great Father," he apologized. "I only obey orders."[22]

Meanwhile, as soon as Howard's peace mission was over, Crook began his twice-delayed campaign against the tribes in the mountains of western Arizona. It began on November 15, 1872. The winter that followed appears in army reports as a succession of

command there or at the military post, but he did have authority as a special agent of President Grant.

21 Barrett, *Geronimo's Story of His Life*, pp. 128–29.
22 Thrapp, *Victorio*, p. 149.

hardships, individual exploits, pursuits, and the destruction of *rancherias*, in all of which the Apache scouts demonstrated Crook's confidence in them as trailers and guerrilla fighters. By spring the defeated raiders began to come in and settle on the reservations. Some eventually broke away, but Crook continued to comb the mountains and canyons for them. After they surrendered, he treated them with fairness and compassion. The Apaches learned that Nantan Lupan (Chief Grey Wolf) was a relentless enemy, but that they could trust his word.[23]

The general still itched to get his hands on Cochise, but Howard's peace pact prevented operations against the Chiricahua chief. He did send a mission to the chief in February, 1873. The party included Jeffords, who served as interpreter; George H. Stevens, acting agent at San Carlos, a prominent Arizona rancher married to a White Mountain Apache woman; and Bourke. Bourke was impressed by Cochise's sincerity and his efforts to keep the peace with the Americans. But regarding the Mexicans, "he said he considered them as being on one side in this matter, while the *Americans* were on the other. The former had not asked for peace as the latter had done. He did not deny that his boys were in the habit of raiding on Mexico, but this he could not prevent as it was no more than was done from all the Reservations."[24]

Cochise's homeless Warm Springs relatives also found the Chiricahua Reservation a convenient place to leave their families while the warriors went on to raid in Mexico. Jeffords learned that whether or not he fed them, they stayed. Then when the warriors returned and joined them, they all came in to share the rations. Jeffords was in a quandary. If he should refuse to feed them, hunger would drive them to more raiding. He believed that rationing, by supplying their needs, at least reduced it.[25]

At the same time, Cochise guarded the trails and protected the ranches on the American side of the line, not only from his own

[23] Thrapp, *Conquest of Apacheria*, pp. 119–43; Bourke, *op. cit.*, p. 112; Ball, *In the Days of Victorio*, p. 184.
[24] Bourke, *op. cit.*, p. 235; Thrapp, *Conquest of Apacheria*, pp. 145–47.
[25] Thrapp, *Victorio*, p. 166.

people but also from lawless raiders coming down from the north. But complaints were coming from the governor of Sonora to Governor Anson P. K. Safford of Arizona. On March 31, 1873, the harried Safford sent the communication to Crook. He added that "so far as the people of Arizona are concerned, I believe that Cochise has kept his word with us," but he feared that any attempt to halt the raids on Mexico would start another war with him.[26]

There is no record of Geronimo's actions during this period. It seems to have been a quiet interlude in his turbulent career. He may have been referring to it when he said, "It was a long time before we again went into Mexico or were disturbed by the Mexicans."[27] He was closely associated with Cochise (it may be, in fact, that it was at this time that he married She-gha), and Cochise did discourage, though he did not prevent, the Mexican raids. The chief's personal relationships with the white Americans can be glimpsed by the reminiscences of old Al Williamson, who as a youth of eighteen clerked in a trading post at Fort Bowie. There he often saw Cochise and his sons, Taza and Naiche. The chief was grave, never smiled, and, although he would drink with the officers, always left the post before sundown and required his people to do the same. Taza had a pleasant, smiling face, and like his grandfather, Mangas Coloradas, was very large. One day Al put him on the scales, and he weighed 199 pounds. Young Naiche resembled his father in his slender build and reserved manner.[28]

Cochise died in June, 1874. Before his death he called in his headmen and in their presence designated Taza as his successor. As the Apaches remembered it, he had carefully trained Taza for this responsibility. He exacted a promise from him and Naiche that they would preserve the peace. New Mexican Superintendent Levi Edwin Dudley had visited him in his stronghold during his last illness, hoping to persuade him to remove to the Alamosa. Later, Dudley hoped to persuade Taza.

In preparation for this removal the area had already been set

26 *Ibid.*, p. 165; Thrapp, *Conquest of Apacheria*, pp. 168–69.
27 Barrett, *op. cit.*, p. 85.
28 Lockwood, *op. cit.*, pp. 124–26. Lockwood talked with Williamson in 1934.

aside as a reservation by an executive order on April 9. But in any case, Dudley recommended the abandonment of the Tularosa Reservation (it had been a failure from the beginning, he said) and the location of the Warm Springs tribe in their homeland. To keep squatters from flocking there in order to claim reimbursement from the government, he issued an order reserving the tract, subject to approval. The approval was granted, and in July instructions came to remove the Tularosa Agency to that place. By the end of the summer, about four hundred Indians had assembled in the loved region.[29]

Thus, by a combination of Crook's efficient fighting methods and the overtures of peace commissioners, the Apache wars were in process of settlement. Of course, not all was sweetness and light on the reservations. Some of the agents placed in control were weak and unable to restrain their wild charges. Others were corrupt, entering into collusion with contractors to cheat on the quantity and quality of rations or even selling the Indians' supplies to the mining settlements. There were lawless spirits among the Apaches unwilling to settle down, and still more lawless white men, often leading citizens, who deliberately stirred up Apache wars in order to profit from fat army contracts—two million dollars annually to the Southwestern economy. But although there remained some police work by the army to bring in outlaws, and a more efficient management of the reservations by the civilian agents, Apache depredations no longer threatened normal development of the Southwest.

A demonstration of good reservation administration was furnished when John Philip Clum came on August 8, 1874, as agent on the San Carlos Reservation. This reservation had had a turbulent history, with seven hundred wild Indians, a succession of short-term agents, including a notorious swindler, and two companies of cavalry unable under the circumstances to keep order. The agency was a log hut with an earthen floor and canvas doors

<hr>

[29] Thrapp, *Victorio*, pp. 165–68, 170, 352 n. 42. The feeling the Warm Springs Apaches had for the place is shown throughout the accounts by James Kaywaykla and Jason Betzinez (Ball, *op. cit.*, and Betzinez, *I Fought with Geronimo*).

situated on the gravelly, wind-swept flat above the junction of the Gila and San Carlos rivers. Clum immediately got rid of the soldiers and assumed control. He lacked three weeks of being twenty-three years old, but he was honorable, able, and efficient; and he had all of Crook's single-minded confidence that he could manage all the Apaches by himself if only the wicked rival service (in Crook's belief, the civilian "Indian ring"; in Clum's the army) would keep out of it.

Clum liked the Indians and treated them fairly, and they reciprocated. He set up crude but effective courts with the leading chiefs as a council of judges, and he enrolled and trained the warriors as police to enforce order. He called in the Indians for a regular count, not only to ensure against their straying, but also to give them an air-tight alibi when they were falsely accused of raiding. On every weekly ration day he issued three hundred pounds of beef, fifty pounds of flour, eight pounds of sugar, four pounds of coffee, one pound of salt, and two bars of soap for each hundred Indians. There, friends and relatives pooled their shares and made a gala social gathering of the occasion. Beyond this, Clum encouraged industry by buying supplies from their little farms and hiring them in the construction of adequate adobe buildings at the agency. He found them eager to work, and he observed that they took naturally to livestock raising. Thus, he looked forward to a time when their rations could be discontinued.[30]

By 1875 Apache-white relations were in the most hopeful state since the wars began in 1860. All the tribes had guaranteed titles to protected refuges, usually comprising their former heartlands. It had been demonstrated that a reservation could be managed for the welfare of its inhabitants and that good order and contentment could prevail there, with eventual self-support a not impossible goal. The army would still be needed—Clum to the contrary not-

[30] Thrapp, *Conquest of Apacheria*, pp. 147–54, 162–65; Clum, *Apache Agent*, pp. 132–40, 148–49, 163–64. John P. Clum was writing his reminiscences when he died suddenly in 1932, and his son, Woodworth Clum, completed the book from these unfinished notes. I agree with Thrapp, who finds his account "wildly inaccurate" but a valuable source if carefully checked.

withstanding—to search out "renegades" from their mountain hideouts, but Crook had developed the techniques. As he expressed it, "I knew if I were to permit a party, even if small, to remain out it would get accession to those on the reserve, who, in turn, would become dissatisfied, and it would not be long before they would be pretty much all out in the mountains again. So frequent expeditions were sent out, and destroyed several small parties."[31]

But in that same year of 1875 the Indian Office began to carry out the concentration policy so often recommended by planners and theorists. This cruel and stupid uprooting of barely tamed hostiles, so recently guaranteed a settled homeland "forever," was to bring about eleven more years of Apache wars with the most arduous military campaigns in American history, the death of hundreds of civilians in the United States and Mexico, and damage and suffering without reckoning to the Apaches.[32] As a direct result, Geronimo became a "renegade," and his career from this time on becomes an epic of the Southwest.

[31] Schmitt, *op. cit.*, p. 182. For these mopping-up expeditions see Thrapp, *Al Sieber*, pp. 117–55.
[32] For a historical evaluation, see Thrapp, *Conquest of Apacheria*, p. 166.

CHAPTER 6

GERONIMO IS BRANDED
A RENEGADE

Economy in administration was the reason given for consolidating the subdued hostiles of Arizona and southwestern New Mexico on one reservation. It cannot be argued that it was done to prevent the raids into Mexico; most of the tribes were moved *closer* to the border. The bureaucratic tendency to organize human beings into neat compartments no doubt had its influence. But it is fairly certain that land hunger was the underlying motive of even the most humane administrators, for the vacated reservations were regularly restored to the public domain.

The reservation chosen was the San Carlos, probably because it was convenient to the greedy contractors at Tucson, at that time the territorial capital. Clum welcomed all the new arrivals to his "happy family" (his words), ignoring the fact that during the transfer the less submissive invariably slipped away and became "renegades." Crook, who had rounded up many of the hostiles in the first place, strongly opposed the measure. Bourke later wrote, "It was an outrageous proceeding, one for which I should still blush, had I not long since gotten over blushing for anything the United States Government did in Indian matters." But the civilian administration was in control. In March, 1875, Crook was transferred to the northern plains to fight the Sioux and their Cheyenne and Arapaho allies. His successors, brevet Major General August V. Kautz and later brevet Major General Orlando Bolivar Willcox, were left to cope with the inevitable hostilities.[1]

Crook was still in command at the time of the first removal— that of some Apache and non-Apache tribes of western Arizona from their recently guaranteed reservation. Crook declined to use force, but Dudley, who had been placed in charge, pressured the Indians into consenting. They were launched on their journey on February 27, 1875. On the way they started fighting each other. Several were killed, and the battle was stopped only by the courageous intervention of Al Sieber. This was an earnest of what would happen when mutually hostile tribes were crowded together in one "happy family." Another ominous sign: of the 1,476 Indians who started out, only 1,361 were turned over to Clum at San Carlos. Some of the missing 115 could be accounted for, but most of them had fled into their old hideouts.[2]

The White Mountain and Coyotero tribes of the Fort Apache Reservation were the next to be uprooted. These Indians had even invited the military to establish the post in their homeland and had gratefully added the distributed rations to their hunting and farming economy.[3] But such a feud developed between the civilian agent and the army officer in command there that Clum was instructed to bring the Indians of that reservation to San Carlos. With sixty of his San Carlos Indians and George H. Stevens, then a trader at his agency, he rode up to Fort Apache "on a big white horse," showing a "paper" from Washington—as old John Rope, a member of the band, told it in later years—and induced those tribes to remove. They made the sixty-mile journey and arrived at their new location on July 31, 1875. A few remained, especially

---

[1] Thrapp, *Al Sieber*, pp. 158–59; Schmitt, *General George Crook, Autobiography*, pp. 183–84; Bourke, *On the Border with Crook*, pp. 216–17.

[2] For this removal, see Thrapp, *Al Sieber*, pp. 156–69.

[3] The account of their first meeting with white soldiers, the establishment of cordial relations, and the Indians' assistance in locating the post were related by John Rope, who was present throughout (Goodwin, "Experiences of an Indian Scout" [part I], pp. 36–40).

the families of scouts in army service at Fort Apache, but the agency was closed. This time the abandoned land was not restored to the public domain but was added to the San Carlos Reservation and administered by the San Carlos Agency, a consolidation that was to remain in effect until 1897. Clum now had forty-two hundred Indians of unrelated tribes, many hostile to each other, collected on one reservation.[4]

Next, in 1876, came the Chiricahuas. In their case an incident furnished the pretext for the move. It involved a warrior named Skinya and his brother and supporter, Pionsenay. According to Clum, Skinya, who had been one of Cochise's leading warriors, contested young Taza's position as chief. In any event, a factional fight broke out, and the tribe divided, with Skinya and about a dozen of his followers living in the Dragoons and the majority under Taza camped near the agency. Jeffords had warned the station keeper at Sulphur Springs on the California Trail near Skinya's camp that he would be removed from the reservation if he should sell whiskey to the Indians. He sold a supply, however, to Pionsenay. The brothers and their small band of followers became intoxicated and went on the warpath, killing the station keeper, his assistant, and another white man and stealing their horses and ammunition. Jeffords and the military trailed them to their Dragoon refuge but were unable to capture them.

An aroused public opinion then clamored for vengeance on the tribe. The *Arizona Citizen* of Tucson declared that "the kind of war needed for the Chiricahua Apaches, is steady unrelenting, hopeless, and undiscriminating war, slaying men, women, and children, . . . until every valley and crest and crag and fastness shall send to high heaven the grateful incense of festering and rotting Chiricahuas."[5] Governor Safford wired Washington demanding the abandonment of the reservation and the removal of the Indians.

4 *Ibid.*, p. 41; Clum, *Apache Agent*, pp. 153–63; Thrapp, *Conquest of Apacheria*, pp. 166–67; Ralph Hedrick Ogle, *Federal Control of the Western Apaches, 1848–1886*, pp. 149–59.
5 April 15, 1876. Quoted by Ogle, *op. cit.*, p. 166, n. 87.

Equally "undiscriminating" was the decision of the Indian Office to uproot the whole tribe for the deeds of this small, repudiated faction. Clum was instructed to carry it out. With a military force supplied by Kautz in the background, he arrived with fifty-four of his armed police at Sulphur Springs on June 4. On the same day the outlaws entered Taza's camp and tried to induce the tribe to join them. A fight ensued in which Naiche shot and killed Skinya, Taza wounded Pionsenay, and six other members of the small band were killed. The following day Clum met with Taza and Naiche at the agency and obtained their consent to the removal. But Jeffords informed him that another band under Geronimo, Juh, and a warrior named Nolgee were also living on the reservation, having been included in the settlement with Howard, and that these leaders wanted to meet with him.

This conference was accordingly held at the agency on June 7 or possibly June 8. Geronimo seemed to be the leader. (Clum did not know that he spoke for the band because of the impediment in Juh's speech.) He told Clum that he was willing to go to the San Carlos Reservation, but that his people were about twenty miles distant, and he asked permission to bring them in. Clum consented, but sent some of his police to shadow the two leaders. Upon reaching camp, the leaders gave brief orders, and the band killed their dogs to prevent their barking, broke camp, and fled—the first of Geronimo's many breakaways. By the time the scouts reported to Clum and Clum alerted the soldiers, the Indians were far on their way. Juh and Nolgee went to their Sierra Madre hideouts, but Geronimo had other plans. On July 21, with a party of about forty, he appeared on the Warm Springs Reservation.

Meanwhile, on June 12 the agent left Apache Pass with 325 good Chiricahuas for their new home on the San Carlos. These included 37 members, mainly women and children, of Pionsenay's small band, but their wounded leader himself escaped. There were, in fact, only 60 warriors in the entire party. Their more turbulent relatives were with the Nednais in Mexico; about 135, including Geronimo and his band, joined their Warm Springs friends on the

Alamosa; and an unreckoned number were hiding out in their ancestral mountains. Between the closing of the Chiricahua agency in June and the following October, they had killed—according to Jefford's official report—more than 20 people and had stolen 170 head of livestock.[6]

This was Clum's introduction to Geronimo. From that time on he became the elusive warrior's nemesis. In his lively writings he attributed every raid before and after this meeting to Geronimo. His solution to the whole Apache problem was simple: hang Geronimo. He attributed every reverse to, "If only Geronimo had been hanged———." Other Southwesterners adopted the same simplistic interpretation. Thus, Geronimo acquired a fame—or notoriety—far out of proportion to his deeds or misdeeds.

In his own account Geronimo touched briefly on the murder of the station keeper by "a band of outlawed Indians" and concentrated on the factions within the tribe. As he told it, "some Indians at the Post were drunk on 'tiswin,' which they had made from corn. They fought among themselves and four of them were killed. There had been quarrels and feuds among them for some time, and after this trouble we deemed it impossible to keep the different bands together in peace. Therefore we separated, each leader taking his own band. Some of them went to San Carlos and some to Old Mexico, but I took my tribe back to Hot Springs and rejoined Victoria's band." As for his flight from Clum, he reasoned, "I do not think that I ever belonged to those soldiers at Apache Pass, or that I should have asked them where I might go."[7]

Thus, by the closing of the Chiricahua Reservation a fairly compact tribal unit that had observed a precarious peace was dispersed through the mountains, impossible to contact or control. Clum knew that lawless spirits among them were committing depredations, which typically he blamed on Geronimo, but all

6 John P. Clum, "The San Carlos Apache Police," *New Mexico Historical Review*, Vol. V, No. 1 (part 2), pp. 79–80, and "Geronimo," *New Mexico Historical Review*, Vol. III, No. 1 (part 1), pp. 8–9, 13–19; Clum, *Apache Agent*, pp. 176–84; Lockwood, *The Apache Indians*, pp. 214–18; Ogle, *op. cit.*, pp. 164–68; Thrapp, *Victorio*, p. 180.
7 Barrett, *Geronimo's Story of His Life*, pp. 129–30, 132.

Naiche, "the tall, handsome son of Cochise," who came with his Chiricahuas to San Carlos. Photograph taken there by A. Frank Randall in the spring of 1884.

seemed serene on the San Carlos. He wanted to marry a girl in Ohio, and he conceived the hare-brained idea of paying his transportation by engaging in show business. With about twenty of his Indians, including Taza, he toured the East, visiting the Centennial Exposition at Philadelphia and ending at Washington. In Washington Taza died of pneumonia and was given an elaborate funeral with General Howard in attendance. There, Clum ran out of funds, and the commissioner of Indian affairs paid the way of the party back to Arizona. (Incidentally, Clum married the girl, and she became the only white woman on the reservation.)[8]

Naiche was decidedly hostile to Clum when he learned of the death of his brother. He appeared pacified when other members of the party told him of the burial ceremonies, and the agent did not suspect that for years thereafter the band believed that the young chief had been poisoned.[9] This belief contributed to the Chiricahuas' growing dissatisfaction with the new location and their resentment over the loss of their homeland.

Naiche was recognized as his brother's successor, but he never attained the stature of his father or other great chiefs of the Apaches. As it was told to Kaywaykla, "When Tahza was poisoned Naiche was too young to become the leader. He had not been trained for the place as had his brother because Cochise wanted his younger son to be loyal to Tahza."[10] As he grew older it was apparent that although he was a brave and able warrior, he was temperamentally unfitted to exercise authority. Some of the Apaches tried to explain it. Sam Kenoi, an elderly Nednai, characterized him to Opler: "He liked his Indian dancing, and he liked his fighting, and he liked his drinking. You could make a good soldier out of him, and that was all. He was always influenced by Geronimo."[11] Young Lieutenant Britton Davis, who knew him well on the reservation, gave a similar evaluation: "Nachite was a good warrior

8 Clum, "Geronimo" (part 1), p. 23; Clum, *Apache Agent*, pp. 185–98, 201–203; Howard, *My Life and Experiences*, p. 215.
9 Clum, *Apache Agent*, pp. 198–201; Ball, *In the Days of Victorio*, pp. 51–52.
10 Ball, *op. cit.*, p. 127.
11 Morris E. Opler, "A Chiricahua Apache's Account of the Geronimo Campaign of 1886," *New Mexico Historical Review*, Vol. XIII, No. 4 (Oct., 1938), p. 369.

101

with no peace scruples; but he was fond of the ladies, liked dancing and a good time generally, and was not serious enough for the responsibilities of leadership."[12]

Certainly he lacked the drive of Geronimo, the statesmanship of Mangas Coloradas, and the military genius of Cochise or Victorio. More serious to his tribesmen, he had no Power—no ceremony that would reveal enemy plans, deflect bullets, or cure sickness. But in his mature years as a prisoner of war, the officers in charge found him dependable and cooperative, affable and courteous in his manners, and possessing a quiet influence over his people. In the period of relatively normal living at Fort Sill he produced notable paintings and wood carvings.[13] In another culture he would have been a creative artist, but there was no place for one of his temperament under the hard conditions of Apache life:

Nevertheless, Naiche was the recognized chief, and Geronimo always deferred to him in that capacity. This deference can be seen even in the photographs, in which Naiche invariably is placed on the right. It was true, though, as Sam Kenoi said, that Geronimo dominated his more sensitive superior. At that time, however, they were separated, with Naiche on the San Carlos Reservation and Geronimo at the Warm Springs Agency.

The Warm Springs Reservation was under a very weak administration, and it was soon apparent that bands of "renegades" were using it as a refuge between raids while they carried on a lively business of stealing horses from Arizona and selling them to New Mexico ranchers or in the Mexican towns on the Rio Grande. The Warm Springs people were aware of what was happening, but they seemed unable to prevent it. As one of them explained it to Opler in later years:

>>>>>>>>>>>>>>>>>>>>>>>>>

We were on friendly terms with the towns around us and we

---

[12] Davis, *The Truth about Geronimo*, pp. 71–72.
[13] Hugh Lenox Scott, *Some Memories of a Soldier*, p. 198; Burbank and Royce, *Burbank among the Indians*, p. 34.

were causing no trouble there. But the [Chiricahuas] and the [Nednais] came around. They used to bring in horses stolen from the south and they got us into trouble.

Some of our leading men said, "There are too many [Nednais] and [Chiricahuas] here. They are bringing in horses. They will get us into trouble." But our leader, Victorio, wouldn't do anything about it. He said, "These people are not bothering us."

Then a bunch of them came with some horses from the south. There were about seven [leaders] in the bunch. They had stolen horses from the Pima Indians around Tucson.[14] [The Pimas were a sedentary, agricultural tribe, long-time enemies of the Apaches.]

><><><><><><><><><><><><

Apparently Ponce and other well-known "renegades" were in the party with their followers, but probably Geronimo was the leader. (At least he got the blame.) On March 17, 1877, an army officer reported seeing him at the agency with one hundred horses, very indignant that he was not permitted to draw the rations he had missed during his absence. This brought matters to a head.

On March 20 the commissioner of Indian affairs wired Clum to "take Indian Police and arrest renegade Indians at Southern Apache [that is, the Warm Springs] Agency," remove them to San Carlos Reservation, "and hold them in confinement for murder and robbery." Clum called on General Edward Hatch, commander of the Department of New Mexico, and was notified that three companies of cavalry would meet him at the agency on April 21. He accordingly set out on the four-hundred-mile journey with about one hundred of his trusty police and arrived with an advance contingent of twenty-two on the evening of April 20. There he found a telegram saying the cavalry would be delayed until April 22. He knew that if he waited, the "rengades" would take flight. Reasoning that they knew of only the twenty-two men they saw

---

14 Opler, *An Apache Life-Way*, pp. 462–63. I have substituted the tribal names used by the Apaches for the terminology—Eastern, Central, and Southern Chiricahuas —of ethnologists.

The site of the Warm Springs (Ojo Caliente) Agency. Through the cleft in the center background the Alamosa River flowed down to the Mexican town Cañada Alamosa. Here on April 21, 1877, Geronimo for the only time in his life was "captured"—by a ruse. "We thought they wanted a council and rode in to meet the officers." Photograph by Dan L. Thrapp.

with him, he sent a courier to his chief of police, Clay Beauford, to bring up the others during the night.

The adobe buildings at Warm Springs faced a large parade

ground. On the west side was the agency, and about fifty yards to the south of it was a large vacant commissary building. Along the south side stretched a row of employee quarters. The east and north sides terminated in a deep ravine. The reserve police arrived at about four o'clock in the morning and were concealed in the commissary building. At daylight Clum sent a message to Geronimo and the other "renegade" leaders in camp about three miles away, summoning them to come in for a conference. They came, clearly not expecting a confrontation, for they brought their women and children. As Geronimo told it, "The messengers did not say what they wanted with us, and as they seemed friendly we thought they wanted a council and rode in to meet the officers."[15]

With Beauford and half a dozen of his police, Clum took a position on the porch of the agency building facing the parade ground. The others of his small force were lined along the parade ground on each side of him, half of them north towards the ravine, half south to the commissary building. The "renegade" warriors, fully armed, gathered in a compact group before him, with Geronimo, Ponce, and five (or six, as Geronimo told it) other leaders in front. He directed his charges mainly at Geronimo, but he spoke to the group. He accused them of killing men and stealing cattle in violation of the Howard-Cochise peace and of breaking their promise of the preceding year to come in to San Carlos; now, he said, he had come to bring them in. Geronimo answered defiantly: "We are not going to San Carlos with you, and unless you are very careful, you and your Apache police will not go back to San Carlos either. Your bodies will stay here at Ojo Caliente to make food for coyotes."

In later years Clum admitted that just at that time he would have liked to see the cavalry. He and Beauford and two agency employees were the only white men there. But he gave a prearranged signal; and the commissary doors burst open and the reserves emerged running, in single file, rifles at the ready, and formed a line along the south side of the parade ground. The "renegades"

---

15 Barrett, *op. cit.*, p. 131.

were caught between a threatened cross fire. A few stragglers started to move away, but were halted by Beauford's raised rifle. Thereupon a woman in the crowd sprang upon the chief of police, threw her arms around his neck and shoulders, and pulled down his gun. He threw her off, and by the time he raised it again, all the reserves were in place ready to halt any attempt at escape. (One would like to know the name of this Amazon. There were some women warriors among the Apaches who fought regularly alongside their men.[16])

Clum had been watching Geronimo's thumb creeping toward the hammer of his rifle. Now it moved back, and the agent realized that he had won. He handed his own gun to one of the police and ordered the "renegade" leaders to lay their rifles on the ground. They shuffled their feet and made no move to comply. Clum motioned to Beauford, and Beauford aimed his gun straight at Geronimo. Then Clum stepped down and disarmed him. To the end of his long adventurous life—for he was to become the founder of the *Tombstone Epitaph* and the mayor of that wild town in its heyday—Clum never forgot the concentrated hatred in Geronimo's face as he was relieved of his rifle. (With typical arrogance the agent kept it the rest of his life and handed it on as a family heirloom.) Beauford disarmed the other leaders, and their followers laid their rifles on the ground. Clum then asked Geronimo and "his sub-chiefs" to come up on the porch for a conference, and the main body—men, women, and children—dispersed in groups over the parade ground.

On the porch, as the leaders squatted around in the favorite Apache position, Clum again berated Geronimo for his flight the year before, informed them that they were prisoners, and ordered them to the guardhouse. Geronimo then leaped to his feet, "erect as a lodge-pole pine, every outline of his symmetrical form indicating strength, endurance, and arrogance." At the same time the other

---

[16] See Ball, *op. cit.*, for the exploits of the famed woman warrior, Victorio's sister Lozen, and of James Kaywaykla's own mother in her service as a warrior fighting beside her husband.

six sprang to their feet, as did most of the warriors in front. Geronimo's hand crept toward the knife in his belt, and in his fierce eyes Clum read his indecision, whether to surrender or to draw the knife and die fighting. While he hesitated, one of the police sprang forward and snatched the knife, and the guns of the others clicked as they were pointed at the seven leaders. Geronimo flashed one defiant glance at his captors. Then he relaxed and said, "In-gew" ("all right").

Clum had forgotten that the agency had no guardhouse; therefore, he decided to use the corral. He had intended only to disarm and imprison the leaders, but Geronimo's attempt to draw his knife decided him to have them shackled. He marched them to the blacksmith shop while their followers looked on. Geronimo watched impassively while the irons were being heated. Did he expect to be tortured? Then the irons, connected by chains, were riveted on the ankles first of Geronimo, then of the others. When the shackling was completed, they were led to the corral, given beds of hay, blankets, and food, and placed under strict guard. Then Beauford, with twenty police, marched the band to their camp, made them gather up their belongings, and brought them back with their stolen horses and cattle before sunset.

This was the only time that Geronimo was ever captured, and then by a ruse. At the end of his career he could taunt the army with the undeniable fact that "you never have caught me shooting."[17]

The next morning Victorio and two other Warm Springs leaders came to the agency to see what was happening. Clum ordered them to bring in their people that evening for counting, explaining his reasons. Soon the cavalry arrived. Clum showed their commander around. He saw Geronimo and the other "renegade" leaders shackled and guarded in the corral and their followers, disarmed and with their guns locked up, gathered under the trees in groups fraternizing with the police. (Clum always believed that his police were effective in spreading propaganda about the happy situation on the San Carlos Reservation.)

17 Opler, "A Chiricahua Apache's Account," p. 379.

The only known photograph of Victorio, possibly taken in the unsettled period following his removal from Warm Springs in 1877. It is said that he had to be physically restrained and lost his headband in the struggle. "We should not have been driven from our homes. We were not to blame for what Geronimo did." Courtesy National Archives and Records Service.

The Warm Springs people were counted without incident. They numbered 343. Then the police started counting the "renegades." All was going smoothly until a young warrior named Nulah sat on the ground and refused to be counted unless Clum would take the chains off Geronimo. Clum ordered two of the police to take him to the corral and place him under guard. He wrenched free and sat down again. Victorio's people and Geronimo's people were watching, many of them laughing heartily, while the cavalry officers were sitting on the porch observing the spectacle. Clum had been a boxer and a wrestler in college. He jerked the Indian to his feet, parried a knife thrust, and finished his antagonist by a blow with his rifle barrel. Then the counting was resumed. The total, including the seven shackled leaders, was 110. The following evening Nulah was first in line while his companions watched with amused smiles. (One would like to know more about this courageous and loyal follower of Geronimo. If he survived the hazards of Apache life, he must have become a notable warrior under some other name.)

The next day a telegram from Tucson informed Clum that Ponce and Nolgee were raiding in southwestern Arizona. And Ponce was in irons in the corral! But Clum could not ignore the appeal; he immediately dispatched Beauford with seventy-five of his police to catch the real or imaginary raiders. At the same time he told the Indians, especially Ponce, about the telegram to make them realize the importance of having an alibi; there was no more objection to the daily count. Then a telegram from the commissioner of Indian affairs instructed him to remove not only the captured "renegades" but also the Warm Springs band to San Carlos. After all their wandering and pleading for a title to their homeland, this buffeted people had enjoyed secure possession only three years. Their removal could, of course, be justified on the ground that they had harbored the raiders, but it was not only cruel but unwise, and would bring terrible consequences. Clum talked with Victorio and secured his consent. Perhaps the chief was influenced by the good reports he heard from the police about San Carlos. Perhaps he simply reasoned, "What's the use?"

As late as the 1950's members of the tribe who were still living in Oklahoma insisted that their uprooting was unjust. Old Sam Haozous, great-great-grandson of Mahko and grandson of Mangas Coloradas, said with an intensity of feeling impossible to convey in print: "We were innocent and should not have been driven from our homes. We were not to blame for what Geronimo did. The United States didn't give this land to us. It was ours." And Jason Betzinez said with tragedy in his voice and tears in his eyes: "That was *our* country. It had always been our home."[18]

All of this was invisible to Clum as he made his energetic preparations for the journey. "There was no sadness," he said, only a band of "hopeful people." He decided that with his reduced police force he was warranted in accepting twelve troopers as an escort. Wagons were provided for the shackled leaders and for any who might become ill on the journey. The others were to walk, except that a few thrifty families with horses loaded their possessions on travois. (The ill-gotten herds of the raiders were, of course, confiscated.) Preparations were all completed by the morning of May 1. Then, just as they were ready to start, Clum found a very sick Indian sitting on a step in front of one of the employee quarters. The man had smallpox. Clum hastily improvised an ambulance from a wagon and put the patient in the charge of one of the police who had had the disease.

The journey was uneventful, even pleasant, as Clum described it. He found that even Geronimo had "become a most tractable prisoner and did not give his guards the slightest inconvenience during the long trek." (In later years, throughout all their captivity, army officers were to marvel at the docility of the Apache prisoners.) During the first days, the children romped, chasing lizards and playing tag, and the dogs ran after rabbits; then all quieted down to the daily march. Four babies were born en route. Clum ordered a baggage wagon to stand by and bring them in with their mothers. More cases of smallpox developed, and the pest

---

[18] Haozous interview, January 27, 1955; Jason Betzinez interview, January 26, 1955.

wagon became crowded. The original patient recovered, but eight died. The long train reached San Carlos on May 20.[19]

This trip accomplished, the hanging of the shackled leaders came next on Clum's list of things to be done. In after years, he always wrote as though this were a mere matter of routine, but at the time he thought it was necessary to offer some hearsay evidence that he had collected from Apache gossip along the trail. He wrote officially to the sheriff at Tucson: "I have personal evidence against some of these prisoners, and will be glad to testify against them. Through my Apache police, and information they have obtained by fraternizing with the renegades, ample evidence is now available to convict each of the seven chiefs on many counts of murder. This evidence should be used while details are still fresh in the minds of witnesses." Half a century later he wrote of the "vast amount of expense, tribulation, distress and bloodshed" that would have been avoided if Geronimo's arrest "had been swiftly followed by prosecution, conviction and execution."[20]

Geronimo did not magnify his danger when in his old age he said of this imprisonment that it "might easily have been death to me."[21] And the suspicion growing out of this traumatic experience was to influence him throughout his life. Exasperated army officers, government officials, and Indian-hating frontiersmen—not to mention historians—never understood how strongly it entered into his subsequent flights.[22] At the same time, ever present but not so clearly expressed, was a deep-seated preference for the untram-

19 In this whole story I have followed Clum's account (Clum, *Apache Agent*, pp. 204–49), and Clum, "Geronimo" (part 1), pp. 26–39. He may have embroidered it a little for dramatic effect, but it seems, in the main, accurate. Eve Ball's informants discredit it as pure invention and deny that Geronimo was ever "captured." See Ball, *op. cit.*, p. 50. But they admit that Geronimo and the others were shackled, and until they explain how these warriors were induced to hold still for irons to be riveted on their ankles, Clum's account will have to stand. Also, it is supported by the testimony of John Rope, who got the story from a member of the police force. See Goodwin, "Experiences of an Indian Scout" (part 1), p. 42.

20 Clum, "Geronimo" (part 2), p. 125; Clum, *Apache Agent*, p. 250.

21 Barrett, *op. cit.*, p. 133.

22 In an analysis of Geronimo's character, Morris Edward Opler gives fear and suspicion as his motivation. See "Some Implications of Culture Theory for Anthropology and Psychology," *American Journal of Orthopsychiatry*, Vol. XVIII (Oct., 1948), pp. 617–19.

meled freedom, in spite of its dangers, of the old Apache life-way. He would settle down under pressure, but the wild urge was there; when his suspicion was aroused, it was easy to break away.

Clum kept the seven shackled leaders (eight, according to Geronimo) and twelve other prisoners locked in the agency guardhouse. He told the rest of the band that they were free from arrest and might establish their camps anywhere on the reservation, and he instructed their leaders to bring them in once a week to be counted and receive the issues of food and clothing. He recruited four of them for his police force and added Victorio to his council of judges. But members of the band continued to die from smallpox. (Nobody seemed to think about vaccination.) When they brought the disease, the other tribes fled in terror to the mountainous areas of the reservation. Probably this fear added to the resentment that soon developed between them and the newcomers. The unaffected among the latter also sought refuge in the mountains. But the arid flats along the Gila, where a sub-agency was established for them, presented a disheartening appearance. "We were completely downcast over the prospect of having to live in this hot, desolate country," said old Jason Betzinez. "I well remember our feeling of indignation and helplessness over this ill turn in our fortunes."[23]

With Clum's good administration of the reservation they might have become reconciled to the change, but he was having his own frustrations. When he returned from Ojo Caliente, he found a company of soldiers camped just outside the agency under orders to inspect and manage his Indians. This raised his ever-present hostility against the army to the boiling point. He informed the commanding officer that *he* was in charge, and he fired off a telegram to the commissioner of Indian affairs at Washington. He had another grievance. During his three years' tenure he had consolidated five Indian agencies into one, saving the government $25,000 on each, and his own responsibility had increased from

---

[23] Clum, *Apache Agent*, p. 249; Clum, "Geronimo" (part 1), p. 38; Goodwin, *op. cit.* (part 1), p. 42; Betzinez, *I Fought with Geronimo*, pp. 46–47.

the supervision of eight hundred to that of five thousand Indians, with no increase in salary. His telegram, dated June 9, read:

IF YOUR DEPARTMENT WILL INCREASE MY SALARY SUFFICIENTLY AND EQUIP TWO MORE COMPANIES OF INDIAN POLICE FOR ME, I WILL VOLUNTEER TO TAKE CARE OF ALL APACHES IN ARIZONA—AND THE TROOPS CAN BE REMOVED.

When this arrogant proposal became known, the War Department went into a tantrum equal to his own, and the Arizona newspapers joined in condemning him. But one of his friends, a leading Tucson merchant, revealed the real motive behind some of the attacks. "What are you trying to do?" he asked, "ruin my business? If you take the military contracts away from us, there would be nothing worth staying for. Most of our profit comes from feeding soldiers and army mules." The Indian Office rejected his overconfident offer, and he resigned in a huff, leaving at the end of July.[24]

James Kaywaykla's early childhood was a nightmare of flight and terror, the result of Clum's removal of the Warm Springs band, but he made a surprisingly perceptive evaluation of the agent. "As agents went, John Clum was one of the best," he said. "The Apaches conceded that; but they knew also that he was responsible" for the consolidation policy. (This policy, of course, did not originate with Clum; he only carried it out—with enthusiasm.) "And they knew, too, that his motive for attempting to bring all Apaches under his rule was an increase in salary." (They misjudged him here also; his motive was excess energy and the exhilaration of using it.) But—"They respected the arrogant young man in spite of that, for he was both courageous and honest. . . . They liked his using Indian police and Indian judges . . . [for] it was commendable to have a man who realized that our standards differed from theirs and felt that a man should be judged by the mores of his people."[25]

Meanwhile, Geronimo remained shackled in the guardhouse.

24 Clum, *Apache Agent*, pp. 249–55; Clum, "The San Carlos Apache Police" (part 1), pp. 210–11.
25 Ball, *op. cit.*, pp. xiii, 50–51.

The sheriff at Tucson failed to claim him, and soon after Clum left, the succeeding agent, Henry Lyman Hart, removed his shackles and set him free. Thus, according to Clum, he received no punishment for having murdered at least one hundred men, women, and children. And if he had been hanged, five hundred more human lives would have been saved, to say nothing of twelve million dollars and the most humiliating military campaigns in American history. His shackles "never should have been removed, except to permit him to walk untrammeled to the scaffold."[26]

Geronimo's own account of his arrest is more restrained. He told how after he was invited to come in, he was disarmed, and "Scouts conducted me to the guardhouse and put me in chains. When I asked them why they did this they said it was because I left Apache Pass." He made no mention of Clum's other accusation: that he had been on raids, killing people and stealing livestock. It is even possible that he had observed the peace as he interpreted it—applicable only to Anglos—and had confined his raids to Mexicans and Pimas. He was not the liar he was represented to be by his detractors. He sometimes used deception of an adversary for strategic purposes as he had done with Clum at Fort Bowie, but if one can untangle his wild logic, his account of events rings true. He went on to say: "I was kept a prisoner for four months, during which time I was transferred to San Carlos. Then I think I had another trial although I was not present. In fact I do not know that I had another trial, but I was told that I had, and at any rate I was released. After this we had no more trouble with the soldiers [that is, the police], but I never felt at ease any longer at the Post [the agency]. We were allowed to live above San Carlos at a place now called Geronimo. . . . All went well for a period of two years, but we were not satisfied."[27]

This unstable situation was to erupt in a succession of breakouts.

26 Clum, "Geronimo" (part 1), p. 34.
27 Barrett, op. cit., pp. 132–33.

CHAPTER 7

A PATTERN OF BREAKOUTS IS SET

After Clum's departure, things went from bad to worse on the San Carlos Reservation under weak or corrupt agents.[1] The Warm Springs band, starving and poorly clothed, dying from smallpox, ill from malaria bred by the mosquito-infested Gila flats, and pining for their mountain homeland, became increasingly dissatisfied. At the same time, Pionsenay, having recovered from his wounds, was happily raiding with Nolgee in Mexico or hovering around the reservation making contacts with his Chiricahua friends. The miserable captives began saving up flour from their scanty rations and hiding away other supplies.

On the night of September 1, Pionsenay and his adherents came in rich with plunder and full of boastful tales of successful raiding. Early the next morning, with 22 of their women and children who had been living on the reservation, they headed back towards Mexico, and Victorio and Loco broke away with 323 of *their* followers and escaped into the mountains to the northeast, leaving 143 of their band, including some members of their families, at San Carlos. In comparison with subsequent Apache breakouts, the

---

[1] Details of their speculations are given by Ogle in *Federal Control of the Western Apaches*, pp. 194–213 *passim*.

Warm Springs fugitives at this time acted with restraint, fighting the soldiers only to cover the escape of their women and children and killing civilians only when necessary in obtaining supplies. Late in September the two chiefs appeared at Fort Wingate in the Navaho country of New Mexico and offered to bring in their people. They had not intended to go on the warpath, they said, but were only seeking a refuge. Assured of protection, most of their followers, who had been scattered through the mountains, collected there during October. Nana, however, with a small band joined the Mescaleros.

The refugees at Fort Wingate begged above all to return home, but they said they would go anywhere except back to San Carlos. Indian Inspector William Vandever came from his office at Santa Fe and conferred with Victorio and Loco. As he reported it, they complained of the hostility of the other tribes at San Carlos. "They said further that the water was bad . . . it made their people sick, and therefore they determined to go somewhere else to live. My reply to them was, that, they must learn to stay wherever the Government chooses to put them." He concluded that it was "wholly out of the question to yield to their desire to return to Ojo Caliente," and he recommended that they be permanently located in the Indian Territory (present Oklahoma), meanwhile being subsisted on the Mescalero Reservation until their removal.

The Washington officials decided that allowing them to return to Ojo Caliente would be "a sign of weakness" and "establish a bad precedent"; their short-lived reservation had been restored to the public domain in August, and the agency buildings were in process of being sold. But while the Indian Office wavered between driving them back to San Carlos or sending them to Fort Sill in the Indian Territory, the army permitted them to drift back to their beloved homeland. They remained there through the winter of 1877/78, carefully keeping the peace, while settlers, travelers, and prospectors were secure in their persons and property.[2]

2 Thrapp, *Conquest of Apacheria*, pp. 177–78; Thrapp, *Victorio*, pp. 193–207; National Archives and Records Service, Inspectors File No. 1732, Vandever's Report, October 23, 1877. For Kaywaykla's account of the flight, see Ball, *op. cit.*, p. 52.

Naiche and most of the Chiricahuas remained on the San Carlos Reservation. Geronimo also did not go out with either his Warm Springs friends or Pionsenay. On the evening of September 23 (or possibly September 25) Hart held a conference with him and made him "captain" of the remaining Warm Springs band. Geronimo promised that he would not leave the reservation and would inform Hart of any contemplated breakouts. At the same time the Chiricahua leaders made the same promises.[3]

Some of Geronimo's close relatives were among the Warm Springs people who did not go out with their leaders. Among them were his widowed "sister," Nah-thle-tla, and her teenaged children, Betzinez and Ellen. They recognized Geronimo as "the senior member" of their family group and were "under compulsion" to follow his leadership. Apparently Nana's wife, Nah-dos-te, and their son also remained, probably for the same reason. Although a man of tribal prestige like Nana might become independent of his wife's family, the bond was still there.

The promises made by Geronimo and the Chiricahuas did not last long, as the dissatisfaction on the reservation continued to mount. The warriors began stealing guns and ammunition, preparing for a breakout, and Juh came up from Mexico to encourage it. Geronimo is credited with being one of the leaders in the plotting, but Betzinez gives an interesting personal reason for his immediate decision to leave. He and his family had been camping in the mountains north of the sub-agency. There, during a *tizwin* drink, he scolded his nephew—apparently the son of Nana and Nah-dos-te—"for no reason at all." The young man, with typical Apache sensitivity to disapproval, thereupon committed suicide. Geronimo, blaming himself for his relative's death, then left with Ponce and other noted irreconcilables for Mexico. The date was April 4, 1878.

Betzinez with his mother and sister remained on the reservation. He has left a revealing account of the indecision they felt as they were torn between their obligation to the head of their family group

[3] National Archives and Records Service, *loc. cit.*, enclosure, Hart to Vandever, September 24 (or 26), 1877.

and their own peaceable inclinations. Geronimo, of course, took his immediate family. According to Betzinez, he had two wives. These must have been Chee-hash-kish, with her two children Chappo and Dohn-say, and She-gha. If he had only two, he had not yet married Shtsha-she.[4]

As Betzinez told it, Geronimo and Juh were in command of the escaping band. They intercepted a wagon train, killing the drivers and obtaining food and ammunition. They were attacked by troops, but beat them off and reached the border. Once in Mexico, they joined the band of Juh and Nolgee in their Sierra Madre hideout, from which they set up a lively traffic in stolen goods with the conniving citizens of Janos.[5]

Another band of Apache raiders was soon loosed on the ranchers and travelers of New Mexico and Arizona. In the summer of that same year (1878) the Indian Office requested the army to drive the Warm Springs band to San Carlos. The officer in command at Ojo Caliente reported on their cooperative attitude and their earnest desire to stay, but the order went out. When the attempt was made to remove them, they fled to the mountains. Finally, the army collected twenty men, seventy-eight women, and seventy-five children, including the peaceable Loco, and delivered them to the Indian police at San Carlos in November. Among those who remained out were fifty irreconcilable warriors under Victorio. They began of necessity to rob and kill. Their hunted existence, with their flight from pursuing soldiers and their losses in killed and captured, as remembered by three-year-old James Kaywaykla, is an epic of courage and determination.

Finally, early in January, 1879, Victorio called down from the heights to the officer in command at Ojo Caliente and asked for a talk. The officer, unarmed, climbed the mountain with an interpreter for a conference. It was eventually decided that the band

---

4 Betzinez also said that he took along the young Mescalero girl Ih-tedda, whom he afterwards married, but this seems improbable. Not only in his book, but also in personal conversations I have found Betzinez confused about Geronimo's family.
5 Thrapp, *Conquest of Apacheria*, pp. 189–90; Betzinez, *I Fought with Geronimo*, pp. 47–49; Griswold, "The Fort Sill Apaches," s.v. "Nah-dos-te."

should settle with the Mescaleros. By late July the Mescalero agent reported that 145 had collected there, and arrangements were being made to permit their people who were at San Carlos to join them. Plans were even being considered to establish them once more at Ojo Caliente. But Victorio learned that indictments had been found against him in Grant County for horse stealing and murder. (It appears that Pionsenay was the actual culprit. And considering the murders and livestock rustling by white men in the contemporary Lincoln County War and throughout that lawless period, one wonders why the Apaches were picked out for prosecution.) Just then a party from Silver City, including a judge and the prosecuting attorney of Grant County, came to the reservation on a hunting and fishing trip. (Nobody ever considered that killing the game on the Indians' land was exactly the same as their killing the livestock of the ranchers.) Victorio thought they had come to arrest him, and the whole band fled, along with some lawless spirits among the Mescaleros. It was August 21, 1879.[6]

Now the killings and robbings on both sides of the border surpassed anything previously experienced in Apache raids. They began before Victorio was well out of the Mescalero Reservation when two Mexican sheep herders were killed and their horses were taken. Then came a dreary succession of wagon trains captured and livestock—horses, cattle, sheep—swept away from ranches, always with every defender killed. Even the cavalry mounts were captured, and the troopers were set on foot. Troops were pulled out from everywhere for the arduous campaigning, only to be lured into deadly ambushes while the Apaches melted away. The harassed white officials suspected that Juh and Geronimo joined Victorio, but this seems untenable. Understandably, when every rock exploded with death the soldiers saw too many Indians, more than Victorio alone could have had—a common miscalculation in Indian fights. But the keen-eyed child Kaywaykla never saw any

6 Ball, *op. cit.*, pp. 3–10, 52–53, 64–66; Thrapp, *Victorio*, pp. 208–20; Sonnichsen, *Mescalero Apaches*, pp. 161–71; Thrapp, *Conquest of Apacheria*, pp. 179–81. For an account of non-Indian murders and livestock rustling in contemporary New Mexico, see Lily Klasner, *My Girlhood among Outlaws*, pp. 169–91 and *passim*.

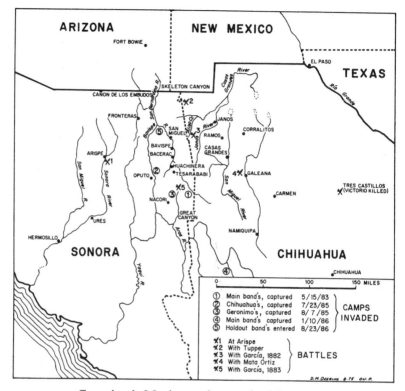

Geronimo's Mexican refuge and raiding range

of these supposed allies until they all gathered in Juh's stronghold the year after Victorio's death. No doubt some of the raids were separate exploits of Juh, possibly even of Geronimo, slipping up from the Sierra Madre. In some of the captures of wagon trains, teamsters were tortured by suspending them head-down over the burning wreckage.[7] This was the punishment reserved by Apache custom for their own witches after a trial and conviction by a council.[8] Extending it to white victims was the practice of some Apaches, but it was not the trademark of Victorio.

[7] Thrapp, *Conquest of Apacheria*, pp. 182–89; Thrapp, *Victorio*, pp. 220–48; Ball, *op. cit.*, pp. 71–73, 79–86.
[8] Opler, *An Apache Life-Way*, pp. 252–54.

"I was with Victorio until his death, with Nana for years, and Geronimo several months," said Kaywaykla. "I do not like to think of the things I witnessed." But he went on to say, "I have seen hundreds of people killed, but nobody tortured." He felt horror when a wealthy Mexican family—two men, a woman, and a little boy—were brought into camp and summarily executed; and his grandmother was shaking as she took him in her arms and tried to comfort him. He saw a small detachment of Mexican soldiers lured into a trap and exterminated. "The warriors walked among the bodies collecting rifles and ammunition belts . . . shirts and saddles," he said, but "The men were not tortured; the bodies were not mutilated. I know, for I lay on my belly and watched this thing happen." He went on to say, however, that mutilation of a body might occur after death to avenge such mutilation as was "perpetrated on the body of Mangas Coloradas."[9]

In the fall of 1879, while Victorio was slashing his bloody way across northern Chihuahua, Geronimo and Juh were holed up in a hidden camp at McIntosh Spring in the Guadelupe Mountains near the Arizona–New Mexico line. From this place they sent a runner to ask General Willcox to "be their friend." This envoy contacted the general's aide-de-camp, Captain Harry L. Haskell, then at San Bernardino conducting a scout in the southeastern corner of Arizona. Haskell, seeing the importance of this overture, decided at once to visit the hostiles' camp. They had imposed the condition that he bring no soldiers, and he went accompanied only by an interpreter, probably Jeffords. (In spite of the treachery the Apaches had experienced when they came under supposed safe conduct to confer with white men, they still observed their savage code of honor.) He held a conference with the leaders and then went back to San Bernardino while they considered his proposals. The next day they called him back, and he went with Jeffords and Archie McIntosh.

9 Ball, *op. cit.*, pp. 13, 46, 77–78, 119. For a historian's account of the annihilation of this Mexican force, see Dan L. Thrapp, *Juh: An Incredible Indian*, pp. 18–19. Thrapp believes that Juh participated and bases his conclusion on the report of the American consul at Chihuahua.

As he reported it, "The Indians say they have heard that General Willcox has always treated their people well and they have come to live at peace, that they shall not go on war-path nor break out from the agency, that they have not been with Victoria and do not know where he is." They asked that the scout companies be withdrawn while they collected their band, and that Haskell remain with them until they should be settled at San Carlos. They wanted to be located with their own people at the sub-agency (probably to avoid the hostility of the other tribes on the reservation) and asked that Nolgee, who had already gone in, might visit them there.

The agreement was made without difficulty, and the hostiles settled down on the reservation. It was in December, 1879, or perhaps the following January. The *Arizona Star* at Tucson hailed the good news. "These Indians belong to Cachise's old tribe—the worst in the deck. They deny having fought with Victorio and his band, but own up to having done deviltry under their own chiefs, Hoo and Geronimo. . . . We take it that the people of southern Arizona and Sonora are resting easier, since the surrender of these 'disturbing elements.' "

But the Mexican consul at Tucson was alarmed at the prospect that they would use the reservation as a safe base for more intensive raids into Mexico. Willcox assured him that "Hoo and his followers . . . will be kept at San Carlos, where they can harm neither Americans nor Mexicans, and like the rest of the Indians on the reservation will be treated friendly as long as they behave themselves and will be used as auxiliaries for the subjugation of hostile bands across the border."[10]

Everything indeed seemed at peace at San Carlos. Reuben Hood, who operated a trading post there, reported in late May that the hostiles were "perfectly content with their new home, and instead of being in sympathy with Victorio's band, they exhibit

10 Thrapp, *Juh*, pp. 19–21, citing Office of Indian Affairs, Letters Received, 1821–81, Roll 581, File No. W67–1880, Haskell to AAAG, December 14, 1879, and Roll 582, File No. W1354, Willcox to Prieto, November 8, 1879, and January 31, 1880; and *Arizona Star*, January 7, 1880.

hostile feelings towards them." He cited Jeffords as confident that they would not assist Victorio even if he should appear there.[11] In fact, some of Victorio's warriors had already reached them, possibly with the idea of enlisting assistance. Earlier that spring a dashing leader named Washington, said to be a son of Victorio, made a swift raid into Arizona with fourteen well-armed warriors. They reached a camp of Juh's and Geronimo's people, now good reservation Indians, and apparently skirmished with them. Then they were attacked and pursued by the soldiers, who suffered some casualties but inflicted no damage. Killing and pillaging as they went, the raiders returned to Victorio's camp in New Mexico without, as far as is known, losing a man.[12]

But by that time the great Apache was approaching the end of his career. On May 24 in a box canyon at the head of the Palomas River in the Black Range of New Mexico he was trapped by a force consisting mainly of Apache scouts and suffered his first tactical defeat. He lost about thirty of his people—men, women, and children—and according to the scouts was himself wounded. He set out for the border, killing everyone he met on the way, but on June 5 before he reached it, the army came up with him again, killing ten of his band and wounding three. (Every such loss reduced his small fighting force, while the army manpower seemed limitless.) One of the slain was Washington. In fact, Victorio lost three sons at one time or another during the wars, leaving only a small boy, Istee, hidden out in the Black Range with his mother. Mangus, who had married Victorio's daughter, also left his wife and little son, later known as Frank Mangus, in the same refuge. The child Kaywaykla was not so shielded. His father had been killed during a raid, but the rest of the family remained with the band.[13]

Now south of the border, Victorio raided deep into Chihuahua, once striking within thirty miles of the capital. Officials of the two

11 Thrapp, *Juh*, p. 21, quoting *Arizona Star*, May 27, 1880.
12 Thrapp, *Conquest of Apacheria*, pp. 198–99; Thrapp, *Victorio*, pp. 275–76.
13 Thrapp, *Victorio*, pp. 277–82; Thrapp, *Conquest of Apacheria*, pp. 199–203; Ball, *op. cit.*, pp. 15, 58–60, 113.

countries prepared for "the biggest manhunt in the history of the Southwest" (Thrapp's words), as military forces were put into action on both sides of the line. In September plans were developed for enlisting Juh and others in his band to aid in the operations.[14] Juh's response to the suggestion, had it been made, cannot be conjectured. It is impossible to believe that Geronimo, with his strong family and tribal ties to the Warm Springs band, could have been enlisted. There was also mention of approaching Naiche, who probably would not have responded either. But Victorio for once relaxed his vigilance and led his weary people to a supposed resting place at Tres Castillos, where three rugged hills rise above the plain far east of the protecting Sierra Madre.

There, a strong Mexican force under Colonel Joaquin Terrazas, a cousin of Governor Luis Terrazas of Chihuahua, lay hidden. It was October 14, 1880. When the Apaches started to relax and make their camps, Terrazas sprang the trap. The Indians were almost out of ammunition. Kaahteney, a popular young warrior soon to become prominent in Apache history, had been sent out with another man to capture some, but they had not yet returned. Everything was soon over. The Mexicans' casualties were only three killed and ten wounded. They killed and scalped for the bounty seventy-eight Indians, of whom sixty-two were warriors, the rest women and children; they captured sixty-eight women and children to be sold into slavery; they took 120 horses, 38 mules, and 12 burros; and they recovered two Mexican boy captives. They were given a triumphal entry into the city of Chihuahua with the seventy-eight scalps borne on poles and the captives following. It is said that the scalp bounty added up to fifty thousand dollars, but the cheering multitude thought the victory was well worth the price.

Only seventeen Apaches—men, women, and children—escaped the massacre. These included Nana, who was with the rear guard, and Victorio's son-in-law Mangus. Victorio was among the dead.

[14] Thrapp, *Juh*, p. 21, citing Record Group 393, Records of U.S. Army Continental Commands, 1821–1920, Department of Arizona, misc. papers re Victoria's campaign, roll 36, 2715, Carr in the field at Bowie, to AG, Whipple, September 1, 1880.

Kaywaykla and his mother, Guyan, escaped, but his baby sister was lost; his grandmother and his young girl cousin Siki (Sy-e-konne) were among the captives. (Siki was a daughter of Loco. Her mother, Guyan's sister, had died and the girl had been brought up by her grandmother.[15]) A woman who was then, or who afterwards became, a wife of Mangus was also captured. Later, under the Spanish name of Huera, she was to figure largely in a crisis of Geronimo's life. A hunting party sent out before the attack and the two warriors on the ammunition raid eventually joined the survivors, but even so, it was a tragically diminished band.[16]

The white men of the American Southwest also had their losses to consider. In his report for 1881 William Tecumseh Sherman, the commanding general of the army, reckoning the price of the Victorio war in the hundreds of civilians slain and the millions of dollars expended, sarcastically remarked that while he did not know why the Interior Department had insisted on removing these Indians to Arizona, the reasons must have been very good to justify the cost to settlers and the government.[17]

In contrast, Juh and Geronimo and their followers were living quietly on the reservation. Even Clum, writing of that time, credited the two leaders with peaceable intentions.[18] It may have been at this period that Geronimo's daughter, Dohn-say, received some sort of Apache accolade as one of the three outstanding young women of their band. This must have pleased Geronimo, for he loved his family. (The other two were Betzinez' sister, later known as Ellen, and the young woman who became the wife of Geronimo's "brother," actually his second cousin, Perico.)[19]

But the survivors of Victorio's band did not come in to share the peace with their friends and relatives on the reservation. Nana

15 Ball, op. cit., p. 87.
16 Ibid., pp. 87–102; James Kaywaykla interview, July 29, 1959; Thrapp, Victorio, pp. 293–307, 310–11. Thrapp, who has examined the site of the massacre, is impressed by the accuracy with which the four-year-old Kaywaykla's memory fits the terrain.
17 Thrapp, Victorio, p. 314.
18 John P. Clum, "Apache Misrule," New Mexico Historical Review, Vol. V, No. 3 (July, 1930), pp. 226–27.
19 Jason Betzinez interview, August 21, 1959.

gathered the broken fragments and led them to hidden places in the Sierra Madre to rest and recuperate.[20] The next year (1881) they made cautious overtures to return. In April Loco reported to the San Carlos agent that they had communicated with him, offering to come in and join his band and refrain from raiding if they could be assured of protection. Apparently the assurance was not given, although Loco said he would be responsible for their future good behavior. Then in July, according to the Mescalero agent, they made four attempts to contact *him*, hoping to settle there; but each time they approached they were driven back by the soldiers. Rebuffed, they went on the warpath.[21]

If it was Nana who initiated these overtures, one can hardly credit his sincerity. Kaywaykla, who heard all the adult conversation at the time and afterwards, represented him as implacably committed to vengeance for the disaster at Tres Castillos. "Nana . . . was not content with an eye for an eye, nor a life for a life. For every Apache killed he took many lives."[22] In either case, in late July, with fifteen warriors of his own band and about twenty-five Mescaleros who joined him, he began a series of slashing raids through the mountains of south central and southwestern New Mexico. Old and crippled as he was, he seemed tireless, riding as much as seventy miles a day, striking army units and citizens' posses, killing miners, herders, Mexican-Americans—every person encountered—and capturing horses and supplies. Altogether eight companies of cavalry, eight companies of infantry, and two companies of Indian scouts were called out to run him down, but his hostiles inflicted casualties and melted away unharmed. Finally, in late August they crossed the border, and "on positive orders from the government," said the official summary, "the chase was abandoned."[23]

Geronimo and Juh and their people on the reservation were not directly affected by Nana's raid, but the panic into which it threw

20 Ball, *op. cit.*, p. 113.
21 Thrapp, *Victorio*, p. 310; Secretary of the Interior, *Annual Report*, 1881, p. 5.
22 Ball, *op. cit.*, pp. 119–20, 123.
23 Thrapp, *Conquest of Apacheria*, pp. 212–16; Sonnichsen, *op. cit.*, pp. 191–94.

the government officials may well explain the irrational actions that were to drive these scarcely tamed bands into hostility. It all began, innocently enough, with one of those religious revivalist movements that have broken out spontaneously among frustrated Indians at various times and places, linked only by a fervent faith in the disappearance of the white man and the return of the old order.[24] This time the "prophet" was Noch-ay-del-klinne.

This frail, mild ascetic was living with his family on Cibecue Creek in the western part of the former Fort Apache Reservation. The Indians removed by Clum from this area had been permitted to return to their homeland by an effective temporary agent,[25] and many had gone there, preferring the opportunities for self-support in this bountiful region to dependency on government rations. There was a garrison at Fort Apache to keep them in order, but they remained under the authority of the distant San Carlos Agency. The Chiricahuas and their Nednai associates were still held there in the vicinity of the sub-agency farther up the Gila, and a few miles beyond that, off the reservation to the east, was Fort Thomas.

Released from close herd on the Gila, the White Mountain and Coyotero Apaches discovered the extent to which white intruders were overrunning their land.[26] The boundaries of the combined reservation had in fact been moved back several times to accommodate mining interests, and towns had sprung up on land thus lost to the Indians. Out of their frustration they turned to religion. By the spring of 1881 Noch-ay-del-klinne had convinced them (and probably had convinced himself) that he could commune with the spirits of the dead and even had the power to bring their dead chiefs back to life. He taught his followers a new dance, in which the performers were arranged like the spokes of a wheel, all facing inward, while he stood at the hub and sprinkled them with

---

24 The historian will recall the Shawnee movement headed by Tecumseh's brother and the "ghost dance religion" that swept the Plains tribes in the 1890's. Less well known nativist revivals have occurred in other widely separated tribes.

25 Ogle, *op. cit.*, p. 197.

26 *Ibid.*, pp. 130, 203–204.

the sacred *hoddentin* as they circled around him.[27] The Indians flocked to him and danced with a religious ecstasy frightening to white observers. It was reported that he linked the return of the dead chiefs to the disappearance of the white men and foretold that the consummation would occur at the time of the corn harvest.

It is not known to what extent the hard-headed Geronimo was affected by these emotional orgies. Apparently he did at least visit the prophet. He must have been referring to him when he said later at Fort Sill, "Once while living in San Carlos Reservation an Indian told me that while lying unconscious on the battlefield he had actually been dead, and had passed into the spirit land." There he saw Indians he had known in life camped in a green valley with plenty of game, and "was sorry when he was brought back to consciousness."[28]

As he remembered it from his boyhood, Asa Daklugie stated that his father Juh and Geronimo were present when the religious excitement reached its tragic climax. He was probably mistaken about this. The army made an investigation of the incident, and no evidence of their presence was found. But Daklugie also said that Geronimo told him at Fort Sill shortly before his death in 1909 that he had never understood how he and Juh could have been influenced by the prophet's incantations. This is entirely typical of Geronimo's healthy skepticism. Nana apparently had greater faith. According to Daklugie, who as an adult knew that leader well at Fort Sill, Nana once visited the prophet, attended at least one prayer session, and on a misty predawn saw him call up Mangas Coloradas, Cochise, and Victorio. "The word of Nana could not be questioned," said Daklugie.[29] One may question his vision, but there is no need to question his visit. Nobody knew where the invisible Nana was except when he struck. While he was collecting his people and recuperating he could have taken a side trip to Cibecue.

[27] James Mooney, *The Ghost-Dance Religion and the Sioux Outbreak of 1890*, pp. 704–705.

[28] Barrett, *Geronimo's Story of His Life*, pp. 208–11.

[29] Dan L. Thrapp, *General Crook and the Sierra Madre Adventure*, p. 40 n.; Thrapp, *Juh*, pp. 21–25.

The dancing and the emotional fervor were at their height at the very time Nana was splashing blood over the map of New Mexico. Officials responsible for good order on the reservation and the safety of civilian lives outside were understandably nervous. White men have seldom sensed the meaning of such religious manifestations among unhappy Indians grasping at nostalgic memories of their past.[30] Joseph Capron Tiffany was the agent at San Carlos. According to inspectors sent out from Washington, he not only sold immense stores of goods supposed to be issued to the Indians, but also established a ranch where he put his private brand on issued cattle, fed them issued grain, and detailed an agency employee to herd them.[31] Certainly in the Cibecue emergency he exhibited ineptitude and lack of discernment. The commander at Fort Apache was Colonel Eugene Asa Carr,[32] who, though a competent officer, had no sympathy for Indians. He tried, however, to calm the situation. In a post order he issued on August 17 he said he had heard that "some silly or evil disposed soldiers" had been telling the Indians that the army was planning to attack them or drive them from the reservation, and he warned against such "foolish or wicked" boasts.[33]

As the excitement increased, even the enlisted scouts at Fort Apache demanded passes to attend the dances, and they returned as converts. Tiffany sent his Indian police to arrest the prophet, and they came back empty-handed, grumbling about white aggression. The prophet evaded summonses from both Tiffany and Carr to come in for a conference. Finally, after considerable vacillation, the agent on August 14 sent this demand to the officer: "I want him arrested or killed or both."

Carr accordingly set out on August 29 with 117 men, including 23 scouts. They arrested Noch-ay-del-klinne, who submitted quietly, but his followers attacked the troops, and even the scouts defected and joined them. The prophet, an estimated 18 other

---

30 For example, the massacre of the Sioux ghost dancers at Wounded Knee in 1890.
31 Ogle, *op. cit.*, pp. 211–13.
32 Brevet rank, major general.
33 Thrapp, *General Crook and the Sierra Madre Adventure*, p. 14.

Indians, and 8 of Carr's men were killed. Carr slipped away by night and reached Fort Apache, and the Indians then made a futile attack on the post. Small bands also struck out, killing several soldiers and civilians they found in the vicinity of the reservation. It is clear, however, that there was no plan for a general uprising; it was only that the Indians revered their prophet and were furious over his arrest and death. Major General Irvin McDowell, who commanded the Department of the Pacific, which included Arizona, came to this conclusion: "The fact of the troops finding the medicine-man and his people in their homes, where they had been planting corn,[34] shows that they were not then for war."

After their first angry reaction, the Indians settled back into disillusionment. Their prophet was dead. No miracles had intervened. Their dream was over. But the whole Southwest was unnerved by the fear of a general outbreak. General Willcox rushed all available Arizona military forces to the area. Reinforcements were sent in from New Mexico and California—cavalry, infantry, artillery—twenty-two companies in all. The huge consolidated reservation swarmed with armed men. The Indians involved in the Cibecue fight, including the mutinous scouts, began to surrender. Possibly the presence of the soldiers did hasten their submission. It had the opposite effect on the Chiricahuas and their relatives.

According to Tiffany's report, these bands had been "perfectly quiet during the whole White Mountain trouble," but there had been no soldiers in their area since Clum had informed the military in 1876 that he was in charge of the agency. Now soldiers were marching and countermarching all over the place. The Indians there, especially those like Geronimo and Juh, who were uneasily conscious of past depredations in Mexico, became nervous. About the middle of September they came to ask Tiffany "what was going on, and what so many troops meant about the agencies. I explained it to them and told them to have no fear, that none of the Indians who had been peaceable would be molested in any way." They said

---

[34] He did not mean that they had been planting corn in August, but that they were a settled people with corn fields.

they had been on the war-path and had come in in good faith and were contented, that they did not want war or to fight. . . . They inquired if the movement of troops had anything to do with what they had done in Mexico. I assured them it had not. They shook hands, much delighted and went back" to the sub-agency.[35]

But two bands that *had* engaged in the fighting were in the area. One had five members, who are usually classed by historians as Chiricahuas but apparently were White Mountain Indians. Their leader was Benito (Bonito), who will be heard from hereafter.[36] The other was a White Mountain band of twenty-six under a leader known as George. On September 25 the two leaders came to Ezra Hoag, the employee in charge of the sub-agency, and surrendered. General Willcox, at Fort Thomas, then released them on parole, but five days later, for no discernable reason, it was decided to take them into custody. September 30 was ration day at the sub-agency, and all the Indians were assembled there in the happy confusion of the distribution. Suddenly three companies of cavalry appeared. George and Benito, not wanting to miss their rations, sent word that they would voluntarily appear later at Fort Thomas, but the commander deployed his troops and advanced on their people. The two bands then fled to the Chiricahuas and Nednais, the latter took flight, and seventy-four warriors under Juh, Geronimo, and the formerly peaceable Naiche set out with their families for Mexico. Among them were Benito and his tiny band.

Incidentally, George and his band also escaped. They bolted in the opposite direction and hid out in the northern part of the reservation, but they were eventually captured. Altogether, the army collected about one hundred suspects during the weeks following the Cibecue fight. A general hanging of the participants was at first contemplated, but through McDowell's influence all were eventually released except five scouts. The latter were court-

---

35 Department of the Interior, *Annual Report*, 1881, p. 5.
36 For a biographical sketch of Benito as a White Mountain Indian, see Griswold, *op. cit.*, s.v. "Benito." But Willcox regarded him as a Chiricahua who had been planting with the Coyoteros living on Turkey Creek; Secretary of War, *Annual Report*, 1882, pp. 145, 148. Whatever his tribe, he became a member of the band in Mexico.

martialed; three were hanged, and two were sentenced to long terms in the army prison at Alcatraz.[37]

The army officers were completely baffled about the cause of the Chiricahuas' and Nednais' stampede, but the reason is evident. As Hoag said, they were "literally scared away." Even Geronimo-hating Clum passionately supported this judgment.[38] Few white men ever understood the fears of this volatile people, who had centuries of good cause to fear. Two and one-half years later, when the runaways had been brought back after a gruelling army campaign, Geronimo explained his reasons.

He said he "left on account of the trouble on the Cibecu. Some Indians from the White Mountains came to us when that trouble took place. A White Mountain Chief called 'George' came to us and told us a great many things and we left on that account. . . . We were treated very badly by the Agents here also, and that made us want to leave. We were given rations but not all that we should have had, not all that belonged to us. They gave us a little manta and cloth, but not enough. . . . We were not allowed to go to the mountains to bake mescal. [The large fleshy bulb of the century plant—the same plant from which the Mexicans made their fiery intoxicant—was steamed in pits over heated stones by the Apache women, and it constituted one of their most important foods.] . . . The manta they gave us was not enough to make a breech-clout. On account of these things we were dissatisfied."[39]

On their way to the border the fugitives killed everybody they encountered, picking up supplies and horses as they fled. The army pursued them, striking them twice in inconclusive actions but otherwise failing to catch up with them.[40] Their trail took them close to Tombstone, and Mayor Clum, with a posse, including

[37] Scholarly accounts of the entire Cibecue affair and its aftermath are in Thrapp, *Conquest of Apacheria*, pp. 217–30; Thrapp, *General Crook and the Sierra Madre Adventure*, pp. 3–50; and Ogle, *op. cit.*, pp. 203–209. For the Indian Office version, see Secretary of the Interior, *Annual Report*, 1881, pp. 5–7.

[38] Clum, "Apache Misrule," pp. 226–39, and "Geronimo" (part 2), pp. 126–30.

[39] National Archives and Records Service, 1601 AGO 1884, F/W 1066 AGO 1883, Geronimo to Captain Emmet Crawford, March 21, 1884.

[40] Thrapp, *Juh*, pp. 26–28. Geronimo's account of the flight is in Barrett, *op. cit.*, pp. 134–35.

three of the famous Earp brothers and other frontier notables, set out to follow them. Clum blamed Geronimo for the whole affair—even for being the source of Noch-ay-del-klinne's visions. Geronimo would not be set free this time, he said, but turned over to the authorities in a box with a paper lily on his chest. But that involved catching him, and the posse never came in sight of the speeding Indians.[41]

The life of Geronimo and his friends and relatives was now centered in the Sierra Madre.

41 Clum, *Apache Agent*, pp. 265–67.

CHAPTER 8

THE BANDS GATHER IN
THE SIERRA MADRE

The observant child Kaywaykla has given a good description of the Apache leaders as he first saw them assembled in the Sierra Madre. He had a photographic memory of the physical appearance and character traits of the people he met, and these first impressions were reinforced by subsequent acquaintance. Juh and Geronimo had already settled in those mountains when Nana arrived with his small following. After his revenge raid in New Mexico, that incorrigible hostile had rested his people in hidden *barrancas* on the west side of the great uplift. Then, far to the south, they "camped near a stream at the foot of a mile-high mountain," where they could see a zigzag trail leading up to the flat top, which was Juh's fabulous stronghold. In that relaxed situation the meeting with Geronimo began with an expression of the broad Apache humor.

Juh first came riding in, "a powerful figure on a sturdy war horse. . . . He was very large, not fat, but stockily built." As he dismounted, he towered above Nana, who himself must have been close to six feet tall, and "his body was twice as thick. . . . His heavy hair was braided and the ends fell almost to his knees. His features differed from those of the Warm Springs. They were what people would now call Mongoloid." He and Nana greeted each other cordially. Soon Geronimo approached at the head of a party of horsemen. Juh suggested that they "play a joke on him." The fire was hastily covered, and all sought hiding places behind boulders and along the walls of the canyon. Geronimo rode unobserving into the trap, taking no precautions in that secure refuge. Then Nana emerged with good-natured banter.

Geronimo was not above a white lie in such a situation. "I knew all the time you were here," he countered. "You did not," said Nana. "And you the sly fox of the Apaches!" But warm greetings followed. Geronimo's "erect compact figure was smaller than that of Juh, but blocky and muscular," as Kaywaykla saw him. After him came "a tall stately young man . . . the tall, handsome son of Cochise."

Apparently the united band never climbed to the stronghold, but remained at the foot of the mountain for the days following. Kaywaykla observed them in their dances and councils. He watched Juh come to the dance at the head of his warriors, wearing only a breechclout and gorgeously beaded moccasins. On his head was "the tight-fitting skull cap of the Nednhi Medicine Man," from which "floated long streamers of eagle plumes that dangled almost to his heels." His speech impediment did not appear in his singing. "He had a soft, deep voice and was skillful in improvising rhythmic accounts of the exploits of his band."

Among Geronimo's warriors were his "brothers" Perico and Fun. The two were sons of the same father. Fun's mother was Geronimo's first cousin, who went by the Spanish name of Bonita. The name of Perico's mother is not remembered, and the ancestry that made him Geronimo's second cousin has not been traced. Possibly Geronimo had a fifth "sister," whom—following the Apache tendency to keep to the mystic number four—he did not mention.[1]

In subsequent events Perico was to appear as Geronimo's chief lieutenant, and even at this time "to many Apaches, Fun was the

---

1 Griswold, "The Fort Sill Apaches," s.v. "Mahko," "Perico," "Fun."

bravest of all the band."[2] Kaywaykla also observed, "For the first time I saw Yanosha, another mighty warrior," Geronimo's brother-in-law. The members of this related group were to be with Geronimo at the time of his last break to the mountains and his final surrender.

Yahnozha "was followed by a small thin boy, little more than half-grown," an orphan named Kanseah. Through some unexplained relationship this youth was Geronimo's nephew, and Yahnozha, by an Apache custom not unlike the page-squire apprenticeship of nobles' sons in medieval Europe, was training him to be a warrior. Kanseah also was destined to be present when Geronimo's last holdout band reached the end of its tangled trail. Another boy noticed by Kaywaykla was Daklugie, who followed his father's warriors to the dance. Kaywaykla was already intimate with two boys of his own band. When Nana was collecting his people after the tragedy of Tres Castillos, he had picked up from the Black Range the wife and young son of Mangus, and Istee, the son of Victorio. Istee was "a handsome and intelligent lad about three years older than I," as Kaywaykla characterized him. Mangus' son was also slightly older than Kaywaykla. The eager child, aspiring to begin his warrior's training, had watched with longing as the two carried on their duties at camp or on the trail.

In this meeting of bands, Kaywaykla was impressed by the recognition given his "grandfather" (actually his granduncle, his grandmother's brother), the revered elder statesman Nana. And among the young warriors rising to prominence in Nana's following was Kaahteney, who had married the widowed Guyan.[3] Kaywaykla was delighted to learn that his adored stepfather had been chosen by Nana to succeed him as leader of the band. A few years later that spirited young warrior was to figure in a crisis of tribal history.

Although the boy's eager interest was centered on the warriors

---

[2] Other informants have made the same statement about Fun's courage.
[3] For the marriage, and Kaywaykla's happiness over the event, see Ball, *In the Days of Victorio*, p. 106.

136

and their sons, he was aware of the quiet influence exerted by Juh's favorite wife, Geronimo's "sister" Ishton, the mother of Daklugie. She was "not a warrior." (This was relevant to the child's experience, for Guyan had shouldered a rifle and fought by her husband's side until his death.) But in other ways Ishton was "powerful." It was believed that she suggested "much of the strategy employed" by Juh and Geronimo, but was "far too wise to admit it." Nothing is known of Juh's other wives, but Daklugie's older half-brothers, Delzhinne and Daklegon, had already attained the status of warriors.[4]

Thus, Kaywaykla saw his people as a child admiring the war leaders and loving his family elders and as an adult looking back with affection and understanding on a small, intimate group. But he was completely out of character in presenting one Chiricahua member of Geronimo's band, an "insolent young man" named Chatto, whom he saw as a greedy opportunist, scheming for position, treacherous, and thoroughly unreliable. Even Chatto's manners were bad—rude, pushing, devoid of respect for his superiors. It could only be said that he was a brave and able warrior, and for that reason he was tolerated.[5] He was to become a controversial figure in subsequent tribal history, and Kaywaykla's memory of his early impressions were certainly affected by that development.

The united bands soon decided in council to bring Loco's people from the reservation. According to Kaywaykla, Geronimo was the originator and leader of the movement, and this judgment seems to be correct. As the boy remembered it, the plan was purely a rescue mission to save friends and relatives from the sickness, starvation, and discomfort they would experience with the approaching summer if they remained penned up on the sun-scorched, malarial Gila flats with no means of self-support and cheated on their ration issues by a corrupt agent.[6] No doubt he did hear ex-

---

4 For Kaywaykla's characterization of the Apaches assembled below Juh's stronghold, see *ibid.*, pp. 113–14, 121–27, 136, 146. See also Griswold, *op. cit.*, s.v. "Yahnozha." For Juh's family I am indebted to Eve Ball, letter, July 13, 1973.
5 Ball, *op. cit.*, pp. 136–39.
6 *Ibid.*

pressions of sympathy for their plight, but rescue was scarcely the motivation. Geronimo was more realistic in assessing it: "In 1884 [1882] we returned to Arizona to get other Apaches to come with us into Mexico. The Mexicans were gathering troops in the mountains where we were ranging, and their numbers were so much greater than ours that we could not hope to fight them successfully, and we were tired of being chased about from place to place."[7] In other words, they wanted reinforcements, though in looking back he may have exaggerated the need at that particular time. And although most of Loco's people were women and children, according to army estimates there were thirty warriors in his band. Women and children were also valuable assets to a tribe in building up its strength. And as for the Mexican menace, it was soon to appear.

Several times during the winter the assembled bands in the Sierra Madre sent messengers to Loco urging him to join them, warning that if he should refuse they would use force. One such contact made in the middle of January, 1882, was reported to Willcox by an inspector of the Indian Office and the army officer in command at Fort Thomas, and he moved his forces to keep "a closer and more vigorous watch" on the border. Similar preparations were made by the army in New Mexico. All this military activity, however, caused no inconvenience to the invaders, who slipped invisibly past the defenses through the mountains on the western edge of New Mexico and crossed through the Steins Peak Range into Arizona. Apparently they traveled in small parties before assembling in the Apache manner for their final dash to the reservation.

According to the army officers, Juh, Geronimo, and Naiche were the leaders,[8] but since nobody saw them this is only a guess. In the Apache accounts, Juh is mentioned only by Kaywaykla, and that child, of course, remained in the Sierra Madre refuge. John Rope, who also was not present but who had talked with many

[7] Barrett, *Geronimo's Story of His Life,* pp. 105–106.
[8] Secretary of War, *Annual Report,* 1882, p. 72.

who were and who gave circumstantial details of the advance of the party, made no mention of him. Neither did Betzinez, who was one of the kidnaped band. This makes it extremely doubtful that Juh participated in the raid.[9] In either case it is apparent from all Apache accounts that Geronimo was in command. Nana remained in the Sierra Madre to care for the women and children.[10]

On the San Simon River northeast of Fort Bowie, according to Rope, two of the raiders (he gave their names) stole two good horses from some cowboys at a ranch and decided to take them back to Mexico before joining the party. Rope traced their route to "a little over towards Janos where there is a high mountain with pine trees on it." There they were captured by a Mexican army unit. Questioned by the officer (probably the notable Indian fighter Colonel Lorenzo García) they revealed the route of the expedition, which would require about four days to reach San Carlos and about twelve days to return to the vicinity of the Mexican camp. The officer held them captive with a promise to release them if their report should prove accurate and a threat to kill them if the return should fail to materialize. Then the Mexicans laid their trap,[11] with results that would be fatal to Loco's people.

Meanwhile, the other raiders continued on their way. Near Ash Flat, about twenty miles north of Safford, the united band came to a sheep ranch belonging to George Stevens, at that time the sheriff of Graham County with his home in Safford. There are four accounts of the massacre that followed. Three, all told at second or third hand, came from the eyewitness story of a well-known White Mountain Apache named Bylas, a close relative of Mrs. Stevens. Two of these—one told by Clum and the other told in his old age by Jimmie Stevens, the young son of George Stevens—are enlivened by dramatic touches and colored by the narrators'

9 Dan L. Thrapp, whose judgment is entitled to great consideration, is convinced that he did. He bases this conclusion on the opinion of the army officers; the established fact that Juh was seen at Corralitos, near the Mexican border, a month before the party reached San Carlos; and the masterly conduct of the expedition, typical of Juh's tactics (Letter to Angie Debo, Dec. 8, 1972).
10 Ball, *op. cit.*, p. 139. Britton Davis, who knew the Apaches well, also stated that Geronimo was the leader (*The Truth about Geronimo*, p. 142).
11 Goodwin, "Experiences of an Indian Scout" (part 2), pp. 41–42.

hatred of Geronimo. The third, by Rope, who knew all the people involved, sounds like an exact report. In addition, there is a contemporary newspaper account quoting a grieving small boy who survived. The four stories differ widely in details, but all reveal the ruthless spirit of Geronimo and his absence of all faith and pity when dealing with Mexicans.

Stevens' foreman was a Mexican named Victoriano Mestas (or Bes-das) who had been captured in boyhood by Geronimo on one of his Mexican raids. Geronimo apparently had treated him well, as the Apaches regularly treated their adopted children, giving him a pony and saddle and supplying him with shirts, but soon he traded him off to a white rancher, and Mestas had grown up as a Mexican and had married a Mexican woman. As chief shepherd of Stevens' ten thousand sheep, he was in charge of nine (some stories say ten) Mexican and three White Mountain Apache herders. (Rope named the Apaches—names like Hac-ke-ha-da-dol-ni-he.) Bylas was also at the sheep camp with his wife and children and other White Mountain families. With the Mexican herders were Mestas' wife and three children and two other Mexican women.

The war party came riding up to the camp with Geronimo, Naiche, and Chatto in the lead. Jimmie Stevens also mentioned the leader of a small Chiricahua band who went by the name of Chihuahua—a warrior relatively unknown at the time, but destined to figure largely in later Apache history.[12] Stevens said there were seventy-six men in the party. The army guess was "about sixty."[13] Even if the number was exaggerated, it was a major expedition.

The raiders began killing Stevens' sheep, and because Geronimo liked horsemeat better than mutton he shot a sorrel pony belonging

---

[12] Juh was not present there, else he would certainly have been mentioned, but that fact does not entirely preclude the possibility that he was one of the leaders. The most direct army mention of him is a statement by the commander of Fort Apache that a Cibecue participant named Na-ti-o-tish "met Hoo according to agreement near Eagle Creek. . . . This information can be relied on" (Thrapp to Angie Debo, Dec. 8, 1972). That conference on nearby Eagle Creek, if it occurred, could have taken place while the main party was raiding the sheep camp.

[13] Ogle, *Federal Control of the Western Apaches*, p. 213.

to Jimmie Stevens, and they told the women to prepare the meal. Some of the stories indicate that Geronimo promised not to harm the Mexicans, that Mestas in particular trusted him, and that there was some talk and fraternizing. Mestas was wearing a fine shirt elaborately embroidered. Geronimo asked him for it, not wanting it to be bloodied, and Mestas tremblingly complied. Then at Geronimo's signal his men seized and bound the Mexicans— Mestas and his herders, his wife and two of his children, and the other women who had helped to cook the meal—and dispatched them by stabbing, clubbing, and shooting them or beating out their brains with stones.

Mestas' third child, a boy about nine years old, escaped by hiding behind Bylas' wife or under her long skirt. When he was discovered, it was Naiche, according to Clum, who protected him, even threatening to kill Geronimo if the woman were harmed; in Jimmie Stevens' account, it was an unnamed warrior of the band who braved the killer. It was this young Mexican boy's story that appeared in the newspaper account. He said that he saw his parents and brothers killed, his father after excruciating torture (the newspaper may have added this detail), and that he himself was saved through the pleas of Bylas' wife.[14]

The war party then resumed their journey. As a precaution against discovery they left two men at the sheep camp to guard the White Mountain women and compelled Bylas and the other White Mountain men to accompany them as far as the reservation. In the evening they camped on the south side of Ash Flat. There Geronimo sang four songs, consulting his Power to learn the situation at San Carlos, and was assured that the raid would be successful. His Power also helped the good work along by laying a deep sleep on Loco's people and the agency employees. By this time Geronimo's access to such supernatural aid was an important asset to his generalship. Fifty years later his followers told Opler that he would go through his ceremony and announce, " 'You should go here;

14 Clum's account is in Clum, *Apache Agent*, pp. 272–76; Jimmie Stevens' is in Ross Santee, *Apache Land*, pp. 167–71; Rope's is in Goodwin, *op. cit.* (part 2), pp. 42–46; and the newspaper story is in Thrapp, *Conquest of Apacheria*, pp. 237–38.

you should not go there.' That is how he became a leader."[15] No doubt, like superstitious people in white society, he and his warriors overlooked the occasions when the signs failed.

After this assurance, the party made a night ride to the reservation, arriving before dawn in the brush along the Gila east of the agency. They cut the telegraph wires connecting the agency with the sub-agency and with the nearby mining camp of Globe, just off the reservation to the west. It also appears that they sent agents to alert confederates in Loco's camps, for a rider with a Nednai accent came "long after midnight" to the tent where Betzinez lived with his mother and sister to ask directions to the lodge of Gil-lee. (This Gil-lee, or Zele, a Chiricahua, was to become prominent in the Apache wars as an associate of Chatto and Benito.) Geronimo, in fact, threatened to infiltrate the entire reservation. There were about forty police there, living at their homes scattered throughout the various camps, and he had said he would send three men into every camp to kill them all. Perhaps this was idle boasting, for he made no attempt to carry out his threat. While the band waited on the river for daylight, one of the men, using an Apache technique, threw a pebble into the air. It was visible, and thus they knew that dawn was approaching. At daybreak they crossed over to the Warm Springs camps.[16] It was April 19, 1882.

Loco and his people were living three miles east of the agency on the same gravelly bench between the Gila and San Carlos rivers. Except for some brush and scrawny cottonwoods along the streams, the area was bare of vegetation. The Indian agents regularly gave glowing reports of irrigation works and bountiful crops raised by their charges, but these stories can be discounted. Still, Loco had pledged his word to stay there, and he stayed. His people were at least at peace. Now at daybreak they heard shouting and saw a line of armed warriors between them and the agency, while others, swimming their horses, were approaching from across the river. One of the leaders was shouting, "Take them all! . . . Shoot

[15] *An Apache Life-Way*, p. 200.
[16] Goodwin, *op. cit.*, (part 2), pp. 46–47; Betzinez, *I Fought with Geronimo*, p. 55; Griswold, *op. cit.*, s.v. "Gil-lee."

down anyone who refuses to go with us! Some of you men lead them out."

"We did everything they told us to do," said Betzinez. They were driven away on foot with barely time to snatch up a few belongings. It is said that Loco was forced at gunpoint to lead the evacuation.[17] Geronimo went in front, guiding them east along the foot of the hills north of the Gila. Others stayed behind as a rear guard against any help that might come from the agency. Soon they heard shooting behind them. Chief of Police Albert D. Sterling, with one member of his Apache force, had ridden up to see what was happening. According to official reports the telegraph operator at the sub-agency had managed to repair the break in the wire and alert the agency; according to Rope the Warm Springs people had fired two shots to call him.[18] He and his Apache policeman were both killed.[19]

The killing of the policemen convinced Loco's people of their helplessness. "We told ourselves that our safety depended on keeping quiet and not trying to escape," said Betzinez. "We were filled with gloom and despair." Their captors herded them along the river for several miles, then turned northeast into the Gila Mountains. Near sunset they were given a short rest near a spring, then were started out on a night journey. Loco, a resourceful and brave warrior in spite of his peace policy, was admitted to the council of the leaders. Naiche, Chatto, and others were prominent, but clearly Geronimo was in charge. At midnight, during another brief rest, some volunteers were sent to a sheep camp for food with instructions as to the morning's rendezvous. At sunrise these raiders came with several hundred sheep, and the band ate and rested for two days.

There the leaders in council discussed plans to escape to Mexico with this great company and avoid combat with the troops, who

17 Thrapp, *Juh*, p. 30.
18 At least I think Rope meant that it was the Warm Springs people, not the invaders, who fired the signal shots.
19 Betzinez, *op. cit.*, pp. 56–57; Goodwin, *op. cit.* (part 2), p. 47; Thrapp, *Conquest of Apacheria*, p. 236.

were certainly scouring the country for them. There were probably about one hundred warriors and three to four hundred women and children[20]—a difficult number to conceal. They saw that they would have to make better time. It is in fact evident to one who reads Betzinez' firsthand account of their journey that they were showing little of the speed and endurance typical of Apache movements. Probably Loco's people had become soft during their enforced idleness on the Gila flats. Betzinez' mother had systematically trained him and his sister in physical fitness, but probably few had been so rigorously kept in condition. And although by his own reckoning he was twenty-two years old, he had received no training as a warrior, and he traveled with the noncombatants. Probably other young men did, also. After all, how could a youth serve the necessary apprenticeship while cooped up at San Carlos with no opportunity even to hunt? Thus, the abductors were burdened with hundreds of helpless people.

Several men were accordingly sent north up the San Francisco River to raid a ranch for horses and mules for the captives to ride. They came back driving the animals and spent another day or so breaking them to be ridden bareback or with improvised saddles made of bundles of reeds. Then men were sent to another ranch for more mounts while the main band waited out of sight on the other side of a hill. Just at that inconvenient time one of the girls reached puberty, and her womanhood ceremony was observed in an attenuated form while shots were heard from the ranch. By this time the ranging parties had killed more than fifty people—prospectors, wagon train drivers, ranchers, lone travelers, everyone they encountered on their raids. Loco's people were now deeply committed as hostiles.

Once mounted, the company set off for another night journey. The abductors surrounded their captives as they rode, but some managed to slip away and head for the Navaho country. By morn-

[20] The well-informed George Stevens estimated the number of warriors at 90. Crook, after careful calculation following the exodus, set the number at 176, and the total in the band is usually placed at 700—estimates that are probably too high. See Thrapp, *General Crook and the Sierra Madre Adventure*, p. 77, and *Al Sieber*, p. 237.

ing, completely exhausted, they stopped to rest at a spring in the rugged Steins Peak Range. From this place a dozen warriors were sent out on a scouting expedition while the rest of the party moved halfway up the mountainside. Lieutenant Colonel George A. Forsyth, out hunting the hostiles, discovered the trail of these scouts and sent his scouts to find them. The finding came the other way. The hostile scouting party ambushed Forsyth's scouts in the mountains and killed four of them. Then the officer came to the rescue with six companies of cavalry. There in a canyon—"I never saw a more rugged place," he reported—he attacked the whole hostile force while the noncombatants watched from the heights. Although he claimed to have "won" the engagement, he hastily pulled out, leaving the Indians in possession. He thought he had killed two. Later, Crook's careful investigation showed that the Indians had lost one warrior.[21]

After driving off Forsyth's vastly superior force, the hostiles made another long night march, moving down the mountainside and crossing the wide, open San Simon Valley to the southwest. Perhaps in this extremity Geronimo again summoned his Power— to delay the morning. Fifty years later one of his followers related such an event to Opler. Geronimo was crossing a level place and wanted to reach the mountains before the pursuing enemy could sight him, "So [he] sang, and the night remained for two or three hours longer. I saw this myself."[22] By morning they reached their assembly point in the Chiricahua Mountains southeast of Fort Bowie. There they rested during the day while some of the warriors stationed on a peak kept the post in view, half expecting to see troops coming out in search of them. But nothing happened, and after another night march through rugged arroyos and foothills along the east edge of the range and a recrossing of the San Simon Valley to the southeast, they entered Mexico. There in the Sierra de San Luis, just south of New Mexico, they rested another day. They had continued to leave a trail of blood behind them.[23]

21 Thrapp, *Conquest of Apacheria*, p. 248.
22 Opler, *An Apache Life-Way*, p. 216.
23 The inside story of their experiences is in Betzinez, *I Fought with Geronimo*, pp.

They had conducted their exodus with almost incredible skill and success, and now they believed themselves safe. They had escaped the American soldiers, and they never had much regard for the fighting qualities of Mexicans. In the evening their leaders summoned them to another night journey. This time it was a pleasant excursion free—they thought—from pursuit. They rode in bright starlight southeast across the Janos Plains, laughing, breaking into snatches of song, calling to companions, challenging each other to short races. Several times they stopped at springs to rest. By morning they reached the base of the Sierra Emmedio, "a very rough, small mountain in the middle of the Janos plains."[24] They camped on the west side at a fine spring, with the uplift rising behind them. Between them and the mountain was a rocky ridge overlooking their camp. To the south a jumble of rocks formed a small, round hill. Away to the west and south stretched the level plain. For two days they rested and relaxed, spending their nights dancing in celebration of their deliverance. The women even gathered the fleshy crowns of the mescal and placed them in pits for the prolonged cooking.[25] They had long been deprived of this food during their virtual captivity at San Carlos.

But unknown to them, Forsyth had decided to disregard international law and cross the border. With his large force of four hundred soldiers and fifty scouts he kept at a safe distance, but Captain Tullius C. Tupper was hot on the trail, picking it out through mountain and plain. He had thirty-nine troopers and forty-seven lynx-eyed Apache scouts under the indefatigable Al Sieber. On the night of April 27 they saw the fires of the hostiles' camp five miles ahead. Sieber and four of the scouts crept up to investi-

---

57–66. The civilian casualties and the army pursuit based on original sources is given in Thrapp's books: *General Crook and the Sierra Madre Adventure*, pp. 76–84, includes his study of the terrain, and excellent photographs of the localities in the Steins Peak Range follow p. 70; and a more detailed account is in *Conquest of Apacheria*, pp. 235–46.

24 The words of Al Sieber.

25 Ball, *op. cit.*, p. 141. Kaywaykla's account of the flight, which he received second hand, is confused and inaccurate. He said that the mescal roasting was interrupted by the fight in the Steins Peak Range.

gate. The Indians, with their guard relaxed in their supposed sanctuary, were dancing around their big fire, and the spies were undiscovered. They reported the lay of the ground to Tupper, and he brought his force—still undiscovered—into position during the night. The scouts were to man the ridge at the back while the cavalry was to advance on the plain in front to make a concerted attack on the unsuspecting camp. They arrived just before dawn. The Indians were still dancing. They might have annihilated the band except for the cooking mescal.

The scouts were taking their position on the ridge when a man and three women appeared within twenty-five feet of them, laughing and talking as they came to see about their mescal. Even in the dim light the officer in command recognized the man as the son of Loco. Knowing that discovery was imminent, he gave the order to fire. All four were killed, and the premature shots aroused the camp. So says the army account.

Kaywaykla told the same story as he heard it from the Indian man who was supposed to have been killed. He was not the son but the youthful grandson of Loco; his mother was Loco's daughter, and his father, who had been killed by Mexicans, had been a son of Mangas Coloradas. In later years he was known as Talbot Gooday. In spite of differences in detail, the two accounts of the incident as seen from opposite sides are striking in verisimilitude. As Gooday told it, the band planned to make an early start on their travels that morning if the mescal had finished cooking. His mother called him and two young women to go with her to inspect it. One of the girls stooped over to make the test when a shot rang out and she fell across the pit. The other girl started to run and was picked off. Gooday pulled his mother behind a rock. He had no weapon except a knife.[26]

At the sound of the shots the Apache camp sprang into action. The scouts fired down upon it from the ridge, and the troopers

---

26 Gooday's account is in Ball, *op. cit.*, p. 141. For his biography, see Griswold, *op. cit.*, s.v. "Gooday (Talbot)." Kaywaykla cites Frank Gooday, a slip of his speech or of Mrs. Ball's pen—Frank Gooday was not born until years later at Fort Sill. Elsewhere, Kaywaykla's informant is correctly identified as Talbot Gooday.

The site of Tupper's attack on Loco's band, taken from the ridge from which the scouts fired on the Apaches, who fled to the rocky hill in the center. *Geronimo's venture to abduct Loco's people had indeed cost them dearly.* Photograph by Dan L. Thrapp.

attacked from the front, killing six warriors. The whole band made for the rocky hillock at the side, the warriors firing as they ran, but in their excitement they shot too high and inflicted little damage. There they took refuge, the women and children hiding in the rocks, the men firing from cover. Loco called across to the scouts, urging them to defect, but they answered with insults. He was slightly wounded as he leaned against a rock. Some of the warriors tried to save their horse herd but were driven off. Desultory firing continued for several hours, with Tupper unable to dislodge the Indians on the hill and the Indians unable to drive off the attackers.

Early in the afternoon four young warriors circled to the south and east, came up behind the scouts on the ridge, and began firing on them from the rear. The scouts then withdrew and joined the troopers on the plain, and the four warriors, ducking behind rocks, continued firing. This diversion gave the Indians on the hill a chance to escape to the east into the foothills that ringed the mountain. Possibly Tupper had already ordered the scouts to join him, for he withdrew his whole command. His men were exhausted and almost out of ammunition, and it was clearly impossible for his outnumbered force to encircle and destroy the Indians. Taking along the Indians' horses, he retired to his camp of the previous night. There, Forsyth finally arrived and assumed command.[27]

According to Crook's later investigation, the Indians lost fourteen men in the day's fighting.[28] At dusk they came out from the foothills and assembled for their flight to the south. They were in a desperate plight. The few scanty supplies—blankets, utensils, other necessities—they had brought when they left the reservation had been left behind that morning when they fled from their camp. Many of them were wounded, and they lacked transportation. They drank from a spring they found and distributed a little food that some of them had snatched up. Just before they started, some of the warriors came in with a few horses they had recaptured from the retreating soldiers, but most of them were on foot.

As they dragged themselves across the level Janos Plains they became so utterly exhausted that they had to rest and sleep for an hour or so. A few warriors who had horses, Naiche, Chatto, Kaahteney, and about a dozen others, did not stop but rode on. Early in the morning, according to Betzinez, they saw some Mexican soldiers, but they went on into the foothills without returning to warn the company. Betzinez may have been mistaken about their seeing the Mexicans, but their subsequent conduct is hard to

---

27 A summary of the army pursuit and the battle, with a careful description of the terrain, is in Thrapp, *General Crook and the Sierra Madre Adventure*, pp. 84–90, with photographs following p. 70; a more detailed account is in his *Al Sieber*, pp. 225–37. The Apache version, which harmonizes well with the army account, even in day-to-day incidents, is in Betzinez, *op. cit.*, pp. 66–69.
28 Thrapp, *Conquest of Apacheria*, p. 248.

explain. Meanwhile, the main band resumed their journey. By morning they were close to their chosen assembly point. They had traveled twenty-nine miles that night.[29] With daylight the band was straggling in an irregular column about two miles long. They had reached a country of low hills and were paralleling Aliso Creek, a dry stream bed in a small arroyo. Visible ahead were the blue shapes of the Sierra Madre. A few warriors were out in front leading the way, but they stopped to rest, and the laboring column passed, unaware of danger from that direction. The other warriors were in the rear, guarding against possible pursuit by the American soldiers. Suddenly, García's men emerged from a ravine and struck the long line from the side. As Betzinez remembered it: "Almost immediately Mexicans were right among us all, shooting down women and children right and left. People were falling and bleeding, and dying, on all sides of us. . . . Those who could run the fastest and the farthest managed to escape. . . . my mother and sister and I were among them, being excellent runners. . . . I had no weapons of any kind, not yet having been made a warrior. We headed rapidly for the mountains. As we ran, my mother and I heard Geronimo behind us, calling to the men to gather around him and make a stand to protect the women and children. We learned later that thirty-two warriors responded to Geronimo, around whom some women and children assembled for protection."

The Mexicans fired on the ones who were fleeing, but a number ran over a hill and escaped. There, on the other side, sitting under a tree smoking, was the party that had ridden ahead. They had heard the shots but had made no move to return. Betzinez was a truthful witness, and Al Sieber, who examined the site the next day, found evidence that some "young bucks . . . put spurs to their horses and made escape."[30] Why did they do it? The three Betzinez named were warriors of undoubted courage. Had they quarreled with Geronimo and disassociated themselves from the expedition?

29 Betzinez, op. cit., p. 70.
30 Thrapp, General Crook and the Sierra Madre Adventure, p. 92.

Had something occurred during the previous day's battle to alienate them? Were they disgusted by the rest stop in the night? Apaches were individualists in their wars; if they trusted their leader, they carried out his orders, but he could not enforce obedience.

Betzinez called to the fugitives, and they came from hiding places until a considerable band was collected. Then they moved to the rendezvous point on the steep side of a mountain, where other fugitives had preceded them. Meanwhile, Geronimo and Chihuahua and the warriors they had assembled, with a few women and children, had taken their stand in the dry creek bed. There the real battle was fought as the Mexicans made repeated efforts to dislodge them. There are three accounts of this fight—all remarkably similar—by Geronimo himself; by Kaywaykla, who got the story from Talbot Gooday; and by Betzinez, who heard it when the participants rejoined the fugitives on the mountainside.

The women dug holes in the banks for shelter, and the men cut footholds so they could step up and fire. By digging in the sandy soil they found water to drink. When their ammunition ran low, a woman ran out in a hail of bullets and retrieved a bag that had been dropped a few yards away. As the Mexicans charged, the officers rallied their soldiers with the hated name of Geronimo. The Indians understood their Spanish: "Geronimo is in that ditch. Go in and get him!" and the taunt, "Geronimo, this is your last day!" This time the Indians' marksmanship was steady. They killed three officers and eighteen or nineteen men and wounded many more of García's 250-man force.

The battle continued until dark. Then somebody set the grass on fire. (The Indians did it, said Geronimo, in order to drive off the Mexicans; the Mexicans did it, said Betzinez and Kaywaykla, to smoke out the Indians.) The Indians prepared to slip out unseen. And then, according to Gooday, Geronimo called out to his men, "If we leave the women and children we can escape." Fun, who had been the bravest of the brave throughout that hard-fought day, was unable to believe his ears. He asked the leader to repeat it.

Geronimo gave the order to go, and Fun raised his rifle. "Say that again and I'll shoot," he said. Geronimo climbed to the top and disappeared.[31]

This incident is as hard to explain as the desertion of the mounted warriors in the morning; even Geronimo's most severe detractors conceded his courage.[32] But could it be a significant revelation of his practice in extremity? Three times in battle he lost, or was to lose, wives and children while he escaped. Was this merely a series of coincidences? It should be pointed out, however, that Gooday was not an impartial witness. Throughout his long life—he died in 1962—he held a strong resentment against Geronimo for the death of his Warm Springs relatives because of Loco's forced exodus. But Kaywaykla was convinced of the truth of his story,[33] and it gained some credence throughout the tribe. Opler heard it in garbled form in the 1930's.[34]

And some groups creeping to safety did abandon the babies. Betzinez said that the warriors "asked the consent" of the women to choke them "so that they wouldn't give away their movements by crying," and he implies that it was done. Sam Haozous told of one mother who strangled her baby rather than leave it to grow up in Mexican slavery. But Fun was credited with holding off the Mexicans until the babies in his sector could be carried out.

The party on the mountainside suffered much from cold. Since it was unsafe to build fires, they pulled grass for covering. There was no help for the wounded and no food. Throughout the night the sound of wailing and mourning for lost relatives was heard. In the morning they looked far into the valley and saw the Mexican and American armies come together. They expected a fight, but nothing happened. Their leaders gave orders for them to move, and halfway down the mountain they met Geronimo and his

[31] Ball, *op. cit.*, pp. 144–45.
[32] See, for example, Santee, *op. cit.*, p. 167, for a statement by the ardent Geronimo-hater, Jimmie Stevens.
[33] He told it to me as a fact without mentioning the source: "Geronimo wanted to desert the women and children and Fun said he would shoot him if he did" (interview, July 29, 1959).
[34] "A Chiricahua Apache's Account of the Geronimo Campaign of 1886," p. 368 and n. 12.

party. There was much excited conversation and comparison of experiences. Then Geronimo gave the order to resume the march.[35]

When the Apaches observed the meeting between the Mexican and American forces they were vaguely aware of the international issues involved. Forsyth, as he admitted later, "had strict orders in my possession not to enter Mexican territory," but when he came up with Tupper's force and learned of the Sierra Emmedio battle he decided to continue the pursuit. The following morning he reached the site and found the Indians gone. He followed their trail across the plain and camped for the night not far from the place where García had attacked them that very day. The next morning García confronted him, demanded his authority for invading Mexico, and peremptorily ordered him to leave. Forsyth said he was following orders to exterminate the hostile Apaches. García informed him the job was already done and showed him over the battlefield. It was a ghastly sight, strewn with the bodies of nineteen soldiers (García in his report said eighteen) and three officers of the Mexican force and seventy-eight Indians. In addition, the Mexicans had captured thirty-three women and children, one of the women, it is said, being a daughter of Loco. Of the Indians killed, only eleven were warriors; most of the others were victims of the first attack before the warriors came to their rescue. In fact, the Indians afterwards told Crook that they had won the real battle, the fight on Aliso Creek.

The two commanders parted amicably, and Forsyth returned to the United States. Washington was not informed that its armed forces had invaded Mexico. Forsyth's report was stopped by his immediate superior with the advice that "the less said about it the better." Tupper located his fight in the mountains of New Mexico, and so it appears in the War Department's *Annual Report*.[36]

35 For the Apaches' account of the ambush and the fight on Aliso Creek, see Betzinez, *op. cit.*, pp. 71–75; Ball, *op. cit.*, pp. 143–45; and Barrett, *op. cit.*, pp. 106–109. Geronimo's story of the fight is accurate and detailed, but the rest of his account is confused—probably by Barrett. Haozous's taped interview is in the Duke Oral History Material in the Western History Collections of the University of Oklahoma Library.

36 For the army's account of the García fight, see Thrapp, *Al Sieber*, pp. 236–41 and nn. 26 and 32; Thrapp, *General Crook and the Sierra Madre Adventure*, pp. 92–95 and photograph after p. 70; Secretary of War, *Annual Report*, 1882, pp. 72, 148–50.

To the Indians the meaning of all this was that Forsyth was on his way back to the border and that García lacked the resources to follow them into the mountains. Their day's journey after their night on the mountainside took them through successive ranges of hills. They had to travel slowly because of the many wounded, who had to be helped or carried. Geronimo, meanwhile, had sent some men out to distant ranches to steal cattle, and these foragers came driving beeves to the next rendezvous. Thus, they had their first good meal since the night before Tupper's attack three days before. They rested there for two days.

When they resumed their journey, three badly wounded members of the band, a woman and two men, remained at the camp to recover. The identity of the woman is not known, but one of the men was Tsoe (Tzoe), a young White Mountain Apache married to two Chiricahua women, both of whom had been killed in the García fight,[37] and the other was Kayihtah (Kieta), a cousin of Yahnozha. Each of the men was destined to play a decisive role in ending Geronimo's career. Geronimo sent a man back the following evening to help them, but he proved to be unreliable and reported that the place was occupied by the Mexicans. The company moved on in great anxiety, but the three managed somehow to sustain themselves, and a month later, fully recovered, they rejoined their people.

Meanwhile, the main body soon reached the camp of Juh's Nednais. These people were not at their fastness deep in the Sierra Madre, but, moving about as their custom was, they had established their base high in the mountains about thirty miles southwest of Casas Grandes. When Loco's people arrived, destitute and defeated, carrying their wounded, they found many strangers, but there were some happy reunions with friends and relatives in the two bands. "They gave us food and blankets and by talking to us cheerfully tried to take our minds off our losses," said Betzinez. Geronimo's venture to abduct Loco's people had indeed cost them

[37] At least that was what Crook understood him to say when he subsequently became a captive (Bourke, *Apache Campaign*, p. 31; Thrapp, *General Crook and the Sierra Madre Adventure*, p. 121). He seemed a little young to have two wives.

dearly—twenty-six fighting men out of about one hundred and great destruction inflicted on Loco's women and children. Still, the largest number of these related Apaches that had come together in many years were now assembled in one camp, and among them were many experienced warriors.[38] And their mountain refuge had never been invaded by an enemy.

Mexico and the southwestern United States could well beware.

[38] Betzinez, *op. cit.*, pp. 75–77.

CHAPTER 9

LIFE IN THE SIERRA MADRE

The united band under the leadership of Juh and Geronimo soon moved to a new location close to the San Miguel River, where they were joined by a party returning from a successful raid. There, Loco's peaceable people saw a victory dance performed by the honored raiders surrounded by a circle of their women—a new experience to Betzinez and probably to other young members of the group.[1]

After a few days of relaxation and recreation, the leaders held a council and decided to take a trading trip to Casas Grandes. About one-third of the band joined the expedition. Juh had established fairly constant peaceable relations with this Mexican town,[2] which no doubt furnished a market for the spoils of his raids. But this understanding was not recognized by the state of Chihuahua, and after the Indians had reached an intoxicated condition, the Mexicans struck. Betzinez attributed the act to treachery on the part of Casas Grandes, but Geronimo said that "two companies of Mexican troops from another town attacked us." Probably

---

[1] Betzinez, *I Fought with Geronimo*, p. 77.

[2] Kaywaykla said that after Victorio's survivors joined Juh's band Nana was very careful not to raid Casas Grandes in deference to this relationship. See Ball, *In the Days of Victorio*, pp. 129–32.

they were state troopers from the town of Galeana, about twenty miles southeast. Juh, in fact, did not hold Casas Grandes responsible, for he continued his peaceable trading relations with that community.

"We fled in all directions," said Geronimo. He and Juh escaped, and among others who got away were the fleet-footed Betzinez and his mother and sister. Some of the warriors—probably led by Juh and Geronimo—fought the attackers, but the rout was complete. The Mexicans killed many of the Indians (twenty, said Geronimo) and carried thirty-five into captivity. Among the captives were the wife and two children of Chatto and Geronimo's beautiful wife Chee-hash-kish, the mother of his teenaged son and daughter. In after years Chatto made vain attempts to recover his family, and Geronimo never saw his wife again, although word drifted back to the Apaches that she married a fellow captive.[3]

The band waited at their camp four days for their missing people to come in. Then they moved southwest into the heart of the Sierra Madre and made their camp on the brink of an immense canyon through which flowed a branch of the Yaqui River. But they soon became restless and started moving west towards Sonora. It required a whole day for even the sure-footed Apaches to make the perilous descent into the awesome depth of the canyon and the difficult climb to the opposite side. They continued on through the mountains, crossing another branch of the Yaqui River and then the river itself. Coming out in less rugged country, they planned a raid on a Sonora town. There, Geronimo asked Betzinez to become his assistant. Thus the young man entered his apprenticeship. Several such warriors in training were in the party. Among them was a youth later known as Lot Eyelash. Geronimo's son Chappo was there also; probably he, too, was an apprentice

3 The most detailed account of the Casas Grandes massacre is in Betzinez, *op. cit.*, pp. 77–80. Briefer references are in Barrett, *Geronimo's Story of His Life*, pp. 103–104, and Ball, *op. cit.*, p. 133. The story that reached the American side of the border is in Thrapp, *Conquest of Apacheria*, pp. 263–64 and notes 31 and 32. Mention of the fighting by some of the warriors is in Griswold, "The Fort Sill Apaches," s.v. "Ny-ith-shizeh," and the fate of Chee-hash- kish is in *ibid.*, s.v. "Geronimo." It was unusal for an adult male captive to be spared, but this did sometimes occur. See Ball, *op. cit.*, pp. 20–21.

and not a recognized warrior. As it happened, the raid was abandoned because too many soldiers were in the vicinity,[4] but other raids were to follow.

It was probably during this time when all the bands were united, even more probably after the loss of Chee-hash-kish, that Geronimo married a diminutive Nednai girl named Zi-yeh, whose father seems to have been a white captive, an Apache in all but blood, and whose mother was related in some way to Kaywaykla's mother, Guyan.[5] Later, she was to share Geronimo's captivity, and his affectionate concern for her and their young children was evident throughout the Fort Sill period.

But the consolidation of the bands was short-lived. An amicable difference of opinion arose among the leaders, and in typical Apache fashion they separated. Juh and his Nednai followers turned back into their heartland, while Geronimo, Chihuahua, and Kaahteney, with their contingents of Warm Springs and Chiricahua relatives totaling about eighty men, women, and children, went on to raid in Sonora. Betzinez and his mother and sister were, of course, in the latter group. Apparently a child was born to one of Geronimo's wives during this time, for at one stage of the journey she and her baby rode Betzinez' big mule—the only ones who rode, a probable concession to a recent delivery.[6]

Their raids took the band south almost to Ures and north to the bend of the Bavispe not far from the Arizona line. While the warriors went out to plunder villages, drive in cattle, horses, and mules, and capture pack trains, the women were safely hidden in the mountains, where they dried beef, gathered and stored wild products, and made clothing from the bolts of cloth abundantly supplied by their men. If one did not consider the feelings of the Mexicans, it was an idyllic life, requiring hardihood and caution, filled with adventure but not too much danger, and enlivened by

---

4 Betzinez, *op. cit.*, pp. 81–83, 106; Griswold, *op. cit.*, s.v. "Eyelash, Lot."
5 Griswold, *op. cit.*, s.v. "Zi-yeh." For Zi-yeh's father, see *infra*, pp. 182–83, 187.
6 Betzinez, *op. cit.*, p. 86. Betzinez told me he did not remember which wife this was. It would have solved a subsequent identity problem if he had known (interview, August 21, 1959).

victory dances. For his part, Geronimo *did* consider the feelings of the Mexicans. Betzinez, who was closely associated with him during this period, said that he was still motivated by bitterness against the state of Sonora for the massacre of his family. There were garrisons in the towns, but the raiding parties easily evaded them or drove them off. They observed the usual precautions—posting lookouts, obliterating their trails, concealing their camps, planning rendezvous ahead—but the military made no attempt to hunt them out. Only once a hidden Mexican soldier killed a warrior who was charging past. They labored over some rough terrain, but in other places they "traveled slowly, enjoying the trip and the pleasant surroundings." As Betzinez remembered it, much of the country "looked as though it belonged to us." At the northern end of their journey in the late summer or early fall they "settled down for an indefinite stay. It was just like peacetime. We had plenty to eat, good clothing taken from the stolen stocks, and no enemies nearby."[7]

There was only one disturbance, but this indicates that not all the Indians brought from the reservation in April were reconciled to their forced membership in the band. While close to the border, a San Carlos man and his Chiricahua wife started to run away. The girl's father was so enraged that he told the men to hunt them down and kill them, but the couple evaded their pursuers and made their way back to the reservation.[8]

This proximity to the border gave an opposite idea to the band. The warriors held a council and decided to invade southern Arizona for ammunition. Their guns were of late American make, and the Mexican cartridges did not fit. They hid their women and children at the foot of a mountain under the care of the apprentice warriors and, no doubt, of the older men. The raiders soon rejoined them, bringing great quantities of ammunition and "many articles useful for camp life," but their success was shadowed by the loss of a young warrior who died from wounds received on the raid.[9]

7 Betzinez, *op. cit.*, pp. 83–88.
8 *Ibid.*, p. 88.
9 *Ibid.*, pp. 88–89.

Thus, with the man killed by the Mexican soldier, the expedition cost the band two warriors. And the Apaches always regarded such losses seriously.

Strangely enough, the raid into Arizona seems to have been largely overlooked in army reports and the usually volatile Arizona press.[10] Possibly the party made one fortunate haul, such as wiping out a freight train, with little other disturbance. And probably attention was focused on a circumstance unknown, but ominous, to the Apaches: General Crook had been recalled from the North to the Department of Arizona, arriving at his headquarters, Whipple Barracks outside Prescott, on September 4. Convinced that raids of this kind would continue as long as the Indians remained in Mexico, he began making plans for invading their sanctuary.

Meanwhile, the band started back to their interior fastness. On the way Geronimo's Power served them well. When they were close to Oputo he told them that some Mexican soldiers were on their trail, and he predicted the exact time and place of their appearance. Thus forewarned, his warriors attacked and captured all the Mexicans' horses and supplies. At the victory dance that followed, a young warrior and a woman companion caused much merriment by a comic impersonation of a Mexican couple, he as a soldier with a gun over his shoulder and she as a simpering senorita.

Without further incident the party returned laden with spoils to the "great canyon." Juh's band soon appeared on the opposite side, and they heard the beating of each other's tom-toms across the gorge. Finally, Geronimo's band made the difficult crossing to rejoin their friends. "It was a very happy time for us all, exchanging presents and reminiscences," said Betzinez.

Juh also had a story to tell. With a skill typical of his military genius he had won a battle with Mexican soldiers. For two days his warriors had skirmished with the pursuing troops until their ammunition was exhausted. He then led them up a steep mountain,

10 The easiest explanation is that Betzinez confused this raid with a widely publicized one made the following spring, but his account is carefully written, and the details of the two are at variance.

leaving a plain trail, and concealed them just above a section that ran parallel to the ascent. There he had them roll a line of big rocks into position. When the Mexicans reached that stretch of trail, the warriors rolled the rocks down on them. Not many escaped from the falling boulders and the trees uprooted by the descending mass. Then the Apaches gathered up the guns and ammunition. They had not lost a single warrior.[11]

After camping several weeks beside the "great canyon," the leaders held a council and decided to attack Galeana, probably in revenge for the massacre at Casas Grandes. Also, the Apaches may have known that the commander of the garrison there was the hard-bitten Indian fighter Juan Mata Ortiz, who had been second in command of the force that destroyed Victorio, for the ever-vengeful Nana, who had not been at the Casas Grandes disaster, joined the expedition. The party traveled by easy stages, holding dances on the way, and formed a camp with their women and children on the mountain range that overlooked the town. There they held another council and planned their strategy. This battle was not in the usual Apache style, for they used the tactic common to many other Indian tribes of decoying the enemy into an ambush. "Everything went according to plan," said Betzinez. Its faultless execution furnishes striking proof of the discipline observed under the leadership of Juh and Geronimo.

Warriors were placed in groups along a ravine that paralleled the highway that connected Galeana with Casas Grandes, and the main body was concealed in a depression beyond this ambush. Some volunteers rode up close to the town and started driving several Mexican horses up the road. A small body of Mexican cavalry rode out in pursuit. The Apaches fled, keeping just out of range until they reached the hidden warriors ahead. Suddenly the pursuers encountered a withering fire from the front, and at the same time the warriors concealed in the ravine sprang out and attacked them from the rear. The Mexican commander then swerved off the road to a rocky hill a short distance away, where

11 Betzinez, *op. cit.*, pp. 89–92.

161

Cerrito Mata Ortiz, the rounded hill on the right, where Geronimo and Juh annihilated a small Mexican force. "Everything went according to plan." Photograph by Dan L. Thrapp.

his men dismounted and began piling up rocks at the apex to form a breastwork.

The Indians rode to another hill close by and turned their horses over to the apprentice warriors, of whom Betzinez was one. They then stole invisibly to the base of the hill which the Mexicans were fortifying, encircled it, and began crawling up the slope, each rolling a stone in front of him as a shield. Geronimo, Juh, Nana, and others of the older men and some of the best marksmen, including Kaahteney, took a sheltered position near a lone cedar tree at the base and fired a few shots to distract the enemy's attention. Finally, at the very summit, the Apaches sprang to their feet and charged the works in a hand-to-hand fight. They lost two of their warriors but killed the officer and twenty-one men, all but one of the Mexicans. To their immense gratification they found that the officer was Ortiz. (The hill is still known as Cerrito Mata Ortiz, and the little plaza in Galeana is called by his name.[12])

As the Mexican survivor fled towards the town, Geronimo shouted, "Let him go. He will tell the rest of the soldiers and they will come out and we can kill more." Soon another Mexican force did emerge. The Apaches mounted and rode towards them, and the soldiers started digging in. Since it was nearly sunset, the Indians decided not to attack. They watched them dig until dark, then joined their women and children on the mountainside.[13]

There was no victory dance. The band was too deeply grieved over the loss of their two warriors. That same evening word came to them that Mexican soldiers were on the way from Casas Grandes to attack them, and they fled into the mountains. After camping there in security several days, the band again divided, Juh going back to his stronghold and Geronimo and Chihuahua establishing a base camp on the headwaters of the Bavispe River.

After staying some time in this pleasant place of good water, firewood, and abundant game, Geronimo and Chihuahua decided to acquire some needed supplies by another raid into Sonora. This

---

12 Thrapp, *Victorio*, pp. 311–12. Thrapp has visited the site and examined the terrain.

13 News of this fight reached the United States, and a garbled account was published in the Albuquerque *Star* of December 8, 1882 (Thrapp, *Conquest of Apacheria*, p. 262). There are two eyewitness narratives—one by Betzinez, who saw it from the hill where he was holding the horses, told in *I Fought with Geronimo*, pp. 93–96, and the other by the child Kaywaykla, who watched it from the camp on the mountainside, in Ball, *op. cit.*, pp. 134–35. Kaywaykla added some conversation of the leaders, which he could not have heard. For Kaahteney's skill with the rifle, see Ball, *op. cit.*, p. 142.

time they left the women and children in camp while the warriors and the young apprentices made a rapid dash across the Bavispe and circled the area to the west where the pack trains passed through on their way to Ures. Butchering cattle and acquiring horses as they went and slipping undetected around the towns, they succeeded in capturing a pack train heavily loaded with dry goods and other supplies. During the journey Betzinez was greatly pleased by a compliment from Chihuahua on his handling of the captured animals, and in the victory dance upon the return he was included with the warriors in the center of the circle.[14] But although he was capable and dependable in carrying out such responsibilities, it is clear that he had no liking for the life of a warrior, and he was never to attain that status.

The band remained in the area for several months, then went back to the camping place on the brink of the "great canyon." Juh's party finally joined them there. They had suffered a great misfortune. The Mexicans had attacked them, killing some of their people and capturing many women and children. Juh's wife, Ishton, and his four-year-old daughter had been killed, and his older daugther, Jacali, was severely wounded.[15] This loss of his favorite "sister" was, indeed, a grief to Geronimo.

The remnants of Victorio's band had been with Juh at the time, and the child Kaywaykla carried throughout his life a flashing picture of the encounter. The camps of Kaahteney's and Juh's families were close together near an arroyo. When the soldiers attacked, Kaahteney fought them off while Guyan went for the horses, calling to Kaywaykla to run down the arroyo. When he passed Juh's camp, he saw Ishton and the two girls fall, the boy Daklugie kneeling beside his mother, and an older brother standing over them firing at the soldiers. As he fled down the arroyo, he heard hoofbeats behind him. His step-father raced past, sweeping him to a place on the saddle before him, and the family reached the mountain in safety. Three days later, when the scattered mem-

14 Betzinez, *op. cit.*, pp. 96–101.
15 *Ibid.*, pp. 101–102. Betzinez did not mention the little girl.

bers of the band assembled, Juh's two older sons were carrying their sister on a stretcher made by fastening a blanket to two lances. She had been wounded in the leg and was a cripple thereafter.[16] After Juh arrived at the "great canyon," the united bands, in spite of their losses, included more than eighty fighting men. They remained there until spring. Then two new raids were planned, one into Sonora for pack trains and the other into Arizona and New Mexico for ammunition. Juh and his people did not join these parties. They had become demoralized by their misfortunes, and their band was breaking up in mutual ill feeling.[17] As nearly as can be determined, Juh, his three sons, and his few followers struck out on their own while Jacali, probably because of her wound, remained with the main body,[18] which established its base camp for the women and children on the headwaters of the Bavispe. That place was a natural amphitheatre surrounded by towering mountains with a sparkling stream running through.[19]

With their families settled, the men made the usual careful preparations for the raid—cleaning and greasing their rifles, making new moccasins (Apache warriors took good care of their moccasins), plaiting good rawhide ropes, sharpening their knives, even washing their hair with the saponaceous roots of the yucca.[20] Then they set out on the familiar raiding trail into Sonora.

After the first night's stop, Chatto and Benito, with twenty-six warriors, turned north towards Arizona. Chatto was in command. In the party were the youthful Naiche, Tsoe, and Tsoe's close friend Beneactiney, the son-in-law of Chihuahua. Beneactiney was

16 Ball, *op. cit.*, pp. 146–47. Daklugie also told this story in more vivid detail to Mrs. Ball (Eve Ball to Angie Debo, July 13, 1973). The Fort Sill records identify a woman named Ish-keh who died at Fort Sill in 1897 as the same person as Ishton, but this identification is certainly an error. Kaywaykla could have been mistaken about the identity of the woman he saw fall, but Daklugie saw his mother killed by Mexican bullets.
17 Betzinez, *op. cit.*, p. 102; Secretary of War, *Annual Report*, 1883, p. 176. These statements are supported by Tsoe, who told Britton Davis that only three men and five women remained with Juh; quoted by Thrapp, *Conquest of Apacheria*, pp. 272–73. See also Bourke, *Apache Campaign*, p. 95.
18 This is surmised on the basis of where they were when they next appeared.
19 Bourke, *op. cit.*, p. 79; Thrapp, *General Crook and the Sierra Madre Adventure*, map in back pocket made from field notes of an army engineer.
20 Bourke, *op. cit.*, pp. 39–40, 62; Betzinez, *op. cit.*, pp. 85, 102.

Betzinez' cousin and was regarded as the head of the family of the widowed Nah-thle-tla, since Betzinez had not attained warrior's rank.[21]

The main body, said to number eighty men,[22] warriors and apprentices, continued west into Sonora. This time they penetrated far into enemy territory, passing through a well-settled region to a point one hundred miles southwest of Ures. They committed the usual depredations, plundering the towns, taking cattle and horses, and killing the people they encountered (most of the Mexicans stayed out of reach), but they failed to find a pack train.

There were diverting incidents. Once they approached a walled town, "riding in column of twos just like cavalry, with Geronimo and Chihuahua at the front." Two mounted Mexicans saw them coming and galloped madly back to warn the inhabitants. Then Geronimo placed his warriors in a line outside to jeer at the people cowering on their flat rooftops. At another time there was the incident of the traveling saddle. On a dark night they had stopped to rest until moonrise. Chappo unsaddled his horse and laid the saddle on a rock. When the moon came up and the band was preparing to start, both saddle and rock were gone. Finally they were found in the bushes, the "rock" an armadillo still carrying the saddle on its back.[23] Chappo was subjected to much laughter and teasing by his young friends.

On their return journey the raiders did find and capture a pack train. It was loaded with dry goods, blankets, and other needed articles, but it also contained mescal. At the camp that night many of the older men got drunk, but the young apprentices stood guard and no enemy appeared. Before they reached the base camp two messengers met them with the news that Beneactiney had been killed. He had been the special protector of Betzinez. Chihuahua

---

21 Betzinez, *op. cit.*, pp. 88, 97, 107, 116. The participation of Naiche rests on a statement later made by Tsoe, given in Thrapp, *Conquest of Apacheria*, p. 273. Some writers have credited Chihuahua with the leadership, but Betzinez, a reliable witness, gives several instances of his presence on the Sonora raid.

22 Tsoe's statement.

23 The Apache saddles, of course, were not the heavy stock saddles used by Southwestern frontiersmen.

came over and laid his hand on the shoulder of the grieving young man, urging him not to mourn too deeply, for "He was a very brave warrior." The party soon reached the base camp, where Betzinez found his mother and sister saddened by the death of their relative. A few days later Chatto and Benito came in from their successful raid with guns and ammunition and a small white boy they had captured.[24]

The raiders had indeed been busy on the American side of the line. On March 21 they struck a charcoal camp near Tombstone, killing three of the four men they found there. Next, at a second camp they killed one man and fired into a tent. When no one responded, Beneactiney and Tsoe ran towards it, and a man inside shot and killed Beneactiney. The next victims of the raiders were three miners. They raced on, killing a lone man here, a small party there, stealing fresh horses to replace their worn-out mounts. All the border country was in an uproar, with violent newspaper editorials and futile pursuits by army units and citizens' posses.

The reservation braced itself for an invasion. It had been transferred from civilian control to the military when Crook was sent back to Arizona. He had put able Captain Emmet Crawford in charge, with headquarters at San Carlos. Among Crawford's subordinates were the experienced Second Lieutenant Charles B. Gatewood at Fort Apache and young, ardent Second Lieutenant Britton Davis in command of the scouts at San Carlos. Now there was the prospect of another kidnaping of reservation Indians by hostiles or perhaps some voluntary recruitments to swell their number. Davis saw his Indians guarding their camps with guns and ammunition he had not suspected them of having and even establishing outposts in the neighboring hills.

But the raiders did not reach the reservation. They sped north along the San Simon Valley to the Gila and turned east to enter New Mexico north of Steins Peak. They traversed the Burro Mountains and then on the road between Silver City and Lordsburg they came upon a buckboard carrying Federal Judge H. C.

24 Betzinez, *op. cit.*, pp. 102–108.

167

McComas and his wife and six-year-old son, Charlie. They killed and stripped the two adults and took the child along. This was the boy Betzinez had seen; his fate would become for many years an unsolved mystery of the Southwest. The prominence of these latest victims shocked the nation. The judge was a well-known jurist, and Mrs. McComas was the sister of Eugene F. Ware, the Kansas historian and poet who later served as pension commissioner.

After this it was believed that the raiders were heading west and would shortly attack San Carlos. Instead, they bore south, dodged their pursuers, and escaped into Mexico. In a foray lasting only six days they had ridden fully four hundred miles, sometimes traveling seventy-five or one hundred miles a day, and had killed twenty-six persons. They had not even been sighted except by their victims and a few intended victims who escaped. Members of the band later told Davis that Chatto slept only on horseback, standing vigilantly on guard while the others snatched brief pauses for rest.[25] But one member defected, with results that may well have been the determining factor in Crook's subsequent success in invading their refuge.

As Betzinez told the story, which of course he heard at second hand, Tsoe had been deeply grieved by the death of Beneactiney at the charcoal camp. Shortly afterwards, when the party stopped on a high mountain, he started crying as he looked off towards the reservation where his mother and other relatives lived. He told his companions that he could not go on. They gave him some supplies and wished him well, and he set off alone. But Tsoe later told Crook that he had been taken to Mexico against his will and now took the opportunity to steal away from the raiding party during the night. Both stories may be true. Tsoe and Chatto were close friends, and Chatto might have helped him to leave without the knowledge of the rest of the party.[26]

But the reunited band in the Sierra Madre was unaware of the consequences of his defection. Fifteen volunteers soon went out

---

25 The whole story of their raid is in Thrapp, *Conquest of Apacheria*, pp. 267–71. For Davis' experience, see *The Truth about Geronimo*, pp. 34–35, 56.

26 Betzinez, *op. cit.*, pp. 116–18; Ball, *op. cit.*, p. 175; Bourke, *op. cit.*, pp. 30–32.

towards Oputo and returned with one hundred cattle. There was a busy day of butchering followed by a feast and a victory dance. Then at this camp a fire broke out and spread through the tall, dry grass, sending a great cloud of smoke high above the mountains and marking the locality for any Mexican soldiers who might be following the raiders. Apparently Juh also had joined the band by this time, for Betzinez stated that he and Geronimo were in command. They sent back sentinels who reported that Mexican soldiers were indeed following the broad trail made by the cattle. The Indians then crossed a deep canyon and established a camp beyond it while the warriors prepared an ambush. Some, armed with guns, were posted on the ridge along the gorge, the best fighting men were deployed astride the trail, and still others were sent to a steep slope at the nearby head of the canyon to roll rocks down on any of the enemy who might attempt to climb up there to outflank them.

The soldiers descended into the gorge while the hidden warriors waited impatiently. Finally they emerged on the ascent. When they reached the brink, the warriors posted along the trail ahead opened fire. The Mexicans retreated and ran into the ambush, while rocks were rolled down on them from the head of the canyon. They rallied and fought bravely, making several attempts to dislodge the Indians, but they eventually withdrew after serious losses. In the melee the Apaches shot one of their own men, their only casualty. They sent out parties to shadow the movements of the retreating enemy, but the Mexican withdrawal was complete.[27]

It is enlightening to read the official Mexican report of this battle. The able García was in command, marching from Moctezuma with eighty-six federal troops and fifty auxiliaries and absorbing another force of auxiliaries on the trail. On April 25, deep in the mountains at "a point whose name is unknown," they found the Indians "in two positions in impregnable points and difficult of access." They divided and made a frontal and a flanking assault (here one remembers the warriors with rocks at the head

27 Betzinez, *op. cit.*, pp. 110–11.

of the canyon) and drove off the Indians, killing eleven and wounding many "according to the bloody tracks they left."[28]

After the battle the Apaches, unaware of their reported casualties, traveled on and made their camp in a pleasant location under the pines on a very steep mountain. There, secure from enemies and with plenty of meat, they relaxed for a time. Then the principal men held a council and decided to make a raid on Chihuahua to take Mexican prisoners to exchange for their people captured at Casas Grandes and in the attack on Juh's camp. A party of thirty-six volunteers accordingly set out with Geronimo as leader, traversing the mountains and coming out on the plains to the east. They crossed the main highway south of Galeana, walking on their heels in the dust to leave little round holes not recognizable as human tracks. Continuing east, then turning north, killing cattle for food and all the time watching the roads for travelers, they finally sighted a party of two men and six women near the village of Carmen, not far from the Mexican Central Railroad. They killed the men and captured the women, one of whom was carrying a nursing baby. The women were the wives of soldiers stationed at one of the towns.[29] Geronimo told them not to be afraid, that they would not be harmed, but understandably they were terrified. He sent the oldest one to the officials to report his purpose for an exchange of prisoners. Meanwhile, the raiders continued on their way, watching for other travelers.

One evening all were gathered around the fire eating. Geronimo was sitting next to Betzinez with a knife in one hand and a chunk of beef Betzinez had cooked for him in the other. Suddenly he dropped the knife and exclaimed, "Men, our people we left at base camp are in the hands of U.S. soldiers. What shall we do?"

"This was a startling example of Geronimo's mysterious ability to tell what was happening at a distance," said old Jason Betzinez,

---

[28] Thrapp, *General Crook and the Sierra Madre Adventure*, pp. 141–42 and note 21, quoting the official Mexican report.

[29] Betzinez said their husbands were stationed at Casas Grandes, but this statement must have been a slip of his pen.

looking back. "I cannot explain it to this day.[30] But I was there and saw it. No, he didn't get the word by some messenger. And no smoke signals had been made."

In response to Geronimo's question, every man replied that they should return to their base camp immediately. They were at least one hundred and twenty miles away and completely out of touch with it. They started that very evening and traveled all night. Their captives slowed them down. "We tried to help the women and get them to walk faster but we really didn't expect Mexican women to walk as far and as fast as Apache women."

Before they again reached the road south of Galeana, the men captured some cattle to drive back. The last night out Geronimo made another prophecy. He said that on the following day's journey a man standing on a hill to their left would report the capture of their camp. It came out exactly as he had predicted. In the middle of the afternoon a man hailed them from a hilltop and then came down the rocks to report that Crook had indeed captured their camp and had taken their people into custody. They held another council and decided to investigate. Abandoning their captives and their stolen cattle, they made their stealthy way to the summit of a high mountain overlooking Crook's camp. There Geronimo disposed them in firing positions among the crags.[31]

Would there be a battle or a conference there in the mountains?

30 Neither can I. One can usually attribute Geronimo's Power to a lucky guess and the tendency of superstitious people to disregard all adverse evidence. But Jason Betzinez in his old age was entirely free from superstition. He simply told what he saw.

31 Betzinez, *op. cit.*, pp. 112–16; Bourke, *op. cit.*, p. 109; Secretary of War, *Annual Report*, 1883, Crook's report to the Military Division of the Pacific, July 23, 1883, p. 178. Crook obtained his information from the Mexican women captives. See also Goodwin, "Experiences of an Indian Scout" (part 2), p. 67.

CHAPTER 10

THE SANCTUARY IS INVADED

The capture of the Indians' camp was the culmination of developments on the American side of the line of which they were blithely unaware.

As soon as he arrived in Arizona, Crook began in his systematic way to study the situation. First, he held conferences with the reservation Indians. As he reported it, "The simple story of their wrongs, as told by various representatives of their bands, under circumstances which convinced me they were speaking the truth, satisfied me that the Apaches had not only the best of reasons for complaining, but had displayed remarkable forbearance in remaining at peace."

Even their life, such as it was, seemed insecure. Their reservation had been cut down five times to satisfy intruding miners and ranchers. The western boundary had been moved back because of the discovery of silver and later of copper in that area, and the riotous mining towns of Globe and McMillenville had sprung up there. On the east, where their reservation had once extended to the New Mexico line, a large strip had been cut off for the benefit of copper mining interests, and the town of Clifton had developed as the center of the industry. Now white exploiters were eyeing

172

their remaining land, and the Apaches "were constantly told . . . that they were to be attacked by troops on the reservation and removed from the country." Four thousand of them were confined to the pestilential flats near the agency at San Carlos, wholly dependent upon the scanty supplies left after the grafters had taken their share. A more fortunate fifteen hundred, living in the mountains around Fort Apache, were nearly self-supporting, killing game, collecting and storing wild products, and tending their little fields in the valleys. Crook gave the others permission to choose their own locations, and they began to move out and settle in bands and family groups under the direction of their leaders.[1]

There were no depredations of any kind by the reservation Indians after Crook took over, but he had no illusions about the bands in Mexico. As he went about enlisting scouts and organizing pack trains to invade their stronghold, Chatto's raid confirmed his analysis. But he must have wondered how he would find their hideout. Then came his lucky break.

On the night of March 28 a telegram came to San Carlos with the report of the McComas outrage and the belief that the raiders were headed towards the reservation. As it happened, Captain Crawford had been called away to assist Crook, and Davis was in charge. The young officer watched in suspense for a repetition of the Loco kidnaping, possibly even the massacre of all the whites at the agency. Five trusty Indians had been enlisted there as "secret scouts"—actually spies—to report to the officers any indication of unrest or hostility so that potential disturbances might be nipped in the bud. Now close to midnight on March 30 one of them slipped noiselessly into Davis' bedroom. "Chiricahua come," he whispered. (By this time all the related bands were known as

1 Secretary of War, *Annual Report*, 1883, Crook to Military Division of the Pacific, September 27, 1883, pp. 160–64; Davis, *The Truth about Geronimo*, pp. 32–34, 41–44, 48; Ogle, *Federal Control of the Western Apaches*, pp. 130–31, 189; Lockwood, *The Apache Indians*, p. 258. The changes in reservation boundaries are shown in Charles C. Royce, "Indian Land Cessions in the United States."

Chiricahuas.) He reported that the hostiles were in the camp of a White Mountain or Coyotero leader named Nodiskey twelve or fourteen miles away. (Nodiskey was regarded as a bad Indian.) It was believed that there were fifteen or twenty of them. That would mean Chatto's whole party. Davis had thirty scouts under Sam Bowman to keep order on the reservation. He and Bowman hastily collected them and with a few other Apache volunteers, set out through the night, and cautiously approached the camp. At daylight from a hidden position they called on the occupants to surrender. Thus they captured the entire force—the unruffled, smiling Tsoe. He said he had come to the camp to get news of his relatives, and he talked freely about the raid and the location of the various bands in the Sierra Madre. Davis wired Crook, Crook instructed him to find out whether the Indian would act as guide for the invasion, Tsoe readily consented, and Davis sent him on to the general.[2]

All Crook needed now was permission to enter Mexican territory to search out the hostiles. He traveled by train to confer with the officials and military commanders of Sonora and Chihuahua, and reached a cordial understanding with them. The Mexicans were unable to protect their people and Chatto's raid into the United States showed that the Americans were equally helpless so long as the band remained in their refuge.[3]

Crook then set out on the Mexican campaign, crossing the international boundary on May 1. Captain Bourke as usual served on the General's staff and kept a day-by-day diary of the expedition. In the carefully selected force were 9 officers, 42 enlisted men, and 193 Apache scouts; and it had five pack trains of 266 mules with 76 civilian packers. A few of the scouts were Chiricahuas, but most of them belonged to White Mountain and other reservation tribes unfriendly to the outlaw band. Al Sieber served

---

[2] Davis, *op. cit.*, pp. 16, 56–59; Thrapp, *Conquest of Apacheria*, pp. 272–73, and *General Crook and the Sierra Madre Adventure*, pp. 118–21.

[3] Secretary of War, *Annual Report*, 1883, Crook to Military Division of the Pacific, September 27, 1883, p. 163; Thrapp, *General Crook and the Sierra Madre Adventure*, pp. 123–27.

as chief of scouts with Archie McIntosh and Sam Bowman as his assistants; and Crawford, assisted by Gatewood and another officer, was in command. Mickey Free and a Mexican named Severiano, captured in youth and brought up as an Apache, were the interpreters. Accompanying the expedition was A. Frank Randall, a correspondent of the *New York Herald*. He carried photographic equipment that would have preserved a pictorial record of the confrontation in the Sierra Madre, but it was destined to be destroyed when the mule carrying it rolled over a precipice.[4]

Besides Bourke's diary, there is a scout's-eye view of the campaign given by John Rope—"we were scouts in order to help the whites against the Chiricahuas because they had killed a lot of people," he said.[5] Tsoe proved to be a congenial spirit, truthful, reliable, and cooperative throughout, and his knowledge of the terrain was invaluable. He was given the sobriquet of "Peaches," because although he was considered a full-blood Apache, he had a fair complexion and rosy cheeks, probably inherited from some forgotten captive white ancestor. "He was one of the handsomest men physically, to be found in the world," wrote Bourke. "He never knew what it meant to be tired, cross, or out of humor."[6]

Bourke was equally impressed by the scouts as they fanned out ahead, each one an individual working independently, "the perfect, the ideal, scout of the whole world," with eyes keen as a hawk's, tread as stealthy as a panther's, ears that heard everything. An artist might call them undersized, he said, but otherwise they were physically perfect. "Their chests were broad, deep, and full; shoulders perfectly straight; limbs well-proportioned, strong and muscular, without a suggestion of undue heaviness; hands and feet small and taper [*sic*] but wiry; heads well-shaped, and countenances often lit up with a pleasant good-natured expression." On the march they laughed and joked. At night they washed their hair;

---

4 Thrapp, *General Crook and the Sierra Madre Adventure*, pp. 128–29, 137, 139; Bourke, *op. cit.*, pp. 56–57; Secretary of War, *Annual Report*, 1883, Crook to Military Division of the Pacific, July 23, 1883, pp. 174–75.
5 Goodwin, "Experiences of an Indian Scout" (part 2), p. 56.
6 Bourke, *op. cit.*, pp. 52–53.

Mickey Free, the interpreter with Crook's Sierra Madre expedition and on the reservation. He was mistrusted by the Apaches as "the coyote whose kidnapping had brought war to the Chiricahuas." Courtesy Arizona Historical Society, Tucson.

Tsoe ("Peaches"), who guided Crook to Geronimo's sanctuary in the
Sierra Madre. Photograph taken by A. Frank Randall at San Carlos in
the spring of 1884. "He was one of the handsomest men physically to
be found in the world." Courtesy National Archives and Records
Service.

177

cut sections of cane and made pipes for smoking or flutes with which they produced a weird music; or built an air-tight hut, poured water on hot stones, and took a sweat bath.[7] But concerning the health and stamina of the scouts, a few ominous indications may be worth noting. Years later, as prisoners of war, the Apaches were to die in appalling numbers from tuberculosis. The physical examination given these scouts at the time of their enlistment may be significant. Said Rope, "They felt my arms and legs and pounded my chest to see if I would cough. That's the way they did with all the scouts they picked, and if you coughed they would not take you." One of them was to die of an unspecified cause after they reached their destination in the Sierra Madre, and a few days later Bourke recorded that two others "were so far gone with pneumonia that their death was predicted every hour."[8] Tubercular pneumonia had not at that time been identified by medical science. Could this infection have been present in their native state, but held in check somewhat by their outdoor living?

Such possible weakness was unmarked, however, as the expedition moved down the San Bernardino River, then up the Bavispe. "For three days," said Crook, "we did not see a human being. The whole country had been laid waste by the Apaches and much land of value and formerly cultivated had grown into a jungle of cane and mesquite." They threaded the canyon of the Bavispe past the river towns of San Miguel, Bavispe, Bacerac, and Huachinera. "The condition of these little Mexican communities was deplorable," said the General. "Apache attacks were to be looked for at any moment. No man would venture away from the vicinity of his own hamlet." The "inhabitants welcomed us with exuberant joy."[9] This was the other side of Betzinez' lighthearted narrative.

Crook camped near Tesorababi, a former ranch abandoned because of Apache raids, and on May 8 turned southeast into the

---

[7] *Ibid.*, pp. 38–40, 46, 51–52, 62–64.

[8] *Ibid.*, pp. 120–21; Goodwin, "Experiences of an Indian Scout" (part 1), p. 43, and (part 2), p. 69.

[9] Secretary of War, *Annual Report*, 1883, Crook to Military Division of the Pacific, July 23, 1883, p. 175; Bourke, *op. cit.*, pp. 56–74.

heart of the hostiles' mountain sanctuary. Here was a complete picture of their life-way. The whole area was an extensive complex of crisscrossing trails beaten by the feet of hundreds of stolen animals, and recently occupied camps on the mountains and along the streams. Only the planted fields that typically marked Apache settlements were missing; for these Indians' sole support came from gathering wild products and raiding, with their main dependence on the latter. Cached in trees or strewn along the trails with the prodigality of affluence were dried meat, mescal, buckskin, horse-hides, cowhides, and articles taken from the Mexicans—cloth, clothing, saddles, flour, even letters. The camp remembered by Peaches in the natural amphitheater had been abandoned. The invaders made a "terrible" climb up a nearby mountain, where on the summit were forty lodges in one place, thirty in another, two or three in every protected nook—all likewise abandoned. Then after a slide down the face of a bluff they came to an open space also dotted with the frames of dismantled wickiups. At these places were the ashes of fires, the straw of unused beds, play-grounds of the hoop-and-pole game, dance grounds, mescal pits, stones for grinding acorn meal—all the paraphernalia of an active society. Everything seemed secure, but Peaches said the hostiles never relaxed their vigilance, keeping sentinels posted and extin-guishing their fires at night; and it was apparent that they fre-quently changed their campsites.

Travel was difficult almost beyond endurance for the white men, and pack mules rolled down precipices and were dashed to pieces in the chasms below. (One of these mules, alas, carried Randall's photographic equipment.) But the scouts climbed up the heights "like deer." They accordingly held a conference with Crook and suggested that they advance on their own. Crook agreed, and Crawford with 150 scouts started out ahead, sending back messages directing the rest of the command to favorable routes and camping places as it cautiously followed. He believed that the hostiles were unaware of their presence.[10]

10 Bourke, *op. cit.*, pp. 74–91.

While the main body was waiting for these directions, some of the packers and scouts made a side trip into the adjoining mountains and found evidence of a recent battle between Mexicans and the hostiles. This was the fight in the canyon described by Betzinez and reported by García. Their examination of the battlefield gave a remarkable confirmation of Betzinez' account. They concluded that the Apaches had ambushed the Mexicans, killed a number with bullets and rocks, and had put the rest to flight. They even found the grave of one Apache warrior, the one Betzinez reported as killed by their own crossfire.[11]

Meanwhile, on May 15 the advance party of scouts discovered the *rancheria* of the hostiles on the side of a mountain across an intervening valley.[12] In some army accounts it was designated as the camp of Chatto and Benito; in others, as that of Chihuahua. It did, indeed, contain the people of those leaders, but it was the main camp of the entire body of related tribes except Juh's few followers, and Geronimo, at this most influential stage of his career, was the overall leader.[13]

The scouts attempted to surround the *rancheria*, some of them fired prematurely, and the hostiles fled, but they killed at least nine of them and captured five children, three girls and two boys, rounded up the horse herd, and occupied the camp. Chihuahua and other men of the band had just returned with many cattle from a successful raid. They had been butchering, and meat was spread out everywhere on the bushes to dry. Also, there was a quantity of mescal, freshly cooked or drying. The scouts looted the camp and set it on fire.[14]

Meanwhile, a courier from Crawford had reached Crook, who

11 *Ibid.*, pp. 76, 86.

12 There is some confusion in Bourke's book about dates, but this accords with the official map of the expedition reproduced by Thrapp in *General Crook and the Sierra Madre Adventure*, back pocket.

13 Geronimo's leadership is apparent throughout. See, for example, the statement of Loco's family cited in *ibid.*, p. 173.

14 Goodwin, *op. cit.* (part 2), pp. 58–63. Rope's account is circumstantial and personal, with such details as, "The [captured] girl had lots of beads made from Yo-il-tchine, the roots of a kind of bush that grows down there. She had four strings of them," and "I saw someone's heels sticking out of a clump of bushes. I grabbed this person and pulled him out"; it was a little boy with "no blood on him."

came up quickly but did not arrive until the fighting was over. The victorious scouts came into his camp bringing their captives and with their horses grotesquely loaded with plunder—prizes such as gold and silver watches, even some photograph albums, and much American and Mexican money. While they gloated over their wealth, Crook questioned the captives. They "behaved with great coolness and self-possession, considering their tender years." The oldest was a well-grown girl, a daughter of Benito. She said that her people had been dismayed to find their stronghold discovered and would be still more disconcerted when they learned that Tsoe, who knew every hidden fastness, was guiding the invaders. Most of the warriors were out on raids—some had gone out that very day—but she was sure that Loco and Chihuahua would be glad to return to the reservation. She was not so sure about Geronimo and Chatto. Juh was defiant, but his band had been destroyed. Most important of all, she said that a small white boy named Charlie, captured by Chatto on his recent raid, had been in the *rancheria* and had run off with the women. She believed that if she could contact them, she could bring in the whole band, including this boy.

Crook sent her and the older of the boy captives back with a conciliatory message. The next day women carrying white rags as flags of truce began to venture in. Among these, according to Rope, was a sister of Geronimo. This was probably Nah-thle-tla, the mother of Betzinez, although Geronimo had other "sisters" in the camp.[15] She said that Chihuahua wanted to come in and was trying to gather up his people, who had been scattered by the fight. He did come in the next day, "a fine-looking man, whose countenance betokened great decision and courage." He said he wanted to surrender and had sent runners to the bands that were out raiding. No doubt it was one of these couriers that would soon

---

15 Bourke called her the sister of Chihuahua, but Rope was more careful than any white man in identifying Indians. The band that was raiding with Geronimo in Chihuahua had taken their families along and settled them in a temporary camp on the way, but they had started back in advance of their men and could have reached the base camp by this time.

hail Geronimo's party from the hillside. By nightfall that day (May 18) forty-five men, women, and children had come in. The women "showed the wear and tear of a rugged mountain life," wrote Bourke. But the "children were models of grace and beauty."[16] By the next day the number of surrendered hostiles had swelled to an even one hundred. The women tore up flour sacks, tied them on poles, and set them all about the camp to signal to the returning warriors that all was peace. There were indications that Chihuahua was not entirely ready to surrender, and they warned the scouts that the combined forces might attack. "We piled rocks and pine logs up to lie behind," as Rope recalled it, and they held their arms in readiness.

Geronimo's thirty-six raiders did, in fact, arrive that night and took their positions among the rocks a thousand feet above Crook's camp. The women called up to them "and told them not to shoot ... that they did not want any fighting" but only to make friends. At daybreak (May 20) Geronimo sent down two messengers (two old men, said Betzinez; two old women, said Bourke) to find out the general's intentions. If they should fail to return, he planned to attack. There were some other communications back and forth. Geronimo's "sister" went up to the raiders, and they sent her back to request some of the scouts to meet with them. The scouts sent relatives of the raiding party—a brother-in-law of Chatto and a relative of Geronimo's father-in-law Dji-li-kine.[17]

Although Geronimo, with his six marriages, must have had several fathers-in-law, Dji-li-kine was almost certainly the father of Zi-yeh. He was a white man by blood, but had been captured in boyhood by the White Mountain Apaches and brought up as a member of that tribe. He was "like one of us," as John Rope expressed it. Then he had married a Nednai woman and joined her people, "and was just like one of them." According to Rope, he was "not as tall as an old-fashioned long musket," but he was

---

16 The children of their descendants are still remarkably beautiful.
17 Bourke, *op. cit.*, pp. 91–100; Goodwin, *op. cit.* (part 2), pp. 63–66; Betzinez, *I Fought with Geronimo*, p. 116.

"about the best fighter of any of [the band] . . . and they usually did what he advised."[18]

These messengers told the raiders that hostilities had been suspended to give Chihuahua time to bring in his people and the captured Charlie McComas. Finally, the men began to drop down from the mountainside and enter the camp by twos and threes. "In muscular development, lung and heart power, they were, without exception, the finest body of human beings I had ever looked upon," Bourke reported. "Each was armed with a breech-loading Winchester; most had nickle-plated revolvers of the latest pattern, and a few had also bows and lances."

But Geronimo and the other leaders still stayed out. Crook decided to contact them by the most supremely courageous act of his adventurous career. (He suppressed this story, and so did the other officers; it was not known until Rope's reminiscences were published in 1936.) He took his gun and left the camp ostensibly to shoot birds. The hostile leaders confronted him, "grabbed his gun away and took the birds he had shot." Then Mickey Free and Severiano came to interpret. "They all sat on the ground and talked. After about two hours" the general and his former enemies came into the camp together.[19]

Then and in the ensuing days Crook and Geronimo had several conferences. Although the general must have realized that his position was precarious, he professed indifference about whether his antagonist should surrender or fight it out. But he reminded the Apache that his mountain fastness was not impregnable and warned him that Mexican forces also would be coming in to invade it. Geronimo said he had always wanted to be at peace. He had been ill-treated at San Carlos (Crook could hardly deny that in view of his own appraisal of conditions there), and driven away (even Clum conceded that). As for the Mexicans, they were treacherous, made war on his women and children, and ran like

---

18 Basso, *Western Apache Raiding and Warfare*, pp. 110, 165–67.
19 Goodwin, *op. cit.* (part 2), pp. 66–67; Bourke, *op. cit.*, pp. 100–102. Rope's account of Crook's bird-shooting stroll is glimpsed in the reminiscences of another scout. See Basso, *op. cit.*, p. 200.

coyotes from his warriors. He said he was even then trying to arrange an exchange of prisoners. But he admitted that he could not cope with united American and Mexican soldiers assisted by Apache scouts. If he could not make peace, he and his warriors would die in the mountains fighting to the last. Crook remained remote and unconcerned.[20]

The following morning (May 21), Geronimo, Naiche, Chatto, and a leading warrior named Tcha-nol-haye joined Crook at breakfast. "They all seemed to be in a pleasant humor and consumed with relish the bread, beans and coffee set before them; pork they would not touch."[21] Geronimo said he had sent some of his young men out to collect his scattered people. Meanwhile Chihuahua's messages were having their effect, as increasing numbers of "all ages and both sexes" continued to come in; "most of them were mounted on good ponies, and all drove pack and loose animals before them." During the day Kaahteney arrived with his band of thirty-eight, "mostly young warriors . . . driving steers and work animals and riding ponies and burros. All were armed with Winchester and Springfield breech-loaders, with revolvers and lances whose blades were old cavalry sabres. The little boys carried revolvers, lances, and bows and arrows."

Feeding so many Indians was making serious inroads on Crook's supplies. He told them to help out by killing their own cattle and ponies, and the young men began butchering. Bourke watched the process with fascination. Standing within five or six feet of a steer, a young Apache would strike it with a lance immediately behind its left shoulder, and with one short bellow the animal would fall forward upon its knees, dead.[22]

On May 22 the Mexican women captives arrived at the camp, hysterical with relief and gratitude. Although they had not been mistreated by Geronimo, they had suffered much from terror and

[20] Bourke, *op. cit.*, pp. 101–104, 111–12.
[21] The Apaches had a deep-seated aversion to eating pork. It may have been an undefined taboo. See Barrett, *Geronimo's Story of His Life*, p. 62 and n.
[22] Bourke, *op. cit.*, 104–105; Thrapp, *General Crook and the Sierra Madre Adventure*, p. 159.

the hardships of the journey and their three days of wandering through unknown mountains and canyons after being abandoned by their captors. The sympathetic officers ministered to their needs, and when the expedition returned to Arizona they were sent back to their people. Thus, there was no exchange of prisoners, and Geronimo's wife, Chatto's family, and other victims of Casas Grandes remained in slavery.[23]

Perhaps it was the arrival of these captives that inspired the hostiles that night to hold a victory dance, which according to custom was followed by a social dance. By this time the scouts "mixed with [them] like friends," as Rope expressed it; thus, they were invited to the dance. Bourke gave a lively description, saying that "they danced together in sign of peace and good will," but he may have been mistaken, for Rope said that Sieber forbade the scouts to participate. One disobeyed and found himself in an embarrassing predicament. By Apache etiquette the women chose their men partners for these night-long social dances, and at the close each man was expected to give a substantial present to his lady. This time the scout's partner demanded twenty cartridges, and he complied. When the other scouts reported, "the officer [Sieber, no doubt] made him go back and get the cartridges." How he made it up to the woman is not recorded. But in spite of this breach of discipline, the scouts, for all their fraternizing, never relaxed their vigilance, keeping their rifles and cartridges always at hand.[24]

On the following morning (May 23) Crook issued rations to 220 hostiles in his camp. Soon after, Nana came in with 17 of his people. "He has a strong face, marked with intelligence, courage, and good nature, but with an understratum of cruelty and vindictiveness," was Bourke's impression. (This last was never shown to his adoring followers.) He "limps very perceptibly in one leg." He reported that the hostiles were coming in by every

---

23 Bourke, *op. cit.*, pp. 107–11; Thrapp, *General Crook and the Sierra Madre Adventure*, p. 160; Goodwin, *op. cit.* (part 2), pp. 67–68; Secretary of War, *Annual Report*, 1883, Crook to Military Division of the Pacific, July 23, 1883, p. 178.
24 Bourke, *op. cit.*, pp. 114–15, 117; Goodwin, *op. cit.* (part 2), p. 68.

trail and that all would go to the reservation as soon as they could collect their families.[25]

The next day the expedition, with the surrendered hostiles, started back, traveling only a short distance and making camp about noon at a pleasant place on the Bavispe, where they remained several days while the women gathered and steamed a supply of mescal for the return journey. There Loco joined them with a small band. It was probably at this time that he told Crook that some of his people had become separated from the main body during the recent fight with García and had taken the opportunity to return to the reservation. One of them had gone back to bring him, but the aged chief felt unequal to the journey and advised them to go on without him. The party, comprising Loco's immediate family and a few others, totaling six men and fourteen women, had started before Crook entered the Sierra Madre. At this very time they were nearing Fort Apache, where they surrendered to the military. Loco told Crook that he also wanted to return "and obtain a little farm, and own cattle and horses, as he once did."[26]

During this stop, Bourke amused himself by observing the Indians. The scouts gambled with the hostiles, winning hundreds of dollars in gold, silver, and paper money. The women and children bathed in the stream, disporting themselves with "agility and grace." He commented on the "modesty of the Apaches of both sexes, under all circumstances." He thought the leaders—he named Geronimo, Loco, Chatto, Nana, Benito, Chihuahua, Mangus,[27] Kaahteney and Gil-lee (Zelé)—were "men of noticeable brain power, physically perfect and mentally acute—just the individuals to lead a forlorn hope in the face of every obstacle."

He watched some little boys, tired of swimming, who played at fighting Mexicans. Three, representing the enemy, ran, dodged, and hid, trying to elude their pursuers, "who trailed them to their covert, surrounded it, and poured in a flight of arrows." They

---

[25] Bourke, *op. cit.*, p. 115.
[26] Bourke, *op. cit.*, pp. 115–16; Thrapp, *General Crook and the Sierra Madre Adventure*, pp. 162–63, 172–73.
[27] Mangus had probably come in with Kaahteney.

"killed" one and seized the others, carrying them into captivity. In the excitement the "corpse" rose up to watch. "In such sports, in such constant exercise, swimming, riding, running up and down the steepest and most slippery mountains, the Apache passes his boyish years. No wonder his bones are of iron, his sinews of wire, his muscles of India-rubber."[28]

Geronimo urged Crook to remain in the mountains a week longer so he could finish collecting his people. At this time he had not actually surrendered, although according to Crook and Bourke he was fairly begging for the privilege of doing so.[29] But Crook may have overdone his pose of indifference and aroused the deep-seated fears of the wild warriors. According to Rope, they held a council and planned a desperate attack on the expedition. They would invite the scouts to join their girls in a social dance. Then they would start killing their guests. "It didn't matter if they themselves got killed." But because many of the scouts were White Mountain people, Dji-li-kine dissented, saying "the White Mountain people are like relatives of mine." Geronimo argued with him. "My father-in-law, tonight we mean to do as we told you. Whenever we have gone to war before, you have gone with us." But he still refused. "You chiefs don't mean anything to me," he said. "I have been with you many times and helped you kill lots of Mexicans and whites, and that's the way you got the clothes you are wearing now. I am the one who has killed these people for you, and you have just followed behind me. I don't want to hear you talking this way with me again." And he walked away from the council.

But the council went ahead with plans for the dance. Al Sieber may have learned of the plot, or he may have objected to the fraternizing on general principles as he had done before. He knew his Apaches, a people ever mindful of the proprieties. One of the scouts had died that day, and he accordingly sent word for them

---

28 Bourke, *op. cit.*, pp. 116–20.
29 *Ibid.*, pp. 103–104, 112–13, 118; Secretary of War, *Annual Report*, 1883, Crook to Military Division of the Pacific, July 23, 1883, pp. 176–77.

to stop the dance, and they did.[30] Thus, by a thread the expedition was saved. The hostiles could not have wiped out Crook's force, but if they had sprung their trap there would have been one more indecisive battle with Apaches, the whole band would have scattered, and the general would have returned from another futile pursuit. There is no indication that he or any of his officers ever knew how near they came to disaster. Apparently the plot was never revealed until Rope's story was published in 1936.

On Crook's last day in this camp, May 27, an excited scout came in with a story to tell. He had gone out hunting some distance to the north and had discovered a large body of Mexican soldiers driving back the cattle Geronimo had abandoned when he made his hasty return to the captured camp. Crook sent a small party out to communicate with them, but they failed to make contact. By this time the mescal had finished roasting, and on May 28 the expedition broke camp and started back. Late that night Geronimo, Chatto, Kaahteney, and Chihuahua joined them, bringing in 116 of their people. These leaders held a conference with Crook, and again they asked for a few days' delay. Crook admitted the reasonableness of their request, but said his dwindling supply of rations made delay impossible. Geronimo said that if Crook would travel slowly they would try to overtake him at the border; if not successful in that, they would move through the mountains to San Carlos. Crook consented, but warned them "that if they could not catch up with the troops they must take their chances of being killed by any Mexicans or Americans they might encounter."[31]

Loco, Nana, Benito, and Kaahteney remained with Crook,[32] while the other leaders turned back. Geronimo was no doubt sincere in requesting time to collect his people. The charge, often made, that this was a scheme to enable him to continue raiding is untenable; he could not have raided successfully in "a few days" or "a week" with Crook present and watching. Rope even said that

[30] Goodwin, *op. cit.* (part 2), pp. 68–69.

[31] Bourke, *op. cit.*, pp. 120–21; Secretary of War, *Annual Report*, 1883, Crook to Military Division of the Pacific, July 23, 1883, p. 177.

[32] Davis, *op. cit.*, pp. 69–70.

the hostiles asked Crook's permission "to gather a lot of horses from the Mexicans" and that Crook consented and told them to meet him at the border.[33] This is not credible. Geronimo would not have revealed such a plan to Crook; Crook would not have approved it; and in any case Rope would not have been present at the conference. No doubt Rope did hear gossip to that effect around the camp. And after the hostile leaders turned back and found themselves free once more, the opportunity to raid was too good to pass up.

Crook had received the surrender or the promise of surrender of all the leaders except Juh, who with his few remaining followers was in his old stronghold far to the south on the headwaters of the Yaqui. The general continued his journey with 325 captives, 52 men and 273 women.[34] Many of them were glad to return. Betzinez characterized their feeling as "a great relief. . . . No more worries, no more sleepless nights, fearing attacks by an enemy."[35] It is, in fact, apparent that the group forcibly brought to Mexico the previous year had been prevented from returning. Sam Haozous, who had been a boy at the time, recalled in later years that "Geronimo wouldn't let us get back."[36] It is also apparent that the women were tired of the rugged life. It was they who took the initiative in the surrender.

But little Charlie McComas was not present on the return journey. The Indians told Crook, and he believed them, that they had been unable to locate the child after he ran into the brush at the time of the scouts' attack on their camp.[37] For many years his fate was an unsolved mystery, and there were constant reports of his appearance. As late as 1938 a news story stated that an archeological expedition into Mexico had discovered a "lost" Apache tribe

---

[33] Goodwin, *op. cit.* (part 2), p. 69.
[34] Secretary of War, *Annual Report*, 1883, Crook to Military Division of the Pacific, July 23, 1883, pp. 176, 178.
[35] Betzinez, *op. cit.*, p. 116.
[36] Interview, January 27, 1955.
[37] Bourke, *op. cit.*, p. 128.

189

never brought back to the United States, whose red-haired, blue-eyed leader was thought to be Charlie McComas.[38] The Apaches knew all the time, but they were protecting one of their people from possible punishment. Old Sam Haozous said in 1955, "All the people are dead now, so I can tell how Charlie McComas died." Jason Betzinez, who of course was raiding at the time, published the story in his book as he had heard it later from a fellow student at Carlisle. An old woman in the camp was wantonly shot by the scouts during the attack when she was begging to be taken captive. Her son, in grief and anger, then picked up a stone and beat the child on the head. But, according to Sam Haozous, the wound was not fatal. It must have been the following day that Haozous' mother and aunt, making their way down the mountainside through rocks and brush to Crook's camp, came across the boy and found him still living. The aunt was greatly attached to the child. Sam Haozous' voice was very tender and compassionate as he quoted her: " 'Poor little fellow. We can't let him die here. Let's take him along.' But my mother said, 'If we bring him in, the soldiers will blame us.' So they left him. Nobody else went that way, so no doubt he died there."[39]

Crook did not return by way of Sonora, but struggled east through the mountains on the Chihuahua side of the line. Then the expedition descended and camped where "a broad, perfectly distinct trail" led towards Casas Grandes. There, carved on the trunk of a tree they found the message in Spanish, "The 11th Battalion Passed Here 21st of May '83."[40] This reinforced the warning Crook had given to Geronimo. It was the third instance of the Mexicans' penetration of the mountains during the previous six weeks. Although they had not reached the Apaches' inner sanctu-

[38] Federal Writers' Program, *New Mexico: A Guide to the Colorful State*, pp. 417–18.
[39] Goodwin, *op. cit.* (part 2), p. 63; Betzinez, *op. cit.*, pp. 118–19; Sam Haozous interview, January 27, 1955. Betzinez said it was Ramona, the daughter of Chihuahua, who told him the story, but she afterwards denied knowing anything about it (Eve Ball to Angie Debo, February 27, 1973). His informant must have been some other girl.
[40] Thrapp, *General Crook and the Sierra Madre Adventure*, p. 167; Secretary of War, *Annual Report*, 1883, Crook to Military Division of the Pacific, July 23, 1883, p. 178.

190

ary, they were approaching it. Meanwhile, Crook chose a route remote from inhabited areas to avoid meeting any Mexican force that might send his prisoners fleeing to the mountains.

On the way, the expedition passed close to Aliso Creek, where García had attacked Loco's weary people and their abductors the year before. There, some of the scouts braved Apache avoidance of the dead. "We shouldn't have gone to look at this place, but we did it anyway," said Rope. It was a ghastly sight. "There were many bleached-out bones, pieces of women's dresses, and lots of beads scattered on the ground." "Human bones, picked white and clean by coyotes," said Bourke.[41]

Before reaching the international boundary, the expedition entered Sonora. On June 10 it crossed the line and reached Silver Springs near the present Douglas, Arizona, where Crook had established a base camp. From there the Southwest and the nation at large received the first news of the campaign since he had passed out of communication three weeks before. The officers also found their first newspapers. They were full of inflammatory telegrams saying that the government would hang all the men of the hostiles and parcel out the women and children among the tribes of the Indian Territory. Somehow this "news" got to the prisoners, and Bourke believed that it drove the leaders who had promised to follow and surrender back into the mountains. The clamor for their removal, in fact, became so serious that Crook issued a warning against it in his official report. "The glibness with which people generally speak of moving them would indicate that all we have to do is to take them from their camps, as you would chickens from a roost, without reflecting that to attempt their removal would bring on the bloodiest Indian war this country has ever experienced."[42]

The general took no chances. The prisoners and the scout contingent were escorted to San Carlos by Captain Crawford with four companies of cavalry picked up at the border. They arrived on June 23. As Rope remembered it, "All the people at San Carlos

41 Goodwin, *op. cit.* (part 2), p. 70; Bourke, *op. cit.*, pp. 125–26.
42 Bourke, *op. cit.*, pp. 126–27; Secretary of War, *Annual Report*, 1883, Crook to Military Division of the Pacific, September 27, 1883, p. 169.

knew that we were coming that day and waited for us. Right on top of Copper Reef we stopped to line up. From here we could see lots of looking glasses flashing signals to us from San Carlos. . . . Now they put one hundred of us scouts in front, then all the Chiricahuas, then the rest of the scouts, then the soldiers, and last of all the pack train. . . . Sieber rode in front. There was a crowd of Indians on both sides, watching us. . . . All the scouts went to the right and camped. All the Chiricahuas went to the left, and the pack trains were brought to the center. We cooked in eight lots. All our relations came to see us. . . . The second day after that all of us scouts were discharged and got our pay."[43]

Not only to the scouts, but also to some of the 325 former hostiles it was a homecoming. And if Crook had any misgivings about the leaders who still remained out, he refused to admit them. On July 23 he closed his report of the campaign by saying that the fact that they had not yet arrived was "of no significance. Indians have no idea of the value of time."[44]

He would settle the ones he had and wait for the others. The future was to prove him right.

[43] Goodwin, *op. cit.* (part 2), p. 72.
[44] Secretary of War, *Annual Report*, 1883, Crook to Military Division of the Pacific, July 23, 1883, p. 178.

CHAPTER 11

BACK TO THE RESERVATION

The surrendered hostiles were located temporarily at San Carlos until all their people should be assembled. Captain Crawford, again in overall command, was stationed there with Davis as one of his assistants, while Gatewood was back at Fort Apache. Feared and hated by the other reservation Indians, the newcomers turned to the officers for reassurance and sympathy. Then, as Davis expressed it, "we began to find them decidedly human," with a keen sense of humor and full of fascinating tales of their years of warfare.[1]

But not all of the band entered into these friendly relations. This was the first reservation experience for the popular young warrior Kaahteney, and he was dissatisfied and suspicious. He haunted the officers' quarters, standing outside an open window or a door, silent and watchful. Reports reached them through their "secret scouts" that he regretted coming in and was plotting a break as soon as he could collect a sufficient following. They could not arrest and punish him lest Geronimo learn of it and be afraid to return. All they could do was to watch him closely. And al-

[1] Davis, *The Truth about Geronimo*, p. 72. Betzinez also wrote of the hostility of the other tribes (*I Fought with Geronimo*, pp. 122–23).

though they gave no thought to Nana—army officers always disregarded him because of his age and apparent feebleness—one can be certain that he was hand in glove with Kaahteney. The boy Kaywaykla, who heard all the family conversations, understood that the surrender was only a temporary concession to Crook's invasion of their stronghold.[2]

Another member of the party who attracted the attention of the officers was Juh's crippled daughter, Jacali, then about eighteen years old. Her wound had never healed, but had remained a running sore. The leg below it had shriveled to skin and bone "as immovable as a rod of iron," and she "was hardly more than skin and bones herself." But she had ridden the long journey up from the Sierra Madre in that condition. At the reservation the army surgeons persuaded her with some difficulty to submit to an amputation, and she was restored to health.[3] But probably she did not live long, for her subsequent history is unknown.

The friends and relatives of these first arrivals were in no hurry to join them. A little news drifted back of hard-fought battles in which the Mexicans went into the mountains after them but were always driven off.[4] Geronimo later stated that two of his people had been killed.[5] Probably he counted Dji-li-kine as one of these two, for that elusive warrior had remained with the raiders in Mexico and had been shot in the head—so they reported—by a Mexican while they were stealing horses.[6] It was also learned that Juh had died. The reports varied: they agreed that he had got drunk on mescal at Casas Grandes but after leaving the town had

2 Davis, *op. cit.*, pp. 70, 73, 113; Secretary of War, *Annual Report*, 1885, Crook to Division of the Pacific, September 9, 1885, pp. 175–76; Ball, *In the Days of Victorio*, pp. 148, 150. Kaywaykla was completely confused about the events of the surrender, and he implicated Geronimo in a scheme to draw rations on the reservation during the winter and break away in the summer. This does not fit the time of year when Geronimo subsequently came in, but Kaywaykla probably reported correctly the spirit of his own family elders.

3 Davis, *op. cit.*, p. 70.

4 Bourke, *Apache Campaign*, p. 127.

5 National Archives and Records Service, 1601 AGO 1884, F/W 1066 AGO 1883, Geronimo to Captain Emmet Crawford, March 21, 1884.

6 Goodwin, "Experiences of an Indian Scout" (part 2), p. 71. Rope doubted their story—he suspected that they had killed him themselves because of his refusal to join the plot to attack the scouts—but it seems entirely plausible.

fallen off his horse from a cliff or in a stream and had broken his neck or drowned. He may have been drinking, but according to Daklugie, who was present, he must have died from a heart attack or a stroke.

Juh had, indeed, been trading in Casas Grandes. Perhaps Mangus had joined him at this time, for he had a considerable party with him. He sent his men ahead with the supplies he had purchased, while he, with his three sons, remained in the town to ensure that none was left behind. Then he sent Daklegon to deliver a message to his warriors while he followed with Delzhinne and Daklugie. Several miles out, his horse fell into the river. "The banks were not high, the water was not deep, and both boys reached him quickly. He lay in shallow water, apparently stunned by the fall." The two boys were unable to lift him, heavy as he was, to the overhanging bank. Daklugie held his head above water while Delzhinne rode after the warriors for help. He was still alive when they returned. "They built a shelter for him and tried to save his life, but he died shortly after. They buried him beside the river."[7]

"After the deaths of my father and mother I was a very lonely child," said Daklugie in his old age to Mrs. Ball. But his brothers were sympathetic, saying he should always be with them. The three were in Mangus' band, although they sometimes encountered Geronimo and spent some time with him. Geronimo personally directed the training of the young boys of his band, and Daklugie retained a lively recollection of his strict discipline. During the winter in the high sierras, when ice was formed on the streams, he used to have them build a fire on the bank and time after time alternately warm themselves and plunge into the water. He stood there with a stick in his hand, which, however, he never found it necessary to use. Daklugie adored his "uncle" and would have preferred to stay with him, but Geronimo never gave him permission, saying he should remain with his brothers. In after years Daklugie wondered if Geronimo might have foreseen that the boy would be the last of his line and felt that he would be safer with

7 Ball, *op. cit.*, p. 148. Kaywaykla got this account from Daklugie.

the less aggressive Mangus.[8] If Geronimo's Power gave him that forewarning, it was soon realized; Daklegon and Delzhinne were captured by Mexican cavalry and taken to Mexico City, where they died.[9]

Meanwhile, the promise the hostiles had made to come in to the reservation seemed all but forgotten. Finally, in October Crook sent Davis to the border with a pack train and a company of scouts recruited partially from the members of their band who had come in at the time of the surrender. His purpose was to encourage the others to join them and to guard them on their way to the reservation. Although it should have been evident to even the most virulent Apache-hater that as long as they remained in their Mexican sanctuary raids like Chatto's would continue, the newspapers were abusing Crook for bringing some of them back to Arizona and inciting citizens to attack any others that might try to come in. One such occurrence, and the whole band would have fled, with disaster piled on disaster.

Suddenly, eight warriors with five women and children appeared at Davis' camp. Then in late October Naiche and Gil-lee, with nine other warriors, arrived with about twice their number of women and children. On November 16 Chihuahua and Mangus, with about ninety of their people, came in. (No doubt the orphaned Daklugie was in this group.) Other small bands followed. By the end of November, 423 of the former hostiles, including eighty-three warriors, were on the reservation. Another party came on December 20. Chatto and nineteen others arrived on February 7, 1884.[10]

Some of them made their own way back to the reservation, slipping invisibly through the mountains. Davis brought up two companies. Since he was a regular army officer and the scouts were enlisted men, even the most turbulent Arizonans might have hesitated

8 Eve Ball to Angie Debo, July 13, 1973.
9 Griswold, "The Fort Sill Apaches," s.v. "Juh."
10 Davis, *op. cit.*, pp. 73, 77, 79–80; Thrapp, *General Crook and the Sierra Madre Adventure*, pp. 175–76, citing Crook's papers. Davis placed Chatto with Mangus, but his memory probably tricked him.

to attack them; but even so, he kept away from traveled routes, avoided towns and ranches, and made rapid marches of forty or fifty miles daily. The returning wanderers were by no means a beaten people. As they sped uphill and down with their tireless, effortless stride, the young officer marveled at their physical perfection. "The thought of attempting to catch one of them in the mountains gave me a queer feeling of helplessness, but I enjoyed a sensation of the beautiful in watching them." If a baby chanced to be born along the route, the mother soon caught up with the party and moved on.[11]

Geronimo did not arrive until late in February. He had improved his time well. Davis had been sending scouts out daily to patrol the border watching for his arrival. One day they reported that he was approaching. Davis sent two of them down to meet the party and explain his own presence—they "were as wary and suspicious as so many wild animals"—while he rode his mule to the border and waited. He saw a long line of Indians coming up the valley, and following them two or three miles behind was a great cloud of dust.

Geronimo rode up on his white pony. He was in a bad humor. Without checking his mount until its shoulder bumped the shoulder of Davis' mule, he angrily demanded the reason for escorting his people to the reservation. He had made peace with the white men; why did he have to be protected against them? Davis explained that it was bad white men he feared. They might come out of the towns full of whiskey and try to cause trouble, but the scouts were now American soldiers, and if such ruffians should kill one they would be hanged. Geronimo was mollified and shook hands with the young officer.

Davis inquired about the dust cloud. Geronimo spoke to the point. "*Ganado*," he said in Spanish. And indeed they were—about 350 head of beeves, cows, and half-grown calves. That meant slow travel along regular roads with access to water, giving opportuni-

---

11 Davis, *op. cit.*, pp. 80–81, 85; Secretary of War, *Annual Report*, 1884, Crawford to Assistant Adjutant General, Whipple Barracks, p. 134.

ties for citizens to organize and attack. Now at the outset Geronimo demanded a three-day halt for his cattle to rest and graze. To avoid Mexican pursuit he had driven them too hard. Davis consented to rest that day but insisted on starting out the following morning. They traveled eighteen or twenty miles each day, and every evening Geronimo came to the officer's tent protesting that the long marches were running all the fat off his cattle. When they reached Sulphur Springs, long a favorite Indian camping ground because of its fine water and grass, Geronimo balked. Davis could go on if he wanted to, but *he* was going to stay there a few days to rest his herd. Davis had to consent to one day's halt.

Sulphur Springs was then the headquarters of a small ranch. An adobe wall four or five feet high enclosed the springs and a low adobe ranch house with a porch on the front. A small gate in the wall before the house formed the entrance to the enclosure. On all sides the valley stretched away as level as a floor. The pack train camped outside about fifty yards from the gate, the scouts a little way beyond. Several Apache families had made their camping places along the wall running in front of the house, two of them close to the gate on either side. The other families were scattered about the ranch. The cattle, mules, and ponies had been watered and were grazing half a mile away with three mounted Indians on herd to prevent their mixing with the ranch cattle.

Davis had just pitched his tent and was awaiting the cook's call to supper when two men dressed in civilian clothes came out of the ranch house. One, showing his badge, informed the officer that he was the United States marshal for the Southern District of Arizona; the other announced himself as the collector of customs from Nogales, the Arizona port of entry from Mexico. They said they had come to arrest Geronimo and his warriors for the murder of Arizona citizens and to take possession of the cattle smuggled across the border. Davis said he would not obey such orders except from Crook, and the marshal then subpoenaed him as a United States citizen to help in the arrest. He added that in the morning he would subpoena the packers and the five cowhands at the ranch, and if they should refuse to assist him he would go to the village of Willcox, about forty miles north, and organize a posse with every available man in town. "I am going to have those Indians," he said, "and then I am going to see that you answer to the federal court for your refusal to obey my order."

This meant a fight. Davis had orders from Crook to escort Geronimo and his band to the reservation, and he was determined to throw in his lot with them. He could expect no help from the military; Fort Bowie, the nearest post, was thirty miles away to the east, and Camp Grant was still farther to the north. But it would take the marshal some time to collect his posse. If Davis could persuade Geronimo to start at once, they could make some distance on the journey. Then the women and children could continue their flight to the reservation while Geronimo and his warriors and Davis and his scouts would stand off the marshal and his men. But would Geronimo cooperate? He might break back for the border, to be followed by his relatives on the reservation, with the usual bloody trails on the way.

Then came relief. Davis' West Point friend, Second Lieutenant J. Y. F. Blake, was stationed at Fort Bowie. Davis had sent word for Blake to meet him at Sulphur Springs and spend the night, but in his excitement he had forgotten the invitation. Just then Blake rode up. The two young officers began scheming. Blake had graduated a year before Davis and thus was technically his superior. If the Indians would move out, he would be their escort while Davis would remain in obedience to the subpoena. (It is uncertain even now whether the credentials of the civilian "officers" were real or fraudulent, but Davis accepted them as authentic.)

The two young men had just finished supper when the marshal and the collector joined them to do a little gloating. Blake had brought along a quart of whiskey. He offered it to the two civilians and saw hospitably that they drank most of it. They had a good laugh at Davis' expense and went back to the ranch house. One of them brought his bedding outside and settled down to sleep on the porch not more than ten feet from the Indian families by the gate. But his deep breathing was reassuring. Now all depended on Geronimo. Davis sent his scout first sergeant to call him from his bed. The other scouts had sprung up from somewhere and were awaiting orders. Geronimo's warriors joined the tense circle. Davis did not tell him the whole truth. If he had learned of the plan to try and hang him, he would have fled with his people back to the Sierra Madre, and the ensuing campaign to search them out would have been more difficult than the one before. Davis simply said that the customs man had come to collect one thousand dollars on the cattle, and if the payment were not made he would take them. Thus, in order to avoid trouble, the herd should be started for the reservation immediately. His "brother" (Blake) would go along while he himself would stay at the ranch to throw the officers off the trail.

Geronimo angrily refused to start. Staring straight into the eyes of the lieutenant, his lips twitching, and shifting his rifle from arm to arm, he said he had come in for peace but had found nothing except trouble. If those men wanted to take his cattle let them try it. He was going back to bed, and he would take the promised layover. Just then the sergeant, who belonged to a tribe that hated Geronimo and his people, added some rapid words of his own. Davis never knew what he said. Mickey Free had been interpreting, but the moment was too tense for him to interrupt. Whatever it was, it caused Geronimo to wilt. He looked around at his men and the scouts, but found no support. Then Davis slyly suggested that probably he would not be able to get away undiscovered by the men at the ranch. This touched the Apache's pride: "His people could leave me standing where I was and I would not know that they were gone." Davis then reminded him of what a good joke it would be on the officers if they woke in the morning and found that the Indians with all the cattle and ponies had got away. Geronimo almost smiled, looked at his men, and saw that they agreed.

Davis went to the pack train and woke the packmaster, and he started the train silently on its way. When the officer came back to the gate, the Indians had all vanished from their sleeping places along the fence. Geronimo's young nephew Kanseah retained a vivid memory of what happened. As he told the story in his old age, he and his mentor, Yahnozha, who knew many English words, had scouted around and listened. "One man said he was from the Customs and he wanted to take our cattle because we had not paid any tax on them. Our cattle! He hadn't stolen those cattle; why should he get them?" They heard Davis talking to Geronimo. Of course, he said, it would be impossible to move all those people without waking the men. "Dogs would bark, children would cry. . . . If any people knows how to be quiet it is the Apache. . . . We shook with laughter as we got everything ready to move. It did not take ten minutes. Not a dog barked. Not a baby cried. We tied children's feet together under the bellies of the horses. We tied small children to adults. And we started. At first we moved slowly, very slowly. We had to, because of the cattle. But after we got out of hearing we put boys with lances to keep the cattle moving, and we made time. By morning we were far north of that spring. . . ."[12]

Davis took up a lonely vigil by the gate, sitting on an empty box and holding his saddle mule by the bridle. In the morning he saw the man on the porch stir and sit up. Then in great excitement the man ran into the house and called his companion. They climbed to the roof and scanned the horizon through field glasses. There was not even a cloud of dust in sight. They demanded an explanation from Davis. He told them that a superior officer had come, had taken command, and had left with the outfit. He could not say whether they had gone east towards Fort Bowie or north towards Camp Grant or whether, followed by Blake, they had bolted for Mexico, but he was there in obedience to the marshal's orders. There was nothing they could do. The Indians were close to sanctu-ary in one of three places. Davis then struck out, and after two days of hard riding he overtook Blake a few miles south of the reserva-

12 Ball, *op. cit.*, pp. 152–53 and note 3. Mrs. Ball here represents Kaywaykla as the narrator, but she informed me, as her footnote also indicates, that it was actually Kanseah (to Angie Debo, February 27, 1973).

tion line, and they delivered their charges to Crawford without further incident.[13]

But Geronimo lost the cattle he had worked so hard to accumulate to set his people up in ranching. Although all the parties coming up had been riding stolen horses, Crook had overlooked it, but he could not overlook a theft of this magnitude. The cattle were taken by the agency and ultimately sold, and the proceeds were turned over to the Mexican government to undertake the task of sorting out the claimants. Geronimo protested in outraged innocence. He was still protesting twenty years later at Fort Sill: "I told him [Crook] that these were not white man's cattle, but belonged to us, for we had taken them from the Mexicans during our wars. I also told him that we did not intend to kill these animals, but that we wished to keep them and raise stock on our range. He would not listen to me, but took the stock."[14]

In the company that came up with Geronimo were twenty-six warriors and some seventy women and children.[15] Geronimo's three wives and his children were, of course, in the group. One young son, of whom nothing further is known, had died on the journey. Geronimo told Crawford that there were "twenty-five men women and children still out. . . . They said that at the end of the next moon they wanted some of their people to be sent to the line after them."[16] Possibly these were the remnants of Juh's family and his few followers. A small party did arrive in April, and Crawford could truly say that "for the first time since the establishment of the reservation all the tribes of the Apache nation in their entirety were upon it."[17]

---

13 The whole story may be found in Davis, *op. cit.*, pp. 82–101.

14 Thrapp, *Conquest of Apacheria*, p. 294; Barrett, *Geronimo's Story of His Life*, p. 135.

15 Davis, *op. cit.*, pp. 84, 90.

16 National Archives and Records Service, 1601 AGO 1884, F/W 1066 AGO 1883, Geronimo to Crawford, March 21, 1884.

17 Secretary of War, *Annual Report*, 1884, Crawford to Assistant Adjutant General, Whipple Barracks, undated but subsequent to August 21, p. 134. Crawford, of course, was referring only to the Arizona Apaches and their relatives. Crook reported that the last party arrived on May 15, but Crawford, who was in charge, stated specifically that they came in April.

Plans were being made for their permanent settlement even before the arrival of this last small, belated band. On March 21 Geronimo made a formal statement of their position to Crawford for forwarding to Crook. It is apparent that the leaders had held a council, had decided on a policy, and were present indicating their agreement when it was submitted. But although Geronimo voiced a group consensus, this first recorded expression of his views reveals his practical, logical mind, his sense of responsibility, and his sound economic planning—along with considerable adroit diplomacy. (Clearly he had not yet learned that he would lose his cattle.) His statement began: "Geronimo said: That he has come here with the understanding that everything he asked for was to be granted him. When the General was in the Sierra Madre, he met the General and remembers everything that the General then told him."

He went on to attribute supernatural powers to Crook, a form of address often used by Apaches to officials they wished to conciliate.[18] At this distance it is impossible to determine whether this was simply a convention of Apache etiquette or an attempt at flattery, or whether warriors who believed themselves to be the recipients of Power attributed corresponding Power to white men. In any case, Geronimo's statement reveals his shock at finding his sanctuary invaded: "When he saw General Crook then he told the General that he thought he was a God. That he did not believe he was an American, for he did not believe that an American could go there. He was much astonished to see General Crook there and thought that he was so powerful that he could command the sun the moon and everything."

He told of his decision to come in and stated frankly the reason for his long delay: "As soon as he saw General Crook he thought that he would leave the mountains and come to live at peace on the reservation. . . . Now he is very much pleased to be here. He thinks that it is better to live here than among the rocks and thorns in the mountains down there. He remained in the mountains so long

---

18 Crook, who heartily disliked General Howard, was very scornful of similar compliments paid that officer by an Apache chief, but he failed to mention the instances when he himself had been thus addressed. See Schmitt, *General George Crook*, p. 171.

203

because he wanted to get some horses and cattle to bring here. He was poor and did not think that he would have friends here to give him these things." Apparently referring to Crook's scouts, who had talked with him when he was wavering in his mountain stronghold, he said that "all the Indians told him that they went to bed early and got up late and had nothing to fear, here all the Indians have nothing to excite them, and it is good for him; he likes it. All the men who were sent to him told him that . . . everybody here was good to the Indians, and only kept them from doing harm." He wanted the past to be blotted out. (This theme would recur in his subsequent surrenders.) "He wants everything to be done straight. He is saying that so that everything may be forgotten. All made new, so that they can begin again. Before, here in San Carlos, everything was wrong with the Indians and the people here. But now it is all being carried on straight, and he wants it to continue. He will never think again as he used to think before; now he thinks, that the Americans on the reservation want him to live here, and have cooking utensils &c and not run around in the mountains cooking their meat on sticks before the fire."

He realized that it would not be easy for his people to take up "civilized" pursuits: "They are all here now like brancho mules, which it is necessary to teach little by little, until they are all tamed. And he thinks that they are all to be treated well until they all are living well. He feels now as if he were in a big hole and covered up as far as his chest, while he is at San Carlos. He has surrendered entirely, and any orders given him he will obey without thinking of resisting them. . . . If in future some one tells anything bad about him he wants to know right away who it is that is telling bad things about him."

His main concern was in finding a suitable homesite, and he saw no reason for reservation boundaries. "Here in San Carlos it does not seem to him that it is very well, because there is no grass, no good water, and there is some sickness here too. He would like to live where there is lots of water, lots of land, and lots of wild animals. He knows where there is such a place. He wants to know where they are to live. Whether they will have enough land to live all together. He wants this line around the reservation to be taken away. Now that there is no war, there should be no line, except the line at San Bernardino, the Mexican line."

Here, as related above, he told of the small band still out. Then he went into the heart of his message, an earnest appeal to settle on Eagle Creek:

§§§§§§§§§§§§§§§§§§§§§§

There is plenty of land, plenty of grass and his people can all live there. Those Americans who live on Eagle Creek, can't their land be bought from them and given to the Indians? They take great interest in good land, as they want to farm and live like white men, and think that Eagle Creek would be good for them. Now that they are here, and you [Capt. C.] have them [the Indians] in your power,[19] you can do as you please with them, and ought to let them do what they wish to. . . . All of them have the same things as white men, hands, legs, arms &c, just as white men, and are surprised that they are not given the same things as white men when they ask for them. This peace they promised was a legal peace and they expect to get the land they want on account of having made this peace.

§§§§§§§§§§§§§§§§§§§§§§

He used every means he could summon to gain his object—entreaty, adequate presentation to Crook, the united support of his people, justice as he argued it, and the practical advantages:

§§§§§§§§§§§§§§§§§§§§§§

He begs you [Capt. C.] as if you were his father,[20] and asks you to give him what he asks for. He wants that this paper be well written, so that the General will give them this land. All these Indians who [are here] around me knew what I have said, and are very anxious to get this land. They want General Crook to know this so he will give it to them. At Camp Apache it is not good to live as there is

19 Brackets in original.
20 Brackets in original.

no game around there, and he has heard that the Indians around there have come here for rations, and learning that the ground there is not sufficient to live on. There are many of us, and there is not enough land around Camp Apache for us . . . for we want to plant melons, squashes, corn and everything. . . . If we go to Camp Apache we will starve to death there. He is afraid that after he had raised one or two crops, the land will be taken from him. There is no mescal to bake around Camp Apache. . . . He wants to live on Eagle Creek, and if they think that he is going to steal anything, soldiers can be put to watch him. He thought that everything he wanted to do in this country he would be able to do, and he is much astonished to find that he cant get Eagle Creek. . . . When the General was in the Sierra Madre the interpreter told them that the General said they could live on Eagle Creek or on the creeks that come out of the Mogollon Mts.[21] If we cant go to Eagle Creek we want to go to Ash Creek [on Ash Flat] and see how the country is there.

◇◇◇◇◇◇◇◇◇◇◇◇◇◇◇◇◇◇◇

There was the ever-present concern about the captives in Mexico. These, of course, included Geronimo's wife, and possibly Juh's two sons were still alive. He had made another attempt to free them after Crook left the Sierra Madre: "I went to Case Grande and talked with an Officer about the Indian captives the Mexicans have. There were no Americans there. I was not actually in the town, but out near it and two Mexican soldiers came out and talked to me." He returned to the subject later in his statement: "We want all our captives here. They are in Mexico and we believe that General Crook can get them for us. We believe that he can do anything."

He gave the reasons—previously quoted[22]—for the breakaway from the reservation after the Cibecue fight. He said that although

---

21 Crook certainly had not told them that. The general's unbreakable rules were: never lie to an Indian, and never promise an Indian anything you can't carry out. The interpretation may have been faulty, and Geronimo probably heard what he wanted to believe. He must have been sincere in his statement, for it was addressed to Crook.

22 *Supra*, p. 132.

he had heard of "a little white boy" about whom the general inquired, he had never seen him. He ended by stating the objective of his band to choose a place to live apart, away from the unfriendly tribes on the reservation: "If these Indians around San Carlos come here after I leave and talk about me, I don't want you [Capt. C.] to believe them.[23] We are going out to look for some land to farm, and we dont want any [of these] Indians around here with us. We want to be alone, and have no Indians but Chiricahuas with us.[24] Where we are going to live we would like to have a store, so that we can buy what we want in the way of manta &c. We only want a little one just for ourselves."[25]

The large party that had come up with Crook must have had a weary wait, especially during the summer on the sun-scorched flats around the agency, until the arrival of the rest of their people made it possible to locate them. But Crook was not unmindful of their welfare. In January he persuaded them to let him send forty-seven of their boys and five of their girls to the school recently established by Captain Richard H. Pratt at Carlisle. Among the boys were a son of Loco, afterwards known as Dexter Loco, and two sons of Benito.[26] Also, after Crawford took over under Crook's directions, the cheating on supplies was ended. To Britton Davis was assigned the duty of issuing the rations, and he corrected sickening frauds on the Indians.[27]

But the reform of the system was not as easy as a simple change from civilian to army control. There were good men and bad men in both services. The good men, whether civilian agents or army officers, followed identical practices. Besides cleaning up the graft, they recognized the authority of the tribal leaders, maintained

23 Brackets in original.
24 By this time all these related tribes were known officially as Chiricahuas, and that designation accordingly appeared in Crawford's transcript of Geronimo's statement.
25 National Archives and Records Service, 1601 AGO 1884, F/W 1066 AGO 1883, Geronimo to Captain Emmet Crawford, March 21, 1884.
26 National Archives and Records Service, Record Group No. 75, Bureau of Indian Affairs, Letters Received 1881–1907, Secretary of War Robert T. Lincoln to Secretary of the Interior, January 25, 1884; Griswold, "The Fort Sill Apaches," s.v. "Benito" and "Loco, Dexter."
27 Davis, *op. cit.*, pp. 32–35, 41–46.

order by a native force (of police by agency terminology, of scouts in army parlance), and for the trial of offenders set up native courts not very different from the Apaches' own practices.[28] They also made a careful distinction between peaceable Indians and hostiles. At the same time, in both services were men insensitive in their treatment of the Indians and corrupt men who robbed them. But the able Crook, who was close at hand, was more adept in checking irregularities than the distant Indian Office at Washington. This was graphically shown at San Carlos after Davis was sent to the border in October to shepherd in the late arrivals.

Crawford then assigned the rationing to Archie McIntosh. This trusted scout was well liked by the Indians, and his wife, an Apache woman, was related to Chihuahua and others of the band. He had served Crook with unfailing dependability for twenty years, and his hardihood and courage in tight places had sometimes meant the difference between success and disaster, but he failed in this test of integrity. On March 28 Crawford received a tip that he was stealing supplies and hauling them to a ranch he owned on Pinto Creek off the reservation near Globe. Although this report, as Crawford said, "has taken me back entirely," he investigated and found it to be true. Then, as he reported to Crook: "I sent for all the Chiefs & told them about it. They all said they wanted Archie kept. They said it made no difference if he took half of their rations he was a good man & could have them. I sent for Archie & he acknowledged that [the accusation] was true & he had the impudence to tell me that it was done at every Military Post in the Dept.[29] The Chiefs tell me to telegraph you & say they wanted him kept but if you said discharge him all right."

Chihuahua, Kaahteney, and two or three others then left, but Geronimo, Chatto, and Mangus remained for a private word: "They said that they thought what I had done was right, that their women & children ought to have that ration[,] that they received

---

[28] For trials under primitive Apache custom, see Barrett, *op. cit.*, pp. 185–86, and Opler, *An Apache Life-Way*, pp. 252–54. For the Apaches' adaptation to the jury system, see Davis, *op. cit.*, pp. 48–49, and Bourke, *On the Border with Crook*, p. 446.
[29] There was probably more truth in this than Crawford was willing to admit.

enough themselves. Archie I think has been feeding up the Chiefs & principal men but cutting down the rest." Crawford told McIntosh he was fired, but said he might telegraph an appeal to Crook. McIntosh then resorted to a technique as old as federal-Indian relations: he collected the leaders and induced them to make the appeal. The telegram read: "We the undersigned after a council yesterday—we all have said we want Archie McIntosh to stay with us. You put him over us and he is our friend. He gives us all we want to eat and he is good. Capt Crawford told us that Archie stole our provisions from us. . . . We all saw what was taken away in the wagon—We want you to come to us right away to straighten things out for us. He brought us back with you and we want to talk to you." It was supposedly signed with the names of Geronimo, Kaahteney, Benito, Loco, Chihuahua, Chatto, Mangus, Naiche and Gil-lee. The operator would not send it until he could consult Crawford. Crawford read it and ordered McIntosh off the reservation with the warning "that if he ever attempted to again call the Indians together for the purpose of breeding discontent I would put him in irons." In reporting the incident, Crawford said he suspected it was McIntosh who put Geronimo up to requesting a store, hoping to get the lucrative job of running it.[30] The whole episode is typical of the complex forces that made honest administration of Indian affairs virtually impossible.[31]

Geronimo did not get his store. Neither did he get the location he had earnestly requested for his people. All the lower course of Eagle Creek was in the area subtracted from the Indians' holdings. Geronimo was aware of that; hence his suggestion that reservation boundaries be wiped out. This, of course, was impracticable, and as for extending those boundaries and buying out the settlers, that would have reversed the entire course of frontier history. But Crook permitted the Indians to choose any location on the reservation. Apparently they rejected Ash Creek. They selected an area around Turkey Creek, about seventeen miles southeast of Fort

30 Thrapp, *Al Sieber*, pp. 290–93.
31 See Ogle, *Federal Control of the Western Apaches*, pp. 194–96, 201, 210–13.

Apache and close to the settlement of the White Mountain bands, with which some of them had marriage or other connections. It was a beautiful region of tall pines, clear streams, abundant game, and for these mountain people an ideal summer climate, but it lacked extensive farmland and sufficient water for irrigation. Most of the good land on the reservation had, in fact, been taken already by other tribes.

Crawford and Davis favored furnishing these former hostiles with breeding stock for cattle and sheep raising (Geronimo's idea exactly). And they could have planted their usual small patches in the valleys. But the Indian Office was committed to the farming methods of the eastern United States. Crawford himself had ordered two hundred plows, two hundred harrows, four hundred sets of plow harness, and one hundred wagons, but these were no doubt intended for the tamer, already settled tribes. The army had been buying corn and barley for its animals from these Indians, who had to prepare the ground with shovels and harvest their barley with knives.[32]

But distant Washington decreed a uniform pattern, and it was the job of Davis to carry it out. Along with some picks and shovels and some seed, which they truly appreciated, his charges received a dozen light wagons, a dozen plows, and a dozen sets of double harness. Two weeks were spent on the San Carlos river bottom training the wild ponies and wilder Indians in the use of this farm machinery. It was a hilarious experience, with the Indians whooping and laughing as their ponies pulled the plows at a gallop and with the plowman barely holding to the handles and the point only occasionally cutting into the soil.[33]

The former hostiles were engaged in another activity that spring at San Carlos. It is not mentioned, as far as is known, in army or agency reports, but it is of great interest to the historian. A. Frank Randall, now settled at Willcox, brought his photographic equipment and made portraits of the leaders against a contrived background of desert plants. Their poses show that they were willing,

---

32 Davis, *op. cit.*, pp. 102, 137; Secretary of War, *Annual Report*, 1884, Crawford to Assistant Adjutant General, Whipple Barracks, pp. 135–36.
33 Davis, *op. cit.*, pp. 102–104.

Apache family at their wickiup. Probably photographed by A. Frank Randall at San Carlos in the spring of 1884. Courtesy National Archives and Records Service.

even cooperative subjects, and the resulting portraits have found their way into many books.[34]

In general, these photographs convey the impression that the spring of 1884 was a time of relaxation and wellbeing for the assembled bands. Then in late May all arrangements were completed, and the entire company set out with Davis in charge for what was hoped would be their permanent home on Turkey Creek.[35]

[34] Some of these pictures are marked with the name of the notable Southwestern photographer Ben Wittick or attributed to the Army Signal Corps, but Richard Rudisill of the Museum of New Mexico at Santa Fe, who is an authority on Wittick's work, states that Wittick copied and claimed the work of other photographers and that the Army Signal Corps simply collected photographs from many sources in the early 1900's with little attempt to record data. He is convinced from his own studies that the well-known picture of Geronimo kneeling and holding his rifle in the Wittick Collection was originally made by Randall; Rudisill to Angie Debo, July 17, 1972, and July 8, 1975. This finding would put all others with an identical or similar setting in the same category. In addition, copies of seven of these photographs are in the records of the Army Signal Corps in the National Archives and Records Service, and they carry the notation, "Copyright, May 16, 1884, A. F. Randall." The date fits, for the spring of 1884 marks the only occasion in their history when all the Apaches depicted in these photographs were together.

[35] Crawford's report said "in May"; Davis remembered it as "about the first of June." Secretary of War, *Annual Report*, 1884, p. 135; Davis, *op. cit.*, pp. 103, 106.

211

Naiche with his wife, Ha-o-zinne, as identified by her daughter, Amelia Naiche. This and the following seven photographs were taken by A. Frank Randall in the spring of 1884. Courtesy Smithsonian Institution, National Anthropological Archives.

Dos-teh-seh, daughter of Mangas Coloradas, wife of Cochise, and mother of Taza and Naiche. Courtesy *Chronicles of Oklahoma.*

213

Chihuahua, the leader of a small Chiricahua band, who rose to prominence among his people. Courtesy *Chronicles of Oklahoma*.

Loco. *Though a brave and able warrior, he sought peace throughout his life.* Courtesy Smithsonian Institution, National Anthropological Archives.

215

Mangus. He lacked the drive necessary to succeed his father. Courtesy Museum of New Mexico.

Nana. *Army officers always disregarded him because of his age and apparent feebleness.* Courtesy U.S. Army Artillery and Missile Center Museum, Fort Sill.

217

Kaahteney, his wife, Guyan, and the child Kaywaykla. Courtesy Museum of New Mexico.

Gil-lee and his wife, Tzes-ton. Courtesy Museum of New Mexico.

CHAPTER 12

PEACE WITH SUSPICION ON
TURKEY CREEK

As the emigrating party moved up to their new home, they came to the Black River in flood. Davis managed the crossing with the wagons as boats and the energetic Indian men and their ponies as motive power. It furnished the Indians almost as much fun as had their agricultural training. They numbered 521, of whom 127 were men and boys capable of bearing arms. Soon they were joined by some Coyoteros and some of the White Mountain band so that they numbered more than 550.

Crook came to see them immediately after their arrival and was much amused when he learned of the techniques used in the river crossing. They scattered among the trees and streams and began at once to erect their clusters of wickiups. They were pleased with their new homesite. Kaywaykla, with the discomforts of the previous summer of waiting at San Carlos fresh in his mind, found the new place a pleasant contrast: "There was an abundance of good water, wood, and game. There was good grazing. There were no mosquitoes, few rattlesnakes, and no cavalry. There were poles and brush to make shelters, and even the canvas of old tents for covering until hides could be secured. The only use I remember for wagons was to place the beds on the side toward the wind for shelter. In addition, we planted rows of evergreens around the [wickiups] to serve as windbreaks."[1] Davis was in sole charge. He pitched his tent in a little glade under the pines, with a large tent nearby in which to store the rations. He had Mickey Free as his interpreter, and Sam Bowman served as cook and general camp helper. To keep order he had a company of scouts enlisted entirely from the recently hostile bands. Chatto he made first sergeant. "One of the finest men, red or white, I have ever known," was the young officer's characterization of him. Certainly Chatto never violated the pledge of peace he had given Crook in the Sierra Madre, and his loyalty was proved in many tight places. Of Geronimo's relatives, his "brother" Perico became second sergeant,[2] and young Chappo requested and received the job of Davis' "striker" (that is, servant, with pay of five dollars a month more than that of the ordinary scout). Less conspicuous in the officer's entourage were two "secret scouts," a man and a woman he had brought with him from San Carlos.[3]

Geronimo and Naiche, with their people, chose their campsite several miles away from Davis' tent. So did Kaahteney's followers, but the young leader himself settled on a ridge just above Davis, where he could keep the officer under surveillance. Nana was there also, unregarded by Davis but still dominating the friends and relatives of Victorio. The camps of Chihuahua and Mangus were only a short distance away. The fatherless boys Daklugie and Istee lived in Mangus' family. Daklugie was in some way related to Mangus, and Istee, as a son of Victorio, was, of course, a young brother of Mangus' wife. Kaahteney undertook their training as warriors along with that of his step-son Kaywaykla.[4]

The Indians liked Davis. He was honest and fair and treated them as individual human beings. He consulted Chatto daily re-

1 Davis, *The Truth about Geronimo*, pp. 104–107; Ball, *In the Days of Victorio*, p. 156.
2 Perico may have been known here as Juan, or possibly he soon succeeded an Indian named Juan. See Davis, *op. cit.*, pp. 106, 150; and Ball, *op. cit.*, pp. 156–57.
3 Davis, *op. cit.*, pp. 38–39, 106.
4 *Ibid.*, p. 107; Ball, *op. cit.*, pp. 156, 158–59. I have followed Kaywaykla's locations because the boy's memory of sites was more accurate than that of Davis.

221

garding general conditions in the camp and the needs of the scouts. Loco, Benito, and Gil-lee came frequently to his tent for friendly or business talks. Mangus was cooperative and with Loco often backed him in controversies with other leaders. Geronimo, Naiche, Chihuahua, Nana, and Kaahteney held aloof. The officer knew that there was an undercurrent of suspicion stirring in the band, and he believed Kaahteney to be the leader of the discontented faction.[5]

Kaywaykla, looking back, described the situation from their side. They distrusted Davis' helpers. Illogically, they blamed Mickey Free for being the innocent cause of Cochise's trouble— "the coyote whose kidnapping had brought war to the Chiricahuas"—and they believed he interpreted falsely to put all they said to Davis in a bad light. They trusted Bowman, but Davis usually employed Mickey Free. He knew of their suspicions, but as he said, "He may have fooled me on occasion, but if he did it was done so skilfully that I never found it out." They regarded Chatto as a traitor to his people who had become a turncoat because he had failed to obtain the leadership of the band. The bitter rivalry between him and Kaahteney may well have been the basis of the hostility. They hated Chatto's friend Tsoe because he had guided Crook to their sanctuary. Tsoe had remained with the scout company at San Carlos, but he was often sent with messages to Fort Apache. They knew about the "secret scouts," and they were convinced that Chatto was one of them. In this they were mistaken, but no doubt Chatto did inform Davis of things he observed or imagined in the band, coloring his reports by his hatred of Kaahteney. Through it all, they hoped that Davis would eventually discover the treachery of his trusted adherents, but meanwhile they watched—Kaahteney from his camp on the ridge, Perico and Chappo from the scout company.[6]

They had more open grievances: the making of *tizwin* and the

5 Davis, *op. cit.*, pp. 111, 115, 139–40.
6 Ball, *op. cit.*, pp. 154–57, 162–65, 175; Davis, *op. cit.*, p. 37. Kaywaykla believed that Geronimo placed his relatives near Davis for that purpose, but apparently they enlisted in good faith.

control of their families. Crook had issued rules regulating these matters as soon as he first came to Arizona and began settling hostiles on reservations. Now Davis called the chiefs together and laid down the law. Disobedience would land them in jail. They were nearly unanimous in their opposition. Chihuahua was especially outspoken; Kaahteney was silent and surly.

Although *tizwin* drinking unquestionably threw the camps into disorder and violence, they had logical reasons for their stand. They said they had promised Crook that they would keep the peace with white Americans, Mexicans, and other Indian tribes, and they were observing this agreement. The white officers and soldiers, and all white men and Mexicans drank something "to make them feel good," and why should the same thing be forbidden the Indians? They had always made *tizwin*, and they did not want any of their people put in jail for following the tribal custom.[7]

Family discipline involved the punishment of a wife for adultery. This must be understood against the background of the Apaches' culture. The woman occupied an honored and secure place in their society. Typical is the advice given a young married couple by the father of the bride:

‸‸‸‸‸‸‸‸‸‸‸‸‸‸‸‸‸

I talked to that boy her husband. I said, "I'm talking to you. . . . Every day means that you should bring in something to eat. . . . If you have nothing to eat, your wife cannot cook anything for you. . . . Look at her clothes. Many things rest on you. It's a man's duty to bring in the meat and clothes. You can't expect the woman to do that. . . ."

I said, "My daughter, it is your [duty] to keep . . . everything neat about your place. Keep yourself neat the way you were when I was raising you. Keep your husband's clothes clean. Keep your fire going all the time. . . . Don't fuss at each other."

And I said to the boy, "A woman must be treated well because she feeds you; she's the only friend you have. Your mother and father can't treat you better than your wife does. That's the way I

7 Davis, *op. cit.*, p. 123.

Nal-tzuk-ich (Cut Nose), believed to be one of Crook's spies in the Sierra Madre campaign. Photograph taken by A. Frank Randall at San Carlos in the spring of 1884. Courtesy Museum of New Mexico, Santa Fe.

feel about my wife." I told him, "She's the mother of the whole thing, this life you have to go through, and you may have a long life."[8]

〰〰〰〰〰〰〰〰〰〰〰〰〰〰

If a man abused his wife, the fact that he had become a member of her family gave them the right to intervene and protect her.[9] If she was lazy or a nagger, there was nothing he could do except to scold her in private. But she was expected to be chaste. Most Apache women were, but there were occasional exceptions, and the husband was obligated to vindicate the family honor by cutting off the end of his wife's nose. If he failed to take action, he lost face in the band. A few women were seen—one was even photographed —with this disfigurement. Crook sternly banned the practice on all reservations he controlled. Possibly for this reason beating was substituted. In some cases the man even killed his wife and then himself in his grief and humiliation,[10] and no wronged husband could ever be induced to complain. His shame was too great.[11]

Now the leaders, as upholders of public morals as well as law and order, told Davis that neither family discipline nor *tizwin* drinking had entered into their agreement with Crook. The meeting broke up with no acceptance of the general's orders on the part of the leaders and no wavering by Davis in his determination to enforce them.[12]

Soon after that, Davis, on a turkey hunt, was following a trail up a mesa when he heard a gobble in the creek bottom behind him. He turned back and shot a turkey. He always hoped it was not the one that gobbled, for he believed that the gobbler had saved his life. That evening a pebble hit the wall of his tent, the signal of a "secret

---

8 Opler, *An Apache Life-Way*, p. 169.
9 Opler, *Apache Odyssey*, pp. 14–15.
10 Opler, *An Apache Life-Way*, pp. 408–10.
11 Ball, *op. cit.*, p. 176. I myself know of a case where a modern descendant of these Apaches punished his wife for flagrant unfaithfulness. Brought to trial, he gave no justification. Asked if he had any reason to complain of his wife's conduct, he finally admitted that he had—"She wouldn't get up and cook my breakfast"—and he accepted his prison sentence with no further defense.
12 Davis, *op. cit.*, pp. 123–24.

scout." It was his woman spy. As he told it, Mickey Free was with her, but he wrote elsewhere that he always spoke to his "secret scouts" directly without an interpreter because they were afraid Mickey Free would reveal their identity. Possibly Davis confused this incident with another related by Kaywaykla, probably occurring the same evening, in which Chihuahua lay hidden outside and heard Chatto and Mickey Free "fabricate" a story of a planned uprising by Geronimo and Kaahteney.

In any event, the woman told Davis that the good spirit of one of his ancestors was in that gobbler. Kaahteney and his adherents had been having a *tizwin* drink on top of the mesa, and when they saw the officer coming with his gun they thought he was on his way to arrest them and were lying in wait ready to shoot him when he should reach the top. Then they would incite as many more of the Indians as possible and make a break for Mexico.[13]

Davis felt that this called for a showdown. He sent to Fort Apache for four troops of cavalry, about 140 men, to arrive at sunrise. At the same time he sent the scouts to summon all the leaders to his tent. The outcome was uncertain. Kaahteney had thirty-two followers, the most reckless of the young warriors. Chatto, Benito, Loco, Mangus, and Gil-lee could be counted on to oppose the young dissenter. Geronimo and Naiche seemed uncommitted, and Davis typically failed to reckon with Nana. He thought that if the sentiment of the majority was for peace, he would win; if they sided with Kaahteney, let it be war now. And there was the uncomfortable reminder of what had happened at an attempted arrest fewer than three years before at Cibecue.

The dramatic confrontation occurred early that morning of June 22, with the cavalry dismounted and ready, Kaahteney and his followers defiant, twenty of the chiefs and principal men assembled in the tent, and other warriors surrounding it with not a woman or child in sight. All the men were armed. Crook, in fact, had strong convictions against disarming Indians. First, he considered it impossible; they always found ways of concealing their weapons.

13 *Ibid.*, pp. 39, 124–25; Ball, *op. cit.*, pp. 162–63.

Then there were plenty of unscrupulous dealers who would supply them in spite of regulations. And significantly, only by being armed could they protect themselves from "the disreputable class of white men" ready to commit depredations against them and their property on the reservation.[14]

But never before had the leaders come armed to a meeting with Davis. There was a tense moment when Kaahteney's followers fanned out and advanced toward the tent, cocking their leveled weapons. But the scouts stood firm, ready to support Davis even at the risk of their lives, and he arrested Kaahteney without incident. Benito and one of the scouts promised to be Kaahteney's sureties if he were not disarmed. He went quietly with them to San Carlos, where he was tried by an Indian jury and convicted of threatening to start an uprising.

Was he guilty as charged? Kaywaykla passionately insisted throughout his life that his step-father was the victim of malicious lies told by Chatto, Mickey Free, Tsoe, and Davis' spies. It should be noted, however, that Kaahteney had been surly and uncooperative during all the months that Chatto was still in Mexico, and even if his words were "twisted" by a hostile interpreter, his manner was his own. Even Kaywaykla said that Davis had urged him to enlist as a scout and he had refused.[15]

Crawford sentenced him to serve three years in irons in the military prison on Alcatraz Island.[16] But Crook recognized the potential of the energetic young warrior and recommended that "he be kept in irons at hard labor for one month and his confinement then relaxed, and he be permitted to go about the island and the city of San Francisco so that he may observe and become acquainted with the manner of living of the whites and thus learn something which may be of benefit to his people when he is re-

14 Secretary of War, *Annual Report*, 1883, Crook to Military Division of the Pacific, July 23, 1883, pp. 177–78; and September 27, 1883, pp. 168–69.

15 Ball, *op. cit.*, pp. 157, 162.

16 The army's account of his arrest and trial is in Davis, *op. cit.*, pp. 125–30; and Secretary of War, *Annual Report*, 1884, Crawford to Assistant Adjutant General, Whipple Barracks, p. 135. Davis said he was sentenced to five years in prison, but Crawford's contemporary report is no doubt correct.

turned to the reservation."[17] In October Crook suggested to the Indians that he be allowed to return if they would be responsible for his good conduct, but Geronimo and (of course) Chatto opposed the plan, saying that he kept the other Indians stirred up.[18] Crook did have him released after about eighteen months, and he returned willing to cooperate with the military and even able to read and write a little.[19]

But this outcome was not foreseen by Kaahteney's grieving family at the time of his arrest. "Mother made no sound," said Kaywaykla, "but I buried myself in my blanket and tried to stifle my uncontrollable shaking and sobbing. Grandfather . . . sat beside me with head bowed and hand on my shoulder. I knew that Kaytennae was as his right hand, and that he suffered as did mother and I." Soon Kaywaykla was sent to pick up the family's share at a ration issue, and there Chatto told him that Kaahteney was "chained on a rock so far from land that no man could swim across that water." When the boy reported to Nana, he was reassured. Nana "had traveled far and seen all the rivers in the land" and there was no water so wide that Kaahteney could not swim across it. Also Nana had gone to a mountain to pray and Usen had told him that Kaahteney would return. But the fear persisted that he had been put to death, and that Geronimo, Naiche, Chihuahua, Nana, and Mangus would be the next victims. Every time one of these leaders appeared, Chatto and Mickey Free would draw their hands significantly across their throats.[20] The Apaches were, of course, aware of instances when Crook had sent his scouts to bring in the heads of incorrigible hostiles.[21]

Meanwhile, Davis was trying to start his Indians in farming. It was late in June by the time all were settled—too late for intensive planting, they told him, for snow would kill the crops before

17 Quoted by Thrapp, *Conquest of Apacheria*, pp. 308–309.
18 Secretary of War, *Annual Report*, 1885, Crook to Assistant Adjutant General, Division of the Pacific, September 9, 1885, p. 176; *Senate Exec. Doc. 88*, 51 Cong., 1 sess., p. 13.
19 Bourke, *On the Border with Crook*, pp. 472–73, 478, 480.
20 Ball, *op. cit.*, pp. 165–68, 175, 177.
21 See, for example, Thrapp, *op. cit.*, pp. 160–61.

maturity. But Kaywaykla remembered, "All cultivated little open glades and planted corn and vegetables." Crawford reported that they raised that year an estimated forty-five thousand pounds of corn, a considerable amount of barley, and "many melons, pumpkins, and other vegetables" so that he was able to reduce "certain portions of their rations." He said that the work was not "by any means" confined to the women, and he credited Geronimo and Chatto with being the best farmers in the group. Davis, however, thought that the best was not very good.[22]

In his zeal the young officer overlooked the small beginnings. "We especially liked roasting ears," Kaywaykla remembered. "Then there was another food, an oblong thing larger than a turkey egg, and covered with thin brown skin. Mother roasted it in the ashes. We liked potatoes. And how we enjoyed watermelon!" Once his mother sent him to Davis with a melon she had raised, and he received a can of tomatoes in return. His mother also collected Davis' empty cans, cut them into strips, then wrapped them around a tapered stick to make cone-shaped bells which were suspended from buckskin thongs on ceremonial garments to jingle as the wearer walked. The Apache women were still cutting up tin cans to make bells with which to trim their baskets when they were prisoners at Fort Sill.[23]

But these wild people found many problems in adapting themselves to the unfamiliar life-way. Apparently Davis had been using a brand of deviled ham with a well-known trademark. Kaywaykla brought his mother a flat container upon which was pictured "a tall thin man with hooves and a tail. The officer had been eating man meat! My people had been told that sometimes White Eyes [that is, white men] practiced cannibalism, and here was the proof. No more collecting of discarded cans! Nana made Medicine for me and I suffered no ill effects."[24]

When fall came, the Indians prepared to follow their immemorial custom of moving to a lower altitude. Except for their fear

---

22 Secretary of War, *Annual Report*, 1884, Crawford to Assistant Adjutant General, Whipple Barracks, pp. 135, 136; Davis, *op. cit.*, pp. 107–108, 122–23.
23 Lucy Gage, "A Romance of Pioneering," *Chronicles of Oklahoma*, Vol. XXIX, No. 3 (Autumn, 1951), p. 306.
24 Ball, *op. cit.*, pp. 157–58.

of betrayal, they had spent a good summer. They had raised crops and gathered wild food; killed deer, dried the venison, and tanned the skins for clothing and wickiup covers; and ground acorn and corn meal. They held a big dance and feast to celebrate the end of the season and then moved their camps down to the valley of the White River near Fort Apache. Davis' tent was pitched about three miles from the post, and the Indians camped in the surrounding foothills or along the streams. From his large tent nearby he issued the flour, coffee, sugar, and other groceries to them, while their meat ration was issued at the slaughterhouse at the post.[25]

While there, the survivors of Tres Castillos had a happy experience. Crook had indeed responded to Geronimo's appeal on behalf of their people held in Mexican slavery. He urged Washington to act, pointing out that all the Mexican captives held by the Indians had been returned.[26] The administration did make representations to the Mexican government, all without result. The Mexican officials refused to admit that they dealt in Apache slaves, and they even sent photographs of the captives to Crook to show that they were happy and free and could return to their people if they wished.[27]

But five of the captives of the Tres Castillos disaster managed to escape—Kaywaykla's grandmother, his cousin Siki, Huera, and two other women. They had been shipped to Mexico City, where they were purchased by the owner of an extensive hacienda in the vicinity. There they served for more than three years, the older woman caring for the children of the family, the others working in the fields, before they found a chance to slip away. Their journey of more than one thousand miles on foot, hiding out, living off the country, with one knife and one blanket their only equipment, is an Apache odyssey of courage, hardihood, and skill in woodcraft. After reaching the United States they were taken by the army and

---

25 *Ibid.*, pp. 175–76; Davis, *op. cit.*, pp. 130–33, 135–36.
26 Secretary of War, *Annual Report*, 1884, p. 134. For the return of two Mexican boys captured by Kaahteney and adopted into his family, see Ball, *op. cit.*, pp. 113, 158–59, 165, 167.
27 *Senate Exec. Doc. 35*, 51 Cong., 1 sess., p. 42.

restored to their rejoicing relatives. The officers at Fort Apache tried to enlist Huera as an interpreter because of her fluent knowledge of Spanish, but she refused to serve. For some reason she was hostile and never came near Davis, even sending someone to draw her rations. Possibly it was because of the ban on *tizwin.* Just as some women in other cultures are notable cooks, she was a skilled *tizwin* maker, and her product was in great demand.[28]

Also, now that they were settled near Fort Apache, suspicious members of the band found good cause to distrust the army. This distrust was explained to Opler half a century later by Sam Kenoi, who had been a small boy at the time. At the post the soldiers would point to them, asking, "Which is Geronimo? Which one is Naiche?" Then "when the officer wasn't looking," some private with rough humor would pass his hand across his throat. Late at night they would hold secret councils. "They would say to each other, 'That white soldier . . . might be a good man trying to let us know just what they are going to do to us.' . . . They would think that white soldier was a kind fellow, that he was telling them that they were going to have their heads cut off." Then they would listen, trying to find out more. One with a little understanding of English would hear a soldier say, "Those Indians ought to go to jail," or, "Those Indians ought to be killed," and he would report his findings to the others. As Kenoi said, "those Indians were wild. They didn't know any better."[29] Nodiskey, who had joined the band because his wife was a Chiricahua, was especially active in spreading these rumors. Davis believed that he was a disturbing influence but could never find any positive evidence against him. Huera also warned Geronimo that he and Mangus were to be arrested and jailed.[30]

Davis never knew of these fears and of the harassment that

---

28 Ball, *op. cit.,* pp. 168–84; Davis, *op. cit.,* p. 140. Because the women were brought in by a military conveyance, Davis assumed that the American government had secured their release in exchange for the returned Mexican captives.

29 Opler, "A Chiricahua Apache's Account," pp. 365–66. Kenoi stated this as a hypothetical case, but it was based on actual experience. Other informants told Opler of these attempts of the soldiers to terrorize them.

30 Davis, *op. cit.,* pp. 140–41, 202.

Huera, the wife of Mangus. "Huera told me that they were going to seize me and put me and Mangus in the guard-house, . . . and so I left." Courtesy Arizona Historical Society, Tucson.

aroused them. As soon as spring approached (the spring of 1885), he and his Indians moved from the unfriendly vicinity of the post back to Turkey Creek. It fell to Bowman to instruct them in farming. Davis was not impressed by their exertions. He thought Geronimo's efforts were typical. One day the reformed raider came to him, proudly exhibiting a small blister on his palm, and asked him to visit his "farm." Davis went there a day or two later. He found Geronimo sitting in the shade with one of his wives fanning him while the other two were hoeing a patch of sickly corn.[31] But Geronimo may have been ill on that occasion. He and Betzinez did plant a field of barley that spring. The patterns might vary, but whether in raiding, ranching, or farming, Geronimo's economic drive was a constant. In a different culture he would have been a captain of industry.

Whether or not their farming accomplishments were satisfactory, the former hostiles were loyally observing the peace they had made with Crook two years before in the Sierra Madre. There had not been one act of Apache violence in all the Southwest—not one horse stolen, not one man killed. Crook could truthfully say in his 1884 report that "for the first time in the history of that fierce people, every member of the Apache tribe is at peace." But with the apparent end of hostilities the civilian administration began to assert its authority, and the old feud broke out between the War and Interior departments.

The army had been in control of the Indians on the reservation ever since Crook's arrival in Arizona in 1882. Now at San Carlos Crawford and the Indian agent issued conflicting orders regarding farming practices, the arrest and punishment of offenders, and the purchase of cattle. Crook asked to be relieved of his responsibility unless he could have undivided control. His request was not granted, but Crawford, in disgust, asked and received permission to rejoin his regiment, and Crook appointed Captain Francis E. Pierce to succeed him. None of this conflict extended to Turkey Creek, but the band knew of the departure of Crawford, and this

31 *Ibid.*, pp. 136–37.

made them uneasy; they were constantly asking Davis whether Nantan Lupan had gone also. Geronimo, in particular, needed continual reassurance. Also they probably knew of the breakdown of authority at San Carlos, and this may have made them bolder in asserting their own independence. That, at least was Davis' interpretation, although it does not appear in subsequent Indian analyses of the situation.[32]

Whatever the cause, wife beating and *tizwin* drinking reappeared that spring among Davis' charges. A young woman came to him with an arm broken in two places, her hair matted with blood, and her shoulders a mass of welts and bruises. The post surgeon patched her up, and Davis arrested her husband and gave him a sentence of two weeks in the jail at Fort Apache. Several of the leaders came and demanded his release, but Davis refused. Next, he arrested and jailed an Indian responsible for a *tizwin* drink. That afternoon Chihuahua and Mangus came to his tent to protest. He was not surprised at the attitude of Chihuahua, who was a constant protestor against the regulations, but he was puzzled at the attitude of Mangus. That night one of his "secret scouts" told him about Huera and the reason for Mangus' concern. Whether she had been his wife before her capture, or whether he had married her after her return, he was now upholding her interest.[33]

The leaders held a council and decided on concerted action. They prepared themselves by an all-night *tizwin* drink. Then before sunrise on the following morning, Friday, May 15, they assembled with about thirty of their followers before Davis' tent. Many of them were armed, and no woman or child was in sight. The scouts were standing around in groups, all under arms. When Davis came out, the leaders said they had come for a talk. All of them but Chatto, who remained with the scouts, then entered the

---

32 For the entire history of the conflict between the civil and military administration, see Ogle, *Federal Control of the Western Apaches*, pp. 221–31. For the army account, see Bourke, *op. cit.*, pp. 457, 460–63; Davis, *op. cit.*, pp. 34, 138–39, 146–47; and Secretary of War, *Annual Report*, 1885, pp. 170–75, 179–85. For Betzinez's interpretation, see *I Fought with Geronimo*, p. 129.

33 Davis, *op. cit.*, pp. 139–41, 202.

tent and squatted in a half-circle in front of the young officer. Loco began quietly to present their case. Chihuahua, who was plainly intoxicated, sprang to his feet and interrupted him. He repeated the old arguments. They had agreed on peace, but "nothing had been said about their conduct among themselves; they were not children to be taught how to live with their women and what they should eat or drink. . . . They had complied with all they had promised to do when they had their talk with the General in Mexico; had kept the peace and harmed no one. Now they were being punished for things they had a right to do so long as they did no harm to others."

Davis tried to explain the reasons for the regulations. When he got to wife beating, Nana got up, made an angry remark to Mickey Free, and limped out of the tent. Mickey tried to avoid interpreting, but Davis insisted. These were his words: "Tell the *Nantan Enchau*[34] that he can't advise me how to treat women. He is only a boy. I killed *men* before he was born."

Chihuahua went on: "We all drank tizwin last night, all of us in the tent and outside, except the scouts; and many more. What are you going to do about it? Are you going to put us all in jail? You have no jail big enough even if you could put us all in jail."

Davis answered that this was too serious for him to decide. He would wire the general and let them know the answer. Benito and Gil-lee started to say something, but Chihuahua cut them off. The council was over. Neither Geronimo nor any of the others had spoken, and only Chihuahua showed the effects of the previous night's drinking.

Davis worded his telegram to show that it was intended for Crook, but following army practice he sent it to his immediate superior, Captain Pierce, at San Carlos. Pierce had come to his command of the reservation with no knowledge of Apaches, and he was accustomed to ask advice from the experienced Al Sieber. But Al had proved the Apaches' point by spending that same night

34 Stout Chief. Davis was stockily built, in contrast to the lanky Gatewood and Crawford.

gambling and drinking the much more potent white man's *tizwin* and was sleeping it off. Perhaps the sequel proved Crook's point of its harmful effects. When Pierce woke him up and showed him the telegram, he said, "It's nothing but a tizwin drunk. Don't pay any attention to it. Davis will handle it," and he went back to sleep. Pierce returned to his office and pigeonholed the telegram.

The rest of Friday passed with no answer. Saturday came and went; so did most of Sunday. Davis saw the Apache leaders every day, but he had nothing to tell them. Rumors spread through the camp. The leaders would be hanged or have their heads cut off. Probably that had been done to Kaahteney. The whole band would be arrested and taken away somewhere. Davis kept in touch with the scouts. And he waited. It never occurred to him that his message had not reached Crook; he supposed the general was making preparations to deal with the situation and would communicate his orders when he was ready. He and Crook always believed that if that message had gone through, the affair would have been settled as a minor incident. Its neglect was to have tragic consequences to the army, to civilians of the Southwest, and, most of all, to the Apaches.

On Sunday, May 17, Davis was at Fort Apache waiting for a reply to his telegram. At about four o'clock in the afternoon Chatto and Mickey Free came to him with the alarming news that a number of the Indians had broken out from the reservation and were on their way to Mexico. He attempted at once to telegraph Pierce, but the line was dead. The Indians had cut the wire in several places where it passed through the forks of trees and had fastened the severed ends with buckskin thongs. This was Nana's idea, said Kaywaykla; formerly they had torn out a section of wire, and the break was easily found and repaired. This time the damaged places were not located until the following day.

The commander of the troops at the post immediately prepared to take the field while Davis hastened to his camp to summon his scouts to accompany them. He formed the company in front of his tent and prepared to issue ammunition, but fearing that some might be disloyal he ordered them to ground arms (rifle butts on the ground) while Chatto and two others stood ready to shoot any man who raised his gun. Perico, Chappo, and one other then slipped out of ranks and melted into the brush. Afterwards, he was told that they had planned to kill him and Chatto, and he believed that his order to ground arms had prevented it. Later Crook accused Geronimo of planning the killings. Geronimo denied that accusation and appealed to White Mountain witnesses, never his friends, to support his denial. Crook ignored his defense; to him, Geronimo was a liar, and that settled it. But according to Kaywaykla, the three disaffected scouts had remained behind to divert suspicion, intending to overtake the others as soon as the breakout should become known. This seems the more logical explanation. It was to the interest of the runaways to escape unnoticed and put as much distance as possible between themselves and the soldiers. They would hardly have risked a probable fight with the scouts, loyal as those scouts were to Davis. These three defections were the only ones during the campaign that followed.

It was dark by the time the cavalry arrived and set out with Davis and his scouts to pursue the fleeing hostiles. They marched all night, and the next morning they came out on the crest of a ridge. Across a wide valley they saw the dust raised by the Indians' ponies ascending another ridge fifteen or twenty miles away. Davis, with Chatto and ten other scouts, then turned back. At Fort Apache he reported to Crook on the now functioning telegraph and went to his camp to assess the extent of the breakout. He called up all the Indians and counted them. Thirty-five men, eight boys old enough to bear arms, and 101 women and children were missing. Among the men were the leaders, Geronimo, Chihuahua, Naiche, Mangus, and Nana. Among the boys were Geronimo's nephew, Kanseah,[35] and Mangus' protégés, Istee and Daklugie. Three-fourths of the band remained, under Loco, Benito, Gil-lee, and (of course) Chatto.[36]

[35] The presence of Kanseah in the party is shown by subsequent events.
[36] Davis, *op. cit.*, pp. 144–52, 206–207; Secretary of War, *Annual Report*, 1886, pp. 147–48; Ball, *op. cit.*, pp. 175–77.

By this time the ominous message, "The Apaches are out," was burning up the wires and screaming in newspaper headlines throughout the Southwest. Exposed settlers, travelers, and prospectors grouped or fled for safety, often too late. Army units— twenty troops of cavalry and probably two hundred Indian scouts —crisscrossed the mountains, guarded the border and the water holes, and wore themselves out in futile pursuit, while the hostiles, killing as they went, helped themselves to horses and goods, once capturing three wagonloads of army supplies and ammunition.[37]

On the reservation Benito and Chatto were very bitter against the hostiles,[38] and in the ensuing campaign most of the men served as scouts.[39] But some who remained had close ties to the runaways. Nana had decreed that his sister, the "Grandmother" of Kaywaykla's narrative, and her daughter, Kaywaykla's mother, should stay, although his wife, Geronimo's sister, accompanied him. Siki had married Toclanny, a dependable scout who had never been a hostile, and remained with her husband.[40] Betzinez was torn between his peaceable inclinations and his duty to Geronimo. Returning home that Sunday evening from planting barley in the field he and Geronimo were farming together, he was told of the outbreak. With his mother and sister he started out to catch up with the fleeing hostiles. Then, "As I hurried along . . . through the dark moonless night, my thoughts were very troubled. I came to the conclusion that it would be foolish to throw away what I was just beginning to learn of a better way of life." He told his mother and sister of his decision, and they all managed to return to the reservation without being discovered. He shed some tears when he arrived and saw that not one of his young cousins or friends had remained. It did not help his feelings to find that "some greedy Indians" had appropriated all the horses Geronimo's party had left behind. Chatto even claimed the barley field, but Davis supported Betzinez' ownership.[41]

37 Thrapp, *Conquest of Apacheria*, pp. 315–26.
38 *Ibid.*, p. 315.
39 Davis, *op. cit.*, p. 151.
40 Ball, *op. cit.*, p. 177; Griswold, "The Fort Sill Apaches," s.v. "Toclanny, Roger."
41 Betzinez, *op. cit.*, pp. 129–30.

Benito. Although he was largely responsible for the breakaway in 1881, he settled down peaceably after surrendering to General Crook in the Sierra Madre. Photograph taken by A. Frank Randall at San Carlos in the spring of 1884. Courtesy U.S. Signal Corps, National Archives.

Looking back, Davis tried to analyze the causes of the breakout. He attributed it to the dissatisfaction of three factions, totaling no more than twelve or fifteen men, led by Geronimo, Chihuahua, and Mangus. The two last, he thought, had not expected the trouble to go so far. They opposed the wife-beating and *tizwin* prohibitions, the first on general principles, the second on personal grounds—Huera's right to make it and Chihuahua's right to drink it—but they did not plan a breakout. Davis believed it was Geronimo who planned it and took advantage of their dissatisfaction. He had not been active in the wife-*tizwin* controversy. His motivation must have been pure depravity; he was "a thoroughly vicious, intractable, and treacherous man. His only redeeming traits were courage and determination."[42]

Apparently Davis was right in charging Geronimo as the moving spirit in the breakout, but he never understood the wild leader's reasons. Geronimo himself later made a clear and logical explanation to Crook, but to army officers and civilians alike this only indicated his mendacity.[43] Their exasperation is understandable. This was his fourth breakaway, to say nothing of his kidnaping of Loco, and there would be one more before his final capitulation. But every time he had cause—as he saw it.

It is certain that he had come in the year before with every intention of settling down. His loss of the cattle had been a disappointment, but he had observed the peace. He tried to trust Crook, and yet there might be truth in the taunts of soldiers and scouts and the warnings of his associates. And how could he be sure that Crook would not be replaced as Crawford had been? Somehow he learned that the newspapers were clamoring for his death. He knew how close he had come to that death when Clum was in charge. And there was the uncertainty over what had been done to Kaahteney. In the spring he had started to plant his barley, hoping to harvest it. Now, in the crisis, with some unknown punish-

---

[42] Davis, *op. cit.*, pp. 142–43.
[43] *Ibid.*, pp. 200–207.

ment about to descend, he consulted his Power. Naturally, in his suspicious state of mind it confirmed his worst fears.[44]

Later, the Apaches that remained on the reservation told Davis and Crook that Geronimo and Mangus induced Chihuahua and Naiche to break out by telling them that they had killed Davis and Chatto and that troops were coming to arrest the whole band and send them away. As soon as these leaders discovered the deception, they threatened to kill Geronimo and Mangus, and the runaways broke up. Mangus and his few followers left for Mexico and never rejoined the others. Naiche collected his family and tried to return, but they ran into some of Davis' scouts and joined Chihuahua. Chihuahua's people then hid out in the mountains north of the Gila, intending to slip back, while Geronimo went on to Mexico. Then, ten days later, Davis and his scouts came to the place where the trail forked and followed Chihuahua's. They came up with the band, and some shots were exchanged. Chihuahua was now committed.[45]

A hide-and-seek pursuit by the soldiers ensued through the mountains of southeastern Arizona and southwestern New Mexico, with the hostiles breaking up into small parties and dashing out to kill and rob. The soldiers seldom glimpsed them, but the bodies of at least seventeen civilians and about 150 horses and mules worn out and killed or abandoned marked their passing. By June 10 most of them had crossed the international border. Lieutenant Davis, following one party, found two newly born, dead babies on the trail. They had traveled ninety miles on stolen horses without a pause until they camped in Mexico.[46]

It is impossible now to determine the truth of the story Davis heard of conflict among the leaders. There is no mention of it in any of their subsequent recorded statements. It is apparent that after they reached Mexico they operated for a time as separate

44 Opler, "A Chiricahua Apache's Account," p. 367 and n. 8. Sam Kenoi did not state that the warning from Geronimo's Power occurred at this exact time, but certainly it did.

45 Davis, *op. cit.*, pp. 152, 205, 209; Thrapp, *Conquest of Apacheria*, pp. 316–18, citing an article Davis published in the *Army-Navy Journal*, October 24, 1885.

46 Davis, *op. cit.*, p. 153; Thrapp, *Conquest of Apacheria*, pp. 318–26.

bands under Chihuahua, Geronimo, Naiche, and Mangus; but except for Mangus and his party they soon united with no evidence of bad feeling.[47]

Once in Mexico, their raids there went unrecorded, but there could be no peace on the American side of the border as long as they remained at large. This meant that their sanctuary had to be invaded.

[47] Ball, *op. cit.*, p. 181.

CHAPTER 13

HISTORY REPEATS ITSELF
FOR GERONIMO

On June 11 a force under Captain Crawford followed the hostiles into the Sierra Madre. Another command, under Captain Wirt Davis, entered Mexico on July 13. At the same time Crook stationed troops at strategic points on the American side of the boundary in an attempt to seal it off or to pursue any bands that might slip across. To the army the campaign meant hardships that approached the limit of human endurance against an enemy that melted away unseen.[1] To the Indians it was the old story of "run, ride, fight, hide, then ride and fight again."[2] In the 1930's Opler attempted to explore Apache dreams to determine their religious revelations. One informant told him that his dreams had no such meaning, but ran "on the order of war" when the scouts were on the trail of his band. "I dream they are making a raid on my people and I am trying to get away from them."[3] After more than forty years it was still his nightmare.

1 Crook's summary is given in Secretary of War, *Annual Report*, 1886, pp. 147–51; Thrapp's carefully researched account is in *Conquest of Apacheria*, pp. 326–32.

2 Eve Ball, "On the Warpath with Geronimo," *The West*, Vol. XV, No. 3 (August, 1971), p. 62. Mrs. Ball's informant was describing another campaign, but the experience is typical.

3 Opler, *An Apache Life-Way*, p. 191.

Confused reports of the campaign came back to Crook of encounters in the mountains of Mexico—inflated accounts of Apache losses by young officers eager for promotion or uncertain about what actually happened among the rocks and canyons. On June 23 Crawford's scouts under Chatto discovered Chihuahua's camp in the Bavispe Mountains northeast of Oputo. They failed to surround it, and most of the band escaped, but they killed one woman, captured fifteen women and children, and brought back a number of horses and much plunder. Among the captives were a son and a daughter of Chihuahua later known as Eugene and Ramona.[4] On July 29 Captain Davis' scouts ambushed four hostile warriors in the Haya Mountains and killed two. On August 7 a picked detail of seventy-eight of his scouts under an army officer struck Geronimo's camp in the mountains a little northeast of Nacori. They "killed" Nana, three other warriors (one the son of Geronimo), and one woman; "wounded" Geronimo and trailed him some distance by the blood; captured fifteen women and children, among them "three wives and five children of Geronimo's family" and Huera, the wife of Mangus; and overran the camp, acquiring thirteen horses and mules besides saddles, blankets, dried meat, and other articles. Only two warriors and one woman escaped.[5]

The "dead" Nana and Chappo and the "wounded" Geronimo went on their way unharmed. The other "deceased" warriors seem to have survived also. In Crook's final report the casualties had shrunk to "1 squaw and 2 boys."[6] According to Geronimo, "One boy was killed and nearly all of our women and children were captured."[7]

The captives, indeed, were real and may even have been counted

---

[4] Lieutenant Britton Davis, who was serving with Crawford, gives the details of this encounter in *The Truth about Geronimo*, pp. 166–69. The Apache account, as remembered by Eugene and Ramona Chihuahua, is told in Ball, *In the Days of Victorio*, p. 178.

[5] National Archives and Records Service, Consolidated File 1066 AGO 1883 [referred to hereafter as Consolidated File], Crook to AAG Division of the Pacific, August 17, 1885.

[6] Secretary of War, *Annual Report*, 1886, p. 150.

[7] Barrett, *Geronimo's Story of His Life*, p. 136.

correctly. Geronimo lost his entire family except for his warrior son. It is known that his wives Zi-yeh and She-gha were captured. If a third wife was captured, Shtsha-she must still have been living. If so, she soon dropped out of sight, for she does not appear in any later accounts of his family. As for the five children, there was Zi-yeh's infant son, afterwards known as Fenton[8]; a three-year-old girl whose exact identity is not established (was she the baby carried on Betzinez' mule during the Sonora raid in 1882?); and a two-year-old son who died shortly thereafter in captivity at Fort Bowie, and whose grave marker in the post cemetery carried the un-Apache name, "Little Robe."[9] Nothing is known of the two other children reported. Dohn-say may have been counted or even her children (at some unreported date she married a young warrior named Dahkeya). Also among the captives was Hah-dun-key, the wife of Geronimo's "brother" Perico, and their children.

Geronimo had indeed suffered a grievous loss, as had the entire hostile band. In the two encounters they had lost fully one-third of their women and children. (Revised figures of the breakout after some stragglers slipped back indicated that ninety-two women and children were absent from the reservation.) Apaches were devoted to their families. Also, in their well-structured division of labor a man without a wife to prepare food and clothing was as seriously handicapped economically as was a woman without a male provider. Stories of lone outlaws hiding in the mountains who slipped back to steal wives appear frequently in Apache history. The women accepted the situation, and there are cases of stable marriages formed in this way.

Thus, through economic necessity as well as sentiment Geronimo and four of his followers set out to bring back their families, or—if necessary—to steal wives. They slipped through the cordon of troops guarding the international border and worked their way through the mountains to the reservation. Their people who had not joined in the breakout had been moved to the vicinity of Fort

[8]Fenton Geronimo's tombstone at Fort Sill gives 1882 as his birth date but he was born later. See his photograph made no earlier than 1895, *infra*, p. 376.
[9]Charles Fletcher Lummis, *Dateline Fort Bowie*, pp. 83, 87–88.

Apache and were closely guarded for their own protection. The captives had not been confined at the post, but had been permitted to live with them. The White Mountain Apaches were patroling the country, but the five coming on foot singly from the east managed to evade them. They picked up some White Mountain horses, and, finding a White Mountain woman alone, compelled her to take them to the camp of Geronimo's family, reaching it at one o'clock on the morning of September 22. They managed to recover his wife She-gha and his three-year-old daughter and to steal another woman. Scouting parties were sent out immediately in pursuit, but the raiders separated and faded into the mountains to the east.[10]

Perico, unsuccessful in recovering Hah-dun-key, took the stolen woman as his wife. Her name was Bi-ya-neta Tse-dah-dilth-thlilth. (Bi-ya-neta should be sufficient for identification hereafter.) The two were to live harmoniously together in the mountains of Mexico, through the succeeding years as prisoners of war, and after their final release. Three of their five children are buried at Fort Sill; descendants of the other two are probably still living.[11]

On their way back from the raid on the reservation, Geronimo and his party captured some Mescalero women as wives. The Mescalero Charlie Smith, who died at a great age in 1973, has told the story. Although he was a young child at the time, he remembered how a party of his people were permitted to leave their reservation to gather piñon nuts and hunt piñon-fattened deer in the mountains of southwestern New Mexico. While the men hunted, the women divided into small groups gathering the nuts. With Charlie and his mother, Cumpah (afterwards known as Sarah), were a woman with a baby and an unmarried girl who later received the name Ih-tedda (Young Girl). Suddenly horsemen swooped down upon them. Charlie started to run for the

---

[10] Rutherford B. Hayes Library, George Crook Letterbook I (No. 234, L.S. 2320), pp. 227–28, copies furnished me by Dan L. Thrapp. The raid is mentioned in *Senate Exec. Doc. 35*, 51 Cong., 1 sess., p. 50.

[11] Griswold, "The Fort Sill Apaches," s.v. "Tse-dah-dilth-thlilth, Bi-ya-neta." It seems fairly certain that Bi-ya-neta was the woman stolen at this time.

brush, and a bullet struck him in the calf of the leg. (He carried the scar throughout his life.) The two women (one carrying her baby), the girl, and the small boy were scooped up, and each one was placed on a horse behind a captor and taken to Geronimo's camp.[12]

Geronimo took Ih-tedda, and the two older women became wives of other members of the band. The boy lost track of the woman with the baby. He could never be brought to reveal the name of the one who took his mother. This man was kind to his captured wife and seriously undertook the training of his stepson in the skills of a warrior. "I really liked my step-father, and was proud when I learned that he was considered one of the bravest of the Apaches. . . . I could not understand why in his absence my mother cried. And she did not explain."

He was not so appreciative when Geronimo undertook the training of the boys that winter in the Sierra Madre, especially when he was forced to plunge repeatedly into icy streams. Later, as an adult, he was to develop a great admiration for Geronimo for holding out after most of the Apaches accepted peace and reservation life, but in his childhood, "There were times when I just hated him."[13] After the band became prisoners of war, Cumpah and her son were reunited with the boy's own father.[14]

Meanwhile, Geronimo's raid on the American side of the line was closely followed by others during that same fall of 1885. On September 28 a band of about twenty hostiles crossed into southeastern Arizona. They were so closely pursued by the troops through the Chiricahua and Dragoon mountains that they killed "only" three men. They then captured the horse herd of the cattlemen of the area who were gathered for their fall roundup, and, superbly mounted on these crack cow ponies, they escaped into Mexico. Early in November came the most spectacular raid of all.

12 This must have occurred *after* the raid near Fort Apache, for the men had horses, and Charlie Smith remembered that Geronimo had a wife with him.
13 Ball, "On the Warpath with Geronimo"; Eve Ball to Angie Debo, May 31, 1973. Charlie Smith's account of these experiences is apparently based on vivid childhood impressions. In tribal and family history I have found his memory unreliable.
14 Consolidated File, report of Major William Sinclair, August 25, 1887.

It was led by Jolsanny (Josanie), often known as Ulzana, a brother of Chihuahua.

With ten warriors he entered New Mexico, and they made for the mountains, killing as they went, while troops swarmed over the area without sighting them. On November 23 they appeared near Fort Apache and struck the Indians who had remained on the reservation, objects of their hatred because the men had joined the army as scouts. There, by the best count obtainable, they killed five men and boys, eleven women, and four children and captured six women and a child. The next day they killed two herders in charge of the reservation beef cattle and made away with Benito's horses. A party from the post, with Chatto and eighteen scouts, pursued them, but they slipped away. A reservation Indian came back with the head of one raider, but that was their only known casualty.

Troops were alerted all over the Southwest, and Lieutenant General Philip H. Sheridan, who had succeeded Sherman as commander in chief of the army, even came out from Washington to confer with Crook at Fort Bowie. They decided to make a stronger effort to break up the hostile base in Mexico, and the commands of Captains Davis and Crawford were accordingly reorganized and reoutfitted for the invasion. Meanwhile, on the American side of the border Jolsanny and his nine warriors continued to evade the armed forces. At the end of December, mounted on excellent horses, they escaped into Mexico. As Crook summarized their raid, they had "traveled probably not less than one thousand two hundred miles, killed thirty-eight people, [and] captured and wore out probably two hundred and fifty head of stock."[15]

Meanwhile, Crawford crossed the line with his pack train and his scouts on November 29. Entering the Sierra Madre and laboring through its jumble of towering peaks and yawning gorges, they reached the Aros (or Haros) River about sixty miles south of Nacori. This was apparently the area of Juh's legendary stronghold, never before breached by a hostile force. There they found trails, campsites, and other evidences of Apache occupation. On

15 Thrapp, *Conquest of Apacheria*, pp. 332–39; Secretary of War, *Annual Report*, 1886, pp. 150–51.

the evening of January 9 the scouts reported that they had found the hostile *rancheria* ten or twelve miles away on a rugged eminence well calculated for defense. It was decided to make a night march and surround it. "It was a dark and moonless night," as Lieutenant Marion P. Maus, who was second in command, reported it. They followed a trail "over solid rock, over mountains, down cañons so dark they seemed bottomless."

Just before dawn they saw the dim outlines of the hostiles' position and were stealthily moving to encircle it when some burros in the camp started braying and its defenders sprang to arms. Shots were exchanged without damage to either side, and the occupants slipped out, sped down the mountainsides, and melted into the rocks below. The invaders took possession of the camp, acquiring the entire horse herd and stores of provisions. Later they had reason to appreciate its strong defensive position.

Soon a woman came in to report that Geronimo and Naiche wanted a conference. It would be interesting to know her identity, for some of the women were very influential in the band. Confused Apache tradition indicates that she may have been Tah-das-te (Dahteste), a sister of one of Chihuahua's wives, or Lozen, a sister of Victorio who never married and became famous in the band as a warrior and possessor of Power.[16] Crawford agreed to meet them the following day (January 11) on the river below the camp. The whole band was there except Mangus' small party, and it is apparent that Geronimo, with his usual deference to Naiche, was the leader. He afterwards said that the appearance of Crawford's force convinced him that no refuge was safe from invasion.

Even the scouts in Crawford's command were exhausted from the night march and the difficult days that had preceded it. When night came, they threw themselves among the rocks in the captured camp to sleep. Then, in the early dawn of a cold, foggy morning, some of them called out an alarm. At once a volley of rifle fire struck the camp. One of the scouts, still sleeping, was seriously wounded, two others slightly. They started to return the fire, but

16 Ball, *In the Days of Victorio*, pp. 151, 182.

249

Crawford checked them. It was now seen that the attackers were Mexican irregulars, volunteers serving without pay except the plunder they might collect. Apparently they had at first mistaken Crawford's command for the hostile camp, but when Maus and the interpreter, Tom Horn, called out to them in Spanish, and Crawford sprang on a rock waving his handkerchief, they deliberately shot Horn, wounding him slightly, and fatally wounded Crawford. They could not have mistaken these men for hostile Apaches. When Crawford fell, the enraged scouts returned the fire, killing all the Mexican officers and wounding five of the men.

The Apache band by this time had assembled on the height on the other side of the river, from which they had a good view of the encounter. "Geronimo watched it and laughed," said old Sam Haozous with an emphasis impossible to convey in print.[17] The Mexicans apparently found the American force too strong for them to overrun, but they remained in the vicinity, showing their hostility. Maus, now in command, decided to withdraw. He was short of ammunition and supplies and was separated from his pack train, which he feared the Mexicans might capture. He also saw no opportunity for his conference with the Apache hostiles while the Mexicans were near; a woman, in fact, came from the band that afternoon saying they feared to come in. Accordingly, on the following day he started back. In camp that night a woman again came to him from Geronimo requesting a conference.

The meeting was held on the second day after, on January 15. No doubt, although he did not say so, the officer was accompanied by Concepcion, a sergeant of the scout company, a Mexican captured in his boyhood and adopted by the Apaches, who served as interpreter. The hostile leaders had stipulated that Maus come unarmed. (There were too many instances of Indians coming to a meeting with army officers only to be seized and killed.) He found Geronimo, Naiche, Nana, and Chihuahua with fourteen men assembled for the conference. They sat in a circle nearly surrounding Maus, with Geronimo in the center. Every one had his rifle

17 Interview, January 27, 1955.

upright, and every belt was full of ammunition. Maus considered this a breach of faith and was understandably apprehensive. He did not know that never once in his turbulent career did Geronimo violate his wild code' of honor. There was silence for fully a minute. Then, looking the officer straight in the eye, Geronimo asked, "Why did you come down here?"

"I came to capture or destroy you and your band," said Maus. The direct answer seemed to please Geronimo. He rose, walked over to Maus, and shook his hand, saying he could trust him to report accurately to Crook. He then told the story of his grievances —"all of which were purely imaginary or assumed," Maus reported. (They were "imaginary," but not "assumed." No white man ever believed that Geronimo was sincerely convinced of an official plot against his life.) But the band was ready to discuss terms. Their relatives captured the previous summer were still in army possession, and now their fastness had been invaded. Geronimo, as spokesman, designated nine members of the band he would send back with Maus, and he promised to meet Crook near the border in "two moons to talk about surrendering. With this understanding," Maus reported, "I returned to camp."

Geronimo soon sent in the nine "prisoners," as Maus now designated them. He listed them as follows: "Nana and one buck . . . the wife and child of both Geronimo and Natchez [Naiche], and one boy, also the sister of Geronimo and one other woman."[18] Geronimo's sister was, of course, the wife of Nana, who accompanied her husband. The wife he surrendered was the young Ih-tedda.[19] He retained his older wife, She-gha. His child was the unidentified

18 This list was furnished me by Dan L. Thrapp, who found it in the Rutherford B. Hayes Library, Crook's Annual Report, 1886, Appendices I and K. Men and women were usually listed as "bucks" and "squaws" in army records.

19 This is contrary to the statements made by the Apaches, but I began to question the accuracy of their memory when I learned that the wife with Geronimo at the time of his final surrender was estimated to be thirty-five years old. This could hardly have been the "Young Girl" he had kidnaped. Then, considering that Ih-tedda was pregnant at the time of the meeting with Maus, I doubted that in view of Apache sex prohibitions he would have chosen her to remain with him. The final proof came in the birth of Ih-tedda's baby in a Florida prison at the very time Geronimo and the wife he had retained were held in captivity at San Antonio, Texas.

little girl. Was she the captive Zi-yeh's daughter who had somehow become separated from her mother and would now be returned to her? It seems more probable that she was the child of Shtsha-she and that Shtsha-she had indeed been captured with the rest of Geronimo's family and had since died. The wife Naiche surrendered was his oldest wife, Nah-de-yole, and the child was probably her son afterwards known as Paul. His other wives, E-clah-heh and Ha-o-zinne, remained with him.[20] (More will be heard of them hereafter.) The identity of the "one buck," "one boy," and "one other woman" is not known. It is fairly certain that they formed one family.

Although the word was not used, these "prisoners" were, in effect, hostages—given as a pledge of the promised meeting. One would like to know the reasons behind the selection. Perhaps there was a wish to protect them from the precarious existence of the hunted band. Nana was old and crippled. Ih-tedda was pregnant, and the Apaches, whenever it was possible, were careful of their pregnant women.[21] The health of Geronimo's little girl at that time is not known, but soon the army surgeon was to report her condition as "very feeble." In any case, their separation from the band was to last only "two moons."[22] Maus returned without further incident, and his "prisoners" were placed under guard at Fort Bowie. At some undetermined time the earlier captives were also brought there.[23] Now there would be no rescue.

On February 5 Maus was sent back across the border to await the arrival of the main band. He established his camp in northern Sonora about ten miles south of the Arizona line. The hostiles met their schedule; on March 15 they signaled their approach, and by March 19 all had arrived. Maus could not induce them to cross

20 For Naiche's family, see Griswold, *op. cit.*, s.v. "Naiche (Christian)," and "Naiche, Paul."
21 Opler, *op. cit.*, pp. 5–6.
22 For Maus's report of the expedition, see Secretary of War, *Annual Report, 1886*, pp. 155–64. Another account by Maus is in Nelson A. Miles, *Personal Recollections*, pp. 450–67.
23 Ball, *In the Days of Victorio*, p. 179 and note 5; Bourke, *On the Border with Crook*, p. 472.

The hostiles' camp at Cañon de los Embudos "in a lava bed, on top of a small conical hill surrounded by deep ravines." Note the sentinel with a gun. This and the following three photographs were taken by C. S. Fly, March 25–27, 1886. Courtesy U.S. Army Artillery and Missile Center Museum.

the border. They chose a strong position in the Cañon de los Embudos, and Maus established his camp one-half mile away. He had reported their presence to Crook as soon as he received their first message; now Geronimo came to his camp almost daily to ask when the general would arrive. It is apparent that the wild leader had staked everything on this meeting.

Crook set out from Fort Bowie, eighty-four miles away. Preceding him was his inevitable pack train. To soften up the hostiles, he brought along the reformed Kaahteney, now released from Alcatraz, the dependable scout Alchise, and "a couple of old Chiricahua squaws. . . . with all the latest gossip from the women prisoners at Bowie." Probably one of these women was Nah-dos-te, for provision was made for Nana to take his place among the leaders at the conference. There was a good complement of interpreters, and

Eighteen Apaches lined up by Fly for a photograph. Naiche is in the front row, center; Fun is in the second row, standing second from left; Yahnozha is mounted at the back, far right. Warriors of Geronimo's band often drew a line of paint across their faces to distinguish them. *All were in superb physical condition, and well dressed, well armed, and well mounted.* Courtesy Smithsonian Institution, National Anthropological Archives.

Bourke served as the general's aide. There were several other officers and civilians in the party. C. S. Fly, a Tombstone photographer, received permission to join them—a fortunate circumstance, for his photographs constitute an important record. Later, at the meeting place, Bourke, was to note the offhand manner in which Fly requested the hostiles—"as fierce as so many tigers," according to Crook's report—to change positions or turn their faces to improve his portrayal. On the way down Kaahteney demonstrated the marksmanship that had distinguished him among Victorio's warriors. The scouts took off after a drove of peccaries, and he shot one through the head while his horse was going at full speed.

The party settled at Maus's camp, "a strong position on a low mesa." The *rancheria* of the hostiles "was in a lava bed, on top of a

Geronimo with three of his warriors. From the left: Yahnozha, Chappo, and Fun. Soon all four were to break back into the mountains. Courtesy U.S. Artillery and Missile Center Museum.

small conical hill surrounded by deep ravines." Between the two camps were "two or three steep and rugged gulches which served as scarps and counter-scarps." Geronimo and other leaders came into Crook's camp, but only half a dozen at a time, while "the others were here, there, and everywhere, but all on the *qui vive*, apprehensive of treachery and ready to meet it." All were in superb physical condition and were well dressed, well armed, and well mounted—an indication that they had employed their "two moons" to good advantage since Maus had despoiled their camp.

The conference was held on the afternoon of March 25 under some large cottonwood and sycamore trees. Geronimo, Naiche, Chihuahua, and an otherwise unidentified leader named Kutli (Catle or Cayetano) participated, while twenty-four armed warriors listened in the background ready to fire if any attempt should be made to seize them. Geronimo was the spokesman. He pre-

The confrontation. Geronimo is near the left of the picture facing the camera; Crook is second from the right, facing Geronimo, with his gloved hand resting on his knee. Nana can be recognized at the right of Geronimo. Lieutenant Maus with a mustache and wearing a slouch hat is in the angle. Note the vigilant Apaches in the background. "The sun, the darkness, the winds are all listening to what we now say." Courtesy University of Oklahoma Library, Western History Collections, Norman.

sented his case with deadly seriousness; great beads of sweat rolled down his temples and over his hands, and he clutched nervously at a buckskin thong he held. Crook, always honorable in dealing with Indians, had Bourke record every word. Thus, one can follow Geronimo's logic and understand his motivation. First he chose his interpreter. (No more Mickey Frees!) Then he began:

I want to talk first of the causes which led me to leave the reservation. I was living quietly and contented, doing and thinking of no harm, while at the Sierra Blanca [White Mountains]. I don't know what harm I did to those three men, Chatto, Mickey Free, and Lieutenant Davis. I was living peaceably and satisfied when people began to speak bad of me. I should be glad to know who started those stories. I was living peaceably with my family, having plenty to eat, sleeping well, taking care of my people, and perfectly contented. . . . I hadn't killed a horse or man, American or Indian. I don't know what was the matter with the people in charge of us. They knew this to be so, and yet they said I was a bad man and the worst man there . . . I did not leave of my own accord. . . . Some time before I left an Indian named Wadiskay [Nodiskey] had a talk with me. He said, "they are going to arrest you," but I paid no attention to him, knowing that I had done no wrong; and the wife of Magnus, "Huera," told me that they were going to seize me and put me and Magnus in the guard-house, and I learned from the American and Apache soldiers [scouts], from Chatto, and Mickey Free, that the Americans were going to arrest me and hang me, and so I left. . . . I want to know now who it was ordered me to be arrested. I was praying to the light and to the darkness, to God and to the sun, to let me live quietly there with my family. . . .

I have several times asked for peace, but trouble has come from the agents and interpreters. I don't want what has passed to happen again. . . . The Earth-Mother is listening to me and I hope that all may be so arranged that from now on there shall be no trouble and that we shall always have peace. Whenever we see you coming to where we are, we think that it is God—you must come always with God. . . . Whenever I have broken out, it has always been on account of bad talk. . . . Very often there are stories put in the newspapers that I am to be hanged. I don't want that any more. When a man tries to do right, such stories ought not to be put in the newspapers. There are very few of my men left now. They have done some bad things but I want them all rubbed out and let us never speak of them again. . . . We think of our relations, brothers, brothers-in-law, father-in-law, etc., over on the reservation, and from this on we want to live at peace just as they are doing, and to behave as they are behaving. Sometimes a man does something and men are sent out to bring in his head.

257

I don't want such things to happen to us. I don't want that we should be killing each other. . . .

I have not forgotten what you told me, although a long time has passed. . . . I want this peace to be legal and good. Whenever I meet you I talk good to you, and you to me, and peace is soon established; but when you go to the reservation you put agents and interpreters over us who do bad things. Perhaps they don't mind what you tell them, because I do not believe you would tell them to do bad things to us. . . . I want to have a good man put over me. While living I want to live well. I know I have to die some time, but even if the heavens were to fall on me, I want to do what is right. I think I am a good man, but in the papers all over the world they say I am a bad man; but it is a bad thing to say so about me. I never do wrong without a cause. Every day I am thinking, how am I to talk to you to make you believe what I say; and, I think, too, that you are thinking of what you are to say to me. There is one God looking down on us all. We are all children of the one God. God is listening to me. The sun, the darkness, the winds, are all listening to what we now say.

To prove to you that I am telling you the truth, remember I sent you word that I would come from a place far away to speak to you here, and you see us now. Some have come on horseback and some on foot. If I were thinking bad, or if I had done bad, I would never have come here. If it had been my fault, would I have come so far to talk to you! . . . I am glad to see Ka-e-a-tena. I was afraid I should never see him again. That was one reason, too, why I left. I wish that Ka-e-a-tena would be returned to us to live with his family. . . . Now I believe that all told me is true, because I see Ka-e-a-tena again . . . as I was told I should.

※※※※※※※※※※※※※※※

Thus he finished his apologia. Crook bluntly told him he was lying. It would have required more objective reasoning than even this high-minded soldier possessed at the time to see that his wild adversary, from his own standpoint, spoke the truth. Geronimo had promised to live at peace on the reservation; he had broken his promise and had gone out and killed innocent people; therefore, his word was not to be trusted. A dialogue followed, with charges and recriminations between the two.

Geronimo began, "I want to ask who it was that ordered that I should be arrested." Crook answered, "That's all bosh. There were no orders for any one to arrest you." Geronimo suggested that perhaps the orders had come from somebody else, and he continued to seek the source of the plot against him. He appealed to Crook: "There is no other captain so great as you. I thought you ought to know about those stories, and who started them." When Crook still accused him of lying, he said, "If you think I am not telling the truth, then I don't think you came down here in good faith."

In this exchange there is some indication of the surrender terms Crook was considering. He ignored Geronimo's assumption that he could return to the reservation and start anew. "You must make up your own mind whether you will stay out on the warpath or surrender unconditionally. If you stay out, I'll keep after you and kill the last one, if it takes fifty years." Then the general's mind passed immediately to Kaahteney and to the beneficial effect of his punishment. He accused Geronimo of insincerity in expressing relief at seeing Kaahteney unharmed and well, reminding him that "over a year ago I asked you if you wanted me to bring Ka-e-a-tena back but you said no." (This had occurred before Geronimo had become suspicious; now he was truly reassured to see that Kaahteney had not been harmed.)

Crook then tried by cross-questioning to show that Geronimo had frightened the other Indians into leaving the reservation. He asked which ones had been threatened. Geronimo said that all of them were, and "If you don't want to believe me I can prove it by all the men, women, and children of the White Mountain Apaches." Crook then pinned him down to: "They wanted to seize me and Magnus."

"Then why did Natches and Chihuahua go out?" Crook asked.

"Because they were afraid the same thing would happen to them," answered Geronimo.

"Who made them afraid?" Crook persisted, and he wanted to know what Geronimo told them.

"The only thing I told them was that I heard I was going to be seized and killed, that's all," was Geronimo's answer.

Crook next tried to establish the validity of Davis' account of the breakout. He asked why Geronimo had sent some of his people to kill Davis and Chatto. Geronimo denied sending them and offered evidence; if it were true, "these Indians [Naiche, Chihuahua, and Kutli, who were present at the council] would say so." Crook continued: ". . . and you reported that they were killed and that is the reason so many went out with you." Geronimo then referred to the White Mountain Indians present (scouts, in general unfriendly to the hostile band), who would establish his innocence. Finally, he said, "Well, here is a White Mountain sergeant, a man like that won't lie; ask him." Crook ignored these prospective witnesses; he and Davis had got the story from members of the band at Fort Apache, and he was convinced.

Geronimo made one last attempt at justification. "Whenever I wanted to talk with Lieutenant Davis, I spoke by day or by night. I never went to him in a hidden manner. May be some of these men know about it. Perhaps you had better ask them." Crook's reply was to close the conference: "I have said all I have to say. You had better think it over to-night and let me know in the morning."

"All right, we'll talk to-morrow," said Geronimo; "I may want to *ask* you some questions, too, as you have asked me some."

But there was no "talk to-morrow" with Crook. The leaders spent the day in their volcanic fastness in serious discussion. Kaahteney and Alchise circulated among them breaking down their resistance. A few messages passed back and forth between them and Crook. The general had been instructed to insist upon unconditional surrender, but he had been given some latitude, which he interpreted to mean that he should obtain the best terms he could. The Indians at first would consider only a return to the reservation, but the time had passed for such easy forgiveness. Remembering Kaahteney, Crook finally stipulated that all the warriors except the supposedly senile Nana should be imprisoned in the East for not more than two years with such members of their families as might choose to accompany them. No doubt he had old Fort Marion at Saint Augustine in mind; seventy-two hostile warriors of the South Plains had been sent there as prisoners eleven years before and had come back willing to observe the peace.

Chihuahua was the first to break, but Crook left him in the camp so that he might influence the others. Geronimo was the last holdout. Crook's emissaries feared even to mention surrender to him. Finally, after much agonizing, the same four leaders came to Crook at about noon on March 27 and said they "wanted to talk." As Bourke told it, Nana "toddled after them, but he was so old and feeble that we did not count him." Again they sat down under the sycamores.

Chihuahua spoke first. His submission was complete: "I am anxious to behave. . . . I surrender myself to you because I believe in you and you do not deceive us." And he gave Crook some of the fulsome compliments that formed the ultimate expression of Apache good will: "You must be our God. . . . You must be the one who makes the green pastures, who sends the rain, who commands the winds. You must be the one who sends the fresh fruits that appear on the trees every year. . . . Everything you do is right." He asked only that "you send my family with me wherever you send me. . . . I ask you to find out if they are willing to go or not." (Through all the years of their subsequent imprisonment, Chihuahua seemed to grieve the most of any of the band about the separation from his children.) Naiche spoke next, expressing the same submission: "When I was free I gave orders, but now I surrender to you. . . . You now order and I obey. . . . Now that I have surrendered I am glad. I'll not have to hide behind rocks and mountains; I'll go across the open plain. . . . There may be lots of men who have bad feelings against us. I will go wherever you may see fit to send us, where no bad talk will be spoken of us. . . . I surrender to you, and hope you will be kind to us. . . ."

Then Geronimo spoke. He had finally concluded to trust Crook, but he was more restrained than were his associates. "Two or three words are enough," he began. "We are all comrades, all one family, all one band. What the others say I say also. . . . Once I moved about like the wind. Now I surrender to you and that is all. [Shakes hands with General Crook.]²⁴ . . . My heart is yours, and I hope yours will be mine. . . . Whatever you tell me is true. We are all satisfied of that. I hope the day may come when my word shall be as strong with you as yours is with me. That's all I have to say now, except a few words. I should like to have my wife and daughter come to meet me at Fort Bowie or Silver Creek."

Geronimo had two wives and two daughters in army captivity. Probably he was referring to Zi-yeh, with her baby, and his grown daughter, Dohn-say, who had been captured by Wirt Davis' scouts the previous August and whom he still believed to be in the vicinity of Fort Apache. Crook promised that the meeting would occur and advised Geronimo to pay no more attention to unfriendly talk. "There are some people who can no more control their talk than the wind can." (Crook knew what it meant to be abused by a violent population and a frontier press.)

Geronimo then called on Alchise and Kaahteney "to speak a few words. They have come a long way and I want to hear them speak." Kaahteney pleaded a sore throat, but Alchise, secure in Crook's favor, made an earnest appeal on behalf of the hostiles: "They have surrendered. I don't want you to have any bad feelings towards them. They are all good friends now . . . because they are all the same people—all one family with me; just like when you kill a deer, all its parts are of the one body. . . . No matter where you send [them] we hope to hear that you have treated them kindly. . . . I have never told you a lie, nor have you ever told me a lie, and now I tell you that [they] really want to do what is right

---

²⁴ Brackets in original.

and live at peace. . . . I want you to carry away in your pocket all that has been said here to-day."

Crook told them that he would go on ahead to Fort Bowie and that they would follow with Maus and the scouts. Chihuahua promised to send on word to him every day. Crook said, "All right. Ka-e-a-tena can write your letters for you."[25] The next morning he set out early to telegraph the goods news to Washington.[26]

The Apache wars were ended. Or were they?

[25] The transcript of the conference is printed in *Senate Exec. Doc. 88*, 51 Cong., 1 sess., pp. 11–17. It may also be found in Davis, *op. cit.*, pp. 200–212. Bourke's account is in *On the Border with Crook*, pp. 472–79; Crook's report is in Secretary of War, *Annual Report*, 1886, p. 153.

[26] The telegram is on pp. 2–3 of the Senate document and on pp. 199–200 of Davis, *op. cit.*

CHAPTER 14

GERONIMO BRINGS DISASTER
TO HIS PEOPLE

The night after the surrender, the scarcely tamed hostiles went on a drunken debauch. They had obtained the makings from a bootlegger named Tribolett, who operated just on the Mexican side of the border. All through the night Maus heard the sound of shots being fired in their camp. The next morning before daylight Alchise and Kaahteney, apparently sent by Chihuahua, awakened Crook with the news that Naiche was lying on the ground unable to stand and that others were in nearly the same state. They asked permission to take a squad of scouts and guard the bootlegger. But the mischief was already done. It was worse than bootlegging.

Tribolett apparently belonged to that class of scoundrels who profited from the Apache wars and intrigued to foment them. The wars brought not only army contracts, but also the shadier business of smuggling and trading with the raiders for their stolen livestock and other plunder. He was probably well known to the hostiles and trusted by them. Now he convinced the ever suspicious Geronimo that plans had been made to hang him as soon as he should cross the border. He may have been in the pay of profiteers at Tucson known collectively as the "Indian ring."[1] As Crook once

[1] This is the conclusion expressed by Thrapp in *Conquest of Apacheria*, pp. 346–47.

said, "With them, peace kills the goose that lays the golden egg." Unaware of this sinister influence working among the surrendered hostiles, Crook set out that morning for Fort Bowie, leaving Maus to bring them in. Their intoxication was apparent. Near their camp, as he passed it, were saddled mules wandering around without riders, while Geronimo, Kutli, and three other warriors were grouped on two of the other animals—"all drunk as lords," in Bourke's words.[2]

Maus waited for the band to move, but they were slow about starting and traveled only a short distance that day, still watchful and keeping scattered in small groups. Geronimo advised Maus to go on with the scouts or he would not be responsible for his life. When they camped, the officer "went into their camp and found trouble. Natchez had shot his wife, and they were all drinking heavily." During that night, March 28, Maus heard a few shots fired, and the next morning he learned that Geronimo and Naiche, with twenty men, fourteen women, and six children, had slipped away in the night, taking only two horses and one mule from their herd, "and not a soul as far as I could ascertain, knew anything of the time they had gone, or that they intended to go."

The small band that broke away was made up largely of family groups. With Geronimo were his son Chappo and Chappo's young wife; three second cousins, including his "brothers" Perico and Fun; his brother-in-law Yahnozha; and his orphaned nephew, Kanseah. With Naiche were his wife Ha-o-zinne and several of her relatives: her parents, her half-brother, and her first cousin. Thus, eight of the twenty warriors, not counting the youth Kanseah, were related to the two leaders. Many of them were in their teens or early twenties.[3]

This time nobody could accuse Geronimo of starting a mass stampede. Secret plans for the flight must have been made during the day of March 28, for it was at that time that Naiche shot his wife, E-clah-heh. Present-day Apaches remember the incident well

---

2 *On the Border with Crook*, p. 480.
3 For names and descriptions of members of the band, see *infra*, pp. 304–306.

in their traditions. E-clah-heh, as was often the case with the women, dreaded the hard life of the hostiles. She started running to join the soldiers, and Naiche thereupon shot her to prevent a general defection. (His intoxicated state probably contributed to his action.) She was wounded in the leg. Thus unable to travel, she, with her young daughter, afterwards known as Dorothy, remained behind. She was a great-granddaughter of Mahko, hence a second cousin of Geronimo and a first cousin ("sister") of Fun and Betzinez.

Maus detailed an officer and some of his scouts to escort the main body of surrendered hostiles to Fort Bowie. These included the leaders Chihuahua, Jolsanny, Nana, and Kutli. With his remaining scouts he followed the trail of the fugitives some distance into the Mexican mountains, but he never came in sight of them. On his return he was joined by two of the runaway warriors. They had heard people leaving during the night, and, supposing something was wrong, had gone along. In the morning, when they understood the situation, they had turned back.[4]

Years later, at Fort Sill, Geronimo gave a concise account of the breakaway. He told how "with all our tribe" he started to go "back to the United States, but I feared treachery and decided to remain in Mexico. We were not under any guard at this time. The United States troops [mainly scouts] marched in front and the Indians followed, and when we became suspicious, we turned back. I do not know how far the United States army went after myself, and some warriors turned back before we were missed, and I do not care." He was still convinced of Crook's treachery. Probably his trust in Tribolett was based on a long experience of profitable transactions in stolen goods and mescal sales. He told of the argument between himself and Crook at the conference and his final decision to accept Crook's denial of any intention to arrest him. But—"It was hard for me to believe him at that time.

---

[4] For the incidents of the breakaway, see Bourke, *op. cit.*, pp. 480–81, and Maus in Miles, *Personal Recollections*, pp. 468–70. Crook's summary is in Secretary of War, *Annual Report*, 1886, p. 154. A brief biography of E-clah-heh is in Griswold, "The Fort Sill Apaches," s.v. "E-clah-heh."

Now I know that what he said was untrue, and I firmly believe that he did issue the orders for me to be put in prison, or to be killed in case I offered resistance." He was convinced that Crook's death, which occurred four years after the surrender conference, "was sent by the Almighty as a punishment for the many evil deeds he committed."[5]

In after years, the more conciliatory Naiche also told the story of the flight. On January 2, 1890, Crook came to interview the prisoners, who were then held at Mount Vernon Barracks, Alabama. "How did you come to leave that night?" he asked. "I was afraid I was going to be taken off somewhere I didn't like," Naiche answered, "to some place I didn't know. I thought all who were taken away would die. Since then I have found out different. . . . Nobody said anything to me that night; I worked it out in my own mind."

"Didn't the Indians talk about [it] among themselves?" asked the general.

"We talked to each other about it," said Naiche. "We were drunk."

"Why did you get drunk?" inquired the general.

"Because there was a lot of whisky there and we wanted a drink, and took it," was the chief's logical answer. Then he went on, "The other[s] didn't want to go out. I don't know why the others didn't know of it; I thought they all did."[6]

Meanwhile, on that same March 29 Crook reached Fort Bowie and sent out his telegram telling of the hostiles' surrender and stating the terms. Sheridan answered the following day. Citing the highest authority—President Cleveland—he rejected these conditions, instructing the general "to enter into negotiations on the terms of their unconditional surrender, only sparing their lives." He should prevent their escape and "insure against further hostilities by completing [their] destruction, unless these terms are

5 Barrett, *Geronimo's Story of His Life*, pp. 137–40. See also pp. 135–36 regarding his flight from the reservation to escape Crook's designs against his life. It required two footnotes for Barrett to disclaim responsibility for these "exact words of Geronimo."
6 *Senate Exec. Doc. 35*, 51 Cong., 1 sess., p. 33.

267

acceded to." These instructions were, of course, impossible to follow. Sheridan was thousands of miles removed from the conditions of Apache fighting. Crook, for once departing from his aboveboard method of dealing with Indians, decided to conceal from the hostiles the rejection of the surrender terms. The certainty that they would all scatter to the mountains was too appalling.

A courier from Maus informed the general on the same day, March 30, of the flight of Geronimo and Naiche with their small party. He relayed the bad news to Sheridan, and Sheridan replied in an angry telegram, blaming him for laxity. Crook tried to explain; then, failing, he asked to be relieved of his command. On April 2 Sheridan ordered his transfer to command the Department of the Platte and directed Brigadier General Nelson A. Miles to succeed him in Arizona. The next day he ordered Crook to ship the prisoners to Fort Marion "under the terms directed by the President in my telegram of March 30." Two days later he found an excuse for the breach of faith. The settlement had been rejected by both parties— "The present terms not having been agreed to here, and Geronimo having broken every condition of surrender, the Indians now in custody are to be held as prisoners and sent to Fort Marion without reference to previous communications and without in any way consulting their wishes in the matter."[7]

Crook disarmed these new prisoners and conducted them and the prisoners taken previously to Bowie Station on the railroad a few miles north of the post. They numbered seventy-seven— fifteen men, thirty-three women, and twenty-nine children. Among them were two wives and three children of Geronimo then in army hands; two wives, two children, the mother, and other relatives of Naiche; and families or relatives of all the other warriors who remained at large. They reached Fort Marion on April 13.[8]

Miles came to relieve Crook on April 12. He was an experienced

---

[7] These telegrams are in *Senate Exec. Doc. 88*, 51 Cong., 1 sess., pp. 2–10; they were also published by Miles in *Personal Recollections*, pp. 471–75.
[8] Secretary of War, *Annual Report*, 1886, pp. 49, 154–55.

Indian fighter, but was given to glorifying his exploits; he lacked Crook's quiet dedication, his understanding of the Apaches, and—most important of all—his integrity. Crook had said he could not use more than three thousand regular soldiers to advantage.[9] Miles acquired five thousand, one-fourth of the entire army, in his campaign against eighteen warriors with Geronimo and Naiche and a smaller party with Mangus. Rejecting Crook's reliance on Apache scouts, he discharged all of them except a few he used as trailers. First he tried cavalry. When the horses proved unable to climb the mountains, he dismounted his troopers. But only a few of them could stand up to the hardships accepted as a matter of course by Apache women and children. He set up heliograph stations to flash messages from mountain to mountain, a system of communication the Apaches had long been using, having shifted from smoke signals to mirrors.

In his *Personal Recollections*, which covered his whole lifetime, Miles devoted one-sixth of his space to the Apaches, one-tenth (fifty-six pages) to his own military campaign against them. In his account the campaign was a series of difficult pursuits, occasional encounters, heroic exploits—and complete failure. To do him justice, it may be noted that if the enemy had been more numerous he might have had better success in finding them. Mangus remained out of sight. Naiche and Geronimo first struck at points in Sonora, then on April 27 they entered the United States and raided at will, even around Fort Apache and San Carlos. Characteristically, Miles reported this raid as a victory for the army: "They have killed but fourteen persons in the Territories of the United States, the last one June 5, and were on our soil but twenty-three days before they were driven out." On the other side of the border they killed even more Mexicans.[10]

Later, at Fort Sill, Geronimo gave his version of this raid. Pursued by American and Mexican soldiers,

---

9 *Ibid.*, p. 8.
10 For Miles's official report, see *ibid.*, pp. 164–76; for his evaluation of Geronimo's raid across the border, see *Senate Exec. Doc. 83*, 51 Cong., 1 sess., p. 10.

〰〰〰〰〰〰〰〰〰〰〰〰〰〰〰

we finally decided to break up into small bands. With six men and four women I made for the range of mountains near Hot Springs [Warm Springs], New Mexico. . . . We ranged in the mountains of New Mexico for some time, then thinking that perhaps the troops had left Mexico, we returned. On our return through Old Mexico we attacked every Mexican found, even if for no other reason than to kill. We believed that they had asked the United States troops to come down to Mexico to fight us.

. . . We were reckless of our lives, because we felt that every man's hand was against us. If we returned to the reservation we would be put in prison and killed; if we stayed in Mexico they would continue to send soldiers to fight us; so we gave no quarter to anyone and asked no favors.[11]

〰〰〰〰〰〰〰〰〰〰〰〰〰〰〰

There is no doubt that Geronimo killed Mexicans wantonly because he liked to see them die, but the killings on the American side of the border were a necessary part of raiding. The raiders killed to obtain supplies, and they killed every person they met to prevent his reporting their presence. In his 1890 interview Crook asked Naiche why they killed people, and the chief answered: "Because we were afraid. It was war. Anybody who saw us would kill us, and we did the same thing. We had to if we wanted to live."[12]

And as far as the American army was concerned, they continued to live. They did lose one warrior by desertion, a man named Massai, who was destined to become famous in Western legend.[13] They lost another through Mexican treachery. A courier from the officials at Casas Grandes brought the news to Britton Davis, who had resigned from the army to manage a ranching and mining enterprise at the nearby hacienda of Corralitos. According

---

[11] Barrett, *op. cit.*, pp. 140–41.

[12] *Senate Exec. Doc. 35*, 51 Cong., 1 sess., p. 33.

[13] Betzinez, *I Fought with Geronimo*, pp. 143–44; Secretary of War, *Annual Report*, 1886, p. 168; Davis, *The Truth about Geronimo*, pp. 220, 222. According to Davis, the deserter was Kayihtah, and Miles so implied, but this is certainly a mistake. Betzinez knew Massai well, and there is no indication that Kayihtah was ever with the war party.

to this report, the hostiles had sent three men to transact some of their periodic business there, and the Mexicans "stood them up before an adobe wall, and made 'good injun' of them." Two must have escaped, for only one was killed.[14]

But Miles, for all his efforts, did not kill or capture a single hostile. He finally decided to proceed against some Apaches he could catch—about four hundred of them who had remained at peace on the reservation, making a start at farming, accumulating livestock, cutting hay to sell at the post, and serving the army as scouts against the hostiles. But they were hated by the white citizens of Arizona—to whom all Apaches looked alike—and disliked by the other tribes on the reservation. On July 3 Miles suggested to Sheridan that they should be removed and located elsewhere. This policy had been frequently advocated by both the War and Interior departments (in unaccustomed accord),[15] but with bureaucratic insensitivity none of the officials had ever given a thought about where these displaced people should be settled. Crook had objected to their removal, and at first Sheridan also opposed it, citing the disastrous Victorio wars resulting from the uprooting of the Warm Springs band. But now, upon the recommendation of Miles, it became the official policy.[16]

One cannot resist the suspicion that, failing to apprehend the eighteen hostiles with their women and children, Miles needed some "captives" to show. Naturally, he advanced a different reason. He had made "a very careful examination into the condition of the Chiricahua and Warm Springs Apaches . . . and a more turbulent and dissipated body of Indians I have never met." *Tizwin* drinks with "riots and bloodshed" were frequent, "and the stillness of the nights was often broken by the discharge of rifles and pistols in their savage orgies. The indolent and vicious young men and boys were just the material to furnish warriors for the future." He

---

14 Davis, *op. cit.*, pp. 194, 218. Other reports mention the death of only one hostile, and the loss of three cannot be reconciled with the known number remaining in the band.

15 See, for example, Secretary of War, *Annual Report*, 1882, p. 186; 1886, pp. 6–7.

16 *Senate Exec. Doc. 83*, 51 Cong., 1 sess., pp. 2–3.

asserted that the band "had been in communication with the hostiles, and some of them had been plotting an extensive outbreak."[17] Nevertheless, Miles, in spite of his faults, had humane intentions. Seven years before he had any experience with the Apaches he had denounced as "cruel" the removal of hardy, mountain Indians to a warm, malarial climate.[18] Now he pointed out that the prisoners recently sent to Florida "would in a short time most likely die" because of the low altitude if left there. Therefore, the two bands should be relocated on a new reservation. There, they should be started in farming and stock raising, and "most of their children [should be] scattered through the industrial Indian schools." He had a place picked out for them near the Wichita Mountains in the Indian Territory where they would find a healthful climate and fertile soil.

This plan would have placed them in the vicinity of Fort Sill on the reservation owned by the Comanches, Kiowas, and a small tribe closely connected with the Kiowas which bore the misleading name Apaches. Miles had conducted military operations against these South Plains tribes, but he had never learned anything about them. The Comanches were long-time enemies of the real Apaches of the Southwest, and their Kiowa allies shared this hostility. And although the Kiowa-Apaches had a distant linguistic relationship with the true Apaches, they had come down from the north with the Kiowas and had no tradition of any connection with the Southwestern bands. Miles assumed that the two tribes were an identical people and would accept each other as relatives. Nothing could have been more unrealistic.

There was, however, some available land in other parts of the Indian Territory, which comprised all of present Oklahoma except the Panhandle. Although many tribes of Indians driven from their homelands before the advancing frontier had been placed on reservations there, a considerable area remained unassigned. But people of the adjoining states, especially the Kansans, constantly

---

[17] Secretary of War, *Annual Report*, 1886, pp. 170–71.
[18] Nelson A. Miles, *Serving the Republic*, p. 204.

intrigued to have it opened to white settlement; hence, they opposed any addition to the Indian population. In 1879 Congress, at their urging, had adopted an amendment to the Indian Appropriation Bill prohibiting the location there of Apaches or other Indians from New Mexico or Arizona.[19] The administration informed Miles that it would be "impossible" to have this prohibition repealed. He then suggested the present Oklahoma Panhandle, a High Plains tract cut off from Texas by the Compromise of 1850 and left out in forming subsequent state boundaries. This was clearly impracticable. The level, treeless grassland lacked all the resources required for Apache self-sufficiency. (Even for the white man its agricultural productiveness had to wait until the development of large-scale mechanized wheat farming.)

But even with no place in sight to replant them, Miles continued his plans for uprooting the Apaches. Believing that "their consent would be advisable and desirable," he selected ten of their leaders to go to Washington to negotiate the removal. Chatto headed the delegation. Among the other members were Kaahteney, Loco, and a dependable scout named Noche, and three of their women accompanied them. Miles placed Captain Joseph H. Dorst in charge. He wanted them to be shown the Indian Territory as a home site, and they left with that expectation. The administration vetoed this suggestion, but permitted them to go on to Washington.[20] There, they stood as a unit against removal.

Chatto was the spokesman. His appeal to Secretary of War William C. Endicott at a conference held on July 26 reveals the deep currents of Apache feeling. His words, translated first into Spanish and then into English by Concepcion, Mickey Free, and Sam Bowman, were presented in the third person. Captain Bourke, who was in Washington working on ethnological studies for the

---

19 U.S. *Statutes at Large*, XX, 313, February 17, 1879. This was a compromise. The land seekers had tried to close the area against *all* further Indian relocations. They argued that the Indians would attack the settlements in the surrounding states, but their real motivation appears in the debates. See *Congressional Record*, VIII, 311 ff.

20 *Senate Exec. Doc. 35*, 51 Cong., 1 sess., pp. 35, 36, 41, 44, 48; *83*, pp. 4–5, 8, 10, 13; Secretary of War, *Annual Report*, 1886, p. 14.

Chatto at Washington, July, 1886. The picture was by a Smithsonian Institution photographer. "He came here to ask for his country; to ask for his land, where he lives now; to ask that is why he has traveled so far." Courtesy U.S. Army Artillery and Missile Center Museum.

government, [21] was present to assist in the interpretation. Chatto told Endicott:

〰〰〰〰〰〰〰〰〰〰〰〰〰

What he came to look here for was good words, good advice—he is looking for the words as if God is speaking. He has come, too, because he wants to take a paper with him, so as to remember the words that have been told him here. . . .

He came here to ask for his country; to ask for his land, where he lives now; to ask that is why he has traveled so far. At Camp Apache what he plants grows up very well; the water that runs there is very good; that is why he wants to stay there. . . .

The favor he wants to ask of you, is to ask for his land as if he was asking a favor from God, and he hopes that you won't forget his words. It is to him . . . as if God had said that he and you had come together to exchange words; and he thinks now that God is listening to what he says.

〰〰〰〰〰〰〰〰〰〰〰〰〰

Then he went on to speak of his personal problem, of his family in Mexican slavery: "You may have some children. Everybody loves his son, loves him dearly; holds him in his arms and to his heart. . . .

"He says he has a wife and two children in Chihuahua; that Captain Bourke knows it; that he has seen their pictures over there; and he asks . . . that these children may be given back into his hands, so he can take them to his heart again, and have them with him at Camp Apache. He has feelings just like white people, and for that reason he wants to have his people once more with him. He can not make big houses like this, but can only take small sticks and make a house; but still, even if his hands ache, he wants to live that way."

Bourke explained Chatto's meaning: "In speaking of his house, Chato means that no matter how poor a man is, his home, when it is the best he can offer, is the place for his wife and children to be.

---

21 Bourke, *Apache Campaign*, pp. 6, 10–12.

"When he says I have seen their pictures, he is speaking of the photographs which were sent by the Mexican authorities to General Crook to induce Chato to believe that his wife and children were better off where they were in Chihuahua than they were on the reservation."

Chatto continued: "He says he has had his picture taken here [it had been taken by a Smithsonian photographer], . . . and he wants to have some of them sent to the man with whom his family is in Chihuahua. . . . He wants to have his name, Chato, put on the picture, so that his wife will know."

Endicott promised to give him some copies to send, and Bourke explained that the best way to accomplish this was to send them to Crook for forwarding. He said that Crook had been in correspondence with persons in Chihuahua and knew exactly where Chatto's people were.[22] But if this was done, the appeal was futile. Chatto was never to see his wife and children again.

The secretary gave Chatto the "paper" he had requested, a simple statement that he had been in Washington. He also gave him a silver medal. To the delegates this meant that their mission to save their homeland had succeeded. It was far otherwise. Throughout the month of August the telegraph wires between Washington and Arizona were clogged with conflicting orders to prevent the return of the delegates lest they complicate the scheme for removing their people. They were taken first to Carlisle to visit their young relatives (including Loco's son) in school there, and then on their way west they were detained at Fort Leavenworth, Kansas.[23]

Miles, hoping to succeed where Washington had failed in obtaining their consent to removal, entrusted his plan to Dorst, who was still in charge of the delegation at Fort Leavenworth. First, the Indians were told that the white citizens of Arizona and New Mexico were demanding their removal and that the civil authorities were ready to proceed against them for murders they had

22 *Senate Exec. Doc. 35*, 51 Cong., 1 sess., pp. 41–43.
23 *Ibid.*, *83*, pp. 10–26.

committed in past raids. Dorst then presented a draft agreement granting them a reservation of six hundred square miles where they would be reunited with the Fort Marion prisoners and possibly with the still hostile bands of Geronimo and Mangus. Each family would receive six hundred dollars' worth of farm equipment and domestic animals, and fifteen of their leaders would be paid salaries varying from twenty to fifty dollars a month, besides being given "comfortable abodes" and other "valuables." If they would accept these terms, and if the government should ratify them, they would become "*treaty Indians*" living on this reservation; otherwise, they would be treated as prisoners of war. All ten members of the delegation thereupon "touched the pen," and an army officer witnessed their signatures.

Later, President Cleveland asked Dorst "why General Miles wished to give the chiefs and head men money for moving. I replied that it was because it had been the policy of the Government in other cases to purchase the influence of such men." Probably the proposed bribe *was* a consideration in obtaining the consent of the delegates, but it was not the determining one. Chatto, Kaahteney, and Noche talked to Crook freely about it in 1890. "We thought it was good to get $20 to $50 a month," said Chatto. But it is clear that fear of Arizona vengeance and the attractive features of the mythical reservation described by Dorst caused them to agree to the removal.[24]

Throughout the blizzard of telegrams Miles tried to bring them back to influence their people,[25] but Washington was adamant. And no consideration was ever given to the draft agreement they had signed. With the Indian Territory closed against them, there was no other such tract of land available. Miles had suggested that until a homesite should be found for the displaced band, they should be kept on the military reservation at Fort Riley, Kansas, a healthful region of smooth, grass-covered hills. This proposal also received no consideration, and one can imagine the violent objec-

---

24 *Ibid.*, *35*, pp. 34–36, 48–50; *83*, p. 17.
25 See especially *ibid.*, *35*, p. 48.

277

tions of the Kansans against having these supposedly dangerous people set down in their midst. The administration decided on Fort Marion as "the place of confinement" for these additional "prisoners of war." This ancient defensive work, built by the Spaniards as the Castillo de San Marcos, was a subpost of Saint Francis Barracks at Saint Augustine. The War Department wired Lieutenant Colonel Loomis L. Langdon, the commanding officer of the small garrison there, asking if he could accommodate four or five hundred more prisoners. He replied that he could take seventy-five, but he recommended against sending any.[26]

Langdon explained more fully by letter, incidentally revealing the conditions under which his prisoners lived. The small parade ground inside the old fort, he said, was surrounded by walls in which were casemates once occupied by the garrison, but the terreplein above had become so dilapidated that water leaked down into them, rendering them uninhabitable. Therefore, he had pitched tents—eighteen in all—on the terreplein to shelter the prisoners. He could put up twenty more tents to take possibly eighty additional persons, "but the sanitary conditions will be bad." The small military reserve was so closely surrounded by the town that it was impracticable to quarter any of them outside. He warned against the assumption that a camp could be built on the beach or on nearby Anastasia Island. Both these places "are liable to overflow every fall and winter," and "besides the danger of getting drowned" the prisoners would "have to face the diseases peculiar to the low grounds of such localities." He suggested sending the ones he had to the military reservation at Carlisle so that their children might attend school there. Then he could prepare for the new arrivals, possibly accommodating two hundred. Sheridan's endorsement on this letter reads: "The conditions stated by Col. Langdon need not interfere with sending the remainder of the Chiricahua and Warm Spring Indians to Fort Marion."[27]

[26] *Ibid., 83*, pp. 17–18.
[27] National Archives and Records Service, Consolidated File 1066 AGO 1884, telegrams August 21 and letter August 23, 1886.

Sheridan probably did not know that Langdon's humanitarian protest was being reinforced by a commercial one in favor of Fort Pickens near Pensacola. An article in the *Pensacolian* of September 18 told of the expected arrival of "all of the Apaches of Geronimo's tribe" to the state, pointed out the lack of facilities at Fort Marion, and went on to indicate the efforts made by ambitious city builders to secure the prisoners for the local tourist business: "A move has been set on foot to have some of these red devils sent down to this place and incarcerated at Fort Pickens. Congressman Davidson has been consulted and he has sent a strong recommendation in favor of the scheme to the proper authorities in Washington. If Bob succeeds in this he can point with pride as having been instrumental in giving Pensacola an attraction which will bring here a great many visitors."[28] In their wars the Apaches had been an asset to the economy of Arizona through army contracts; now they were eagerly sought to bring prosperity to Florida.

There is no indication that the Pensacola bid was considered by the administration. The only problem was to plan the removal of the Indians cautiously lest they take to the mountains. Then on September 12 the order went out that the delegation detained at Fort Leavenworth should also be sent to Fort Marion "for confinement with other Indian prisoners now there."[29]

Thus, peaceable people living quietly on their reservation, tending their little farms and striving in all ways to conform to government policy were changed by bureaucratic semantics into "prisoners" to be "confined." But as long as they remained unsuspecting, they could be induced to assist the government. During those same early days in July when Miles was advising Sheridan to remove them, he called their leaders together at Fort Apache and enlisted Kayihtah and his cousin and close associate, a Nednai named Martine, to take a message to the hostiles with Geronimo and Naiche to induce them to surrender. Probably it was at this time that Miles chose his Washington delegation. It seems clear that

---

28 *Pensacolian*, September 18, 1886.
29 *Senate Exec. Doc. 117*, 49 Cong., 2 sess., p. 73.

Noche advised him in selecting the messengers to the hostiles,[30] believing that only these two men could approach Geronimo and live. Kayihtah's cousin, Yahnozha, was known to be in Geronimo's band, and Martine had been in training with Geronimo's close friend, Juh.[31]

Miles placed Lieutenant Gatewood in charge, with authority to call upon any officer for a military escort. Gatewood did not share Bourke's and Davis' liking for the Apaches or their confidence in the scouts, but the Indians knew and trusted him as a man of integrity. He had even learned to speak their language, but as interpreter he took along George Wratten, who, as a young boy, had worked as a clerk at a trading post on the reservation and had acquired greater fluency.[32] (Wratten was destined to remain with the Apaches for many years.) A packer and a courier completed the party.[33]

This mission was the real test of Miles's policy. It had been easy to plot against the peaceable Indians on the reservation and to hold the trusting Washington delegation in captivity, but the only hope of ending the war rested on the shoulders of one army lieutenant and two Apaches who had volunteered to help.

[30] Conflicting stories are told of their enlistment and of the rewards promised them. Betzinez, *op. cit.*, pp. 135–36; Opler, "A Chiricahua Apache's Account," pp. 371–73; and Ora E. Musgrove, "A Belated Reward for the Surrender of Geronimo," from National Archives and Records Service, statements by Noche, Kayihtah, and Martine at Fort Sill, May 2, 1911. See also Lockwood, *The Apache Indians*, p. 329, and Thrapp, *Conquest of Apacheria*, p. 364.

[31] Statements by Kayihtah, Martine, and Daklugie furnished me by Eve Ball.

[32] James Kaywaykla, Benedict Jozhe, and Moses Loco, interview, July 29, 1959.

[33] Charles B. Gatewood, "An Account of the Surrender of Geronimo," manuscript in Gatewood Collection, Arizona Pioneers' Historical Society, Tucson.

CHAPTER 15

"THIS IS THE FOURTH TIME
I HAVE SURRENDERED"

Mounted on mules, and with a three-mule pack train, Gatewood's little party crossed the border into Mexico.[1] They joined the command of Captain Henry W. Lawton, who had been combing the mountains in the Aros River vicinity far to the south in a futile attempt to find the hostiles. Then came word that Geronimo had put out peace feelers to the Mexican officials at Fronteras, only thirty miles from the border. By this time it was the middle of August. The entire command moved north by forced marches, Gatewood's little party with an escort of six men arriving first. There he learned that two of the hostiles' women—one of them is said to have been Geronimo's trusted envoy, Tah-das-te[2]—had recently come there with overtures of surrender. They had been permitted to trade and had left with three extra ponies laden with food and mescal.

1 Gatewood, "Account of the Surrender of Geronimo," p. 5. Here, and in the following pages, except where I have indicated otherwise, I am following Gatewood's narrative. Although it was not written until 1895, it is painstakingly accurate, and it is supported by a statement made by George Wratten at Washington, March 5, 1905 (S. M. Huddleson, "An Interview with Geronimo and His Guardian, Mr. G. M. Wratton").
2 Statement by Kayihtah and Martine recorded by Asa Daklugie and furnished me by Eve Ball.

Neither side had been negotiating in good faith. Geronimo afterwards said he had had no intention of surrendering but had talked peace only to obtain supplies. The Mexicans, for their part, were concentrating soldiers in the town, intending to lure the Apaches there and massacre the whole party.[3] The municipal president insisted that Gatewood should not follow the women. The lieutenant accordingly started south, ostensibly to join Lawton, then circled north and struck their trail. He followed them for three days into the mountains, "with a piece of flour sack to the fore as a white flag" carried "high on a century plant pole." But, as he said, "that doesn't make a man bullet proof." He camped in a canebrake on the Bavispe River. The next day—August 23—he sent the two Apache messengers to the hostiles, who "occupied an exceedingly rocky position high up in the Torres Mountains" about four miles away.[4]

As it happened, the half-grown Kanseah was on guard. Through his field glasses—with which the hostiles were abundantly supplied —he saw the two moving dots on the trail. He reported to Geronimo, Geronimo called his warriors, and they seated themselves in council. By this time Kanseah recognized Martine and Kayihtah, carrying a white flag. He told Geronimo who they were.

"It does not matter who they are. If they come closer they are to be shot," ordered Geronimo.

"They are our brothers," protested Yahnozha. "Let's find out why they come. They are brave men to risk this." When Geronimo argued, Yahnozha said, "We will not shoot. The first man who lifts a rifle I will kill."

"I will help you," said Fun.

Then Geronimo grunted, "Let them come."[5]

The envoys came in and delivered their message. Probably Kayihtah was the spokesman. "The troops are coming after you

<hr />

[3] Dan L. Thrapp, "Geronimo's Mysterious Surrender," *Brand Book*, Los Angeles Corrall, Vol. XIII (1969), reconciles the varying accounts in Mexican and American sources.
[4] Gatewood, *op. cit.*, pp. 5–8.
[5] Ball, *In the Days of Victorio*, pp. 185–87. Mrs. Ball got the story directly from Kanseah.

from all directions," he said. Their "aim is to kill every one of you if it takes fifty years." He reminded them that "everything is against you. . . . If you are awake at night and a rock rolls down the mountain or a stick breaks, you will be running. . . . You even eat your meals running. You have no friends whatever in the world." He innocently assumed that they could return to the reservation, and he described the happy situation there: "I get plenty to eat. I go wherever I want, talk to good people. I go to bed whenever I want and get all my sleep. I have nobody to fear. I have my little patch of corn. I'm trying to do what the white people want me to do. And there's no reason why you people shouldn't do it."[6]

They agreed, and Geronimo sent Martine back to Gatewood to ask for a conference, while Naiche sent the officer an additional message assuring him of safe-conduct. There was nothing but the honor of soldiers like Gatewood to assure safe-conduct to the hostiles. On that very day President Cleveland telegraphed the War Department: "I hope nothing will be done with Geronimo which will prevent our treating him as a prisoner of war, if we cannot hang him, which I would much prefer."[7]

Martine arrived at Gatewood's camp in the canebrake just before sundown, while Kayihtah remained that night in the hostiles' *rancheria*. Meanwhile, Gatewood had sent a courier back to Lawton, and Lawton's scouts had already reached his camp, while the rest of the command was not far behind. The next morning Gatewood, with the scouts, started for the hostile camp. They were met by three armed warriors with a message from Naiche that the scouts should turn back and that the officer should meet the hostiles at a designated bend of the river. Gatewood and his small party accordingly proceeded there, unsaddled their mules, and turned them out to graze. The hostiles came in a few at a time and turned out their own mounts. Geronimo was one of the last to arrive. He laid down his rifle and came over to shake hands with

---

6 Opler, "A Chiricahua Apache's Account," pp. 375–77. Opler's informant, Sam Kenoi, was not present, but his account seems accurate except for a spiteful charge of cowardice against Martine, which is plainly untrue.
7 *Senate Exec. Doc. 117*, 49 Cong., 2 sess., p. 4.

Gatewood. The lieutenant passed around tobacco, and soon all were smoking cigarettes rolled in the Apache way, in oak leaves. (Apaches did not use the peace pipe, but they valued tobacco and used it on ceremonial occasions or as a special luxury.[8])

Geronimo opened the council by announcing that the warriors had come to hear General Miles's message. Gatewood gave it to them straight: "Surrender, and you will be sent to join the rest of your friends in Florida, there to await the decision of the President as to your final disposition. Accept these terms or fight it out to the bitter end." All listened attentively, and a long silence fell upon the group. Then Geronimo passed a hand across his eyes, extended his arms, making his hands tremble, and asked for a drink. They had just been on a three days' drunk, he said, on the mescal the women had brought from Fronteras. "The Mexicans expected to play their usual trick of getting us drunk and killing us," he explained, "but we have had the fun." Their spree had passed off happily "without a single fight," but "now I feel a little shaky." Gatewood answered that he had brought no liquor. Geronimo then got down to business.

He said that he would leave the warpath only on the condition that the band could return to the reservation and live as before. Gatewood said that Miles's message was final. Geronimo then "narrated at length the history of their troubles," while Gatewood remained unimpressed. The warriors then "withdrew to one side in the cane brake, and held a private conference for an hour or so." When they returned, they all ate a noon meal, probably supplied by Gatewood's packer. After it, they resumed their places, and the council continued. Looking Gatewood square in the eye, Geronimo delivered his ultimatum, the result of their deliberation: "Take us to the reservation or fight." Surrounded as he was by armed enemies, the officer was decidedly uncomfortable, but Naiche, who had said very little so far, spoke up to assure him "that whether they continued the war or not," his party "would be allowed to depart in peace." Gatewood then informed the

8 Opler, *An Apache Life-Way*, pp. 441–43.

hostiles that they had no reservation to return to, that their people had been sent to join Chihuahua in Florida. This removal had not yet occurred, but Gatewood supposed that it had. The news was a real blow. The Apaches withdrew for another private council. After they reassembled, Geronimo announced that they would continue the war, but that they wanted to kill a beef and remain in conference through the night. The tired Gatewood had to consent, but to his relief they found no beef to kill.

Then, after some smoking and general conversation, Geronimo asked Gatewood what kind of man the new general was. He wanted to know his age and size, the color of his hair and eyes, whether his voice was harsh or agreeable. Did he talk much or little, and did he mean more or less than he said? Had he many friends among his own people, and did they generally credit his word? Did the soldiers and officers like him? Had he had experience with Indians? Would he keep his promises? They all listened intently to Gatewood's answers. Even at this distance of time and culture one can sense the desperate earnestness of the Indians and how much depended upon the quality of the man in whose hands they were asked to place their lives. Geronimo summed up their conclusions: "He must be a good man since the Great Father sent him from Washington, and he sent you all this distance to us."

Toward sunset Gatewood suggested that his party repair to the camp of Lawton, who had arrived that day (August 24), while the hostiles should continue their discussions. To this they agreed. Then Geronimo, out of their anguished indecision, made a strange appeal to the enemy soldier: "We want your advice. Consider yourself one of us and not a white man. Remember all that has been said today, and as an Apache, what would you advise us to do?"

"I would trust General Miles and take him at his word," Gatewood answered. At this, "They all stood around looking very solemn," as the lieutenant remembered it, "and no further reference was made to the matter, except Geronimo said he would let me know the result of their council in the morning." Only the future would reveal the extent to which Gatewood had unwittingly betrayed them.

Before he left, they asked him to go alone or with one man to the nearest army post to communicate with Miles in an attempt to gain a modification of his terms. They would send several of their warriors as a hidden escort to protect him from Mexicans or others. He told them that the general had made up his mind and would not change it. Then, "After shaking hands all around, we bade them a solemn good-bye and rode to Lawton's camp." On the way young Chappo overtook them, and after riding along for a mile or so, Gatewood asked him where he was going. "With you," he replied, "I'm going to sleep close to you to-night, and tomorrow I'll return to our camp," and he added, "I have my father's permission to do so." Gatewood, knowing the unfriendly attitude of the scouts toward Geronimo's band, feared that some of them would stick a knife in Chappo during the night, with fatal consequences to the mission. He explained his fear to Chappo, and the youth reluctantly returned. Later, Gatewood learned that his action had made a favorable impression on the hostiles.

The following morning in Lawton's camp, the scout pickets passed in a call for Bay-chen-daysen (Long Nose; that is, Gatewood). The lietutenant came out and met Geronimo and several of his warriors a short distance away. As he approached, they dismounted and unsaddled their ponies, and all but Geronimo, who wore a large pistol in front of his left hip, laid their arms on the saddles. He told Gatewood that they had decided on surrender.

Betzinez, who heard the story from his close relatives in the band, told of this final weakening. It was Perico who said, "I am going to surrender. My wife and children have been captured. I love them, and want to be with them." Then a second and a third of Geronimo's "brothers" expressed similar decisions. One of them, of course, was Fun. The other was Ahnandia, a second cousin of Geronimo by a different line of descent from Mahko. (His wife was Geronimo's messenger, Tah-das-te.)

At these defections "Geronimo stood for a few moments without speaking. At length he said slowly, 'I don't know what to do. I have been depending heavily on you three men. You have been great fighters in battle. If you are going to surrender, there is no use my going without you. I will give up with you.' "[9]

The deadly seriousness of the band was apparent throughout their conferences with Gatewood; they well knew that everything in their lives hung on the issue. And the deliberations of these eighteen wild warriors in a mountain hideout indicate the strength and stability of Apache institutions. There was the democratic manner of reaching decisions, and the influence, but never the despotic power, of their leaders. Every time Geronimo spoke to Gatewood, he expressed a conclusion they had reached in council.

They had worked out the conditions of their surrender before they presented themselves at the army camp. They would travel armed to the United States and surrender to Miles, provided Lawton would accompany them to protect them from Mexican and American troops. Gatewood should remain with them and, when convenient, sleep in their camp. Gatewood consented, Lawton approved the agreement, and the whole band—men, women, and children—moved close to the army camp. Miles was informed of the arrangement, and Skeleton Canyon, the rugged, age-old raiding route between Old Mexico and the Arizona mountains, was chosen as the place of meeting.[10]

The cavalcade then started for the border, the Indians with Gatewood and Wratten traveling independently in front, Lawton's command following. On the third day out a Mexican force of about two hundred infantry appeared from the direction of Fronteras. While the command remained to parley with them, the Indians, with Gatewood, raced on through brush and rocks, protected by flankers and a rear guard under Naiche. After an hour's run, they halted to see if there would be a fight between the Ameri-

9 Betzinez, *I Fought with Geronimo*, p. 138. Ahnandia was Betzinez' first cousin. The two had been "raised together, just like brothers," according to Betzinez' identification of a photograph in the Fort Sill collection.
10 Gatewood, *op. cit.*, pp. 8–14. Gatewood always referred to twenty-four warriors. Actually there were only eighteen, the whole band of men, women, and children numbering thirty-eight. Lawton gave the correct number in his report to Miles.

can and Mexican soldiers, in which case the warriors intended to join the Americans. Soon a courier from Lawton informed them that the Mexican commander demanded a meeting with Geronimo in order to be assured that the Indians indeed intended to surrender. It was arranged that a meeting should take place close to the Indian position far from the Mexican force, with each of the principals to be accompanied by seven armed men. The Mexicans arrived first and were received by the American officers with due formality. Then Geronimo and his party came through the bushes, Geronimo dragging his rifle and with his six-shooter in place. Gatewood introduced the two principals, and they greeted each other. Then the Mexican officer shoved his revolver around to his front. Instantly, Geronimo "drew his half way out of the holster, the whites of his eyes turning red and a most fiendish expression on his face." The Mexican hastily put his hands behind him, and Geronimo dropped his hand to his side.

The Mexican asked Geronimo why he had not surrendered at Fronteras. Geronimo retorted that he did not want to be murdered. The Mexican then asked, "Are you going to surrender to the Americans?" Geronimo answered, "I am, because I can trust them. Whatever happens, they will not murder me or my people."

"Then," said the Mexican, "I will go along and see that you *do* surrender."

"No," retorted Geronimo, "You are going south and I am going north. I'll have nothing to do with you or any of your people." A Mexican soldier was finally permitted to go along with the command, and after the surrender was consummated he took back an official statement from Miles to that effect.[11]

The journey was resumed without further incident. At one time Gatewood and his Indians became separated from Lawton's pack train. That night Perico's wife—the stolen Bi-ya-neta—was preparing "a toothsome repast" of newly killed venison and "flour, sugar, and coffee the thrifty woman had brought with her." Perico,

---

11 Gatewood, *op. cit.*, pp. 14–15.

"with considerable grace and dignity," invited Gatewood and two other officers with him to share the meal. Bi-ya-neta "made everything clean, the edibles were well cooked, and it pleased her to see us eat so heartily."[12]

One of the officers was the surgeon, young Dr. Leonard Wood, who was destined for future fame in Cuba and the Philippines. That evening Geronimo became interested in Wood's gun, a model new to him, and asked to examine it. Wood was a little apprehensive, but he handed it over with some ammunition and explained the mechanism. Geronimo shot it off, barely missing one of his men. He thought that was very funny, saying "good gun" between bursts of laughter.[13]

A day or so later they came to Guadelupe Canyon on the American side of the line. The Indians had killed some of Lawton's troopers in a fight there, and now they were uneasy, fearing the army would seek revenge. As it happened, Lawton was absent most of the day, communicating with Miles, and the trigger-happy officer who was second in command expressed an inclination to attack them and settle the surrender right there. When they learned of this, they mounted their ponies and broke out of the canyon, the women and children at the front. Gatewood caught up with Geronimo and rode along with him, while the troops followed slowly. Geronimo asked the lieutenant what he would do if the soldiers opened fire. Gatewood said that he would ride back to stop them, if possible; otherwise, he would run away with the Indians. Naiche, who had joined them, then said, "You must go with us, for fear some of our men might believe you treacherous and try to kill you." The two leaders proposed that they should all run into the mountains near Fort Bowie and that the Indians would remain there while Gatewood would go down to the post and confer with Miles. Gatewood advised against it; he knew that Miles was not at Fort Bowie, and he was afraid that before he

---

12 *Ibid.*, p. 15.
13 Wood's story of the campaign is included in Miles, *Personal Recollections*. See pp. 513–14 for the account of this incident.

could reach there some army unit would attack the band and drive them back into the Sierra Madre.

They camped a few miles farther on. Lawton joined them, but they spent an uneasy night. Several young officers were suggesting that Geronimo should be murdered. This talk was enough if he should hear of it to put him to flight again, and neither Lawton nor Gatewood wanted to risk what had happened to Crook. Gatewood attempted to leave, saying he had carried out his mission. Lawton, his superior in rank, ordered him to stay, and he stayed.[14]

The glory-seeking Miles was in the worst quandary of all. He ardently wanted credit for Geronimo's "capture," but if the elusive raider should slip away again, he did not want to bear Sheridan's censure. For six days, from August 28 to September 3, messages raced back and forth by courier, heliograph, and telegraph wire, with Lawton desperately entreating the general to come and accept Geronimo's surrender and with Miles stalling and demanding reassurance. On August 31 Miles suggested that Lawton "secure the person of Geronimo and Natchez . . . by any means, and don't fail to hold them beyond the possibility of escape." In a second communication that same day he explained the "means." Lawton could "send for them saying you have a message from me and from the President." Then, having lured them into his camp, he could disarm and hold them, "or you can do whatever you think best." Clearly, this last hinted at murder. A third message that same day was more emphatic: "You will be justified in using *any* measures." As for Miles's meeting the hostiles, "If you have any guarantee or hostages . . . I will go down, but if they are going to put their camp in the hills it might result as other talks have." And he said in his third message, "I am ready to start but not unless I am sure it will do good."

Geronimo then sent his "brother" Perico with George Wratten as interpreter to Fort Bowie to tell Miles that the band indeed wanted to surrender. The general now had his hostage, but even when he learned of this—he was still not at Fort Bowie—he con-

14 Gatewood, *op. cit.*, pp. 15–17.

tinued to express his doubts. Lawton replied on September 2, explaining that the Indians were "alert and watchful, and to surprise them is simply impossible. I could by treachery perhaps kill one or two of them, but it would only make everything much worse than before." Truly, such an act would have set off a bloody vengeance that would have made previous Apache wars seem mild. That day the Apaches again proposed to Gatewood that they make a dash for the vicinity of Fort Bowie and wait there for Miles, but on the same day Miles finally started for Skeleton Canyon after protecting himself by reporting to his superiors that he did not "anticipate any favorable result. They are still in the mountains and not within the control of our forces." Late on the afternoon of September 3 he arrived at the rendezvous.[15]

Geronimo immediately rode down unarmed from his camp high in the rocks to greet him. Dismounted, he approached the general, shook hands with him, "and then stood proudly before the officers," waiting for the conference to start.

"General Miles is your friend," the interpreter began.

"I never saw him, but I have been in need of friends," said Geronimo. "Why has he not been with me?"

When this was interpreted, general laughter broke out among the officers.[16]

Miles was impressed by his wild antagonist. Although he had no scruples against winning Geronimo's confidence through treachery, and tricking and deceiving him, it is apparent that after he had him in his power he respected his strength and regarded him with good will. As the general saw him, "He was one of the brightest, most resolute, determined looking men that I have ever encountered. He had the clearest, sharpest, dark eye I think I have ever seen, unless it was that of General Sherman when he was at the prime of life. . . . Every movement indicated

---

[15] These messages may be found in Odie B. Faulk, *The Geronimo Campaign*, pp. 139–45.

[16] Barrett, *Geronimo's Story of His Life*, p. 172. The account comes from W. T. Melton, who was employed at a ranch in the vicinity.

power, energy and determination. In everything he did, he had a purpose."[17]

His purpose now was surrender. Miles stated the terms. The hostiles would be sent to Florida, but he emphasized the part that concerned them most: "Lay down your arms and come with me to Fort Bowie, and in five days you will see your families now in Florida with Chihuahua, and no harm will be done you." He drew a line on the ground, saying, "This represents the ocean." Then, putting a small stone beside the line, he said, "This represents the place where Chihuahua is with his band." He picked up another stone and placed it a distance from the first and said, "This represents you, Geronimo." Next, he placed a third stone, saying, "This represents the Indians at Camp Apache." Then, picking up the last two stones, he placed them with the one representing Chihuahua, with the words, "That is what the President wants to do, get all of you together."[18]

It was probably at that moment that Geronimo turned to Gatewood, smiled, and said in Apache, "Good, you told the truth." He kept close to Miles as if afraid he might be left behind.[19] No doubt he knew that he was surrounded by soldiers and civilians who thirsted for his blood. He told the general of the imaginary plot by Chatto and Mickey Free that had caused him to leave the reservation. For once he found an officer who would listen. Miles not only listened but apparently was convinced.[20]

Meanwhile, Naiche remained out in the hills with most of the band, mourning for his "brother" who had gone back into Mexico to look for a favorite pony and, it was feared, had been killed by the Mexicans. Naiche, of course, had no brother; the missing warrior may have been his brother-in-law, Zhonne, the half-brother of Ha-o-zinne. The next day, at Geronimo's suggestion, he

17 Miles, *Personal Recollections*, pp. 520–21. To most army officers Geronimo's eyes expressed cruelty and low cunning.
18 *Senate Exec. Doc. 117*, 49 Cong., 2 sess., pp. 22, 29.
19 Gatewood, *op. cit.*, p. 17.
20 At least he so reported it. See Secretary of War, *Annual Report*, 1886, p. 173. He may have used it as his justification for making prisoners of Chatto and the other scouts.

and Gatewood went out to talk with Naiche. They explained that the big white chief had arrived and that even in this time of grief it would be discourteous to keep him waiting. Naiche, ever mindful of the amenities, consented, and later Geronimo rode out and brought him in.[21] He impressed Miles as "a tall, slender young warrior, whose dignity and grace of movement would become any prince."[22] The same terms were presented to him, and he also surrendered. It was now late in the afternoon of September 4.

Miles made the ceremony impressive. As Geronimo told it in later years, "We stood between his troopers and my warriors. We placed a large stone on the blanket before us. Our treaty was made by this stone, and it was to last till the stone should crumble to dust; so we made the treaty, and bound each other with an oath." As he said, "We raised our hands to heaven and . . . took an oath not to do any wrong to each other or to scheme against each other." Lawton then built a monument on the spot—of rough stone ten feet across and six feet high. Some cowboys later tore it down and found only a bottle containing a sheet of paper with the names of the officers present. Even so, it lasted longer than the agreement did. But looking back nineteen years, Geronimo could truly say, "I do not believe that I have ever violated that treaty."[23] Few white men ever understood how seriously the Apaches took such pledges.

By the following morning, September 5, all the hostiles had come into the camp. Early that day Miles, accompanied by a military escort, started out with Geronimo, Naiche, and three other leaders in his ambulance for Fort Bowie,[24] leaving the rest of the band for Lawton to bring in. He made the sixty-five-mile journey in one day. On the way, Geronimo looked out towards the familiar Chiricahua Mountains and remarked, "This is the fourth time I have surrendered." "And I think it is the last time," answered Miles.[25] Upon their arrival, the general flashed his exultant mes-

21 *Ibid.*; Gatewood, *op. cit.*, pp. 17–18.
22 *Serving the Republic*, pp. 228–29.
23 Barrett, *op. cit.*, pp. 145–47, 173–74.
24 So said his telegrams. In other places he reported four. Perhaps he included Perico, who was already at the post. But army officers were never able to count Apaches.
25 Miles, *Personal Recollections*, pp. 526–27.

Fort Bowie in 1886. In the extreme rear angle is the commanding officer's quarters, occupied by both Crook and Miles. Courtesy Arizona Pioneers' Historical Society.

sages across the country. He waited until the following day to wire the secretary of the interior: "The indians surrendered as prisoners of war on sept fourth. I returned here last night bringing Geronimo Natchez hereditary Chief and three others Lawton will bring in the remainder tomorrow about forty in all—Indians are perfectly submissive and will do whatever I say—I intend to ship them to Florida in a few days unless otherwise ordered— Geronimo says reason he broke out was that Chatto and micke free had laid plot to kill him That statement is Confirmed by others and not disproved by [illegible]."[26]

At Fort Bowie, Miles continued his friendly reassurance to the leaders, again using graphic figures. Extending one hand horizontally with the open palm towards them he traced the lines with the

[26] National Archives and Records Service, Record Group No. 75, Bureau of Indian Affairs, Letters Received 1881–1907, 27984—1886.

finger of the other hand, saying, "This represents the past; it is all covered with ridges and hollows"; then rubbing it with his free palm, he said, "This represents the wiping out of the past, which will be considered smooth and forgotten." Again clearing a piece of ground with the back of his hand, he told them that "everything you have done up to this time will be wiped out like that and forgotten, and you will begin a new life." He held out the prospect of a happy reunion of the whole band: "Leave your horses here, maybe they will be sent to you; you will have a separate reservation with your tribe, with horses and wagons, and no one will harm you."

Questioned about those promises later, Geronimo and Naiche said that they "did not believe Crook because he talked ugly" to them, but that "Miles talked very friendly to us, and that we believed him as we would God." Looking back after nineteen years as a prisoner, Geronimo summed it up: "I looked in vain for General Miles to send me to that land of which he had spoken; I longed in vain for the implements, house, and stock that General Miles had promised me."[27]

Miles, of course, knew that his promises to the Indians would not be kept. He probably hoped that things would work out that way eventually. He had indeed argued with the administration throughout July and August trying to find a home for the displaced tribes, or, failing that, a Western place of detention for them. As late as September 2 he had made a last-ditch attempt to have the reservation Indians sent to Fort Riley and Fort Leavenworth in Kansas, but the following day—the very day when he met Geronimo in Skeleton Canyon—a peremptory order from the War Department directed him to send them to Fort Marion.[28] As for the hostiles with Geronimo, it was the consensus reached at Washington on September 7 that Miles should hold the men as "close prisoners" at some point in Arizona, "subject to such trial and punishment as may be awarded them by the civil authorities of

27 *Senate Exec. Doc. 117*, 49 Cong., 2 sess., pp. 22, 30; Barrett, *Geronimo's Story of His Life*, pp. 144–47, 178.

28 *Senate Exec. Doc. 117*, 49 Cong., 2 sess., p. 36.

the Territories of Arizona and New Mexico. The women and children of his party should go to Fort Marion."

Nothing would have pleased the local authorities more than to get their hands on the hostiles. One can understand their feelings, considering the killings and robbings these raiders had inflicted, but any trial, as Miles pointed out to his superiors, would have been "simply a mockery of justice." To his wife he wrote that the Apaches had "surrendered like brave men to brave men," and "we were in honor bound not to give them up to a mob or the mockery of a justice where they could never have received an impartial trial."[29]

Unaware of all this, the six hostile leaders at Fort Bowie serenely awaited the arrival of the rest of their party. They even did some shopping at the trader's store, purchasing boots and other finery with the ample funds involuntarily furnished by the Mexicans, or, as another story has it, receiving them as a gift from the government by the grace of Miles. In either case, the new garments were worn proudly in contemporary photographs.

Lawton arrived with the rest of the band on the morning of September 8. They had one new member. The evening before they started, a baby girl was born to the young wife of Chappo. Her husband carried the child, but that was the only concession made to the mother; she mounted her horse unaided and traveled with the others. But, as Crook had learned, even surrendered Apaches were hard to hold. During the last night out, three men, three women, and a boy crept from Lawton's camp and escaped.[30] They were reported killed by Mexican forces—in some accounts it was the American army that wiped them out—but like other "deceased" Apaches, they continued to raid. A year later, on October 7, 1887, Britton Davis reported that they had made away with some horses from the Corralitos Ranch. They were joined from time to time by a few outlaws from the San Carlos Reserva-

---

[29] *Ibid.*, pp. 8, 10, 21, 44; letter quoted by Faulk in *The Geronimo Campaign*, p. 170.
[30] This is the army's story. But Wood said that in the darkness an officer rode suddenly down on the camp and stampeded the band, and when daylight came, the seven were missing. See Miles, *Personal Recollections*, p. 514.

Geronimo and Naiche at Fort Bowie after their surrender to Miles on September 4, 1886. Notice the new boots and other finery. Courtesy University of Oklahoma Library, Western History Collections.

tion, and their descendants probably still live in some hidden retreat of the Sierra Madre.[31]

But Miles's immediate problem was to spirit the hostiles in his possession out of Arizona and the jurisdiction of its courts before

31 *Senate Exec. Doc. 117*, 49 Cong., 2 sess., pp. 12, 44; W. T. Melton in Barrett, *Geronimo's Story of His Life*, pp. 173–76; National Archives and Records Service, Consolidated File 1066 AGO 1883, brief from Adjutant General's Office, October 21, 1887; Betzinez, *op. cit.*, p. 145. Miles failed to include the boy in his report of the hostiles' escape, but he was with them.

an order from Washington could stop him. Misleading as his promises to them had been, he had his own way of keeping faith. As soon as the main party arrived, he placed them all in wagons under heavy guard and set out immediately for Bowie Station. When they left the post, the military band broke into "Auld Lang Syne." They wondered why the soldiers laughed. The train left Bowie Station at 2:55 that afternoon. Lawton was in charge of the detail that guarded them. Kayihtah and Martine were sent along with the "other captives" (their official designation from this time on), and George Wratten accompanied them as interpreter. They were to travel by way of El Paso, San Antonio, and New Orleans to Florida.[32]

It would be hard to find a more mendacious summary of a campaign than that which Miles presented in his official report of their surrender: "The hostiles fought until the bulk of their ammunition was exhausted, pursued for more than 2,000 miles over the most rugged and sterile districts of the Rocky and Sierra Madre Mountain regions, beneath the burning heat of midsummer, until, worn down and disheartened, they find no place of safety in our country or Mexico, and finally lay down their arms and sue for mercy from the gallant officers and soldiers, who, despite every hardship and adverse circumstance, have achieved the success their endurance and fortitude so richly deserved."[33]

But regardless of the means by which the result had been achieved, the various bands were on their way to twenty-seven years of captivity.

[32] *Senate Exec. Doc. 117*, 49 Cong., 2 sess., pp. 30, 34; *35*, 51 Cong., 1 sess., p. 36; Miles, *Personal Recollections*, pp. 527–28.
[33] Secretary of War, *Annual Report*, 1886, p. 174.

CHAPTER 16

ALL TRAILS LEAD TO PRISON

As soon as Miles shipped out the band with Geronimo and Naiche, he started north immediately to check on the removal of the reservation Indians. He had been assured by Lieutenant Colonel James F. Wade, then the commander at Fort Apache, that they were "under good control." On September 5 Wade called the unsuspecting Indians on a pretext to the post, where they were surrounded and disarmed. Looking back seventy-three years, Kaywaykla remembered it thus: "Gooday and my mother told me how the army enlisted scouts when Geronimo went out. They had them line up under the flag and had them raise their hands and swear. They explained, 'If you see your own kin out with Geronimo, kill them.' Then after Geronimo surrendered, they lined the scouts up under the same flag and disarmed them. Then they threw them in with Geronimo's bunch."[1] Wade herded the men into one of the buildings and sent the women and children to pack their belongings. Massai tried to stir up the men to revolt, but none of this peaceable band responded. Their situation was in fact hopeless. They were without arms and surrounded by soldiers, while their families were in army hands.

1 Interview, July 29, 1959.

On the morning of September 7, the day before Miles shipped out his surrendered hostiles, Wade loaded the evacuees into wagons and conducted them under close guard to Holbrook, ninety miles north on the railroad. They reached it on September 12. The next morning the loading began. Most of the Indians had never seen a train before. Some of the old men and women even prayed to it as it approached whistling, and the terrified children fled to the brush. The soldiers caught the women and children and threw them on it, and the men followed. It pulled out at noon on September 13.[2] Miles, who was then at Albuquerque, reported that the ten carloads of Indians passed that place at 2:30 the following morning.[3]

At the front and rear of the train were cars for the military escort. Wade was in charge of the eight officers and eighty-four enlisted men.[4] On the platforms between each two carloads of prisoners, four of the soldiers stood on constant guard. One of the officers, a man who regarded Indians with disdain, in later years described the conditions within the cars. The heat was intense as they crossed the arid reaches of the Southwest, and all the doors and windows were fastened shut. Once he had to pass through the whole train, and "When I think of that trip, even at this time, I get seasick." It was "not possible for any human being, other than an Indian," to endure the stench. It never occurred to him that the army, not the Indians, was responsible for this state. The Apaches were a clean-living people, accustomed to breathing pure mountain air, bathing in clear streams, and frequently changing their campsites. It is possible that the tubercular infection that was to decimate them during their captivity began on this journey. If there was any source of contamination on the train, all were exposed.[5]

The Apaches fully expected to be killed, and the soldiers in-

[2] *Senate Exec. Doc. 117*, 49 Cong., 2 sess., pp. 15–16; Betzinez, *I Fought with Geronimo*, p. 141; Opler, "A Chiricahua Apache's Account," pp. 381–82. Opler's informant, Sam Kenoi, was about ten years old at the time.

[3] *Senate Exec. Doc. 83*, 51 Cong., 1 sess., p. 28.

[4] National Archives and Records Service, Consolidated File 1066 AGO 1883 (hereafter cited as Consolidated File), telegram by Loomis L. Langdon, September 20, 1886.

[5] His account is quoted by Faulk in *Geronimo Campaign*, pp. 164–65.

creased their terror by that significant motion of the hand across the throat. Massai decided to escape. He patiently worked the fastenings loose on a window, and as the train was pulling slowly up a grade before reaching Saint Louis, he dropped out and rolled into the brush. "He was just an average Apache," said Betzinez, using average Apache skills. He traveled undetected through an unfamiliar land of closely settled farms and towns, finding food along the way, and finally reached his mountains. Because his family had remained on the train, he slipped down and stole a Mescalero woman for a wife. He lived many years as an outlaw, stealing out occasionally from his remote hideout to take cattle or waylay a lone traveler. Finally, he was killed, and his widow took the children and returned to the Mescaleros, but the story of the "Broncho Apache" passed into Western legend.[6]

The rest of the prisoners arrived at Fort Marion on September 20. They numbered 381—278 adults and 103 children. Chatto's delegation of ten men and three women were brought there the same day.[7] But the hostile band of Geronimo and Naiche did not join them. As soon as it was learned that Miles had shipped them out, all his superiors jumped on him through channels from Washington on down. Why had he acted "in *direct contravention*" of Sheridan's order of September 7 "*to hold them in close confinement at Fort Bowie*" until the president should decide on their disposition? He answered that they were already gone before it reached him. But why the hurry to ship them without authority? His answer was that he *was* carrying out orders received from March 30 on—to place them "beyond the reach of escape." There was no such safe place in Arizona; hence, he had sent them to a more secure place of confinement.[8]

On September 10 the War Department ordered Brigadier Gen-

---

6 Betzinez, *op. cit.*, pp. 144–45. Betzinez was in the same car with Massai at the time he slipped from the train, and in 1911 he talked with his widow at Mescalero. The story of his escape and a somewhat idealized account of the family life has been told by his daughter, Alberta Begay, in "Massai—Broncho Apache," *True West*, Vol. VI, No. 6 (July–August, 1959).

7 *Senate Exec. Doc. 117*, 49 Cong., 2 sess., p. 75.

8 *Ibid.*, pp. 7–13, 16, 30–32.

Geronimo waiting at San Antonio while Washington was debating his fate. His expression shows the strain of this uncertainty. He fully expected to be killed. Courtesy University of Oklahoma Library, Western History Collections.

Other prisoners waiting at San Antonio. From left: Bi-ya-neta, Ha-o-zinne, Fun, Naiche, and Nah-bay. Courtesy National Anthropological Archives, Smithsonian Institution.

eral D. S. Stanley, commanding the Department of Texas, at San Antonio, to stop the train, take charge of the prisoners, and hold them until he received further orders. The train arrived the same day, and they were accordingly taken off and held there under strict guard.[9] But it soon began to dawn on Washington that the hostiles, "instead of being captured, surrendered, and that the surrender, instead of being unconditional, was, contrary to expectations here, accompanied with conditions and promises." Now the question filled many more telegrams: What terms had been given them? Miles evaded a direct answer, and Stanley was directed to ask the prisoners. By then it was September 29.

Stanley questioned Geronimo and Naiche separately in the

9 *Ibid.*, pp. 13–14.

presence of the post commander. They told him a consistent story, it was confirmed by George Wratten, and he was convinced of its accuracy. They said they had never thought of surrender until Gatewood and the two scouts came to them. They told of Miles's graphic presentations, moving the stones together and sweeping away the past; of his assurance that within five days they would see their families; and of his promise of a reservation.[10]

Stanley was then (on October 11) directed to give statistical data regarding the individual prisoners and to report on their character and conduct. He complied with a census that fixes definitely—against confused Apache memories[11]—the personnel of this last-ditch band of hostiles. The list follows:

∞∞∞∞∞∞∞∞∞∞∞∞∞∞∞∞∞∞

Geronimo, about forty-seven, and wife, about thirty-five; [Geronimo was much older than that, but the estimate indicates his sturdy good health. The wife was She-gha. Zi-yeh, captured the year before by Wirt Davis' scouts, was now in Florida. Ih-tedda, sent back with Maus to Fort Bowie by Geronimo, was also in Florida.]

Natchez [Naiche], about thirty-five, and wife, about seventeen; [This wife was Ha-o-zinne.]

Perico, first cousin of Geronimo, about thirty-seven, and wife, about twenty-eight; [Perico was Geronimo's second cousin, usually designated as his brother or half-brother. His wife was the stolen Bi-ya-neta.]

Fun, first cousin of Geronimo, about twenty, and wife, about nineteen; [Fun, a half-brother of Perico, was Geronimo's second cousin, often designated as his brother.]

Ahwandia [Ahnandia], about twenty-six, and wife, about twenty-one; [Ahnandia was also a second cousin of Geronimo and

---

10 *Ibid.*, pp. 17–22, 29–30.

11 It is a revealing experience to read the lists of names furnished by conscientious old-time Apaches—Daklugie, Kaywaykla, Kanseah, Betzinez, and Charlie Smith—to Eve Ball and Gillett Griswold. Every one of these lists contains errors. Too many years had passed.

a first cousin of Betzinez. He too, was often called a brother of Geronimo. His wife was Tah-das-te, who is said to have served sometimes as Geronimo's messenger.]

Napi [Nah-bay or Nahba], about forty-five, and wife, about thirty-five; [Nothing further is known about this couple. Their two-year-old daughter was with them.]

Yahnozha, about thirty-two, and wife, about twenty; [Yahnozha was Geronimo's brother-in-law, probably the brother of She-gha. He was closely related to Naiche.]

Fishnolthtonz [Tissnolthtos or Tisnolthtos; the printer misread the initial letter T], about twenty-two, and wife, about fourteen; [A daughter born years later at Fort Sill married Charlie Smith and is still living.]

Bishi [Beshe], about forty, and wife, about thirty-five; [The wife was named U-go-hun. The two were the parents of Naiche's wife, Ha-o-zinne. Beshe was probably older than this estimate, for later at Fort Sill he was one of the oldest members of the band. He was known as "Old Man Beshe."]

Chapo [Chappo], about twenty-two, and wife, about sixteen; [The name of Chappo's wife was Nohchlon.]

Lazaiyah [La-zi-yah], brother of Napi, about forty-six, and wife, about thirty-seven; [Nothing further is known about this couple.]

Motsos [Moh-tsos], about thirty-five, unmarried; [His wife and children were in Florida.]

Kilthdigai, about thirty-five, unmarried; [Nothing further is known about this warrior. He may have been called by another name.]

Zhonne, about twenty, unmarried; [Zhonne was the son of U-go-hun, thus a half-brother of Naiche's wife, Ha-o-zinne.]

Lonah [Hunlona], about nineteen, unmarried. [Hunlona was a nephew of Beshe, hence a cousin of Ha-o-zinne.]

Children: Three boys, Skayocarne, twelve years; Gardiltha [Garditha], ten years; Estchinaeintonyah, seven years; and three girls, Leosanni, six years, parents in San Augustine; Napi's infant, two years; Chapo's baby, one month. Chapo is Geronimo's son.[12]

✂✂✂✂✂✂✂✂✂✂✂✂✂✂✂✂✂✂

The boy listed as Skayocarne must have been Kanseah, who was unquestionably in the group. Kanseah was about fifteen years old, but undersized even by Apache standards, and white men regularly underestimated the age of the small, nimble Apache children. The child given the name of Estchinaeintonyah may have been Charlie Smith, who always asserted that he and his mother and her abductor were there. If his memory is correct, his mother and stepfather must have been one of the less well known couples. The boy, Garditha, was an orphan, according to Betzinez. He was a brother or a cousin of Leosanni, certainly the latter if she had parents at Saint Augustine. (There is no indication as to how this little girl became separated from her parents.)

This description of the band members is supplemented by a photograph showing them resting on the railway embankment outside the train at a stop on the way to San Antonio. The picture shows all but one of the warriors, the two boys Kanseah and Garditha, and four of the women. Unfortunately, not all of them have been accurately identified. Eve Ball and Gillett Griswold have made an earnest attempt to fix their names, and aged Apaches with fading memories and failing eyesight have cooperated, but all of them have located persons in the picture who were not present. Even so, the photograph is a striking representation of that small, valiant band that maintained itself undisturbed against the utmost efforts of a powerful government.

Although Stanley was able to name and describe the members, he was unable to comply with Washington's request for information regarding their character and conduct. "The Indians will not inform on each other," he said, and when he inquired of Wratten,

---

12 *Senate Exec. Doc. 117*, 49 Cong., 2 sess., pp. 25–26; Griswold, "The Fort Sill Apaches," biographical sketches. There is no possible doubt of the accuracy of Stanley's list. The warriors' names—with some variations in spelling—check exactly with a list made independently by Langdon when they came under his supervision as prisoners in Florida. See Consolidated File, report of Loomis L. Langdon, March 24, 1887.

A rest stop on the way to San Antonio. Identified without question: front row, from left, Fun, Perico, Naiche, Geronimo, Chappo, and the boy Garditha; second row, Jasper Kanseah on the left. Probably correct in second row: Yahnozha next to Jasper Kanseah; fourth from left, Ahnandia; extreme right, Beshe. The women at the back, as identified by Jason Betzinez: from left, Ha-o-zinne, wife of Naiche; Bi-ya-neta, stolen wife of Perico; Nohchlon, wife of Chappo; Tah-das-te, wife of Ahnandia. It is known, however, that Betzinez made some errors in identifying the warriors. Courtesy U.S. Army Artillery and Missile Center Museum.

the interpreter told him that "he knows of the character of a few only, and that their character is good." Their conduct "since they have been here has been excellent," he found (Clum's experience exactly). He then reported on "the two enlisted scouts—Kayehtah, about thirty-eight; Martine, about twenty-seven. Character of both is good. Wives of both in Florida."[13]

Eight days later President Cleveland finally announced his decision regarding the band, and the War and Interior departments expressed their concurrence. There was some sense of obligation to honor Miles's promise that their lives would be spared and that they would be sent to Florida. This precluded turning them over to the civil authorities of the two territories.[14] His other promise—that the tribe would be reunited, with the distant prospect of a reservation—did not count. On October 19 Secretary of War Endicott sent the instructions to Sheridan:

By direction of the President it is ordered that the hostile Apache adult Indians [then followed the names of the warriors] be sent under proper guard to Fort Pickens, Florida, there to be kept in close custody until further orders. These Indians have been guilty of the worst crimes known to the law, committed under circumstances of great atrocity, and the public safety requires that they should be removed far from the scene of their depredations and guarded with the strictest vigilance.

The remainder of the band captured at the same time, consisting of eleven women, six children, and two enlisted scouts, you are to send to Fort Marion, Florida, and place with the other Apache Indians recently conveyed to and now under custody at that post.[15]

The cynical mendacity of the wording here is worth noting. Strictly speaking, Geronimo and the warriors of the band had not been "captured," but induced by false promises to surrender; now to Endicott's bureaucratic mind even the scouts had been "captured at the same time."

When Stanley broke the news to Geronimo and Naiche, they

[13] *Senate Exec. Doc. 117*, 49 Cong., 2 sess., pp. 25–26.
[14] *Ibid.*, p. 18.
[15] *Ibid.*, p. 26.

protested that they had been promised reunion with their absent relatives instead of separation from those in the band. Stanley forwarded their statement up through army channels along with his own conclusion that it was correct. At the same time, Wratten tried to obtain special clemency for Ahnandia; he had known him in reservation days as "a sober and industrious man." He also had a personal reason for his concern. Once while he was carrying out his official duties another Indian had tried to kill him, and Ahnandia had saved his life. Wratten said that Ahnandia had left the reservation only through fear that he himself would be killed, had remained in Mexico, and had refrained from raiding across the border. Now as a prisoner he and his wife had worked together, producing articles for sale. He had bought an elementary reading book and had been "studying English very hard," acquiring some proficiency in reading and writing. He and his wife were "very much attached to each other," and Wratten was confident that they would have a good influence on the Indians at Fort Marion if they were permitted to join them there.[16]

Stanley forwarded the appeal with his endorsement that "so far as the good conduct and industry of the indian [sic] and his squaw are concerned," it was "perfectly true to my own knowledge." It worked its way up through channels to Sheridan and the War Department, where it was marked "Disapproved." His endorsement of the statement by Geronimo and Naiche was similarly treated. He had to carry out the order, dividing the prisoners into two groups and placing them in different cars for the journey. The train left on October 22.[17]

The news that the notorious Geronimo and the other warriors were destined for Fort Pickens brought rejoicing to Pensacola promoters.[18] (Apparently their congressman *had* got in some good work.) The prisoners arrived at 2:00 A.M. on October 25.

16 Consolidated File, George M. Wratten to Assistant Adjutant General, Department of Texas, October 20, 1886.
17 *Senate Exec. Doc. 117*, 49 Cong., 2 sess., pp. 28–30; Secretary of War, *Annual Report*, 1886, pp. 13–14.
18 *Pensacolian*, October 23, 1886.

At 8:30 a steamer ran alongside the railroad wharf, and they were loaded aboard for the short trip across the bay to Fort Pickens on Santa Rosa Island. A crowd had gathered to see them. It was noticed that Naiche "seemed much amused" by the staring, pushing onlookers. During the passage "one old brave"—this must have been "Old Man Beshe"—was "delighted" in watching the "dolphins" disporting themselves in front of the boat. The island lay before them, a gleaming stretch of white sand with sparse vegetation growing on its wind-piled drifts. At one end were a few shrubs and scrubby trees, and there stretched a low, rambling structure, its walls of solid brick masonry discolored by time and weather, the old fortification "from which place," opined the local press, "they will never emerge, unless they are taken out feet foremost." It was said that as they were leaving the boat, one of them was heard to remark in a plaintive tone, "Won't see Mexico no more."[19] (The speaker must have Ahnandia, using his conscientiously acquired English.) Meanwhile, the train was carrying their wives and children three hundred miles across the state to Fort Marion, where they arrived the same day.

Mangus and his band were still to be brought in. The army had searched for them in Mexico, but no trace of them had been discovered. Seventy years later, Daklugie told their story. They hid in the foothills with the high sierras close by in case of need. Once they went as far south as the great Canyon de Cobra. They lived largely on deer killed with the bow and arrow to avoid the betrayal of gunfire, but they killed Mexican livestock when necessary. Mangus avoided conflicts with Mexicans, but had some trouble restraining the almost grown boys, his son Frank and Daklugie. After the capture of Dalzhinne and Daklegon, he had only two recognized warriors, an aged Mescalero named Fit-a-hat and a very young man named Goso.

Early in October, while Geronimo and his band were waiting at San Antonio, Mangus started north for New Mexico. Crossing the plain, the two boys, without Mangus' consent, drove off the

---

19 *Ibid.*, October 30, 1886.

mule herd from the Corralitos Ranch. Davis followed the trail and found they were heading north. He telegraphed Miles, and Miles sent Captain Charles L. Cooper out from Fort Apache to find them. In the mountains east of the post Mangus discovered Cooper's camp and sent Daklugie to make overtures of surrender.[20] It was the capture of the mule herd that had decided him to come in. As he told it in 1894, "I didnt want to do any harm to anybody so I took a bee line for camp apache [sic] but before I reached there—I met some soldiers who took us in."[21]

On October 19, three days before Stanley shipped out Geronimo's band, Cooper arrived at the post with his "captives": Mangus and his two warriors; three women, one of whom was Mangus' wife, the daughter of Victorio; five children, including the two well-grown boys; and the mule herd, which Miles in due course returned to Davis. Cooper also brought a heroic story of pursuit and capture, which found its way into army reports.

The prisoners were started out from the post on October 30 and placed on the train at Holbrook. The aged and feeble Fit-a-hat died while they were passing through New Mexico and was buried at Fort Union. In Colorado Mangus managed to open a window and escape from the train. He was stunned by the fall, so he was easily captured although he was not seriously injured. He and Goso arrived at Fort Pickens on November 6. The women and children were taken on to Fort Marion.[22]

Summing it up, Miles reported that his victorious campaign had closed the Apache wars, ending "the terrible depredations which the Chiricahuas and Warm Springs Indians had for so many generations instigated"; permitted the discharge of over four hundred Indian scouts and the transfer of army units to the departments

20 Eve Ball to Angie Debo, July 13, 1972.
21 Consolidated File, Hugh Lenox Scott's report to M. P. Maus, August 29, 1894.
22 Ibid., O. O. Howard, October 20, 1886, and Loomis L. Langdon, March 24, 1887; Davis, The Truth about Geronimo, pp. 231–32; Senate Exec. Doc. 117, 49 Cong., 2 sess., pp. 75–77; Secretary of War, Annual Report, 1886, pp. 14, 49; 1887, pp. 156, 158. Typical of the army's inability to count Apaches is Miles's manipulation of these figures. Learning that two of the children were "large boys capable of bearing arms," he added them without subtracting them from the "children." Thus he had "2 large boys" and five children.

of California, Texas, and the Platte; and reduced military expenses in Arizona *"more than one million dollars per annum"* [italics his].[23]

The cost to the Apaches would appear in the years ahead.

[23] Secretary of War, *Annual Report*, 1887, p. 158.

CHAPTER 17

THE APACHES SETTLE DOWN AS PRISONERS

Langdon, a humane officer, had done the best he could with Chihuahua's band at Fort Marion. He had been placed in charge there on June 16. Up to that time the prisoners had been camped on the beach. Although the agency of mosquitoes in malarial infection had not yet been discovered, the unhealthfulness of such localities was generally known, and it was also believed that the water there was contaminated. One man had already died of malaria ("remittent fever") complicated by dysentery, and a number of others were infected. But a well was being drilled at Fort Marion, and Langdon was able to move the prisoners there on June 19.[1]

In his first report, on July 4, he recommended the adoption of measures "for the education of the children and the placing of the adults in permanent homes." And even before he had been asked to add the reservation evacuees to his crowded enclosure, he had begun to think of Carlisle. In his communication of August 23, previously referred to, he drew up a careful statement recommending the transfer of all the present captives to that place, where

[1] National Archives and Records Service, Consolidated File 1066 AGO 1883 (hereafter cited as Consolidated File), Langdon's report, July 4, 1886.

they could live on the reserve while their children attended school. He pointed out that it was unwholesome to keep these formerly active people in indefinite idleness. The women had some light duties preparing their simple meals and—with the assistance of charitable ladies of the town—making their clothing, but the men had nothing to do beyond policing the place, although they would willingly work if given the opportunity. They had been confined long enough to learn the power of the government, and they were entirely docile. Two sisters of the local Convent of Saint Joseph had been coming in for an hour each day to teach the children, but these youths needed vocational training.

He did not recommend sending them to Carlisle unless the whole party, or at least those with children, should be sent. They were in constant dread of having their children taken from them. Even a present of clothing to a half-clad child excited their mistrust—"it looks to them like preparing them for a journey, a separation from their parents." There would be no problem of guarding the band on the reserve, "if there is a reserve of any size at Carlisle."[2] The fourteen men prisoners under the command of Chihuahua would be sufficient, "as the only object of having a guard is to keep the white people away from the Indians."[3]

When this recommendation worked its way up to Sheridan, Langdon was informed "that the final disposition of these Indians will doubtless be determined by the Interior Department and in the meantime all that is expected of him is to hold them as prisoners of War."[4] The Interior Department gave no consideration to such "final disposition," then or later, but suggestions had already been made for placing the children in an industrial boarding school. When Captain Pratt was consulted, he showed some decent hesitation about taking them without the consent of their parents. He proposed sending young Benito to live with them for a few

---

[2] It comprised only about thirty acres (John J. Slonaker, Research Historian, Carlisle Barracks, to Angie Debo July 9, 1973). Probably all of this area was used by the school. Even so, it offered more space than the enclosing walls of Old Fort Marion.
[3] Consolidated File, Langdon's report, August 23, 1886.
[4] *Ibid.*, Sheridan's endorsement, September 3.

weeks in order to tell them about conditions and opportunities at the school and overcome their reluctance.[5] (This boy was probably the one known as Lorenzo Benito. Benito's other boy died at Carlisle. Benito himself as a White Mountain Apache was to escape the roundup of the reservation Indians.[6]) As far as is known, Pratt's suggestion was not followed.

Meanwhile, the prisoners were marking time at Fort Marion. By the end of August three of their young children had died. One of these was the four-year-old daughter Geronimo had sent back from the Sierra Madre with Maus. She had been "very feeble" when she came, and the best efforts of Langdon and the post surgeon in furnishing her with milk and other special food as well as medical care failed to restore her health. In general, the group seemed cheerful and contented. This typical conduct of Apache prisoners grew out of their experience as a hunted people. From earliest childhood they had been trained to accept hardships and disappointments without complaint.[7] They were allowed to go out in small parties under the escort of a guard to make purchases in the stores of the town.[8] They developed a brisk traffic in the sale of beadwork and other articles made by the women and bows and arrows fashioned by the men, and it is evident that the people of Saint Augustine were friendly and sympathetic.[9]

On September 20 Langdon was swamped by the arrival of the 381 evacuees from the reservation and the thirteen members of the Washington delegation. He put up tents and packed them into the space as best he could. Young Sam Kenoi remembered the place well:

We arrived . . . at night, moonlight, about ten or eleven o'clock. It's a big place made out of cement and stones. It has a great dungeon under it. . . . There is a big place about fifteen yards wide

5 *Senate Exec. Doc. 73*, 49 Cong., 2 sess., pp. 4–5, 10, 12.
6 Griswold, "The Fort Sill Apaches," s.v. "Benito."
7 See, for example, Ball, *In the Days of Victorio*, pp. 6, 73, 91.
8 Consolidated File, Langdon's reports, August 20, 23, 1886.
9 See, for example, Betzinez, *I Fought with Geronimo*, p. 146.

all around on top, with a cement wall about four feet high so you couldn't fall over. On each corner of that wall is a square, a little tower made out of stone and concrete with windows on each side. It was a lookout tower, I believe. On that run-around they had been setting up army tents thick. We were up there on a cement floor, and we had no privilege to move our tents. We had to stay right there.

And they had a big gate down there where they brought us in, and it was guarded by soldiers. The Indians were not allowed to leave that gate without permission. . . . Wood was given, a little, and a place to cook was provided in one of the dungeons below. We had to sleep on the hard cement floor. It was warm there in Florida. . . . Many died . . . . We were not used to the climate.[10]

∞∞∞∞∞∞∞∞∞∞∞∞∞∞∞∞

Eighteen of them died there before the year was over.[11] But that was only the beginning.

Of the 394 new arrivals, 70 were adult men, 221 were adult women, 41 were children between the estimated ages of five and twelve, and 62 were under age four.[12] Among them were fourteen scouts whose enlistments had not expired. Langdon asked whether they should continue to draw pay or be mustered out. The latter, said Washington. They were mustered out on October 8, becoming prisoners like the others. Of the interpreters who had accompanied the Washington delegation, Sam Bowman and Concepcion were employed for a time at the post; Mickey Free was returned to Arizona.[13]

Langdon's report of October 1 is eloquent of the patient endurance of the prisoners. Although the place was "excessively crowded," the Indian men, as sanitary police, kept it "scrupulously

10 Opler, "A Chiricahua Apache's Account," pp. 384–85. See also Betzinez, *op. cit.*, pp. 145–46.

11 *Senate Exec. Doc. 35*, 51 Cong., 1 sess., p. 37.

12 Consolidated File, Telegram by Langdon, September 20, 1886. I have added to his figures the number in the Washington delegation. Obviously he classed all over twelve as "adults," and the children "under age four" included the four-year-olds.

13 *Ibid.*, Langdon to Adjutant General, September 29, 1886, and endorsements. Washington had a hard time figuring out who these scouts were.

clean." Two bath tubs (provided for 469 persons) were "in constant use." There had been no instance of disturbance or disobedience during their confinement, and all seemed "harmonious in their relations with each other." There had been seventy-six cases of illness treated during the previous month, of which sixty were of "intermittent fever," and one aged woman had died.[14] (Langdon believed the malaria had been contracted in Arizona, but in this he was almost certainly mistaken.)

An ominous circumstance barely mentioned in the October 1 report was to contribute to the lowered vitality of the prisoners. They had been receiving the regular army ration; then, on September 22 a drastic reduction had been made by the War Department upon the recommendation of the commissary general of subsistence. Langdon protested that the amount was insufficient, but new regulations issued on December 11 and April 23 were to have the effect of cutting it further.[15]

For the time, however, the number of prisoners remained constant, for one birth was recorded for the month—a daughter to Geronimo's wife, Ih-tedda, on September 13. Langdon named the child Marion,[16] but somehow she acquired the name of Lenna, by which she would be known throughout her life. Geronimo, still at San Antonio, was, of course, unaware of this addition to his family.

During that same month of October the Interior Department formulated plans for educating the youthful prisoners. Carlisle was selected to receive those between the ages of twelve and twenty-two, and the possibility of local schooling for the younger children was being considered. A count indicated twenty-four boys and fifteen girls in the older group, forty boys and sixteen girls in the younger.[17] The War Department thereupon rounded up the

---

14 *Ibid.*, October 1, 1886. This report is also found in *Senate Exec. Doc. 73*, 49 Cong., 2 sess., p. 8.

15 Consolidated File, Report of Adjutant General R. C. Drum, June 15, 1887; report of Major William Sinclair, September 30, 1887.

16 Information compiled by the National Park Service, Tallahassee, Florida.

17 Probably the imbalance in numbers between girls and boys was due to the girls' early marriages, and the officers may have underestimated the age of the boys they placed in the younger group.

older youths for delivery to Carlisle. The selections were made by Lieutenant Stephen C. Mills, who had been placed in direct charge of the prisoners, and the post surgeon examined the youths for physical fitness. Mills later said that the separation of these children from their families was the most disagreeable task he had ever performed. The desperate parents tried to hide them, and in one case they succeeded. It was a puzzle how they managed to secrete their children in this crowded place on this and other occasions. Years later it was revealed that the women concealed them—probably the smaller ones—under their long full skirts.[18]

They would have been still more unwilling to part with them if they had known that Carlisle was a death trap, an even more deadly center of tubercular infection than the crowded camp at Fort Marion. Pratt had founded the school in 1879 with young South Plains Indians who had completed their sentences at Fort Marion as its first students; and it is known that some of them were infected with tuberculosis when they came.[19] The school was, of course, well administered, and sanitary principles as understood at the time were observed. The infection probably was spread in the dormitories and classrooms. Certainly it was rampant there before the arrival of the Apache prisoners.[20]

Four of the youths at Fort Marion were not well enough to go with the first contingent. The others reached the school on November 4. The boys' hair was shorn, and all were dressed in conventional clothing. They received the given names by which they have been subsequently known. Among them was Jasper Kanseah, separated less than two weeks before from his Uncle Geronimo at San Antonio. Enough adventure had already been packed into his short life to fill several biographies. Then, two days later, on November 6, the children of Mangus' band arrived

18 Consolidated File, Eli D. Hoyle, Post Adjutant, October 26, 1886; Stephen C. Mills, October 29, 1886; and R. B. Ayres, November 2, 1886. David Michael Goodman, "Apaches as Prisoners of War, 1886–1894," Ph.D. diss., Texas Christian University, 1968, p. 135 and note 113, citing Bourke's diary; Benedict Jozhe interview, September 16, 1969.

19 Karen Douglas Peterson, *Plains Indian Art from Fort Marion*, pp. 102, 258.

20 Consolidated File, Report of John J. Cochran, July 1, 1889.

at Fort Marion. They, with the ones who had missed the first enrollment, required a second shipment, which reached the school on December 8. Among them were Asa Daklugie, Ramona Chihuahua, and Dorothy Naiche. The total number at Carlisle was now forty-four.[21]

On January 1 the Indian Office made a contract with the Bureau of Catholic Indian Missions for the schooling of the younger children at Saint Joseph's Convent. For Sam Kenoi it was not a happy experience: "In the morning they strung out those poor children, and without trying to dress them up . . . they sent them to the Catholic school in the city. They wore their loin cloths, wore rags around their heads, and were bare-legged. . . . [They] were turned in as prisoners every evening." Probably he remembered being subjected to some ridicule by the other children. James Kaywaykla took an opposite view: the "Catholic Sisters undertook to teach the children a little English, and provided baths, clothing, and sometimes medicine. . . . I will never forget the kindness of those good women, nor the respect in which we held them. For the first time in my life I saw the interior of a church and dimly sensed that the White Eyes, too, worshipped Ussen."[22]

James Kaywaykla's experience at the day school was brief, for he was taken to Carlisle in the next roundup, which occurred in April, 1887. Captain Pratt came down, bringing along an Apache student to persuade his young relatives to enroll. They were unconvinced; Pratt was forced to have them lined up so he could make his selections. Benedict Jozhe, the long-time chairman of the Fort Sill Apaches, relates the capture of his mother, a granddaughter of Loco. She was playing on the beach and had taken off one of her shoes. The soldiers snatched her up so quickly that she was unable to retrieve it, and she traveled to Carlisle with one bare foot.

21 *Senate Exec. Doc. 73*, 49 Cong., 2 sess., pp. 2, 11–16; U.S. Army Artillery and Missile Center Museum, "Names &c. of Chiricahua Indian Children at Carlisle Indian School."

22 *Senate Exec. Doc. 73*, 49 Cong., 2 sess., pp. 2–3; Opler, "A Chiricahua Apache's Account," p. 384; Ball, *op. cit.*, pp. 196–97.

Apache students at Carlisle Indian School about 1887. Back row: fourth from left, Asa Daklugie; fifth from left, Jason Betzinez; in front of Asa and Jason, Ramona Chihuahua, whom Asa afterward married; in front and slightly right of Ramona, Viola Massai, afterward married to Eugene Chihuahua; small boy in front of Viola, James Kaywaykla. *The boys' hair was shorn and all were dressed in conventional clothing.* Courtesy Mrs. Eve Ball.

Pratt selected sixty-two students from the lineup: thirty-two children, five older girls, twelve married couples, and twenty-seven-year-old Betzinez. Among them were Benedict Jozhe's father, also named Benedict Jozhe, who was the youngest brother of Fun; fifteen-year-old Charles Istee, the only surviving son of Victorio; another young brother of Fun named Burdett Tsisnah, with his wife, Lucy; and Talbot Gooday, grandson of Mangas Coloradas and Loco, with his wife, whose name is not remembered.[23]

Thus, Langdon's hopes for the education of the Apache youths at Carlisle were realized, though not in the way he had recommended. He did not see their painful separation from their parents. Sometime in October, before the first group was selected, he was

[23] Consolidated File, telegram from Romeyn B. Ayres to Adjutant General, April 26, [1887]; Betzinez, *op. cit.*, pp. 149, 151–53; Benedict Jozhe interview, September 16, 1969; Griswold, *op. cit.*, individual biographies.

320

Fort Pickens, Florida, the entrance to the two casemates in which the warriors were quartered. Author's collection.

transferred to Pensacola to command Fort Barrancas on the mainland and Fort Pickens, which was regarded as its subpost, on the island. He was there when Geronimo and Naiche and their thirteen warriors arrived on October 25. Less than two weeks later, Mangus was brought there with Goso.

Fort Pickens had not been occupied since the Civil War. Not only the parade ground and ditch but also the masonry itself was overgrown with weeds, grass, and good-sized trees. A pine tree was even growing out of one of the chimneys. Langdon put the prisoners to work for six hours a day, five days a week, clearing up the place under the immediate command of an officer and the interpreter, George Wratten. On Saturdays and Sundays they were free, except that they were required to attend to the washing and mending of their clothing on Saturday. Two of the casemates were made habitable to become their quarters. In these rather spacious

The leaders at Fort Pickens. From left: Geronimo, Naiche, and Mangus. The first two were painted for the occasion. Courtesy University of Oklahoma Library, Western History Collections.

rooms they ate and slept and spent their leisure hours. In each of them one prisoner was detailed as cook, and the food was prepared at the open fireplace. (It is easy now to identify their living quarters, for only two of the casemates show fireplaces.) Their beds were rough bunks, but they had plenty of blankets and bedsacks, which they filled once a month with fresh straw. They were amply supplied with clothing of the kind worn by enlisted men on fatigue duty.[24]

Two weeks after their arrival, a local newspaper reporter with a party was permitted to visit them, and he recorded his impressions of different individuals. "Of all the Indians at the Fort," he wrote, "Geronimo and Lona [the youthful Hunlona] have the most cruel countenances. Geronimo's face is expressive of inteligence, but he has the coldest eye we have ever beheld in the face of a human being. Natchez is very tall and straight with an air of superiority

[24] Consolidated File, Langdon's reports, January 7, June 28, and August 9, 1887.

about him," as though upholding "the dignity of his chieftainship. He was very reticent, not deigning to notice in any way the presence of visitors. .... Mangus, strange to say, has rather a pleasant face, in fact he is the mildest mannered man that ever burnt a cabin or cut a throat. .... Geronimo is not a chief, being the Big Medicine Man or rather the brains of the tribe, and is obeyed implicitly by the others. He is a great beggar and will ask for anything that strikes his fancy."[25]

Langdon found the prisoners to be "neat and orderly in person, rooms and cooking." The officer in direct charge of them reported that "not once has the least sign of discontent or insubordination been shown. They perform all that is required of them with cheerfulness, alacrity and intelligence." They remained in excellent health, a condition Langdon attributed to their work in the open. In his opinion they "really suffered at first owing to the smallness of the ration. The only one who complained, however, was Geronimo, (the medicine man) and for this he was rebuked by Natchez the chief. The latter is a very manly fellow and exercises a good influence over the others." But although Sheridan had been insensitive to the feelings of the Apaches, starving them was something else. He issued an order, and by the time of Langdon's report of January 7 they were being adequately supplied with food.[26] (Apparently nobody became concerned about the hungry Indians at Fort Marion.)

In this and subsequent reports Langdon urged that the prisoners' wives and children be sent to them. The place was healthful and there were ample accommodations. He knew they longed for their families, but he was unaware of the undercurrent of desperation beneath their outward cheerfulness. In any characterization of them he always designated Geronimo as the "medicine man" of the band. One can glimpse here the constant, fervent appeals to the Power that had apparently failed him and his people.

Meanwhile, the public was becoming aware that something was

---

25 *Pensacolian*, November 13, 1886.
26 Consolidated File, Langdon's reports January 7, June 28, and August 9, 1887.

wrong with the government's whole policy of dealing with the prisoners. Langdon had done his best for them without result, but now disturbing reports from public-spirited citizens reached the Indian Rights Association of Philadelphia, and Herbert Welsh, its executive secretary, took up their cause in earnest. Other Indian interest organizations were enlisted, and General Crook and Captain Bourke told of the indiscriminate punishment of Apaches who had not joined the hostiles. To Bourke, Geronimo was "a depraved rascal whose neck I should like to stretch," but there was "a marked difference" between his case and that of the scouts who had brought about his surrender.[27] Bourke and Welsh finally pressured the War Department into granting them permission to visit Fort Marion. They made their inspection early in March, 1887.

Sheridan also ordered an investigation that month. On March 16 he wrote to Colonel Romeyn B. Ayres, then in charge at Fort Marion, to learn how many of the men had served as scouts. Ayres reported "that of the eighty-two adult male Indians, confined in Fort Marion, Sixty-five, Served the Government as scouts during the whole or a portion of the time that Geronimo was out, viz. from the Spring of 1885, until the fall of 1886." And of the remaining seventeen he named four subchiefs, too old to be enlisted, who had been influential in keeping their people quiet on the reservation. Of the 365 women and children confined in the fort, 284, as nearly as he could ascertain, "make up the families of the scouts and the four friendly indians [sic] mentioned above." His last sentence is of sinister significance: "Care has been taken, in collecting these points, that they be not public."[28]

But the army could not conceal everything. Welsh published his report in April, and it created a sensation. There were also newspaper articles and speeches, and letters from prominent people to government officials. It finally began to dawn on President Cleve-

[27] *Senate Exec. Doc. 35*, 51 Cong., 1 sess., pp. 52–53.
[28] Consolidated File, March 25, 1887. This would leave only thirteen hostile warriors, and it is known that there were fifteen in Chihuahua's band. But at least one and perhaps others had died by the time Ayres made the investigation. In any case, the discrepancy is small.

324

land that peaceable Indians were being punished, that all were living under subhuman conditions at Fort Marion, and that even the holdout hostiles at Fort Pickens had been separated from their families in violation of the conditions of their surrender. He had been exasperated at the breakouts and raids with the robbings and killings and the extensive military campaigns, and he had been told on good authority that the whole body of related tribes was involved. Now he began to learn the facts. And even Secretary of War Endicott began to wilt before an outraged public opinion.[29] This agitation was to continue throughout the weary years that followed.

Although the public outcry did not bring immediate deliverance to the captives, it did bring some amelioration of their situation. During March the War Department considered transferring the entire band at Fort Marion to Fort Pickens. An inspector reported favorably on March 11, and when his recommendation was submitted to Ayres and Langdon they both approved. They contrasted the crowded conditions, the enforced idleness, and the proximity to the town at Fort Marion with the healthful situation and greater space on an almost uninhabited island at Fort Pickens.

Incidentally, the comments of these two officers reveal the extent to which the captives had justified the hopes of the tourist promoters. The sight of these wild people caged was a sensational experience. On their way east every time their trains stopped, staring crowds awaited them, pushing and shoving for the best views, while the escorting troopers formed a cordon around them; and San Antonio had held a Roman holiday, with hawkers selling photographs and souvenirs, while Geronimo's band was detained there.[30] Now at Saint Augustine Ayers complained that they had no opportunity for normal exercise outside the walls; when they were taken out, they were "swarmed about by the curious and idle, making annoying comments, . . . disinclining them often to fresh air and exercise." Even more significant was a suggestion from Langdon at

29 Goodman has told the whole story in "Apaches as Prisoners of War," pp. 84–111.
30 *Ibid.*, pp. 7, 51, 58, 64–65.

Fort Pickens that if it should be decided to remove them from Fort Marion "it would be well to keep [the intention] as secret as possible, because all the railroad interests of Eastern Florida and the influential men of that region will make the most strenuous endeavors to prevent it by beseiging the War Dept. with petitions and remonstrances against the change which will divert a great deal of travel from that country and cause a loss to the railroads and hotels in that side of the state."[31] At the same time, visitors were flocking to Fort Pickens. Langdon began admitting them early in February. He required them to apply to him at Fort Barrancas for a pass so that he might judge their reliability. By the end of March they were coming in great numbers—rarely fewer than 20 a day, on one day reaching 457 (this must have been a planned excursion), and numbering 40 on the day he wrote.[32]

The War Department decided to remove the prisoners from Fort Marion, but chose to bring only the families of the Fort Pickens prisoners to join them there while sending the main body on to Mount Vernon Barracks, a military post in Alabama on the west side of the Mobile River about thirty miles north of the city of Mobile. On April 19 Langdon was notified by telegram to prepare for his contingent.[33] The train passed through Pensacola on April 27, and the families of the Fort Pickens prisoners were removed and taken by launch to the island. They numbered twenty women and eleven children.[34] The families of two or three of the men chose to go on with the main body. It is safe to assume, however, that Geronimo's three wives and their children were among those who joined their men. Geronimo was thus reunited with his little son Fenton, captured with his mother Zi-yeh in the Sierra Madre almost two years before, and for the first time he saw his infant daughter, Lenna. Probably he learned only then of the death of the little girl he had sent back with Maus in anticipation of the

---

[31] Consolidated File, R. Jones, Inspector General, March 11, 1887, with endorsements by Langdon and Ayres.
[32] *Ibid.*, Langdon's report, March 24, 1887.
[33] His answering telegram is in *ibid.*, April 23, 1887.
[34] *Ibid.*, Assistant Adjutant General (signature illegible), April 20, 1887.

surrender he failed to carry out. Chappo's young wife went on to Mount Vernon. Her name appears in a list of the prisoners there in 1887 or early 1888.[35] Probably her baby had died by this time. She herself must have died shortly after. Dohn-say, of course, went to Alabama with her husband, but Geronimo must have received news of her and of other family members and friends in the band. He always showed a surprising ability to keep in touch with relatives and associates from whom he was separated.

One can be sure that Naiche was reunited with his three wives and that Dilth-cley-ih, the daughter of Victorio, also joined her husband, Mangus. Huera came, too, but apparently Mangus did not welcome her. An especially well informed observer who visited the prisoners later referred to her as Mangus' divorced wife, with whom, however, the kindly Mangus did not quarrel although she was "confined within the same precincts." This perceptive visitor found Naiche gentlemanly, though dignified and reticent; he "responds to summons, smiles gravely, shakes hands cordially," ignoring the stares and comments of the curious with studied indifference. He found Mangus "more genial, smiles broadly" in friendly greeting, while "Geronimo steals up unannounced—sly and silent as a mountain lion. Feline is his eye." But he observed that even Geronimo, as well as Naiche, was a good husband and father, and that the affection of the mothers for their children was plainly apparent.[36]

The general public, accustomed to think of Apaches as subhuman, had no conception of what it meant to the Fort Pickens prisoners to be reunited with their families. A letter written the following year by a tourist is revealing: "I had good luck today. . . . Saw Geronimo. . . . He is a terrible old villain, yet he seemed quiet enough today nursing a baby."[37] The baby, of course, was Lenna. Now he could hold her in his arms.

35 U.S. Army Artillery and Missile Center Museum, Archives.
36 Richard Wheatley, "The Caged Tigers of Santa Rosa," *Pensacola Historical Society Quarterly*, Vol. II, No. 2 (April, 1966).
37 B. F. Crary, "Historical Museum Letter," *Pensacola Historical Society Quarterly*, Vol. II, No. 2 (April, 1966).

Langdon settled the families in the dilapidated casemates formerly used as officers' quarters. Thus, each family had a separate apartment. (The men without families were grouped together as before in the company quarters at the opposite end of the structure.) The women performed the household labors while their men worked outside—clearing the ditch of a dense growth of wild indigo, digging and cleaning wells, and clearing a new parade ground and planting it with Bermuda grass. This division of labor accorded with Apache custom, which did not differ materially from that observed in white society; but Langdon, holding the stereotype of Indian women serving as "slaves" doing all the work, while "the men hunt, smoke, and loaf," was amazed that "there has never been a word of remonstrance on the subject."

There had, in fact, been "no occasion to reprimand, much less to punish a single one of these Indians since their arrival here." Their good conduct went beyond an enforced submission. Langdon commended them "for their cheerfulness of demeanor, for their prompt alacrity in obeying orders and for the zeal and interest shown in the duties assigned to them." But upon a return to more normal living with the presence of their wives and children they were emboldened to express hopes for their future. Two or three of them—no doubt Naiche, Geronimo, and perhaps Mangus— went to Wratten and asked him to tell Langdon that "they were very desirous of going into permanent homes on lands they could cultivate as their own."

Langdon was not ready to encourage even such timidly expressed demands. He sent back the stern message "that they had had that chance" once and had "lost it deservedly." Their lives had been "spared by a strong but merciful government and they should be thankful" to be forgotten for a while. Otherwise, "it might be remembered they had not as yet been punished for their crimes." After that warning, as Langdon reported it, "nothing more has been said about farms."[38] So *he* thought! They got Wratten to write to General Stanley at San Antonio asking him how much

[38] Consolidated File, Langdon's reports, June 28, August 9, 1887.

longer they would have to stay in prison and when they would get the good land Miles had promised them.[39] It would be twenty-six more weary years before their hopes would be realized. "I am an old man now," said Naiche at Fort Sill, and he still asked for "homes to ourselves where we can be to ourselves."[40]

Langdon, of course, was unware of these promises, and it was undeniable that these warriors had raided and killed. He did, however, try to salvage the youngest of them. Very soon he became interested in Goso, whose age he estimated at seventeen, and recommended that he be sent to Carlisle. Afterwards he sought the same opportunity for Chappo. His recorded impressions give the only known characterization of this tragic warrior son of Geronimo. In his first list of prisoners Chappo stood out as "a very intelligent young Indian." More than a year later, in recommending him for Carlisle, the officer gave this description: "Chappo. Age 23. This Indian is unusually intelligent; has learned considerable English and is ambitious to improve his mind and study subjects that will [be] of use to him in the future."[41] No doubt his father concurred. Throughout his later life Geronimo advocated equipping the youth of his band with the white man's techniques.

Sheridan gave his immediate approval to Langdon's first request regarding Goso. And eventually four of the young warriors were selected for educational training, but the red tape was not untangled until after the prisoners were removed from Fort Pickens. And now, with the arrival of their families, Langdon found three of their children who needed schooling. One was a son of Naiche, almost certainly the boy known as Paul. He was eventually sent to Hampton Normal and Agricultural Institute, the famous Virginia school for the training of Negroes, which at that time also accepted Indian students. The others were a brother and a sister (or possibly cousins) of Hunlona, orphans with no other relatives: a fifteen-year-old girl known as Katie and a small boy called Mike.[42]

[39] Goodman, *op. cit.*, p. 334.
[40] Berlin Basil Chapman, "Notes—Apaches."
[41] Consolidated File, Langdon's reports, March 24, 1887, and April 6, 1888.
[42] *Ibid.*, Langdon's reports, December 30, 1887, and April 23, 1888; Griswold, *op. cit.*, s.v. "Naiche, Paul."

Langdon soon became disturbed about Katie. An observance celebrated by the band in early June was unquestionably her womanhood ceremony. The Indians had wanted to hold it earlier, but Langdon, cooperating with the local tourist business, set a later date and invited visitors. About three hundred spectators joined the excursion, arriving on two steamers from Pensacola the evening of June 10. They thought they were seeing a Corn Dance designed to keep evil spirits from damaging the crop—a custom foreign to Apache practice—but in spite of his gross misinterpretation the reporting journalist unwittingly gave a clear description of the puberty rites. The party arrived late and missed part of the ceremony. No mention was made of the ritual involving the girl— it is even possible that the Indians managed to carry it out in private —but the Dance of the Mountain Spirits was clearly depicted.

A huge fire was blazing in the center of the parade ground so that even the interior of the extensive old fortress was lighted. A large buffalo robe had been placed on the ground with the skin side up, and Geronimo, Naiche, and about eight other men with switches in their hands formed a circle around it. In front of one of the men was a rude drum. As the spectators waited, they were startled by a strange cry rising in unison from the women inside the fortress—a reverent imitation, if they had known it, of the cry of White Painted Woman when her son, Child of the Water, returned from slaying the monsters of Apache mythology. As the reporter described it, "It was a peculiar cry, commencing very low and rising until it became very shrill, then dying away with a low wailing sound."

This was the signal for the men in the circle to begin "a wild kind of chant" accompanied by rhythmic beating on the hide and drum. Then two masked dancers appeared wearing the ceremonial costumes and pronged headdresses of the Mountain Spirits and performed the rite of "worshiping the fire"—to the undiscerning spectators, "a mimic warfare with the evil spirits." They were accompanied, as always, by a clown, whose actions were designed to create merriment but who at the same time was supposed to be invested with curative Power.

After about two hours the visitors returned to the city, but the Indians continued through the night. To the spectators it had been an entertaining exhibition of savage customs. In actuality, it can be seen as a moving revelation of the Apache spirit. Circumscribed as they were, these prisoners, far from their mountains and facing an unknown future, living in a grim old fortress on a narrow strip of sand with the sea closing them in, were still true to their ancient faith.[43]

As for Katie, she was now eligible for marriage. Although Langdon did not report his making an exhibit of the prisoners, he expressed his concern about her "in the interest of morality." He stated that Ahnandia, "who is living in the fort with his present wife wants to marry Katie—and her people [these would include Hunlona's relatives in Naiche's family] are said to be not averse to the 'marriage' so called." After a year of struggle with official regulations, he succeeded in sending her to Carlisle. She arrived on April 22, 1888, and died a year later—on May 27, 1889.[44]

Eventually, the four young warriors were also sent to Carlisle. Ira Goso, Chappo Geronimo, Eli Hunlona, and Calvin Zhonne entered the school on July 8, 1888. With them was Hunlona's young brother, who was enrolled as Bruce Patterson.[45] He remained there until 1898, when, having developed tuberculosis, he was transferred to the Indian service school at Albuquerque in the hope that the change of climate would benefit him. But he died there after slightly more than a month from a hemorrhage of the

43 *Pensacolian*, June 11, 1887.

44 Consolidated File, Langdon's reports, December 30, 1887, February 18, 1888 (with enclosed letter from Captain Pratt, February 13, 1888), and April 23, 1888; Acting Secretary of War (signature illegible) to Secretary of the Interior, March 8, 1888; and National Archives and Records Service, Record Group No. 75, Bureau of Indian Affairs, Records of the Carlisle Indian Industrial School, student record card of Katie Dionta.

45 U.S. Army and Missile Center Museum, "Names &c. of Chiricahua Indian Children at Carlisle Indian School."

Chappo Geronimo (left) and Jason Betzinez (right). The photograph was taken at Newtown, Pennsylvania, where Jason and possibly Chappo worked on farms between school sessions at Carlisle. Courtesy U.S. Army Artillery and Missile Center Museum.

The grave of Geronimo's wife, She-gha, under a tree in Barrancas Military Cemetery. *Geronimo's travels were marked by the graves or the mutilated corpses of the members of his family.* Author's collection.

lungs, at about the age of seventeen.[46] Three of the four young warriors were also to succumb to the tuberculosis that lay in wait for them at Carlisle. Hunlona was to die at the school, Goso was to end his life while working on a Pennsylvania farm during vacation, and Chappo Geronimo was to rejoin his band to die with his family.[47] Five out of six was an unusually high death rate even for Apache youths at Carlisle.

But at Fort Pickens the prisoners, including the children, continued in good health. The post surgeon visited them at least twice a week and found few cases of illness. There was one exception. Geronimo's wife She-gha had been "very ill" when she came, and

[46] National Archives and Records Service, Record Group No. 75, Bureau of Indian Affairs, Letters Received, 1881–1907, No. 42481–1898; and Records of the Carlisle Indian Industrial School, student record card of Bruce Patterson.

[47] Biographical sketches of the four warriors are in Griswold, *op. cit.*, which, however, mistakenly places Goso in Geronimo's band instead of the band of Mangus.

she never recovered her health. She died on September 28. Geronimo and a few other Indians were permitted to accompany the body across the strait to Fort Barrancas, where it was buried in the post cemetery. The cause of her death was ascribed in a current news account to Bright's disease, but the cemetery records show it to have been pneumonia. In June a woman who may have been She-gha had been reported as ill with "cold or rheumatism in the chest." It seems probable that she had become infected with tuberculosis at Fort Marion. Hers was the only death that occurred during the entire period at Fort Pickens.[48]

Finally, the War Department decided to remove this party also to Mount Vernon Barracks. On May 13, 1888, they were taken across the bay to Pensacola and placed on the train. They reached their destination on the same day, leaving the train at the railway station in the small town of Mount Vernon, one-half mile from the military post. Thus, they got their first view of the locality that was to become drearily familiar to them in the ensuing years.

The post was built on a ridge in a location considered healthful. Its buildings, constructed in the 1830's, were of brick, and it was enclosed by a massive brick wall. The military reservation of 2,160 acres and the surrounding land were covered with small pine timber growing on sand ridges interspersed with low-lying swales and swamps. The soil was unsuited for agriculture, and the region was sparsely populated, with here and there a log cabin occupied by a poor white or black family supported by working at a sawmill or by gathering turpentine.[49]

The newly arrived prisoners, with Geronimo leading, were taken up the hill to the post. There, in front of one of the gates of the barracks wall, they were grouped, sitting on their baggage awaiting orders and looking down on the village that had been

---

48 Consolidated File, Langdon's reports March 24 and June 28, 1887, and March 17, 1888; Goodman, *op. cit.*, p. 66, quoting from *Army and Navy Journal*, XXV (October 15, 1887), p. 223. The date on the grave marker, where her name appears as Ga-ah, is September 29, but this apparently indicates the date of burial.

49 *Senate Exec. Doc. 35*, 51 Cong., 1 sess., pp. 38–39, Report by Guy Howard, December 23, 1889; Joseph K. Edgerton, "A Glimpse of the Sunny South," *Plattsburgh Republican*, February 25, 1893.

built to house their compatriots. For some obscure reason these friends and relatives had not come out to meet them. This may have been a formal decision. Sam Kenoi remembered a council in which some members, blaming the holdout band for their own plight, objected to their return.[50] But this tribal division, if it occurred, was soon to disappear.

At the time, Geronimo advanced a few steps and surveyed the encampment. Not a soul was in sight. Finally, a woman emerged from a distant dwelling and came toward him with slow steps and bowed head. It was his daughter Dohn-say. Still following Apache convention, he appeared to be oblivious to her approach. But when she came close, her feelings overcame her. She ran to him, threw her arms around his neck, and burst into wild weeping. Not a muscle of his face relaxed, but his emotion must have been as deep as hers.[51]

Other reunions as keenly felt took place throughout the group. Except for the exiled youths at Carlisle, the band was one. But the years ahead would be bleak.

[50] Eve Ball furnished me notes of her interview with Sam Kenoi.

[51] Walter Reed, "Geronimo and His Warriors in Captivity," *The Illustrated American*, Vol. III (August 16, 1890), p. 232. Reed's knowledge of history and Apache character was faulty, but he gave a careful account of events he witnessed.

CHAPTER 18

LIFE AT MOUNT VERNON BARRACKS

Mount Vernon Barracks had a small garrison of infantry commanded by Major William Sinclair, who thereby became responsible for the Apache prisoners. When the main body arrived from Fort Marion on April 28, 1887, he marked their lassitude and attributed it to their scanty rations. They had been able to buy some food in Saint Augustine with the money they earned from the sale of souvenirs to tourists, but even so they had been hungry. Now they had lost even that market. A few still had some money they had brought along, and with it they bought cattle and sheep to butcher, but it was soon exhausted.

The post surgeon, J. H. Patzk, put it bluntly. On June 30, reporting on the health of the prisoners, he stated that he had found "a degree of debility perceptible in many of them and probably the cause of some deaths. I consider this condition due to previous hardships, privations and especially insufficient feeding." One man and two women had died since their arrival. Strictly speaking, they had not died from starvation. Two of the deaths had been caused by tuberculosis and one from debility, probably unrecognized tuberculosis.[1] Throughout their imprisonment the medical

[1] National Archives and Records Service, Consolidated File 1066 AGO 1883 (hereafter cited as Consolidated File), Patzk's report, June 30, 1887.

officers were baffled by this infection, the causes of which were not understood at the time, but this period of semi-starvation must have contributed to the Indians' susceptibility.

On May 5, only a week after their arrival, Sinclair began a single-handed fight on their behalf against the intrenched power of the War Department.[2] Some sharp exchanges took place between him and his superiors in the months that followed.[3] He was backed up by Dr. Walter Reed, destined for future fame, who came on August 15 as post surgeon.[4] Finally, a report Sinclair wrote on September 30 worked its way up to Sheridan. In it he told how the prisoners were selling or trying to pawn their possessions for food. Sheridan quoted it with this comment: "It is certainly a disgraceful condition of affairs . . . when the prisoners are compelled to part with their private effects; the blankets required to keep them warm, and their crosses and other religious articles [probably given them by the nuns at Saint Augustine] to obtain sufficient to eat." This time the War Department listened and sent out an order on October 27 authorizing the issuance of full army rations.[5]

But the prisoners continued to die. Although Reed, after the manner of army and Indian service personnel, wrote optimistic reports, the improvement he expected did not occur. By the end of the year two men, ten women, and nine children had died out of the 352 prisoners committed to the post eight months before. The causes of death were even more ominous: ten from "consumption," five from "debility from old age . . . most probably affected with latent disease of the lungs," one from pneumonia, and one from tubercular meningitis. There were also "readily observed manifestations of diseases of a scrofulous type," at that time not known to be tubercular in origin.[6] Wherever or however they had picked it up, the disease had fastened itself upon the prisoners. Even the

2 *Ibid.*, Reports of May 5, 21, and 26, 1887.
3 For example, *ibid.*, Report of August 24, 1887, with comments by commissary general of subsistence.
4 *Ibid.*, Reed's reports, August 31 and October 31, 1887.
5 *Ibid.*, Sinclair's report with endorsements by Sheridan and the War Department.
6 *Ibid.*, Report of Walter Reed, December 31, 1887.

The first Apache village at Mount Vernon Barracks. *The site was in a hollow surrounded by thick timber, cutting off the air and sun.* Courtesy Alabama Department of Archives and History, Montgomery.

relatively high birth rate—sixteen during the same eight months—could not take up the slack.

The prisoners were no longer subject to the crowding they had experienced within the ancient walls of the Castillo de San Marcos. At first they lived in army tents just outside the barracks walls.[7] Then in September the men were put to work cutting down trees and constructing log cabins to form a village near the gate of the post. The cabins were completed and occupied as the winter progressed—thirty-five during January, twenty-seven during February, and so on. Additional housing was required when Geronimo and his band arrived from Fort Pickens in May. The work was virtually finished during June.[8]

Each dwelling had two rooms, each ten feet square, with a covered open space between like the settlers' double log cabins

[7] Ibid., Isabel B. Eustis to "Mrs. Hemenway," January 5, 1888.
[8] *Ibid.*, monthly reports by Sinclair.

(exactly suited to Geronimo's family—Zi-yeh and Fenton in one room, Ih-tedda and Lenna in the other). They had earthen floors and no furniture. The Indians slept on the ground or on boards, cooked over open fires, and sat on the ground. The spaces between the logs were chinked with clay, and a Sibley stove and a circular hearth with no chimney provided some heat. The site was in a hollow surrounded by thick timber, cutting off the air and sun.[9] The dwellings were cold and damp in winter, hot and close in summer, probably less conducive to health than the easily moved native wickiups. Still, anything was an improvement over Fort Marion. Reed was able to report a decline in the death rate during the year 1888—only thirteen, of which only four were from "consumption," while during the same period there had been thirteen births. He began to hope that the mortality had been checked by "the healthfulness of the location" and the fact that the prisoners had been "well housed and properly clothed and rationed."[10]

But philanthropic friends of the Indians still worked to improve their unproductive captivity. In December, 1887, the Massachusetts Indian Association, a women's society of Boston, sent two women experienced in teaching Indians at Hampton to investigate and report. As interpreter they brought along fourteen-year-old Parker West, one of the young boys sent to Carlisle from San Carlos by Crook four years before.

They found the Apaches "a keen and intelligent people." Also, "As we went about their camp they seemed to us a kindly gentle folk, and their affection and confidence were not hard to win. . . . An intense love of their children is their most striking characteristic. . . . Our only obstacle came from [their] fear that we had come to take more of their boys and girls from them. . . . The arguments and appeals that were made to us on this account made us glad that this was not our errand. . . . They kept letters and reports from Carlisle which were months old wrapped in pieces of cloth they had embroidered."

9 *Ibid.*, Report July 25, 1892, by Lieutenant W. W. Wotherspoon, then in charge of the prisoners; Goodman, "Apaches as Prisoners of War," pp. 122–24.
10 Consolidated File, Reed's report, December 31, 1888.

The visitors believed that the work the men did in building cabins furnished training in industry, and in their judgment the final solution of the Apaches' problem lay in settling the families capable of self-support on farms of their own, preferably in the vicinity of Hampton or Carlisle. They talked with the leading men about their hopes for their future. It was apparent that "Arizona is a country which the Apaches almost worship," but realizing the enmity of the people there, they were reconciled to remaining in the East if some opportunity were offered for themselves and their children. "Only old Nana refused to be reconstructed." When he joined the conference, "the other men waited with reverence while he talked long and eloquently." The young interpreter faltered, then said "with great emphasis 'he wants to know Do you *love* your own HOME?' " One of the women showed him a globe of the world and explained that it was covered with people, so the Indians could no longer roam widely, but they and the white men must live and work together like brothers. "The old chief sat with his head buried in his hands and said with a heavy sigh, . . . 'I'm too old to learn that.' "

In reporting on their visit, the two women pointed out the need of a "missionary teacher" to carry on social and religious work among the prisoners, but they made no attempt to influence government policy regarding the Indians' final settlement.[11] Crook was more aggressive. He went to Washington and presented their case to President Cleveland and Secretary of War Endicott, and he rode over to Hampton and inspected a farm in the area that might serve as a reservation for them until they could be removed to Fort Sill.[12] But no official action was taken, and Cleveland was defeated for reelection that year. This meant a new administration unfamiliar with the situation.

Meanwhile, the Massachusetts Indian Association raised the money and with the permission of the War Department sent two "missionary teachers" to conduct a school for the children.

11 *Ibid.*, Report of Isabel B. Eustis to "Mrs. Hemenway," January 5, 1888. See also Reed, "Geronimo and His Warriors in Captivity," p. 235.
12 Goodman, *op. cit.*, pp. 130–32.

The teachers arrived on February 14, 1889. These two or their successors, Sophie and Sylvia Shepard, continued this work as long as the prisoners remained at Mount Vernon. They used a one-room building furnished by the post for the eighty-or-so children until the fall of 1892, when an additional room was added. It is apparent that the children enjoyed the school and loved their teachers.[13]

Geronimo was an enthusiastic supporter of the school. Always practical-minded, he recognized the importance of the white man's skills of learning, just as in earlier days he had replaced the bow and arrow with the gun and had sought to acquire a start in cattle raising. Apparently self-appointed, he brought in the children and spent much time with them, training them with the same strict discipline he had once used in preparing the boys to become warriors, policing the schoolroom with a stick in his hand to intimidate any youngster who might be tempted to misbehave. His interest was noticed by General Howard, now in command of the Division of the Atlantic, who came in April to inspect the prisoners. Remembering the meeting in Cochise's stronghold and the good years following, Geronimo ran and threw his arms around the general and broke into excited Apache. Then he found an interpreter and began to tell him about the school. "We have fine lady teachers," he said. "All the children go to their school. I make them. I want them to be white children." Later the mild-mannered Chihuahua was assigned to work as janitor and to "maintain order," a change that must have been welcomed by the pupils.[14]

Geronimo's son Fenton became old enough to attend the school before the prisoners were removed from Alabama. Also of school age were his granddaughter and probably a grandson, Nina and Joe Dahkeya.[15]

13 Consolidated File, Report by Sinclair, February 28, 1889; by Wotherspoon, October 13, 1891, July 25 and September 30, 1892, and October 1, 1893.
14 *Ibid.*, Report of Wotherspoon, July 25, 1892; Norman B. Wood, *Lives of Famous Indian Chiefs*, p. 550; Schmitt, *General George Crook*, p. 293; Howard, *Famous Indian Chiefs I Have Known*, pp. 358, 361–62; Edgerton, "A Glimpse of the Sunny South."
15 I am estimating the ages of Fenton and Nina by a photograph made in 1895. The age of Joe is not known. He died in 1899. See biographies in Griswold, "The Fort Sill Apaches."

Although he loved his family, Geronimo at that time deprived himself of the companionship of one wife and child. The Mescaleros had been importuning the government to return some of their people who had been caught in the roundup of reservation Indians at Fort Apache, and early in 1889 the War Department consented to send them home. Geronimo saw this as an opportunity to release Ih-tedda, as a member of that tribe, from the hopeless status of the prisoners. According to present Apache memories, she loved her husband and protested against leaving him, but he pointed out that the people were dying around them and that this was the only chance to save her life and Lenna's. Then she consented to go. The party, numbering twelve, left in February. Among them were Charlie Smith and his parents. His father, Askadodilges ("Hides His Foot," that is, "conceals his trail"), also named Charlie Smith, was the leader of the party. Thereafter, on the Mescalero Reservation he was known as "Alabama Charlie."[16]

A son, Robert, was born to Geronimo after Ih-tedda's return to New Mexico probably on August 2.[17] Through a reunion with Lenna fifteen years later, Geronimo received news of the family. As he told the story to Barrett, "So many of our people died that I consented to let one of my wives go to the Mescalero Agency in New Mexico to live. This separation is according to our custom equivalent to what the white people call divorce, and so she married soon after she got to Mescalero. She also kept our two small children, which she had a right to. The children, Lenna and Robbie, are still living at Mescalero, New Mexico."[18]

The sequel was to vindicate Geronimo's judgment in sending Ih-tedda back to their mountains. Her children were the only ones who were to live to perpetuate his family. Before the year 1889 was over, Reed had to admit that his hopes that the prisoners

16 Consolidated File, Reports of Sinclair, August 25, 1887, and February 28, 1889; Eve Ball, interview, July 23, 1971.
17 Robert Geronimo interview, August 7, 1957. He told me this was his birth date, but Apache dates are uncertain.
18 Barrett, *Geronimo's Story of His Life*, p. 178. For Geronimo's meeting with Lenna, see *infra*, pp. 412–14.

"were at last shaking off the disease which has been such a scourge to them" had been "premature and not well founded." On November 18 he reported that during the previous four months three of their wives, "all strong young women when my former report was made," and a girl of thirteen had died of pulmonary consumption and that three men and three women were ill with the same disease, "and within 90 days not one of these will be alive." Once contracted, it had proved "incurable"—"not one case has shown any improvement under treatment." He regarded the mortality as "simply appalling; this too amongst a people who, in Arizona, were remarkably exempt from lung troubles." (In this Dr. Reed was writing from his own experience; he had been stationed at Fort Apache and knew the Indians in their native surroundings.[19]) He could have added that nine of their children had recently been brought from Carlisle to die, the beginning of many such sad homecomings. And a compilation of school statistics made on July 1 that year showed that 27 of their original 112 had died there, 25 from tuberculosis, and that 2 of the remaining 76 were ill with scrofula (one of these last was Ira Goso).[20]

Without taking account of Carlisle, Reed attributed the trouble to the change from the dry air of the prisoners' homeland to "the excessive atmospheric moisture" of the coastal areas. Their transfer to Hampton, he felt, would be "very inadvisable." There had been a suggestion that a tract of land be purchased for them in the North Carolina mountains, where a holdout band of Cherokees had maintained themselves ever since the main body of that tribe had been driven to the Indian Territory half a century before. He was not prepared to say whether the high altitude and the distance from the coast of this region might make it a suitable location, but he was certain "that a dry climate must be the first consideration. I cannot urge this too strongly."

He said that the number of fatalities had caused "anxiety and alarm amongst the Indians." And adding to this "mental depres-

19 Ogle, *Federal Control of the Western Apaches*, p. 194 note 83.
20 Consolidated File, Report of John J. Cochran, July 1, 1889.

sion" was their conviction "that the Government does not propose, in the near future, to improve their condition." He said that Howard had told them during his visit in April that he was authorized by the president to find them a home. Then others, including Captain Bourke, had come to confer with them regarding a location. (They told these visitors that they would need good land, pasture, timber, and a start in livestock, and they especially wanted to go where a river flowed and where it snowed.[21]) These conferences, said Reed, had given them a hope for deliverance, but as the months passed "with nothing accomplished, as far as they can see, this feeling of hopefulness is rapidly subsiding."[22]

Nevertheless, efforts were still being made in their behalf. Later that year General Howard sent his son, Lieutenant Guy Howard, to investigate. The younger Howard reported on December 23 that he had found the camp at Mount Vernon "as good as a prison camp can be, but [it] can not be made a home." He presented the appalling mortality statistics—eighty-nine deaths in the camps and thirty at Carlisle, almost one-fourth of the total population in the three and one-half years since the first party came with Chihuahua in the spring of 1886. The men were put to work regularly, but "their labor is prison labor" without personal incentive. He recommended that Congress be advised to set them up in farming on "a suitable tract of land" by the following spring. "Another year's delay would be criminal."[23]

His report was duly forwarded to Secretary of War Redfield Proctor, who sent Crook on another investigation. Crook inspected the North Carolina tract late that same December and came on to Mount Vernon early in January, 1890. He arrived at the post unannounced and went at once to the home of the commanding officer. There, a young Indian spotted him and spread the news, and soon Chihuahua and Kaahteney appeared, overjoyed to see him. They all started to walk over to the Indian village, and outside the gate of the post they found a crowd wait-

---

21 Goodman, *op. cit.*, pp. 156–58.
22 Consolidated File, Reed's report, November 18, 1889.
23 *Senate Exec. Doc. 35*, 51 Cong., 1 sess., pp. 37–39.

ing. Chatto came up to shake hands with the general, and with his other hand made an instinctive motion as though to clasp him about the neck, then withdrew it, remembering rank. "It was a touching sight," said Crook's aide. Other Apaches crowded around, delightedly shaking hands with the general, while more came running to join in the greetings.

Soon the general settled down for a council with the headmen. Geronimo, accustomed to leadership, pressed forward to speak, but Crook said to Wratten, "I don't want to hear anything from Geronimo. He is such a liar that I can't believe a word he says."[24] He questioned Naiche, as related in a previous chapter, as to his reasons for breaking away after surrendering to him. Then he asked why this runaway band had finally decided to come in. Their response wrecked Miles's claim that he had conquered them. As was his custom, Crook had every word recorded. The colloquy follows:

General CROOK. How did you come to surrender. Were you afraid of the troops?

NATCHEZ. We wanted to see our people.

General CROOK. Did troops force you to surrender?

NATCHEZ. We were not forced to do it. We talked under a flag of truce.

Wratten then told how the surrender had been accomplished. "Could the surrender have been made without the scouts?" asked Crook.

"I do not think so," said Wratten.

Members of the group then related their experiences: their observance of the pledge they had made to keep the peace, their losses when they were taken from their small economic ventures on the reservation, their ever-present hope for a viable future.

Chatto took from his breast the medal given him at Washington,

24 Schmitt, *op. cit.*, pp. 292–93.

and, holding it out, he said, "Why did they give me that to wear in the guard-house? I thought something good would come to me when they gave me that but I have been in confinement ever since I have had it." He told how he had left everything to make the trip: "I was working on my farm and had one field planted in wheat and another in barley. . . . I had a wagon and could make a good deal of money with that hauling hay, supplies, etc. I didn't leave these of my own accord. I had sheep, about thirty head, that were increasing all the time; I had to leave them. I made money by shearing them and selling the wool; I had horses and mules which were worth a good deal of money. . . . You told us about farms; I got a plow and took good care of everything."

Others told of the property they had been forced to abandon on the reservation. Some of their livestock had been gathered up and sold, and the army, with much paper work, had kept account and doled the money out to them in five-dollar monthly payments,[25] but all had suffered losses. Noche said he had been paid for his horses but not for ninety cords of wood he had piled up for sale. Kaahteney said he had lost his crop and his wagon. Chatto gave figures to show that the payment for the livestock was grossly inadequate. Humble beginnings, but important to them, had been wiped out.

Kaahteney reminded Crook of how he had used his influence to induce the hostiles to surrender at the Cañon de los Embudos— "I talked your talk to them and your mind to them." He went on to say, "I never did anything wrong and never went on the warpath since I saw you. I tried to think as you told me to and was very thankful to you, and was very glad to see you again this morning; all the Indians were, even to the little children." He described his unproductive labor in the prison camp: "I help build roads, dig up roots, build houses, and do work all around here. Leaves fall off the trees and I help to sweep them up. I was working this morning

---

25 These payments were recorded in the reports of the post commanders until the last one was made on May 1, 1890. See, for example, Consolidated File, reports by Sinclair, December 5, 1887, and Major W. L. Kellogg, May 1, 1890.

when you came here. I don't know why I work here all the time for nothing. . . . I have children and relatives, lots of them, and I would like to work for them before I get too old to work. I'd like to have a farm . . . long enough to see the crops get ripe."

Chihuahua also said he would like to have a farm "and go right to work so that my children can have plenty to eat. . . . I have a daughter away at school and two other near relatives. I want to see them soon. Won't you make it so I can see them very soon?" And with the smothering pines surrounding him, thinking of the wide vistas of his homeland, he ended his appeal: "There are trees all about. I would like to go where I can see."

In his report Crook asserted that by the "most ordinary justice" those Indians who had served the government should not be held as prisoners: "Their farms have been taken from them, and others should be given to them. I cannot too strongly urge that immediate steps be taken to secure a reservation for them," where they could "work for themselves" and receive "the full benefit of their labors." Their mortality, he thought, was "due to home-sickness, change of climate, and the dreary monotony of empty lives."

He did not recommend sending them back to Arizona. If any trouble should break out so that they would again take the war-path, "it would be utterly impossible ever to get them to surrender again," and the cost in lives and property would be enormous. But he was convinced that no matter where they were placed they would be as law-abiding as any community in the country. He thought the North Carolina region the most suitable of any locality in the eastern United States, but he preferred the Indian Territory as more nearly like their homeland. Finally, he said he considered it a mistake to send their children to Carlisle, "a place which, from whatever cause it may be, proves so fatal to them. . . . Apaches are fond of their children and kinsfolk, and they live in terror lest their children be taken from them and sent to a distant school."

The secretary of war immediately recommended to the president that the prisoners be settled in one of the two suggested locations. Either would be satisfactory, but the Indian Territory seemed the

347

better choice provided Congress could be induced to repeal the prohibition of 1879.[26]

Neither Crook nor Proctor understood the significance of recent events in the Indian Territory. The barrier that had reserved it for Indians had been broken the previous April when a tract in its heartland had been opened to white settlement. The very session of Congress that would be urged to admit the Apaches was creating a Territory of Oklahoma to embrace the new frontier, and plans were rapidly being pushed to break up all the Indian reservations there in preparation for additional land openings.[27] A resolution to put Proctor's Indian Territory plan into effect was introduced in the Senate and hotly debated, but there was never any chance of its passage. Crook, who had been leading the fight, died of a heart attack on March 21, but his death scarcely affected the outcome.[28] The prisoners remained in Alabama.

The War Department then attempted to "improve their condition where they now are located and are likely to remain." In June Lieutenant William W. Wotherspoon was sent to take special charge of them. He initiated plans for converting a mess hall and kitchen into a makeshift hospital. Eventually, the War Department constructed an adequate hospital and staffed it. Wotherspoon managed to use money from savings on the regular rations to buy milk, eggs, and other special foods for the patients.[29]

Even during the first lean days Major Sinclair had been able to hold out and sell some less needed supplies from the rations and buy potatoes and onions, which he hoped would protect the prisoners against scurvy. Then they were put to work clearing land and planting a garden. In spite of the poor soil, this plot produced enough vegetables for their own use and some for sale, besides making more surplus available from the rations. The money thus

[26] *Senate Exec. Doc. 35*, 51 Cong., 1 sess., pp. 29–36.

[27] The rapidity with which the former Indian Territory was settled and developed by white homesteaders and city builders is a familiar story. Oklahoma had a population of 1,414,177, of which Indians constituted only 5.3 per cent when it was admitted to statehood in 1907.

[28] See Schmitt, *op. cit.*, pp. 294–300, for the fight over the measure.

[29] Consolidated File, Wotherspoon's reports, November 30, 1890, and February 28 and April 30, 1891.

accumulated became a special fund used for their benefit—the payment of "salaries" of about ten dollars a month to those performing such services as supervising the gardening and washing the hospital linens, and the purchase of such household conveniences as cooking utensils and knives, forks, and spoons, and even prizes and Christmas treats for the school children.[30]

The gardening was done by the women and older men. The able-bodied men worked six days a week about the post or in improving their own village. George Wratten served not only as interpreter but also as superintendent of the labor crew. He married a young Apache girl, and their two daughters, known as Amy and Blossom White, became the mothers of some of the most gifted of present-day Apaches.[31] Geronimo, for some reason, disliked Wratten,[32] but it is apparent that most of the Apaches trusted him, and it is certain that he presented their case effectively to army officers.

Although the prisoners worked industriously at this forced labor, Wotherspoon believed that their final salvation lay in individual incentive. He held the current theory that Indians in general should disappear as Indians and merge into the general population; and applying this to the Apaches, he hoped that it would end their unproductive status as prisoners. Thus he released them from his labor gang and encouraged them to take employment for wages cutting wood or working on farms. By the following February four of them were working on a farm fifteen miles from the post. They were allowed to take their families along and were prospering.[33]

But Secretary Proctor had another plan for distributing Indians throughout the general population. His idea was to enlist them in the army, and he decided to begin with the Apaches, who

30 The meticulously kept records of these transactions can be traced in all the reports of the officers in charge.
31 See biographical sketches in Griswold, *op. cit.* Wratten and his Apache wife separated shortly before they left Alabama, and he subsequently married a white woman.
32 Barrett, *op. cit.*, p. 179.
33 Consolidated File, Wotherspoon's reports, July 31 and August 31, 1890, and February 28 and March 31, 1891.

had certainly demonstrated their qualifications as fighters. This canceled out Wotherspoon's policy of civilian employment. The able-bodied men responded eagerly; forty-six enlisted in May, 1891, leaving only twenty-eight men remaining in the camp. Some of their young men from Carlisle soon joined them. An additional thirty-one young men from various Apache tribes on the San Carlos Reservation also enlisted and were brought from Arizona. (Three of these last contracted tuberculosis immediately, although they had had very little contact with the prisoners in the village.[34]) These Apache soldiers formed Company I of the Twelfth Infantry. They were put to work at once building barracks. They lived under the same conditions as other enlisted men, receiving the same pay, and were subject to the same regulations.

Besides their regular drills they received an hour of instruction in English every day. They wore army uniforms, had their hair cut, and received given names, by which they were known thereafter. Among their noncommissioned officers were Sergeant Burdett Tsisnah and Corporal Larry Fun. Other members of the company were such well-known former hostiles as Naiche, Ahnandia, and Mangus. The company had field work with bridge building, scouting, trailing, and skirmishing (they must have enjoyed this).[35] They also spent much time building houses.

A better site had been selected for a new village on a sand ridge about three-fourths of a mile from the post, and the War Department furnished the building material. The work began early in 1891 while the men were still prisoners and was continued after their enlistment as soldiers. The army employed one or two skilled carpenters to instruct them, and they showed great aptitude and mechanical ability. They built about eighty small, snug houses, painted outside and finished within, floored, and set on adequate foundations, very different from the hovels in which they had

34 *Ibid.*, Report of Post Surgeon W. C. Borden, July 25, 1892. By this time two had died and the other was near death.

35 *Ibid.*, Wotherspoon's reports, May 31 and December 5, 1891, with attached summary, and September 2 and November 1, 1892; Report by D[avid] J. Baker, October 31, 1891. See also Edgerton, *op. cit.*, for the impression these Indian soldiers made on an observant visitor.

Geronimo at Mount Vernon Barracks. "Geronimo is the leading character among these people. He is no longer a savage in appearance or dress." Courtesy U.S. Army Artillery and Missile Center Museum.

351

formerly lived. Each house was furnished with a cooking range and with bedsteads, tables, and chairs made by the men. The women kept their houses neat and showed their pride by adding decorative touches.[36]

Geronimo lived in one of these houses with Zi-yeh, their small son Fenton, and a cherished baby daughter, Eva, born September 23, 1889.[37] An intelligent observer who visited the post in February, 1893, wrote a lively description of him and his family:

Geronimo is the leading character among these people. He is no longer a savage in appearance or dress. I have met him often. He gave me a call a Sunday or two ago, with his wife, quite a young squaw, and their child. All had a holiday look, and the Chief, a man of 60 or more years, instead of compelling his squaw to carry the baby, a clean, good looking one, in the usual papoose cradle or hamper, on her back, was hauling it himself, in a child's little express wagon, and seemed quite proud of his employment. [Eva was three years old at the time.] G. is a large, well formed man, with a good head and strong Apache features, with a keen and crafty look in his eyes, and a certain dignity of bearing, indicating a man of authority and self respect.

The prisoners had complete freedom about the post and the reservation "and are daily met coming and going between their village and the trading stores at Mount Vernon, where they are both sellers and buyers." There was no tourist trade in the area, but passengers arriving on the train furnished a market for their craft articles, some of which this observer characterized as "very handsome and ingenious." Geronimo was very active in this business.[38] The visitor continued:

[36] Consolidated File, Wotherspoon's reports, April 30, June 30, and December 5, 1891, and Baker's report, October 31, 1891.

[37] This date is given in Griswold, *op. cit.*, s.v. "Godeley, Eva Geronimo." It seems to be an exact record rather than an estimate.

[38] See, for example, Howard, *op. cit.*, p. 358.

Geronimo has an eye to thrift and can drive a sharp bargain with his bows and arrows, and quivers and canes, and other work, in which he is skillful. He prides himself upon his autograph, written thus, G E R O N I M O, which he affixes to what he sells, usually asking an extra price for it. He had a curious head dress, which he called, and Mr. Wratten says was his war bonnet. It is a sort of skull cap of buckskin, profusely and tastefully adorned with beads, and thirteen silver ornaments, representing the sun, moon and stars, and surmounted by a beaded cross, between two horn-like ornaments. . . . He seemed to value this bonnet highly, but finally, in his need or greed for money, offered it for sale for $25—his wife strongly objecting. [Probably her clever hands had fashioned it.] I finally bought it for a much less price, with a large bead necklace, which goes with it. . . . I asked him to write his name in the bonnet, and offered him a pen for the purpose, but he declined the pen, and went out and cut a small, dry twig, which he sharpened to a fine point, and then very slowly, and with much pains-taking, printed his name with the stick dipped in ink. This is the extent of his writing. . . . Adorned with his war bonnet and necklace, the old Chief is a picturesque figure, and has his share of personal vanity.[39]

Thus, the prisoners tried to achieve a normal life in captivity. All their supervisors reported on their good conduct, their cheerfulness, their industry. But the women *would* gamble, and too many of the men had no resistance to the intoxicants supplied by a low class of whites and blacks just outside the military reservation. They were sober most of the time, but it was a sobriety enforced by the vigilance of the army officers and the prosecution of the bootleggers.[40] Soon after assuming charge, Wotherspoon appointed Geronimo as a "judge" or "justice of the peace" to try minor

39 Edgerton, *op. cit.*
40 This is a recurring theme in Wotherspoon's reports. See, for example, Consolidated File, January 31, June 30, and August 31, 1891, and October 1, 1893.

offenses at a monthly "salary" of $10.50 or $10.80 paid from his special fund.[41] Geronimo was very severe at first, sentencing one offender to six months in the guardhouse for getting drunk and imposing one hundred years imprisonment in another, more aggravated, case. But given some instruction and training, he learned to assess more reasonable penalties.[42]

Once Wotherspoon, after the manner of officials in charge of Indians, reported an improvement in their moral condition. He referred, of course, to sexual morality, not realizing that Apaches were more strict in this regard than contemporary white society. He was thinking of their polygamy and their informal divorce practices. Four of them had recently been married according to white customs at their own requests.[43] It is apparent that by the time they left Alabama they had abandoned polygamy except for the marriages already in existence. Geronimo never had but one wife at a time after he sent Ih-tedda back to her people.[44]

There were two cases of marital difficulty during the seven and one-half years the prisoners were kept at Mount Vernon. One that affected the family of Geronimo occurred in March, 1892, when Fun, becoming jealous of his young wife, shot her and killed himself. She, being only slightly wounded, recovered.[45] Two years later, in April, 1894, another man shot his wife and then himself.[46] There were also two cases of drunken quarrels between men that resulted in violent deaths.[47] But generally, the Apaches, in spite of their turbulent past, observed harmonious relations with each other.

Always a religious people in their native culture, they were now coming under the influence of Christianity. During at least part of

[41] This expenditure appears in Wotherspoon's reports from October 31, 1891, and was continued through 1894. The "judge" is not named, but it is fairly certain that Geronimo served throughout. See, for example, mention of "the Indian Judge Geronimo" by Wotherspoon's successor, C. C. Ballou, in his report of April 18, 1894.

[42] Edgerton, op. cit.

[43] Consolidated File, Report, February 28, 1891.

[44] Barrett, op. cit., p. 179.

[45] Consolidated File, Wotherspoon's report, March 31, 1892.

[46] Ibid., Report, C. C. Ballou, April 18, 1894.

[47] Ibid., Report of Wotherspoon, June 1, 1893; Report of Allyn K. Capron, June 23, 1894.

the period, the post chaplain conducted two services for them on Sundays—a Sunday school in the morning for their children and a service for the men and women in the afternoon. Both services were well attended.[48] Also the two women "missionary teachers" must have given the school children religious instruction along with the three R's. And some of the Indians apparently retained the impression made by the Catholic nuns at Saint Augustine. In July, 1890, Geronimo's wife Zi-yeh and the baby Eva were baptized in the Catholic Church at Mount Vernon.[49] This may explain the cross on the old warrior's headdress.

Meanwhile, the school was having a problem unrelated to religious instruction. Some of the children had grown up to the age at which they needed a different type of education. Wotherspoon tried to give the older boys some vocational training by taking them out of school half of each day to work at carpentry, but he recommended sending them to Carlisle or Hampton.[50] The War Department took no action, but the Massachusetts Indian Association raised enough money to support four of the older girls at Hampton.

By this time, Wotherspoon had become an aide to General Howard, and his successor, Lieutenant Charles C. Ballou, encountered the objection of their parents. He warned that if the girls remained at home they would soon marry and produce more children to grow up "in a camp of three or four hundred compulsory paupers." But the post commander hesitated "to sever family ties . . . where no crime is alleged," and the question worked its way up to Howard. Wotherspoon's advice to the general is a classic example of heartless official mendacity. He said it was simply a question whether the Indians' future should "be shaped by those in authority, who look" to their "ultimate good" or "by those old squas and men who have only personal motives and slight affection to guide them. . . . Knowing that it is Indian custom for the

48 *Ibid.*, Report of W[illiam] H. Pearson, December 31, 1891.
49 Goodman, *op. cit.*, p. 196 and note 8. The story was sometimes told that Geronimo himself had been baptized five times, but there is no reason to credit it.
50 Consolidated File, Reports, November 1, 1892, and July 1, 1893.

mothers to practically sell their daughters" he could understand their "aim in opposing their education." He had learned "to place little reliance upon Indian family-affection." The War Department agreed, and the girls were sent.[51]

It must be admitted, however, that the Carlisle and Hampton graduates, with a very few exceptions, did not merge into the general population but returned to their people.[52] In this same report Ballou expressed his perplexity regarding the status of three young men recently returned from Carlisle. The acting secretary of war instructed him to tell them that they were "free to live and seek employment wherever they prefer," but they would not be "permitted to remain with the prisoners of their tribe." Since the government had furnished them "ample opportunity to secure an education and learn a trade they must henceforth support themselves." But the order lapsed. At least two of the three remained,[53] and the Carlisle graduates continued to merge with the prisoners.

The officers in charge were also perplexed about the status of the men they had enlisted in the army. Before Wotherspoon left, he reported early in 1894 that the three years' service of most of them would soon expire. Would they revert to the status of prisoners, or would they be free to return to Arizona, leaving their wives and children still in captivity?[54] The War Department decided that they were free, but all but two unattached young men chose to join their prisoner families.[55]

Thus, the War Department was stuck with the prisoners. Its plan

---

[51] *Ibid.*, Report of Ballou, March 31, 1894, with endorsements; Report of Allyn K. Capron, July 5, 1894. Two years before this, Wotherspoon had written to an Indian interest group, "In his home the Indian is a good and faithful husband, a tender and affectionate father" (quoted by Goodman, *op. cit.*, p. 205). One is tempted to discredit all of Wotherspoon's reports, but they fit into the general pattern, which is in the main trustworthy.

[52] This is evident in the biographies in Griswold, "The Fort Sill Apaches." Although a few worked for a time in the industrial plants of Pennsylvania and New York, nearly all eventually joined the prisoners. For Jason Betzinez' satisfactory experience in a steel mill and his final return, see *I Fought with Geronimo*, pp. 159–61, 164.

[53] See biographies of the three—Knox Nostlin, Oswald Smith, and Leonard Kanesewah—in Griswold, *op. cit.* Not much is recorded here of Knox Nostlin; he probably died in Alabama.

[54] Consolidated File, Report, January 25, 1894.

[55] Griswold, *op. cit.*, s.v. "Jose Second" and "Jim Miller."

to find a home for them in the Indian Territory had been rejected by Congress. Next, its intention of dispersing them through educational training, outside employment, and army service had failed. Attempts to check their mortality by adequate housing and hospital care also failed. True, there was less sickness caused by unsanitary living conditions, but the hoped-for decline in tubercular infection had not occurred. In 1892 Wotherspoon concluded that this disease was due mainly to their "hereditary and physical degeneracy."[56] (The "hereditary and physical degeneracy" of Apaches!) Post Surgeon W. C. Borden was more scientific. His reports show serious consideration of the factors involved, and in the following year he published a comprehensive analysis of the prisoners' health problem based on a sympathetic understanding of their culture and the history of their confinement.[57]

The vital statistics from 1891 on are misleading because the frequent deaths of enlisted men were not included and because forty-six unrelated Apache prisoners from Arizona were added to the village population.[58] But a list of deaths by months from January 1, 1893, through July, 1894, shows a dreary pattern of pulmonary tuberculosis, tubercular meningitis, lupus, and intestinal tuberculosis.[59]

By that time, however, the continued efforts of philanthropic friends of the Indians had once more set the War Department to seeking a different location for the prisoners. This was to result in their removal from Alabama.

[56] Consolidated File, Report, July 25, 1892. His conclusion accords with general medical theory at the time as recorded under "Phthisis" in the ninth edition of the Encyclopedia Britannica. For sanitary regulations and problems, see the report of Surgeon-General C. Sutherland in Secretary of War, *Annual Report*, 1892, pp. 501–504.

[57] Borden, "The Vital Statistics of an Apache Indian Community."

[58] These consisted of the celebrated Eskiminzin and his band. I have told their story briefly in *A History of the Indians of the United States*, pp. 268–71, 281–82.

[59] Consolidated File, Report of Attending Surgeon Charles LeBaron, August 1, 1894.

CHAPTER 19

THE PRISONERS ARE BROUGHT
TO FORT SILL

Late in 1893 the War Department began a second attempt to relocate the prisoners. In December, Wotherspoon, accompanied by Captain Pratt, was sent for another inspection of the North Carolina mountains. He reported that the arable land was insufficient, either in the Cherokee tract or in the area adjoining it. But as he observed the industrious and self-supporting Cherokees he was convinced that a similar opportunity should be provided the prisoners. He thought it unnecessary that the farms furnished them "be contiguous, or, indeed, even in the same vicinity. The more these people are broken up, and the sooner they are thrown into association with the whites, the better."

In his endorsement the post commander, Major George D. Russell, suggested that they be located "even in divided bands if necessary" near prosperous farming or manufacturing communities in New England or the Middle States: "The women and children are naturally deft of hand, and some might make fair factory operatives." General Howard proposed sending them "in small parties, to different western reservations," or posssibly land could be found on some reservation for all of them. General John M. Schofield, Sheridan's successor as commander in chief of the army, suggested one limitation, that they be not sent to Texas, New Mexico, or Arizona.[1]

The War Department worked on Congress, and on August 6 the following year it obtained an amendment to the Army Appropriation Act authorizing their transfer to any military reservation under its control.[2] The War Department then considered a plan to distribute them in various locations throughout the country. It was referred to Miles, then commanding the Department of the Missouri, which embraced the eastern half of the Western posts. Although Miles had been largely responsible for the plight of the prisoners in the first place, he had the grace to oppose this policy emphatically, saying it would be "gross injustice and refined cruelty" to separate these families and friends. He again suggested Fort Sill, now in his department, and ordered Lieutenant Hugh Lenox Scott, who was stationed there, to go with Captain Maus, at that time on his staff, to Alabama to confer with the Apaches.[3]

Before Scott left, word of the contemplated move got out. The Comanches and their Kiowa and Kiowa-Apache allies heard of it and held a council, then came to consult with the lieutenant. They knew and trusted him. He had been associated with Indians in war and peace ever since he went out from West Point to serve in the Seventh Cavalry just after its disastrous defeat under Custer on the Little Bighorn; he had become an expert in the sign language; and with tact and understanding he had contained the ghost dance excitement on the South Plains at the very time an inept handling of the situation in the North had culminated in the massacre at Wounded Knee. Now the Indians told him they had never liked the Apaches, but they consented to let them come if they would remain on the military reservation. Even this consent was a concession granted out of typical Indian sympathy for a homeless people, for the post was built on their land, which would revert to them when

1 National Archives and Records Service, Consolidated File 1066 AGO 1883 (hereafter cited as Consolidated File), Wotherspoon's report, December 14, 1893, and endorsements.

2 U.S., *Statutes*, XXVIII, 238.

3 Consolidated File, Miles to Major George W. Davis, Office of the Secretary of War, September 3, 1894.

it should be abandoned.[4] (Its permanent development as an artillery and missile center was not then envisioned.)

Maus and Scott held their conference with the chiefs and leaders of the prisoners on August 29. Second Lieutenant Allyn K. Capron, who was then in charge of them, was present, and Wratten served as interpreter. Scott recorded the proceedings. The Apaches were questioned "concerning their wishes to be removed to some other locality." Geronimo gave their answer. His unadorned statement—Geronimo lacked eloquence—is an accurate summary of their feelings:

I am very glad to hear you talk—I have been wanting for a long time to hear somebody talk that way. I want to go away somewhere where we can get a farm, cattle, and cool water.

I have done my best to help the authorities—to keep peace & good order to keep my house clean—God hears both of us and what he hears must be the truth. We are very thankful to you— these poor people who have nothing and nothing to look forward to—what you say makes my head and whole body feel cool—we are all that way—we want to see things growing around our houses, corn and flowers—we all want it—we want you to talk for us to Gen'l Miles in the same way you have talked to us—

Young men old men women and children all want to get away from here—it is too hot and wet—too many of us die here—I remember what I told General Miles— . . . I told him that I wanted to be a good man as long as I live and I have done it so far. I stood up on my feet and held up my hands to God to witness what I said was true—. I feel good about what you say and it will make all the other Indians feel good—Every one of us have got children at school and we will behave ourselves on account of these children, we want them to learn   I do not consider that I am an Indian any more   I am a white man and w'd like to go around and see different places   I consider that all white men are my brothers

---

[4] Hugh Lenox Scott, *Some Memories of a Soldier*, pp. 182, 184.

Apache leaders at Mount Vernon Barracks in 1893. From left: Chihuahua, Naiche, Loco, Nana, and Geronimo. "Only old Nana refused to be reconstructed." Courtesy National Archives and Records Service.

and all white women are now my sisters—that is what I want to say.

This last assertion that he had taken up white ways and had come to accept white people would have been characterized by Crook in his day as more of Geronimo's lying, but the ensuing fifteen years were to prove his sincerity.

Maus wanted to be sure Geronimo spoke for the group. "I understand it to be your opinion that all of you want to go somewhere," he said.

"We all want to go everybody," Geronimo answered.

He was followed by Chihuahua, Naiche, Nana, Chatto, an Indian named Ruby (he was the son-in-law of Loco, and his young daughter at Carlisle was to become the mother of the future tribal chairman, Benedict Jozhe), Kaahteney, Mangus, and Loco.

361

Geronimo had indeed expressed the sentiments of the group; evidently, they had held a meeting of their own and had formulated their position. Several reminded Maus of their previous meetings with him and told of their changed attitude and their acceptance of the white man's way. Naiche said, "We live just like white people, have houses and stoves just like them and we want to have a farm just like other white people—we have been here a long time and have not seen any of us have a farm yet." Chihuahua said, "God made the earth for everybody & I want a piece of it—I want to have things growing——." And referring to the enclosing timber, he continued, "I want the wind to blow on me just as it blows on everybody else—I want the sun to shine on me and the moon just as on everybody else." Even Nana made one concession; although he was "too old to work," he wanted "to see all the young men have a farm and I could go around and talk to them and get something to eat."

Chatto said, "If anything I could say would hurry up the farms I wish it would—You can find some of the old people yet—the grandfathers and grandmothers, but most of them are dead—that is why I do not like it here. I want to hurry—I want you to tell Gen'l Miles to get them away from here in a hurry." Kaahteney expressed the same desperate concern: "I had lots of friends— cousins brothers & relatives when you saw me but since coming to this country they have all died— . . . I have children here and am all the time afraid that they will get sick and die——." Loco said that "it is just like a road with a precipice on both sides—they fall off on both sides—nobody killed them—sickness did it——."

Chihuahua spoke as usual of his scattered children: "I went to Carlisle to see them [as far as is known, there is no record of this trip] and it made my heart feel good to see them in the white mans road——." But even so, "I want to have all our children together where I can see them," and "I want my children wherever I go——." And thinking of the time Maus brought him back as a hostile, he assured the captain, "I want you to look at me and see that I am not like what I was when you saw me before——."

Mangus told of his life in hiding, of his voluntary surrender (very different from the army tale of his "capture"), and of his being brought to Fort Pickens: "When I got there I have been up to this time a good man and have never stepped of [*sic*] the good path (Lt Capron in charge of prisoners here stated, this man has the best record of any man in Co "I" 12th Infantry) While walking around I always want to look pleasant at everybody————." As for the place where they lived, "here we are in this little bit of a reservation—there are lots of trees here yes—they give shade but when you put your foot on the ground it burns you————."[5]

As Scott remembered it later, some of the prisoners told him the reservation was no larger than a thumbnail and that the trees were so thick one had to climb to the top of a tall pine to see the sun. He assured them that they would be sent to a place where they could not only look up at the sun but see mountains.[6]

Miles sent their statements along with his recommendations to the War Department, and it was officially decided that they would be sent to Fort Sill. They would still be prisoners of war; Oklahoma was no longer an "Indian Territory" with unassigned land out of which a reservation could be carved for a homeless tribe.

The post commander at Fort Sill, angry at the prospect of having to take the prisoners, planned to build a palisaded pen and corral them there under guard. Scott managed to pass the word to Miles, and Miles went over the commander's head and appointed Scott to take charge of them. The commander was soon transferred to the East. Scott believed that if he had remained at Fort Sill he would have driven the prisoners into running away. The resulting war in hunting them out of their native mountains would have been worse than anything that had gone before.[7]

All was now ready for their removal. But before they left, Geronimo suffered a personal bereavement. Chappo, the "unusually bright young Indian," who had been "ambitious to improve his

---

5 Consolidated File, Verbatum report of the conference, Scott to Maus, August 29, 1894.

6 Scott, *op. cit.*, pp. 182–83.

7 *Ibid.*, pp. 187–88.

mind and study subjects that will [be] of use to him in the future" was sent from Carlisle in the last stages of tuberculosis to die with his people; he died on September 9. His body was placed on the train for the short journey to Mobile and, with a sergeant from the post in charge, was buried in the national cemetery there. Geronimo went along "with two of his wives, one the Mother of Crappo [*sic*]," according to a contemporary newspaper.[8] Geronimo had only one wife, and Chappo's mother, if she still lived, was in Mexican slavery. The woman besides Zi-yeh was probably the young man's sister, Dohn-say.

Thus, Geronimo's travels were marked by the graves, or in some cases by the mutilated corpses, of the members of his family. First, he buried his father in peace near the quiet headwaters of the Gila; next, through the violent years, the bodies of his mother. wives, and children were strewn along his bloody trails through Old Mexico and Arizona; then there were the graves of his little girl at Saint Augustine and his wife at Pensacola; and now the son upon whom he had set his hopes lay buried in the cemetery at Mobile. And he, himself, was bound for a last resting place where other graves would surround his own in the prisoners' cemetery at Fort Sill.

The plans for the removal were soon made. The able and humane Capron was in charge of the prisoners during the journey. Early in October they were placed on a special train which brought them by way of New Orleans and Fort Worth to Rush Springs, Oklahoma. At stops on the way Geronimo, in particular, received the usual ovations, to the great disgust of Oklahomans at such honors to a "murderer"—"The old devil should have been hung fifteen years ago." At Rush Springs wagons waited to take them the thirty miles to Fort Sill.[9] They arrived on October 4, a bedraggled looking party numbering only 296.[10] (This was not their entire

8 *Mobile Daily News*, September 12, 1894; article furnished me through the courtesy of Mr. John A. Shapard, Jr.

9 W[ilbur] S[turtevant] Nye, *Carbine and Lance*, p. 380.

10 Secretary of War, *Annual Report*, 1895, p. 34. I believe this is the correct number. Army figures in other places vary because of the inclusion of unrelated prisoners or the omission of the enlisted men.

population; about forty-five of their youths were still at Carlisle or Hampton or in a very few cases living and working in the East.) They had no livestock, not even a dog or cat. They had a few trunks and boxes, but most of their meager possessions had been destroyed by a fire in a railroad freight shed at New Orleans.[11]

Hundreds of Kiowas and Comanches, their enmity forgotten, came to meet them. They tried to talk with them in the sign language, but these mountain people were unfamiliar with this universal system of Plains Indian communication. Scott took some Kiowa-Apaches to see them, but the dialects were too dissimilar for mutual understanding. They called this Plains band "half Apaches" because they could understand only half of what they said. Finally, both sides produced Carlisle boys, and they communicated through the English language.[12]

Capron remained to assist Scott in supervising the prisoners, and Wratten continued as their interpreter. As at Fort Pickens and Mount Vernon Barracks, the men worked under army command. When they arrived, it was too late in the season to build houses; thus, they put up wickiups in the brush along a creek, using army canvas in place of skins for the overall covering. Soon after they came, they learned that mesquite trees grew in southwestern Oklahoma. Beans from these trees were among their favorite foods, but they had not tasted any since leaving their homeland. The nearest grove was forty-five miles away, but they asked Scott for permission to gather beans there. He said they could go if they would leave after noon on Saturday and be back for work by 7:00 A.M. on Monday. They took along a few horses to carry tents, supplies, and beans. They gathered about three hundred bushels of beans, trotted the ninety-mile round trip, and were ready for work Monday morning.[13]

Meanwhile, schooling had to be provided for their children. The Shepard sisters had been willing to accompany them, but the War Department refused to pay their salaries, and their sponsors

11 *Ibid.*, p. 298.
12 Scott, *op. cit.*, pp. 188–89; Nye, *op. cit.*, p. 380.
13 Scott, *op. cit.*, p. 197.

An Apache wickiup at Fort Sill, winter, 1894/95. The prisoners arrived on October 4, too late in the season to build houses. Courtesy U.S. Army Artillery and Missile Center Museum.

decided against sending them. Now arrangements were made with the Indian Office to place the children in the boarding school established for the Plains tribes near their agency at Anadarko, thirty-three miles away. Scott assembled the parents and told them that the wagons would be ready in four days and that he wanted the children to be clean and neat and prepared to start. His announcement was received in complete silence. He asked Chihuahua if he had anything to say. Chihuahua replied that of course they did not want the children to go, but they had been there long enough to know that the officer's orders were carried out. During the term the mothers would buy candy or some other treat for their children and trot the sixty-six miles to present it.[14]

At the same time, the adult men were learning the techniques of the range cattle industry. Congress had appropriated money to buy

14 *Ibid.*, pp. 197–98.

Geronimo and Naiche as cowhands. *The adult men were learning the techniques of the range cattle industry.* This autographed photograph was probably given to Scott during one of his later visits to Fort Sill. It was found in his effects after his death. Courtesy National Anthropological Archives, Smithsonian Instittuion.

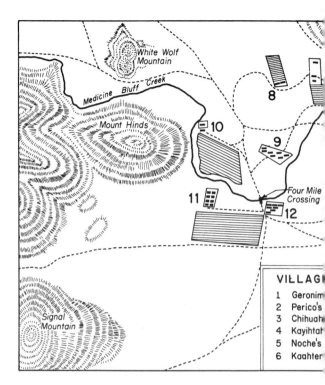

animals to start the herd, but it had to be used at once or it would go back into the treasury. The military reservation was unfenced, and there was no time to fence it or raise winter feed. But if the cattle were allowed to stray on to the surrounding Kiowa-Comanche land it would create bad feeling. That meant that they had to be herded on the grassland and that the Apaches had to be trained as cowboys. Scott and Capron were kept on constant duty. They had been advised against sleeping in the Apaches' camp—the Indians would cut their throats and escape—but the two officers found it necessary in managing the cattle, and they slept there as safely as in their own beds at the post.[15]

15 *Ibid.*, pp. 193, 195–96.

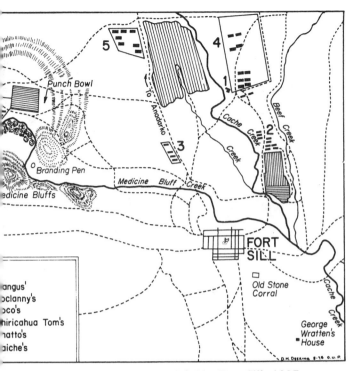

Apache villages and cultivated fields, Fort Sill, 1897

There was much public apprehension that the Apaches would break away for their mountain homeland; and even Scott feared that if some of them should get drunk and commit a crime ("they were homicidal monomaniacs who would kill anybody when intoxicated") they might run away to escape punishment. He consulted a Mescalero who was living with the Comanches and knew all the trails and waterholes along the seven hundred miles to the Mescalero Agency; then he had a good map drawn and sent copies to Miles so the general would be prepared for instant action. He also kept twenty days' rations and a pack outfit in readiness. He told his prisoners of these preparations and warned them that the Comanches, who knew the Plains, were his friends and not theirs

369

Geronimo's house at Fort Sill. Here he lived with Zi-yeh and their children and entertained the artist E. A. Burbank and the writer S. M. Barrett. Courtesy Oklahoma Historical Society, Oklahoma City.

and would join in pursuing them. But they never even considered breaking away.[16]

Various Apaches who had not surrendered were still on the loose, committing depredations in Old Mexico and the American Southwest. The army was chasing them with the usual poor success[17]—"like chasing deer with a brass band," was Scott's opinion. He devised a plan for catching them and obtained Miles's approval. He had made friends with Naiche, Toclanny, and Kaahteney, who knew all their strongholds in Mexico and were willing to search them out. At the same time, their families in Fort Sill would be hostages for their loyalty. He planned to take about fifteen officers and men with the three Indians and set out ostensibly to shoot deer in the Sierra Madre. But the Mexican authorities refused permission, and the plan was dropped. Years later, in 1913, when Scott,

16 *Ibid.*, pp. 186, 193.
17 Secretary of War, *Annual Report*, 1896, p. 4.

Leaders of the old days. From left: Geronimo, Chihuahua, Nana, Loco, and Jolsanny. From S. M. Barrett, *Geronimo's Story of His Life.*

Surviving Bedonkohes. From left: Toclanny, a loyal scout; Nah-dos-te, Geronimo's sister, the wife of Nana; Nah-thle-tla, Geronimo's cousin, the mother of Jason Betzinez; Perico, Geronimo's "brother" (second cousin). From *Geronimo's Story of His Life.*

371

then a brigadier general, was in command on the border, Pancho Villa told him he knew where the Apaches were, but "there were then far worse outlaws on every side of us," and the Apaches were not molested.[18]

As soon as the first winter passed, Scott (now Captain Scott) set his Indians to building houses, using picket construction (upright posts set in a frame). These dwellings were distributed in small villages over the reservation, kindred groups clustered together according to the old Apache custom. (Plural wives were given separate houses closely placed.) A headman was appointed to supervise each village. Since the army had no provision for such officers, they were enlisted for the first three-year period as soldiers, entitled to wear the army uniform and draw the pay of privates, although many of them had passed the age of active service. Their names indicate that they owed their position to natural leadership instead of some white official's artificial selection. The list also indicates the increasing adoption of given names: Geronimo, Martin Kayihtah (later succeeded by Charles Martine), Leon Perico, Chihuahua, George Noche, Jacob Kaahteney, Carl Mangus, Roger (or Rogers) Toclanny, Chief Apache Loco, Christian Naiche, Alfred Chatto, and Chiricahua Tom (or Tom Chiricahua).[19] All these, except the last, had been prominent in Apache history. When one of them died, his son was usually chosen as his successor.

Then, in 1897 a scout detachment was activated, consisting of sixteen men entrusted with special duties such as the supervision of the cattle herd. Finally, in 1911 Noche, Kayihtah, and Martine were enlisted as an act of belated justice for their past services. George Wratten helped them present their claims: Noche's service as sergeant major of scouts under captains Wirt Davis and Crawford (and under Maus after Crawford's death) through the entire 1885–86 campaign, and the rewards Miles promised Kayihtah and Martine for making contact with Geronimo. These claims required

---

[18] Scott, *op. cit.*, pp. 193–95.
[19] Betzinez, *I Fought with Geronimo*, pp. 167–68. I have corrected his list slightly.

Kayihtah (left) and Martine (right) at Fort Sill. From *Geronimo's Story of His Life*.

twenty-eight endorsements, moving up and down through channels and filling eight crowded, single-spaced, typewritten pages before the three were enlisted. Since the men were unable to meet the physical requirements, they were placed on the payroll as scouts, with no responsibilities. After their three-year enlistment expired, they were again forgotten.[20]

Although Geronimo was the headman of his village, the army was careful to cut him down to size. Like Crook, Bourke, and Britton Davis before him, Scott disliked the hard-headed old warrior. He described him as "an unlovely character, a cross-grained, mean, selfish old curmudgeon, of whom . . . I never heard recounted a kindly or generous deed." On the other hand, he found Naiche "a straightforward, reliable person. When he was in charge of the cattle herd I could depend on him completely in every weather, and he never disappointed me." And "Old Chihuahua was called the Apache Chesterfield, from his polite manners."[21] But in spite of Scott's dislike of Geronimo, the energetic old warrior was probably one of his best farmers. With mules the officer had been able to acquire as army surplus when Fort Supply in Oklahoma was abandoned, Scott directed the Apaches in breaking out land and placing it under cultivation. Each man had a plot of his own planted to garden and field crops. They raised more than 250,000 melons and canteloupes on the virgin soil that first year. They ate what they could and sold the surplus at the post. Scott's nine-year-old daughter stationed herself at their wagons and helped them in bargaining and making change. A well-known picture of Geronimo and his family in his melon patch was almost certainly made that season. One doubts that *he* needed any help in making sales.

Scott had seen corn planted by the Kiowas and Comanches under the tutelage of their conscientious civilian agent grow rank

[20] Musgrove, "A Belated Reward for the Surrender of Geronimo." Colonel Musgrove was a young noncommissioned officer at Fort Sill serving as recruiting sergeant. Thus, he prepared the enlistment papers of the three. Later, in his mature years, he found the entire record and the official correspondence in the National Archives and Records Service.

[21] Scott, *op. cit.*, p. 198.

Chihuahua and his family during the Fort Sill years. Apparently the older girl is Ramona. "Old Chihuahua was called the Apache Chesterfield, from his polite manners." Courtesy U.S. Army Artillery and Missile Center Museum.

Geronimo and his family in his melon patch at Fort Sill. With him are his wife Zi-yeh; his daughter Eva, standing next to him; his son Fenton; and probably his granddaughter Nina Dahkeya. *The Apaches raised more than 250,000 melons and canteloupes on the virgin soil that first summer.* Courtesy U.S. Army Artillery and Missile Center Museum.

and green and then crumple under the scorching Southwestern wind. Therefore, he introduced kafir corn, the new grain sorghum that was proving a boon to homesteaders on the Plains, the first grown in that part of Oklahoma. The fodder furnished feed for the Apaches' own livestock, and the surplus was sold to the cavalry at the post. They also cut and baled the hay from the rank prairie grass and sold it to the government. They cut posts and purchased wire and built a fence around the reservation, also enclosing their villages. They then had no need to keep their cattle under herd, but they became adept at roping, branding, and treating the animals for heel-fly, screwworms, and anthrax. Their cattle soon became their chief means of support, with their hay coming second.[22]

Scott remained in charge of the Apaches until 1897. He said that during the whole time they never broke a promise they made him. His successors continued his policy. Everything was so peaceable that when the Spanish-American War broke out in 1898 all the troops were ordered away from Fort Sill except a detachment of twenty men. Then a wild rumor circulated to the effect that the Apaches were plotting an uprising. Panic spread through the post families, who expected a massacre, and troops were hastily sent there. Geronimo, Naiche, and other leaders were questioned. They were incensed at having their loyalty doubted. "I am a U.S. soldier," said Geronimo. "I wear the uniform and it makes my heart sore to be thus suspected." The Kiowas and Comanches were equally incensed; they were able and willing to protect the post against any Apache attack.[23]

Thus, the prisoners were settled, as far as the army could accomplish it, into what seemed to be a good life. They could look at the sun and moon in a big Western sky; they walked on clean grass and breathed pure air; and they saw mountains—not the rugged mountains of their homeland, but mountains. Still, they died. It is enlightening to select a few of their families at random and trace their births and deaths in the Fort Sill records.[24] Small children apparently died from improper feeding after too early weaning, but many deaths came at a usually safe age—of children past infancy, teenagers, returned Carlisle students, and men and women in the prime of life.

The cause was as baffling as it had been to the army surgeons at Mount Vernon Barracks. Jason Betzinez, returning to his people in January, 1900, after working in a Pennsylvania steel mill, blamed the traditional dances. It was bad enough, he thought,

22 *Ibid.,* pp. 186, 191–92, 198–99; Betzinez, *op. cit.,* pp. 168–70, 178. A clear-cut summary of the first two years' work is in Oklahoma Historical Society, Indian Archives, 47403—1896, Scott's report to Adjutant General, October 31, 1896.
23 Scott, *op. cit.,* pp. 197–98, 219–30; Nye, *op. cit.,* pp. 382–83.
24 Griswold, "The Fort Sill Apaches."

for the spectators in the dead of winter to sit on the frozen ground; but for the thinly clad dancers, streaming with perspiration, to drop down there exhausted was highly dangerous, to say nothing of the masks they wore, which they interchanged with each other. (By this time the nature of the infection was known.) He worried about this and then spoke to the officer in charge of the prisoners. The officer, with an understanding rare in white "civilizers," hesitated to interfere with a native custom, but Betzinez pointed out recent funerals which he attributed to exposure at the dances. The officer then forbade them during the cold weather.[25] The family records and the dates on the headstones indicate that this did not work, either.

"We are vanishing from the earth," said Geronimo, "yet I cannot think we are useless or Usen would not have created us." And as they saw their numbers dwindle, always they begged to go home. Geronimo diagnosed their sickness by a reasoning typically Indian. He told how it was "in the beginning: the Apaches and their homes each created for the other by Usen himself. When they are taken away from these homes they sicken and die. How long will it be until it is said, there are no Apaches?"[26]

All this, then, was the background of Geronimo's closing years. In this setting his personal characteristics, barely glimpsed in earlier times, became well known.

[25] Betzinez, *op. cit.*, pp. 175–77, 179, 183.
[26] Barrett, *Geronimo's Story of His Life*, pp. 15–16. By "Apaches" Geronimo referred to his own related tribes.

CHAPTER 20

GERONIMO IS SEEN AS A PERSON

In the publicity that marked his arrival at Fort Sill, Geronimo appeared as the bloody stereotype of the savage Indian. Among the more lurid tales that floated about was the story that when he was "captured" after his last "outbreak" he was wearing a blanket made of one hundred (sometimes it was ninety-nine) white scalps he had collected during that last fling. The account even found its way into serious publications, and writers in search of material sometimes puzzled the old warrior by asking to see the fabulous garment.[1]

But one of these early interviewers had the perception to see the human individual behind the lurid representations. In 1897, Edward E. Ayer, president of the Field Museum in Chicago, sent his artist nephew, Elbridge Ayer Burbank, to Fort Sill to paint a portrait of the fierce raider.[2] With the screaming headlines in mind, Burbank was glad that the "bloodthirsty savage" was in prison so that he could safely paint him behind bars. Arriving at the post, he learned that the captive lived in his own house and enjoyed the freedom of the reservation. A small Indian

[1] Howard B. Hopps, "Lawton," *Chronicles of Oklahoma*, Vol. XXIII, No. 3 (Autumn, 1945), p. 294; Betzinez, *I Fought with Geronimo*, p. 198.

[2] Since writing this book I have learned from the records of Burbank's family that he visited the Fort Sill prisoners in 1897, 1898, and 1899. Clark Hansell, interview, November 14, 1982.

boy, probably Joe or Thomas Dahkeya, helped him locate it. Geronimo was out hunting his horses. He soon came riding up, "an elderly Indian . . . short, but well built and muscular. His keen, shrewd face was deeply furrowed with strong lines. His small black eyes were watery, but in them there burned a fierce light." That face, "so gnarled and furrowed," appealed to the artist as "a wonderful study."

He greeted the old man courteously as "Chief Geronimo." Later he learned that this was fortunate; the soldiers at the post had nicknamed him "Gerry," a name he detested. The boy interpreted the conversation that followed. Geronimo asked the artist where he came from and then wanted to know all about Chicago. Finally he said, "Come," and Burbank followed him into the house. He pulled a photograph of himself out of an old trunk, handed it to the visitor, and said, "One dollar." Burbank meekly paid. This picture gave him the opportunity to ask the old Indian to sit for his portrait. He readily consented, and Captain Scott gave the required permission.

The following morning Burbank found Geronimo ready and eager to pose, but the artist had hardly started when the Apache signaled him to stop, and, calling a little girl—probably Eva—who was playing nearby, he asked her to interpret.

"This man wants to know how much you are going to pay him," she said.

"Ask him how much he wants," Burbank answered.

"You get much money for that picture," said Geronimo. "Maybe five dollars. I want half."

Burbank told him that if he would sit for two pictures, he could have all of the five dollars. The bargain was made.

For that first portrait Geronimo sat on the bed and Burbank on a box. There was no chair in the house until Geronimo inveigled the artist into buying him one. One day a man came by with a sack of grain for sale. Burbank perforce bought that also—for Geronimo's horse. But the Indian was a good sitter, although the habit of vigilance developed in his hunted life was still with him; at the least sound of approaching man or horse he would rush to the door and look out. Sometimes he became nervous from the long sitting, and then Burbank would let him rest. He would lie on his back on the bed and sing in his deep, rich voice—songs "of great beauty," according to the artist. One of them went:

O, ha le
O, ha le
Through the air
I fly upon a cloud
Toward the sky, far, far, far,
O, ha le
O, ha le
There to find the holy place
Ah, now the change comes o'er me!
O, ha le
O, ha le.

Burbank regularly brought his lunch when he worked at Geronimo's house, and he usually brought some extra food to share with his subject. Once during those first sittings Geronimo invited him to take dinner with him. Zi-yeh prepared the meal, which consisted of meat, bread, and coffee. The food was "clean and good," and she served it on a board placed on the ground before the two men. They ate with their fingers, there being no knives, forks, or spoons. Two years later Geronimo again invited the artist to dinner. This time he sat with Geronimo, Zi-yeh, and Eva at a well-set table covered with a linen cloth to an excellent meal topped with dessert.

Zi-yeh was in poor health—no doubt with the tubercular infection that was to lay her low—and Geronimo did all the housework, washing the dishes, sweeping the floor, keeping the place immaculate. Once Burbank tracked in some mud, and the sour look the old warrior gave him as he took a broom and swept it out taught the artist to be more careful in the future. Geronimo idolized Eva. "Nobody could be kinder to a child than he was to her." In spite of his notable thrift in his relations with outsiders, anything in the trader's store was hers for the asking. A small "nephew" also was "invariably about the house." This must have been his grandson, Thomas Dahkeya, the only survivor of Lulu's family. The little girl, Nina, had died in 1895; Lulu herself followed in 1898; and her warrior husband, Mike Dahkeya, and their son Joe died in 1899.[3] No doubt Thomas was living with his grandfather at the time of the artist's later visits. Burbank made no mention of Fenton. This last son of Geronimo's (except for the absent Robert) died in 1897, either before the artist's first visit or before he became acquainted with the family.

As Burbank saw Geronimo in his home, he found it hard to visualize him "as the leader of a band of ravaging savages. To me he was a kind old man." He taught his ponies to come at his shrill note,[4] and he never left the house without putting out a saucer of milk for his cat. (For some reason Burbank could never fathom, he always kept the cat's whiskers closely clipped.) Through the artist he dictated letters to friends in the old homeland, usually requesting that certain native "medicines" be sent to him and invariably closing with the words, "If you are in need, let me know and I will send you money."[5]

Others who knew him at this time testified to his kindly spirit. Oscar Brousse Jacobson, who later became head of the Art School at the University of Oklahoma, commented on Burbank's evaluation of him as "very gentle to his family and kind and generous to his tribesmen": "This is the same impression I had of Geronimo, gathered from several conversations I had with [him]."[6] Miss Ruth Hammond, retired librarian of Oklahoma State University, still remembers him as he appeared to her in her childhood when he

[3] These family records may be found in Griswold, "The Fort Sill Apaches," and also on the gravestones of the Apache cemetery on the military reservation.
[4] Barrett, *Geronimo's Story of His Life*, p. 123, n. 2.
[5] Burbank and Royce, *Burbank among the Indians*, pp. 17–22, 27–31.
[6] O. B. Jacobson and Jeanne d'Ucel, "Art in Oklahoma," *Chronicles of Oklahoma*, Vol. XXXII, No. 3 (Autumn, 1954), p. 276.

came to sell bows and arrows at the officers' quarters when her father was the post chaplain at Fort Sill. "He talked with my father. He did not seem to me like a fierce person, just a kind old man. He spoke a little English, enough to carry on his sales. He charged fifty cents extra for printing his name on the bow."[7]

But one day Burbank saw this kindly Indian turn into a ferocious savage. A magazine editor offered the artist a considerable sum of money if he would get the story of Geronimo's life. Geronimo consented if he were paid half the proceeds. Burbank went to his house, and the old man lay on the bed and began. But as he told of the massacre of his family by the Mexicans, he sprang up in such fury that he was unable to continue. The boy who was interpreting became almost as excited. "He is telling you the truth," he said, "for my father tells me the same story."[8] Apparently the article was never written.

Gambling also brought out Geronimo's latent fierceness. Once he invited Burbank to accompany him to a sports meet, probably the annual Fourth of July field day observed at the post, with horse races and other contests between the soldiers and the Kiowas and Comanches.[9] There he joined a game of monte, dealing the cards expertly with his small, quick hands and shouting at the top of his voice as he raked in his winnings. As they were leaving for home, a white man proposed that they race horses for a ten-dollar wager. Geronimo liked nothing better than horse racing, but his weight was a handicap. Often he pressed his small wife into service; the Apaches long remembered how she tied her hair in a tight knot when she rode.[10] This time he looked around for an Apache boy and found him at bat in a baseball game. He hit a homer just as Geronimo arrived. The old man raced after him all around the diamond and caught him at home plate. The horse race that

7 Interview, March 11, 1973.
8 Burbank and Royce, *op. cit.*, pp. 32–33. Burbank's account of the massacre is understandably confused.
9 Descriptions of these field days are given in Scott, *Some Memories of a Soldier*, p. 199; and Nye, *Carbine and Lance*, p. 375.
10 James Kaywaykla, Moses Loco, and Benedict Jozhe interview, July 29, 1959.

followed was close, but Geronimo's pony won, and he was wildly exultant.[11]

He would, in fact, bet on anything. One time he challenged Burbank to a marksmanship contest with a .22 caliber rifle, in which each man would pay his opponent ten dollars for every successful shot. The artist looked at the old man's watery eyes and was inclined to accept, but Geronimo showed so much eagerness that he said, "No, we'll shoot for fun." It was well for him that he did. Geronimo took a piece of paper about the size of a quarter and pinned it to a tree several yards distant. He hit the target at every shot and once hit the pin. Burbank missed it every time.[12]

Once he came to see Burbank at the post in a peculiar mood. He said that no one could kill him, or Burbank either if he willed it so. He bared himself to the waist, and Burbank was astounded to see the number of bullet holes in his body. Some of them were large enough to hold small pebbles, which he picked up and placed in them as he imitated the sound of a gun. He ended by shouting, "Bullets cannot kill me!"[13] Thus he trusted his Power. Even in his horse racing he relied as much on his "medicine" as on the speed of his favorite sorrel pony. He was in fact, an untamed Apache. His qualities of gentleness and ferocity were those of his native society.

Burbank met other members of this society on his third visit to Fort Sill. He came upon Geronimo riding through the woods with Eva and the little "nephew" on the horse with him. "You make heap money painting my picture," was his greeting to the artist. "You pay me so much," and he clasped and unclasped his hands to indicate twenty-five dollars. Burbank told him he had come this time to paint other chiefs. He persuaded Naiche, Chatto, Chihuahua, Mangus, and Loco to pose for him, and he painted a charming portrait of Eva.[14]

He had been anxious to meet Naiche, and when the meeting

11 Burbank and Royce, *op. cit.*, pp. 24–25.
12 *Ibid.*, p. 23.
13 *Ibid.*, pp. 30–31.
14 Eva's portrait is dated 1898.

Geronimo's daughter Eva at age nine, painted by Burbank, 1898. "Nobody could be kinder to a child than Geronimo was to her." Courtesy Butler Institute of American Art, Youngstown, Ohio.

occurred it was typical of the chief's artistic interests. One day, when the artist was sketching, he noticed "a tall fine-looking Indian" intently watching. He asked him where Naiche could be found. The Indian laughed. "I am Naiche," he said.[15] After that meeting, when Burbank was painting, Naiche used to watch him all day; and Burbank explained his techniques and later sent the

15 He dated Naiche's portrait 1899.

native artist a full set of colors from Chicago. Naiche presented Burbank with a cane he had carved, "beautifully executed, then as finely painted." Burbank wanted to purchase for the museum one of Naiche's paintings done in the Indian way on deerskin, and the chief set the price at three and one-half dollars. Then he learned that the unworldly Indian had paid three dollars for the skin, and he accordingly raised his payment to ten. Later, when the French artist Jean Baptiste Millet visited the museum, he pronounced it "the most beautiful decorative thing he had ever seen." Ayer gave it to him, and he took it back to France.

Although in his subsequent travels to many reservations Burbank saw and appreciated the work of numerous Indian artists, he always regarded Naiche as "by far the best" of all he had known.[16] But he considered all Indians as "essentially artistic." Even the hard-headed Geronimo "had a fine eye for line and color." Geronimo liked Burbank's portraits of him—"You heap savvy," was his judgment—and the two developed a real affection for each other. Their last parting was "quite sad," for both realized that they would not meet again.[17]

This had been Geronimo's first opportunity to form a friendship with a civilian white man. Soon, however, his white contacts were enormously increased. The government had continued its policy of breaking up the Indian reservations in Oklahoma and opening them to white settlement. The Kiowas, Comanches, and Kiowa-Apaches had resisted, but they had finally lost their fight. Each received an individual "allotment" of land, and in 1901 the remainder was given to white homesteaders. This meant a settler on every 160-acre tract, with towns springing up throughout the area and feverish construction of railroads to span it. The city of Lawton came into lusty existence just outside the military reservation and four miles from the post. This development had its bad side for Geronimo: it increased his opportunities to obtain forbidden alcohol. On such occasions he was confined in the post

16 Burbank and Royce, *op. cit.*, pp. 33–34, 207, 223.
17 *Ibid.*, pp. 22, 38, 205.

guardhouse until he sobered up. One of his grievances—a violation, as he saw it, of the peace he had made with Miles—was that "I have been arrested and placed in the guardhouse twice for drinking whisky."[18] At the same time the settlement of the area ended his isolation; the public began to see him as a human being instead of a caged tiger.

In April, 1905, the historian Norman S. Wood, in collecting material for his book on Indian chiefs, came to meet Naiche and especially Geronimo. He first interviewed Lieutenant Purington and then set out to find the old war leader. As he was passing the railroad station, the agent called out to him that Geronimo was there waiting for a train. He was on his way to the nearby town of Cache to visit Quanah Parker, the noted Comanche chief and former hostile, with whom he had formed a friendship. Wood was not a sensational writer expecting to see Geronimo wearing a blanket of human scalps, but he did have to change some of his preconceptions. "I found the noted chief on the platform of the depot; he took my proffered hand with a smile and a hearty 'How!' and pulled me up on the platform. I had expected to see a grey-haired, sour-visaged, skinny-looking old Indian, with a scowl on his face and nervous twitching fingers as if eager to shed blood. But instead I saw a smiling, well-kept, well-dressed Indian about five feet nine inches tall, with square shoulders and deep chest . . . He was dressed in a well-fitting blue cloth suit of citizen's clothes." As Wood was soon to learn, he had an open-faced silver watch in his vest pocket.

The writer found that "while he was quick to understand much that was said to him, he spoke but a few words of English." Wood therefore suggested by signs that they go to Wratten's house, about a quarter of a mile away across the prairie. Geronimo looked up the track and inquired of the station agent, "How much?" The agent pulled out the Indian's watch and ran his finger around the dial and half around again to indicate an hour and a half. "Good," said Geronimo, and the two started off. On the way was a little

18 Nye, *op. cit.*, p. 386; Barrett, *op. cit.*, p. 146.

stream, a good jump across. Wood had excelled in jumping in his college days and saw a chance to test Geronimo's agility by a running leap over this creek. To his surprise Geronimo vaulted across and landed a foot beyond his mark. At Wratten's house he obtained some more information, and with what he had learned from the lieutenant he wrote an accurate sketch of Geronimo's life and experiences at Fort Sill.[19]

All these increased white contacts were good for Geronimo's business. Wood, in fact, had bought one of his bows and arrows at the post sutler's store and brought it to him to autograph. No doubt many others did. And it was through a business contact that he was given the opportunity to present the Indian side of the Apache wars. Lawton School Superintendent Barrett first met him in the summer of 1904 when he was called upon to interpret Geronimo's Spanish and a prospective purchaser's English in fixing the price of a war bonnet. After that, Geronimo always had a pleasant word for Barrett when they met, but it was only after he learned that the educator had once been wounded by a Mexican that he came to visit him and express his hatred of Mexicans. Other visits followed in Barrett's home and Geronimo's. Once the superintendent brought along a Kansas City guest, who mentioned in conversation that he was a friend of General Howard. Geronimo instantly became cordial. "Come," he said, and he led the way to a shade, had seats brought, put on his headdress, and served big chunks of watermelon, all the time talking freely.

By this time Barrett had heard enough tales of Geronimo's adventures that he wanted to publish them. Geronimo said that if Barrett would pay him he would tell the whole story of his life. After the educator finally obtained permission by his direct appeal to President Roosevelt, he began with the help of Asa Daklugie to take down the old warrior's dictation. Daklugie was the ideal interpreter. He had returned from Carlisle in 1895, equipped with the white man's learning but wholly committed to Apache traditions and loyalties. He was Geronimo's main dependence and

---

[19] *Lives of Famous Indian Chiefs*, pp. 550–59.

Asa and Ramona Daklugie and their children. *The home they estab-lished was a model of stability and permanence.* From *Geronimo's Story of His Life.*

Geronimo dictating his memoirs, with Daklugie interpreting and Barrett taking notes. "Write what I have spoken." From *Geronimo's Story of His Life.*

chosen successor, and after many councils the band had recently—in January, 1905—elected him as acting "chief."[20] (Naiche was still the chief; Daklugie succeeded to Geronimo's position as the power behind the throne.) He had married capable, level-headed Ramona Chihuahua, and the home they established was a model of stability and permanence.

With this help Barrett began early in October, 1905, and the three worked through the following winter, sometimes at Geronimo's home, sometimes at Daklugie's, or seated under the trees in some sheltered nook, even riding at a swinging gallop across the prairie. Geronimo refused to accept the presence of a stenographer to take shorthand notes, and Barrett and Daklugie had to

[20] *Lawton Constitution-Democrat* (weekly edition), February 18, 1909.

remember and record his statements as best they could. Every day he had in mind what he would tell and told it "in a very clear, brief manner." He refused to be questioned about details or to add another word; he simply said, "Write what I have spoken." But he would agree to come later to Barrett's study in Lawton or to some other meeting place and listen as Daklugie read it back to him in Apache, and then he would answer questions and contribute additional information.

He soon became tired of the whole proceeding and would have abandoned the task except that he had agreed to complete it. Barrett found that "when he once gives his word, nothing will turn him back from fulfilling his promise." (It would have surprised Crook to hear that!) His good faith was strikingly demonstrated on one cold day in January when he had agreed to come to Barrett's study. Daklugie came alone with the report that the old man was very ill with a cold or, as he feared, pneumonia, and that they must set another date. Just then Geronimo arrived, riding furiously on his exhausted horse. Entering the study, he said in a hoarse whisper, "I promised to come. I am here." Barrett explained that he had not expected him to keep the appointment on such a stormy day, and that, ill as he was, he must not try to work. He stood there for a time, then turned away without a word and mounted his pony for the eight-mile ride against the north wind back to his home.[21]

Geronimo's home that winter was in a state of flux. Zi-yeh had become "a chronic invalid" from tubercular lupus and had died in 1904.[22] On Christmas Day in 1905 Geronimo married again. According to newspaper accounts the woman was an Apache named Sousche or Mrs. Mary Loto, a widow, aged fifty-eight, with a grown son. It was said that the marriage was unknown to even his closest friends until he brought his wife home two or three weeks later.[23] Present-day Apaches know nothing about her, and

[21] Barrett, op. cit., pp. xi-xiii, xx-xxii.

[22] Oklahoma Historical Society, Indian Archives, Chilocco—Fair, Farrand Sayre to S. M. McCowan, September 20, 1903.

[23] Beaver Journal, January 13, 1906; Mangum Star, January 18, 1906; Muskogee Times-Democrat, November 8, 1906.

her name stirs no memory. Apparently she was not a member of their band. They are inclined to think that she may have been a Mescalero or perhaps a White Mountain or other Apache from Arizona, for members of those tribes sometimes visited the Fort Sill prisoners, and she could have been in such a party.

In any case, the marriage did not last long. Mention is made of Geronimo's wife in a letter written on April 11, 1906,[24] but before he had finished dictating his memoirs that spring she had gone. He dismissed the brief episode laconically: "Since the death of Eva's mother I married another woman (December, 1905) but we could not live happily and separated. She went home to her people—that is an Apache divorce."[25]

He had only his daughter Eva with him, he said. She was then sixteen years old, and he had given her an elaborate womanhood ceremony just before he started working with Barrett. Probably Ramona Daklugie helped with the woman's part of the arrangements. He invited all the Apaches, and many Kiowas and Comanches, as well as his friend Barrett. A level place was selected by the south bank of Medicine Bluff Creek near Naiche's village, and the grass on a large circular space was closely mowed. The celebration began on the first night of the full moon in September. For the womanhood rites Naiche led the singing, and Geronimo, with the assistance of the medicine men in charge, directed the dancing. The all-night celebration that closed the observance began with a social dance in which the whole group joined hands and danced in a circle around the fire. Then when the moon began its descent the music changed from the beating of the tom-toms to the plaintive sound of the flageolet. Most of the older people withdrew, and the "lovers' dance" began. The young men formed a circle close to the fire, and the girls formed an outer circle surrounding them. One after another a girl would dance to the inner circle and select a partner, and the two would dance together through the rest of the night. With these young couples this was often preliminary to

---

[24] National Archives and Records Service, Record Group No. 94, AGO 1119665, from 445841, Pawnee Bill to Lieutenant General John C. Bates.
[25] Barrett, *op. cit.*, p. 179.

The site of Eva Geronimo's womanhood ceremony. Naiche's village is on the right, the smooth tract on the left is the tilled field belonging to the village, and far in the middle distance Chatto's village and the trail leading to it can be glimpsed. Courtesy U.S. Army Artillery and Missile Center Museum.

the more businesslike marriage arrangement carried out with the parents of the girl.

When the moon was going down and the sun was rising, the dancing stopped. The gifts were then presented and some betrothals were announced. Soon the gathering broke up. Geronimo and Barrett were among the last to leave. As Barrett remembered it, Geronimo at that time told him that Eva had chosen her husband. If so, she did not marry him. Perhaps Geronimo did not consent. If Asa Daklugie's memory can be trusted, Geronimo hoped she would not marry, fearing that she would not survive childbirth.[26] Possibly the tuberculosis that was to bring her to an early grave was already sapping her vitality.

With the party over and the crowd dispersed, Barrett and

26 Eve Ball to Angie Debo, March 8, 1971.

Eva Geronimo (right), aged sixteen, wearing the costume of her womanhood ceremony. With her is Ramona Daklugie, who probably served as her attendant, wearing her own womanhood costume. Apache women still preserve these dresses throughout their lives. From *Geronimo's Story of His Life*.

A womanhood ceremony painted on buckskin by Naiche at Fort Sill.
Note the girls, each with her older woman attendant, the dancers
"worshiping the fire," the clown, the musicians, and the spectators.
Courtesy Oklahoma Historical Society.

Geronimo prepared to leave. They mounted their horses, Barrett
using the stirrup, Geronimo still agile enough to vault into the
saddle in the Apache way. As his pony struck a canter, the old
warrior started out for home singing his favorite "riding song."

395

Dorothy Kaywaykla, the daughter of Naiche and E-clah-heh, posed in her womanhood costume. From *Geronimo's Story of His Life*.

Later, in dictating his story, he thoughtfully summed up his reactions: "Perhaps I shall never again have cause to assemble our people to dance, but these social dances in the moonlight have been a large part of our enjoyment in the past, and I think they will not soon be discontinued, at least I hope so."[27]

During the same period when his cherished Eva was inducted into the responsibilities of womanhood, Geronimo was able to establish contact with his Mescalero children. The previous year, as will be recounted in the next chapter, Lenna had joined him at the Saint Louis fair. Then the following year—on September 12, 1906—Robert, who had been attending the Indian service school at Mescalero, entered Chilocco, a nonreservation boarding school in northern Oklahoma. The next year Eva also entered the school, and the half brother and half sister became well acquainted. Thomas Dahkeya was already there, having entered at least as early as the spring of 1904; Captain Farrand Sayre, at that time in charge of the prisoners, characterized him as "a promising boy."[28]

After Robert came to Chilocco, he spent his vacations with his father. By this time Geronimo had married again, a widow called Sunsetso or "Old Lady Yellow" by the Apaches who still remember her, or by the Spanish name of Azul (they have forgotten why the colors were different). She had been a Mexican captive, but had escaped. The couple did not live in Geronimo's house but with a family named Guydelkon in Perico's village. There the mother, her niece, had died, and the family consisted of the father and his two sons, her grandnephews. Close by was the home of the Jozhe family. Geronimo used to come over to their house for breakfast and hold their baby, the future tribal chairman (Geronimo liked babies).[29] When Robert came home during vacations, Geron-

<hr/>

[27] Barrett, *op. cit.*, pp. 192–96; S. M. Barrett, *Sociology of the American Indians*, pp. 54–56.

[28] Oklahoma Historical Society, Indian Archives, Chilocco—Deserters, Sayre to Superintendent, March 21, 1904; Frank J. Self, Acting Superintendent, to Angie Debo, February 12, 1973; undated application (probably 1909) by Robert Geronimo to enter Carlisle, furnished me by Eve Ball from Mescalero Agency Records.

[29] Benedict Jozhe and Moses Loco interview, September 16, 1969; Griswold, *op. cit.*, biographies of Azul and the Guydelkons.

Geronimo and his last wife, Azul. The couple lived with Azul's relatives in Perico's village. Courtesy U.S. Army Artillery and Missile Center Museum.

imo settled him first with the Daklugies and then with Eugene Chihuahua, who had married a daughter of Massai.[30] Probably the Guydelkon house was too crowded, even by Apache standards of sharing, to take him in.

Thus, Geronimo was seen in his day-by-day experiences in his home and with his people. But his fame had traveled far, and it attracted visitors interested mainly in sensation. One such incident was remembered by Carlisle-trained Jesse Rowlodge, an Arapaho born in 1886 on the reservation of his tribe, which bordered that of the Kiowas and Comanches. He had relatives among the Comanches in the Fort Sill area and as a young man often visited them, thus becoming acquainted with Geronimo. As he told the story: "Geronimo, he likes to play poker, you know, and montie . . . and a bunch of Comanche boys and myself used to go over there just to be with him. We used to like to play cards. And one frosty morning just as we came out of Ft. Sill into that timber, I picked up a hawk feather that had shed from a hawk. It was about five or six inches long." They found Geronimo at home building a fire. "He was all ready. We said, 'Hello, Geronimo.' 'Ho, ho, making fire,' he said in Comanche. He spoke pretty fair Comanche."

They spread out a piece of canvas, sat down around it, and started to play. Meanwhile, they stuck the feather in the hat Geronimo was wearing. Soon a buggy drove up with a local man and two visitors, a man and a woman from Baltimore. The woman wanted to know whether Geronmo had anything to sell her, and the Comanche boys interpreted. Then "one of those Comanche boys said, 'How's that feather on your hat?' He took his hat off. 'How much you want for that, Geronimo? How much you want for that?' The Comanche boy told him, 'Tell them five dollars.' 'Five dollars,' he said. That lady opened her purse and gave him five dollars. Just for a old feather! Just because he was Geronimo!"[31]

And just because he *was* Geronimo he became a major exhibit in Oklahoma and throughout the nation.

30 Eve Ball to Angie Debo, March 10, 1973.
31 Julia A. Jordan, "Oklahoma's Oral History Collection," *Chronicles of Oklahoma*, Vol. XLIX, No. 2 (Summer, 1971), pp. 167–68.

399

CHAPTER 21

GERONIMO ON EXHIBITION

During the Fort Sill years Geronimo became a commercial property, an exhibit to ensure the success of a celebration. If other Indians accompanied him, they fell into the background. His conduct on these occasions was a lasting demonstration of the code of courtesy and good breeding the Apaches had managed to retain even as hunted outlaws. He appeared self-possessed, alert, and not unfriendly to the people who crowded around him, and all the time he was observing, learning, marking down everything with his fresh curiosity and his active mind. At the same time, he used every opportunity he found to plead for a return to his homeland. Also, being Geronimo, he kept an eye open for business.

His first major experience of this kind was at the Trans-Mississippi and International Exposition held at Omaha from September 9 to October 30, 1898. A number of men, women, and children, including Naiche, his wife Ha-o-zinne, and their two small children, were selected from the Fort Sill prisoners, but Geronimo proved to be the main attraction. When the train stopped at stations on the journey, he cut buttons from his coat and sold them for twenty-five cents each to the eager spectators, and for five dollars he would sell his hat. Between stations he diligently sewed

Geronimo posed for a photograph wearing his ceremonial headdress.
Courtesy U.S. Army Artillery and Missile Center Museum.

Geronimo at Trans-Mississippi Exposition in Omaha, 1898. Courtesy
Kansas State Historical Society, Topeka.

Naiche with Ha-o-zinne and two of their children at Omaha, 1898.
Photograph by F. A. Rinehart of the Bureau of American Ethnology.
Amelia Naiche, the baby in the picture, is still living on the Mescalero
Reservation. Courtesy National Anthropological Archives, Smithsonian
Institution.

Tah-das-te, said to have served in the old days as Geronimo's messenger. Photograph taken for the Bureau of American Ethnology by F. A. Rinehart at Omaha, 1898. Courtesy National Anthropological Archives, Smithsonian Institution.

more buttons on his coat and equipped himself with a new hat from a supply he had thoughtfully provided.[1]

During the fair he carried on a big business selling pictures of himself. But he did not forget the theme that throughout his imprisonment was the major purpose of his life. The story was told by Jimmie Stevens, then grown to young manhood, who had been sent to accompany a party of Apaches from the San Carlos Reservation to the exposition. His account is colored by his hatred for the raider who had killed and eaten his pony at the sheep camp in 1882. (The killing of the Mexicans that day did not seem to count with Jimmie.)

General Miles had come to the exposition to add his official presence to its Army Day, and its promoters saw that a meeting between him and Geronimo would bring good publicity. A crowd gathered to watch and listen. Stevens had been asked to serve as interpreter. At first he demanded that Geronimo pay him fifty dollars for the pony, but he finally decided that his enemy's discomfiture would be sufficient reward. Through all the years since the encounter in Skeleton Canyon, Geronimo had hoped for such a meeting with Miles, but now he trembled, the sweat rolled down his face, and he stuttered until he could not speak. According to Stevens, Naiche taunted him (this is probably not true), and then the words poured out.

First, he accused Miles of having lied in the assurances he gave to induce the surrender. Miles smiled broadly. He admitted that he had lied, but had learned lying "from the great nantan of all liars— from you, Geronimo. You lied to Mexicans, Americans, and to your own Apaches, for thirty years. White men only lied to you once, and I did it." Geronimo then made his plea to return to Arizona: "The acorns and piñon nuts, the quail and the wild turkey, the giant cactus and the palo verdes—they all miss me. . . . I miss them, too. I want to go back to them." When this was interpreted, Miles chuckled again: "A very beautiful thought, Geronimo. Quite poetic. But the men and women who live in

1 Burbank and Royce, *Burbank among the Indians*, p. 23.

Arizona, they do not miss you. . . . Folks in Arizona sleep now at night, have no fear that Geronimo will come and kill them." And he mimicked the old warrior's style, repeating his enumeration: "acorns . . . palo verde trees—they will have to get along as best they can—without you."[2]

One must make allowance for Stevens' bias. Miles had his faults, but he would not have ridiculed a fallen foe even before an audience on an occasion so gratifying to his ever present self-glorification. But there certainly was a confrontation between the two in which Geronimo's appeal failed. Later, however, when Miles visited Fort Sill, Geronimo asked to be released from the prisoners' enforced labor on account of his age, and again reminded the general of the promises made at the surrender. Miles granted this request, and Geronimo was dropped from the work detail. He continued, however, to help with the haying and the care of the cattle, "for, although I am old, I like to work and help my people as much as I am able."[3]

But his sturdy resourcefulness failed him during one amusing episode at Omaha. On Sundays, when they were free, he and Naiche and other Apaches used to get Jimmie Stevens to hire a livery team and take them through the countryside. One cloudy day, as they followed one road after another across the flat land checkerboarded with farms and fields of tall corn, every one exactly like the others, they became lost. "No mountains," said Geronimo, "nothing but corn." They were supposed to return before night, but darkness came with no stars to guide them. Finally, Stevens found a telephone and reported to the officer in charge of the Indians, and he came out and brought them in. They were almost twenty miles from town. Probably this was the only time in his adventurous life that Geronimo was lost.

They returned to find everyone braced for an Indian scare. Geronimo had talked to newspaper reporters about his longing to return to Arizona. Now it appeared that the Indians were headed

---

[2] Woodworth Clum, *Apache Agent*, pp. 287–90; Santee, *Apache Land*, pp. 171–74.
[3] Barrett, *Geronimo's Story of His Life*, p. 182.

ington, Geronimo participated in an event that was, more frankly than the inaugural parade, a Wild West promotion.

Frank Greer, an influential newspaper publisher at the Oklahoma territorial capital of Guthrie, had been able to bring the National Editorial Association to his ambitious young city for its annual meeting in 1905. His inducement was a visit to the 101 Ranch operated by the Miller Brothers, who had leased an immense tract of land from the Ponca Indians in northern Oklahoma. The ranch had not yet entered the show business that was to affect its subsequent history, but it had top cowhands accustomed to winning riding, roping, and bulldogging contests held informally with other outfits. Provision was accordingly made for excursion trains to bring the visiting editors to the ranch for one day's entertainment on June 11, and the Millers exerted every effort to make the occasion memorable. This included the presence of Geronimo, usually billed at such exhibitions as "the tiger of the human race" or "the Apache terror."

Lieutenant Purington had already received the request from the Millers when Norman Wood interviewed him in April, and he was inclined to grant it. "Out of the fifty or sixty thousand people expected on the ground that day," he told Wood, "it is thought that at least ten thousand will come purposely to see Geronimo." The promoters agreed to pay the old warrior his own price, but the amount he exacted is not recorded.

The day came, and so did Geronimo, and so did an estimated sixty-five thousand spectators ranged in grandstands built for the occasion. The Millers had bought some buffalo from Colonel Charles Goodnight's celebrated JA Ranch in the Texas Panhandle, and the main feature of the morning was "the last buffalo hunt," in which Geronimo would kill one of the animals to be butchered and served to the visitors at the noon meal.

The shooting was done from an automobile owned by a Chicago visitor, but from there on the stories differ. According to one account, Geronimo shot and wounded the buffalo, but failed to hit a vital spot, and a Miller cowhand had to finish the job. This could be true. The promoters, as usual, had confused their Indians. Geronimo was not a Great Plains hunter, accustomed to riding a horse especially trained to approach a buffalo on a dead run and swerve at precisely the right instant while the rider launched his arrow at the exact spot for the kill. By the other story, it was the Chicago visitor who wounded the buffalo, and it was Geronimo, riding in the automobile, who sprang out and "finished the animal with neatness and dispatch." Again, this could be true. Geronimo could have used an authentic Apache technique, which astounded Bourke when he saw captured cattle butchered in the Sierra Madre. In either case, the visitors saw Geronimo in action and were treated afterwards to a dinner of buffalo meat. But he did not steal the show that day. The afternoon was filled with feats of skill by the Miller cowhands and was closed by a grand finale in which three hundred obliging Poncas rode yelling from over the hill and engulfed a wagon train.[34]

Lurid accounts of the day's performance were published by the visitors in their home newspapers. As President Roosevelt heard it, Geronimo had participated in a public buffalo hunt in company with army officers. There he drew the line; he wrote an angry letter demanding that whoever at Fort Sill was responsible for this "disgraceful exhibition" should be disciplined. But as it turned out, only two officers had been present, and merely as spectators on leave in civilian clothes.[35]

Geronimo had no qualms about participating in a Wild West spectacle if he could make it pay. As Blaine Kent, an aged Iowa Indian, expressed it: "Old Man Geronimo, well he has good sense just like anybody else in putting on a show. And a lot of people was really scared of him you know." He remembered such an appearance at the 101 Ranch, probably on another occasion (he gave the date as 1906): "He was sitting there. . . . They had a table with a lot of pictures of him and postcards. . . . And they had a ball and chain on him down around the ankle. . . . But then there's guards

---

[34] Wood, *op. cit.*, pp. 553, 559; Fred Gipson, *Fabulous Empire*, pp. 224–31.
[35] Nye, *op. cit.*, p. 385.

behind him with guns, too. He was sitting there and people come by. . . . He don't say a word. Just look right at them. Don't smile. Don't laugh or nothing. Somebody will come along, look at his picture, and throw down a dollar bill, maybe a five dollar bill, and he grabbed that and stick it in a pocket. Won't even give them any change back. Then the man says. Ladies and gentlemen go on by, don't bother him none. (Mr. Kent chuckled at this point.)"[36]

It is safe to surmise that President Roosevelt was unaware of such exhibitions. And if the date 1906 is correct, Geronimo may have taken a side trip in an entirely different character to nearby Chilocco to meet the newly arrived Robert. The Apaches have a tradition that the first meeting between father and son occurred in this way.

Meanwhile, the success of such staged appearances encouraged Pawnee Bill to make another try. On April 11, following the meeting of the Editorial Association, he again applied for permission to take Geronimo with his show, strengthening his request by using House of Representatives stationery and attaching a supporting letter from his fellow townsman, Bird McGuire of Pawnee, Oklahoma's delegate to Congress. The showman stated that he had already made satisfactory arrangements with the old warrior, who requested that his wife and daughter accompany him. (The daughter, of course, was Eva, and the wife was the mysterious Mary Loto.) He promised to give all of them the best of care, protection from intoxicants, "and the benefit of whatever education may be had." This request was also refused.[37]

Geronimo continued however, to make headlines. In 1907 he got into all the Oklahoma newspapers when he disappeared after attending a Fourth of July celebration at Cache. In the evening he apparently started back to Fort Sill, but turned south instead and hid in the timber along a creek. Probably he had simply imbibed too freely at Cache, but it was widely reported that he was on his

36 Martha R. Siegel, "Field Notes," Perkins, Oklahoma, 1965. Used by permission.
37 National Archives and Records Service, Record Group 94, AGO 1119665, from 445841, Pawnee Bill to Lt. Gen. John C. Bates, April 11, 1906; Statement by Arthur Guydelkon furnished by Chapman; *Oklahoman*, April 22, 1906.

way to Old Mexico to join the Apaches still in hiding there. The soldiers found him the next day and brought him back to the post. Thus, another scare story ended without incident.[38]

But although he made no attempt to break away, Geronimo never relaxed his efforts to move the president. Later that same month he went to Lawton, called on a photographer, and ordered a picture of himself to be made. His words, certainly spoken through an interpreter, were rendered by a reporter in the jargon supposed to represent Indian English: "Me want good picture to send to my good friend, President Roosevelt. . . . May be so some time President say: 'Go, good old Geronimo; you killed heap white folks, but Jesus man made you good; be good man all time and war men [that is, the army] hold you no more." The photographer had him sit for the picture, and he went back to the reservation in better spirits than he had shown in many days.[39] This appeal also failed.

In October that year, the old warrior was permitted to attend a big Indian gathering held by the Shawnees at their ceremonial grounds close to the new railroad town of Collinsville, northeast of Tulsa. He went as the guest of his friend the well-known Shawnee leader Spybuck. The *Oklahoman* of Oklahoma City had just installed a new press that had received so much publicity in newspapers of the territory that even Geronimo had heard of it, and when his party passed through the city he expressed a wish to see it operate. As usual, he was keenly interested, but he also saw in the new equipment an opportunity to forward his plea to the president. His words were apparently recorded by the same reporter: "In the paper, write a letter to the great white father in Washington. Say to him: 'Geronimo got religion now. Geronimo fight no more. The old times, he forget.' Geronimo want to be prisoner of war no more. He want free. Tell the great white father that. Tell him in the paper." The *Oklahoman* did write the letter to the "great white father in Washington," and did "write it in the paper,"[40] but the

38 The identical news item appeared in a number of papers. See, for example, *Beaver County Democrat*, July 18, 1907.
39 *Oklahoman*, July 26, 1907.
40 *Ibid.*, March 1, 1953.

reasoning the president explained to Geronimo two and one-half years before still held.

The old man went on to Collinsville, leading the way to the ceremonial grounds in a red automobile. There, about fifteen hundred Indians of different tribes were assembled, wearing the traditional paint, feathers, and blankets they had put on for the occasion. Geronimo addressed them briefly in his native Apache, and interpreters translated it into the various languages. Barrett, always sympathetic to Indian culture, was present and recorded his words: "Brothers, I am glad to see so many of you and see you playing the old games. I shall not keep you long, but you have asked for my advice. Our way of life is gone. Your children must travel the white man's road. Schools and churches will help you and them. I have spoken."

When darkness fell, the grounds were lighted by many campfires, and the dances continued through the night.[41] Geronimo must have thought again that such dances "have been a large part of our enjoyment in the past, and I think they will not soon be discontinued."

His mention of the Christian religion in these later statements indicates the presence of a new Power in his personal experience. This was to lead to an inner conflict that was never resolved.

41 *Ibid.*, October 18, 1907; Barrett, *Sociology of the American Indians*, p. 132.

CHAPTER 22

GERONIMO FINDS HIS POWERS IN CONFLICT

The Christian missionary work among the Fort Sill Apaches was carried out by the direct descendant of the Dutch Reformed Church, the Reformed Church in America. This denomination sent its first missionary, the gifted Choctaw minister Frank Hall Wright, to the Indians of southwestern Oklahoma in 1895, but for a time the army authorities forbade him to work among the recently arrived Apaches. When this ban was finally lifted, Wright and Dr. Walter C. Roe, who had established a mission among the Cheyennes, called a council of the prisoners and with the cooperation of Lieutenant Francis Henry Beach, then in charge of them, presented the plan for a mission. There it was decided to concentrate on a school for the children. Geronimo rose and expressed the consensus of the group: "I, Geronimo, and these others are now too old to travel your Jesus road. But our children are young and I and my brothers will be glad to have the children taught about the white man's God."

The War Department then gave its permission for the construction of mission buildings on the reservation. The site chosen was a sheltered hollow known as the "punch bowl" about two miles northwest of the post. The first building erected was a small frame

Apache Mission of the Reformed Church, attended by Geronimo during his brief Christian commitment. *The conflict between his two life philosophies was to appear in his last hours.* Courtesy U.S. Army Artillery and Missile Center Museum.

schoolhouse with a room for the teacher's residence. Miss Maud Adkisson came in August, 1899, as the first worker with combined duties as teacher, nurse, and home visitor. The first winter fifty-five or sixty children were enrolled in the school. This was a great relief to the parents who would no longer be separated from their small children. The older pupils, however, were still sent away to boarding school, usually to Chilocco.

Religious services were conducted in the same building with Wright and Roe as the ministers. A Sunday school and a Christian Endeavor Society were also organized there. Every summer a camp meeting was held on the grounds. A large tent was set up for the services, and the Indian families camped in smaller tents surrounding it. Eventually, five buildings were constructed. Besides the schoolhouse, now enlarged, there was a church, a teachers' home, and an orphanage with two large buildings used as boys' and girls' dormitories.

429

Regarding the orphanage, the missionaries apparently did find two or three neglected children from undisciplined homes who needed this shelter, but the Apaches in general did not need assistance in caring for their many orphans. Through their losses, first by war, then by disease in captivity, they had had much experience in rearing parentless children by taking them into the homes of friends and relatives. But it was the educational theory of the time to make Indians into white people by keeping them in boarding schools away from native influence; thus, by assuming the support of the orphans, the missionaries had pliable material. The boarding facilities were also a convenience for young children whose village homes were too distant for day school attendance.[1]

Between thirty and forty children were day school pupils, and twenty-four lived in the dormitories. The mission staff increased to a superintendent, two teachers, two dormitory matrons, and several laborers. The pastor lived at the Comanche Mission, off the reservation between Fort Sill and Lawton, and ministered to both tribes.[2] During the first winter an elderly medicine man named Harold Dick set up such a strong opposition with his dances and ceremonies that attendance at the mission services dropped almost to zero,[3] but interest gradually revived.

The loyal scout Noche, although embittered by the injustice done him by the government, was the first convert among the leaders. He was followed by Chihuahua and finally by Naiche. (The last took the name Christian Naiche.) The unhappy Chatto, still hated by Kaahteney and his band, also became a convert. To the missionaries he appeared to be "a bright and interesting man, . . . frequently the spokesman of the people . . . who does his work

---

[1] Amelia Naiche told me that her father was unwilling for her to attend as a boarding school pupil; thus, she made a six-mile walk, there and back, every day.

[2] Richard H. Harper, "The Missionary Work of the Reformed (Dutch) Church in America, in Oklahoma," *Chronicles of Oklahoma*, Vol. XVIII, No. 4 (December, 1940), pp. 329–32; Elizabeth M. Page, *In Camp and Tepee*, pp. 73–75, 130–35; The Women's Missionary Boards of the Reformed Church in America, "The Story of the Apache Prisoners," *Missionary Lesson Leaflet*, Vol. VII, No. 2 (June,, 1906). This last publication has some startling historical errors.

[3] Betzinez, *I Fought with Geronimo*, pp. 172–73.

well, and neither drinks nor gambles."[4] Less influential at the time, but adding to the stability of the congregation, were several returned Carlisle students who had become Christians at school. Among them were Jason Betzinez, the Benedict Jozhes, and James Kaywaykla and his wife, the former Dorothy Naiche. The strong-willed Asa Daklugie remained steadfast to the native religion, but Ramona was an earnest Christian, and Asa, whose love for her had begun in youth across the barriers of Apache etiquette and was to continue unchanged through a life extending beyond their golden wedding anniversary, accompanied her to all religious services.[5]

Geronimo, with his influence slipping, felt left out. He retreated in silence to his village but worked against the mission. Then, at the camp meeting in the summer of 1902 it was noticed that Zi-yeh had set up a tent on the grounds. On Sunday, the last day of the meeting, Geronimo appeared. Wright sought him out, talked to him earnestly, and won his promise to attend the evening service. He came and took a seat in the front row, sitting motionless with his hands folded in his lap until near the close. Then he sprang to his feet and made an impassioned speech, declaring that the Jesus road was best, and ending, "Now we begin to think that the Christian white people love us."

The missionaries encouraged him but did not admit him to church membership because of "a vein of self-importance in his talk." (Crook and numerous army officers would have agreed.) A year passed, in which periods of humility and gentleness alternated with arrogance and drinking sprees. Then in July, 1903, the camp meeting was held in an oak grove on Medicine Bluff Creek. Geronimo had been thrown from Zi-yeh's pony and had been severely injured. He was not present when the meeting started in the morning, but during the hot afternoon he arrived, riding slowly, barely able to sit his horse. He came into the tent, and Naiche came and

4 Page, *op. cit.*, pp. 136–40; The Women's Missionary Boards, *op. cit.*

5 The minutes of the Christian Endeavor Society, kept by Asa Daklugie as secretary, are in the Western History Collections at the University of Oklahoma. Other facts about the religious affiliation of these individuals are known to me through personal acquaintance.

sat beside him. He spoke in Apache, and Benedict Jozhe interpreted: "He says that he is in the dark. He knows that he is not on
the right road and he wants to find Jesus." At this, as the missionaries remembered it, "Naiche's fine, strong face blazed with joy."
During the succeeding days, they spent much time with Geronimo,
explaining the tenets of their faith, and at the last service he
accepted it. "I am old," he told them, "and broken by this fall I
have had. I am without friends for my people have turned from me.
I am full of sins, and I walk alone in the dark. I see that you missionaries have got a way to get sin out of the heart, and I want to
take that better road and hold it till I die."

Dr. Roe examined him and found that under his apparent indifference he had long been listening and learning. He was baptized
a week later. After the ceremony his people crowded around him.
Naiche embraced him, and the women and children clung to his
hands. As the missionaries told it afterwards, his face softened and
became bright with joy.[6]

Thus, his emotions were deeply stirred as he made this commitment. But as he told it to Barrett two years later, he revealed the
working of his independent mind. He had always been religious;
now he compared his old beliefs with the new, finding much
common ground. Barrett may have improved the wording, but the
thought is pure Geronimo:

$$\diamond\!\diamond\!\diamond\!\diamond\!\diamond\!\diamond\!\diamond\!\diamond\!\diamond\!\diamond\!\diamond\!\diamond\!\diamond\!\diamond\!\diamond$$

In our primitive worship only our relations to Usen and the
members of our tribe were considered as appertaining to our religious responsibilities. [Although he did not state it then, even
Christianity did not apply to Mexicans.[7]] As to the future state, the
teachings of our tribe were not specific. . . . We believed that there
is a life after this one, but no one ever told me as to what part of
man lived after death. I have seen many men die; I have seen many
human bodies decayed, but I have never seen that part that is

---

6 Page, *op. cit.*, pp. 142–46.
7 Barrett, *Geronimo's Story of His Life*, p. 110.

called the spirit; I do not know what it is; nor have I yet been able to understand that part of the Christian religion.

We held that the discharge of one's duty would make his future life more pleasant . . . We hoped that in the future life family and tribal relations would be resumed. . . . [He went on then to tell of the man he had known on the San Carlos Reservation, probably Noch-ay-del-klinne, who had told of seeing the spirits of departed friends.] Many Indians believed this warrior, and I cannot say that he did not tell the truth. I wish I knew that what he said is beyond question true. But perhaps it is as well that we are not certain.

Since my life as a prisoner has begun I have heard the teachings of the white man's religion, and in many respects believe it to be better than the religion of my fathers. However, I have always prayed, and I believe that the Almighty has always protected me.

Believing that in a wise way it is good to go to church, and that associating with Christians would improve my character, I have adopted the Christian religion. I believe that the church has helped me much during the short time I have been a member. . . . I have advised all of my people who are not Christians, to study that religion, because it seems to me the best religion in enabling one to live right.[8]

Thus, Geronimo did not discard his primitive beliefs, but supplemented them. It is clear that he found no discrepancy between Christian worship and his people's sacred observances such as the womanhood ceremony he had just celebrated for Eva. (In this belief he was probably more liberal than the missionaries.) His words, "I believe that the Almighty has always protected me," indicate that he still trusted his Power, although he gave it a Christian expression. It was no longer necessary for him to use it to deflect bullets, delay the daybreak, or reveal the location of the enemy; but illness believed to be caused by malevolent influences still afflicted his people, and to that it was applicable.

8 *Ibid.*, pp. 207–12.

It seems impossible to discover whether he used his "curative" ceremonies during his Christian interlude—if he did, the missionaries probably were not aware of it—but it is known that he did practice them during the Fort Sill period. Some of Opler's informants described the procedure as they had observed it in their boyhood. Geronimo permitted these young visitors to be present if they would remain quiet and observe his personal taboo against scratching. (One who scratched himself would immediately experience a choking sensation.)

One informant described a ceremony he had observed for an elderly man suffering from "coyote sickness," a disease caused by any contact with a coyote, a wolf, or a fox—even with the tracks of these animals or the ground where they had lain. This ceremony was held in an arbor outside Geronimo's house, beginning as soon as darkness fell. There a fire burned, with Geronimo and his patient on the west side, Geronimo facing east with the patient stretched out before him. There were several adults present, mainly relatives of the sick man, sitting in a semicircle in the back of the shelter, with an open space towards the east.

In front of Geronimo was a basket tray, holding an eagle feather, an abalone shell, and a bag of pollen. He began his ceremony by rolling a cigarette and sending a puff of smoke towards each of the four cardinal points, beginning at the east. Next, he rubbed certain parts of the patient's body with the pollen, praying to each direction as he did so. Each of his prayers referred to Coyote. Then he started to sing, accompanying his songs by beating on a drum with a curved stick. There were many of these songs, all relating to Coyote: how he was a tricky fellow, hard to see and find; how he had given these characteristics to Geronimo so that he also could make himself invisible; and how he helped Geronimo in curing. The singing continued until the evening star was halfway between the horizon and the zenith—the Apache midnight. The ceremony lasted four nights, each one a repetition of the first.

Another of Geronimo's patients at Fort Sill was an old woman who was helping her dog to follow a wolf; when the wolf ran into a hole, she seized its leg to pull it out. Then she became violently ill, with her body shaking, her lips twisted, her eyes crossed. Geronimo sang over her and cured her. (Anybody familiar with nervous disorders would conclude that *this* cure, at least, was real.) There is another case of his treating a patient for ghost sickness.[9]

Possibly these treatments took place during the early years at Fort Sill before he reached the age when his Power had sinister implications. For while the Apaches admired and trusted the possessor of Power, they feared its ultimate use. As the time of death approached, he might transfer the fatal summons to another person, especially a relative.[10] As Geronimo lived on while others fell away, no doubt such dark suspicions existed regarding him, but if he was aware of them he gave no sign, and certainly they never entered his own thinking. To him, whether pagan or Christian, Power was the central fact of his life.

He would have resolved his scientific-religious conflicts as like-minded men of other cultures have done through the ages, but his favorite amusements were something else. For a time after his conversion he probably refrained from gambling, horse racing, with its feverish wagers, and drinking, but he eventually returned to those forbidden pleasures. (There is reason to believe that some of his contemporaries also had their lapses, but they managed to keep them quiet.[11]) The Reverend Leonard L. Legters, who had become the pastor of the church in 1906, remonstrated with him; and he said that the rules were "too strict" and returned to the uncomplicated faith of his fathers. He was then suspended from membership in the church. This occurred about 1907.[12]

Throughout most of his life Geronimo seemed to be all of one piece—a completely integrated personality—but it is clear that this religious episode brought a spiritual cleavage that was never

9 Opler, *An Apache Life-Way*, pp. 40–41, 224–31, 260. For more details of the symptoms and cure of coyote sickness, see Goodwin, "Experiences of an Indian Scout," Part 2, pp. 33–34.
10 Opler, *op. cit.*, p. 256.
11 Betzinez, *I Fought with Geronimo*, p. 182.
12 *Lawton Constitution-Democrat* (weekly edition), February 18, 1909.

435

closed. At the same time his Power, the sustaining force of his long life, seemed to be breaking down.

As he approached what was probably his ninth decade, it was natural that he would have seen his contemporaries drop off. Old Nana, still unreconstructed, had died in 1896, and his widow, Geronimo's sister Nah-dos-te, in 1907; Chihuahua, the courtly gentleman and earnest Christian, in 1901; Mangus, never very fierce even when a hostile, also in 1901; and Loco, always mild and well disposed, in 1905, with the closing comment that he felt as though he had no country.[13]

But Geronimo's losses went beyond this common experience of old age. He had seen two wives die during his captivity. One by one he had seen his children die—Chappo in Alabama and, within the first five years at Fort Sill, his small son Fenton and his daughter Lulu, with all of her family but Thomas. His feeling for this orphaned grandchild was very strong. At Chilocco the "promising boy" had become "a good student and worker" selected to learn the painter's trade because of his excellent health and vitality.[14] As Geronimo saw him growing into young manhood, all his hopes were centered on this grandson as the remaining scion of his family. (When he finally established contact with his Mescalero son, Robert, the two never became very close; they had spent too many years apart.) Then on March 11, 1908, Thomas died at the age of eighteen. It was a heavy blow to the old man, and he reacted in three ways, all typical.

He retained his clear-cut judgment—and his business acumen. Three days after the youth's death, a Lawton attorney wrote to the War Department, saying that "Chief Geronimo" was "greatly distressed in spirit and brooding over the loss of an only grandson, that was very close and dear to him" and that a "move is on foot to get him a ninety day release" with "a change of scenery." If some promotion scheme was back of this story, it never emerged. The

---

[13] Lockwood, *The Apache Indians*, pp. 324–25; Griswold, "The Fort Sill Apaches," biographies.

[14] Oklahoma Historical Society, Indian Archives, Chilocco—Enrollment, [McCowan] to George L. Puirrington [*sic*], November 21, 1906.

letter traveled to Washington and back to the post commander, who then questioned the old Indian. Geronimo told him "that he does not feel depressed, but does feel the loss of a grandson as any other man would." He said that he had never talked to any person in Lawton about his feelings and that the request had been made without his knowledge. Asked whether he would like to take a trip for a while, he said "he would, if he could get in with some good show where he could make some money." The post commander went on to explain to the War Department that contrary to the implication of the letter, Geronimo was not "held in confinement" there—"he goes and comes at will, with nothing to do but eat and sleep."[15] That ended the matter.

But Geronimo had begun to suspect that some evil influence was destroying his family. By this time his cherished Eva was showing symptoms of debility. In his desperation he sought the cause in the ancient beliefs of his people. The post records and the cemetery headstones show the same succession of fatalities in other families, but he was thinking of his own. Surely someone had "witched" Thomas and probably had "witched" the other children. He called a dance to discover the culprit, with Lot Eyelash in charge. After three or four songs, the dancing stopped, and Lot called out his findings: "YOU DID IT! So you could live on."[16] Geronimo's feelings can only be imagined. He knew, of course, that he was not guilty. But among the more conservative Apaches the suspicion persisted even into recent times that Geronimo indeed used his Power to divert death from himself to his children.[17]

It was probably this crisis in his faith that caused the old man to consider again the Christianity he had renounced. At the camp meeting the following summer he talked to the missionaries, indicating that he wanted to start again, but at the same time he was engaging in his old habits and telling his tribesmen that he held to

15 National Archives and Records Service, Record Group No. 94, AGO 1354977, from 445841, B. M. Parmenter to War Department, March 14, 1908, with endorsements; Assistant Secretary of War Robert Shaw Oliver to Parmenter, April 21, 1908.
16 James Kaywaykla, interview, July 29, 1959.
17 Eve Ball to Angie Debo, December 10, 1957.

the old religion.[18] As it happened, it was the most persistent of these old habits that was to lead to his death, while at the same time the collision between his two life philosophies was to appear in his last hours.

[18] *Lawton Constitution-Democrat* (weekly edition), February 18, 1909.

CHAPTER 23

GERONIMO'S FINAL SURRENDER

As Geronimo's years piled up to the winter of 1908/9, his rugged body began to show signs of breaking down. He was not well that fall, and his sturdy figure had shrunk. His activity was slowing. He had become increasingly absent-minded. To the amusement of his young friends, he would hunt for his hat while he was wearing it. One of them recalled an incident of these last years. Geronimo was fashioning a bow—his deft fingers never lost their skill—when he started to look for his knife, which he was holding in his hand. He asked his wife to hunt it for him. As the amused visitors watched, she refused, saying, "You're old enough to look for your own knife." He became angry. "Boys, you see how she is!" he said, "I advise you not to marry." Finally he saw it in his hand. "Why, I'm nothing but a fool," was his embarrassed admission.[1]

On a cold day in February, 1909 (February 11, according to the local newspaper), he rode to Lawton and sold some bows and arrows. There, he asked Eugene Chihuahua to get him some whiskey. It was illegal to sell liquor to an Indian, but the method of obtaining it was easy. Eugene simply asked a soldier to go into the

[1] *Lawton Constitution-Democrat* (weekly edition), February 18, 1909; Opler, *An Apache Life-Way*, p. 402.

saloon and buy it for him. The young man was to regret his part in the transaction to the end of his long life. Geronimo became intoxicated and, in attempting to ride back after dark, had almost reached his home when he fell off his horse and lay there all night. The next morning Mrs. Jozhe saw the horse standing saddled on the bank of the creek. She and others investigated, and found Geronimo lying partly in the water and partly on the ground. He contracted a severe cold, which became worse.

For three days his friends and family cared for him. Then one of the scouts (probably Benedict Jozhe) reported his illness to the post surgeon, who sent an ambulance to bring him to the little Apache hospital at the post. But the ambulance detail found him surrounded by about a dozen women, no doubt including his wife, and they refused to let him go. So many Apaches had died in the hospital that they called it "the death house" and feared to enter it. The surgeon reported to Lieutenant Purington, and that officer ordered a scout to accompany the ambulance and bring the old man in. By this time he was critically ill with pneumonia. It was Monday, February 15.

Now in these last hours was compressed the totality of Geronimo's life and character. The post surgeon expected him to die that night, but he asked that Robert and Eva be brought from Chilocco and was determined to live until they should arrive.[2] Purington summoned them by letter instead of by wire.[3] Thus, they did not come for two days. Geronimo had many grievances against the army, and this failure to bring his cherished Eva and his newly discovered Robert to his deathbed closed the circle.

Eugene Chihuahua stayed by him through the day, and Asa Daklugie, who was even more than a son, kept the night vigil. During those hours the old man relived the youthful tragedy of the massacre of his first family and his hatred of Mexicans. He talked

[2] *Lawton Constitution-Democrat* (weekly edition), February 18, 1909; Eve Ball to Angie Debo, March 8, 1971; Betzinez, *I Fought with Geronimo*, pp. 179, 198; Musgrove, "A Belated Reward for the Surrender of Geronimo"; Benedict Jozhe, interview, September 6, 1969—"I've often heard my mother tell this story."

[3] Oklahoma Historical Society, Indian Archives, Kiowa—Geronimo, Purington to John R. Wise, February 15, 1909.

440

of the men who were with him on his last war trail. He entrusted Eva to the care of the Daklugies and warned against her marriage. Asa promised to take her into their home.[4]

One experience of this last illness, as he told it to the Apaches at his bedside, indicates how deeply he had been affected by his unresolved religious struggle. Nat Kayihtah, the young son of the scout, had been a schoolmate and friend of Thomas Dahkeya. He had been permitted to go to the Mescalero Reservation to work and had died there of pneumonia on February 10, only the day before Geronimo made his fatal ride to Lawton. Apparently Geronimo had been told of his death. Now in his feverish imaginings, the two youths appeared to him and urged him to become a Christian. He refused, saying he had been unable "to follow the path" in his life, and it was now too late, but he asked why they had not come earlier. They answered that he had had the missionaries and had refused to listen to them.[5]

Throughout his second day in the hospital, his strong spirit staved off death in the hope of seeing his children. Then when night came, and they still had not arrived, he gave up and quietly sank away. His sturdy body held out until 6:15 the following morning, February 17. "I was sitting beside him holding his hand when he died," said Asa Daklugie.[6] This time his surrender was final.

As soon as he died, his widow rushed to his favorite horse, his well-known sorrel racing pony, and would have killed it, but other Indians prevented her. All day long grieving old women, groaning, weeping, and praying, filed in and out of the little stone building where his body lay, while men, dry-eyed and stricken, stood without, silently watching. The funeral was arranged for the following afternoon at three o'clock, and at their request the army gave all the men a half holiday so they could attend.[7]

4 Eve Ball to Angie Debo, July 13, 1973.
5 *Lawton Constitution-Democrat* (weekly edition), February 25, 1909. The Biblical analogy in this last sentence was certainly remembered from a missionary exhortation.
6 National Archives and Records Service, Record Group No. 94, AGO 1490310, from 445841, telegram [Colonel Henry M.] Andrews to Adjutant General, February 17, 1909; Eve Ball to Angie Debo, July 13, 1973.
7 *Lawton Constitution-Democrat* (weekly edition), February 18, 1909.

441

But while Geronimo's body waited in an elaborately decorated Lawton hearse, even his funeral had to be postponed for the arrival of Robert and Eva from Chilocco. They came on the train shortly after three o'clock obviously grief-stricken, and the procession started immediately to the cemetery where so many of the prisoners were buried. His grave had been dug beside that of Zi-yeh, and surrounding it were the graves of the other members of his family. The services were held there, Christian services conducted by the Reverend Leonard Legters. Virtually the entire tribe and many white people from Lawton were present. His funeral furnished an occasion for giving advice to his tribesmen, with his life used to point the moral.

Naiche, tall, erect, intelligent-looking, standing at the very edge of the grave, spoke first, briefly but impressively in Apache. He recalled incidents of the warpath, lauded Geronimo's bravery and skill as a war leader, and told how loyally he had adhered to the peace he made at the surrender. But he had refused to accept Christianity, thus being an utter failure in the chief thing in life. He closed by urging the assembled people to profit by his example.

The missionary, speaking through Eugene Chihuahua as interpreter, then conducted the formal service. He used the parable of the wise and foolish virgins to urge the Apaches to prepare for their own summons. Geronimo, he said, had probably been the greatest war leader the red men had ever known, but he had failed to conquer the pleasures of the body, and like all men he had been unable to conquer death. He told his hearers they might never become as great leaders as he had been, but they could conquer self so as to be ready for this last unconquerable experience. Then, just before the grave was filled, the relatives of the dead leader solemnly placed his riding whip and blanket in it.[8] Before he died, he had told them to tie his horse to a certain tree and to hang up his belongings on the east side of his grave, and in three days he would come and get them, but his widow decided to bury his

8 *Ibid.*, February 25, 1909.

Robert Geronimo at his father's grave in the Apache Cemetery at Fort Sill, January 13, 1964. Courtesy U.S. Army Artillery and Missile Center Museum.

possessions with him.[9] (Regarding his possessions, it was said that the balance to his account in his Lawton bank was more than ten thousand dollars at the time of his death.[10])

An impressive rock monument surmounted by a stone eagle was erected at his grave by the Field Artillery School at Fort Sill

9 James Kaywaykla, interview, July 29, 1959.
10 Burbank and Royce, *Burbank among the Indians*, p. 24.

443

in 1931. Later, small headstones were set to mark all the graves in this tragically populous cemetery. Near the entrance a sign points out that the burials there form the "roll call" of "the most famous names in Apache history": Geronimo, Loco, Nana, and Chihuahua; and the sons and grandsons of Mangas Coloradas, Victorio, Cochise, Naiche, and Juh, and of such noted scouts as Kaahteney, Chatto, Kayihtah, and Martine.

All this history was in the minds of the Apaches that gathered that February day at the graveside of Geronimo. And the question persisted: Would this be the end of their trail, too?

EPILOGUE

Robert Geronimo never returned to Chilocco after his father's death, but transferred to Carlisle. Eva went back and finished the term, but that was the end of her schooling.[1] She came home and lived with the Daklugies. Although they tried to dissuade her, she soon married Fred Golene, a young member of the band who had been one of her fellow students at Chilocco. A daughter, Evaline, born to them on June 21, 1910, lived scarcely two months, dying on August 20. They buried the child close to Geronimo, but left a space between. Eva followed within a year, dying of tuberculosis on August 10, 1911, the last of Geronimo's prisoner descendants.[2] She was buried between her father and the baby, with her mother on the other side of the old war leader and her brother Fenton nearby. Not far away are the graves of her half sister, Lulu Dahkeya, and her family.[3]

Robert Geronimo rejoined his mother and step-father on the Mescalero Reservation after spending several years at Carlisle.

[1] Frank J. Self to Angie Debo, February 12, 1973.
[2] Oklahoma Historical Society, Indian Archives, Chilocco—Enrollment, [M. S. McCowan] to George L. Puirrington [sic], November 21, 1906; Chilocco—Students Returning Home, [McCowan] to Puirrington, September 30, 1907; *Beaver Herald*, August 17, 1911.
[3] Visit to cemetery, August 16, 1971.

445

By that time many of the former prisoners were living there. Several considerations had brought about their release from captivity and their settlement with the Mescaleros. When they were brought to Fort Sill, it was expected that the post, like other frontier posts of Indian war days, would soon be abandoned, leaving the reservation available as a permanent home for the prisoners. This policy was expressed officially as late as 1904.[4] And the Apaches themselves, in spite of the relative comfort in which they lived, still held an unchanged longing for freedom. Typical is a statement made by Asa Daklugie in answer to a questionnaire sent out by Captain Pratt to check on the welfare of the Carlisle graduates. He gave the requested information regarding his marriage, work record, housing, and so on, but to the final question, "Tell me anything else of interest connected with your life," he answered in his sturdy penmanship: "The 'interesting thing in my present life' is That, I wished to see, that 'Apaches people' get a freedom, from being a prisoner of War, under the Government. 'So they can have they own home.' "[5]

At the same time, friends of the Indians were still urging some provision for them. As time passed, an increasing proportion of them had been born in captivity or had been young children at the time of the wars of which they were supposedly prisoners. The death of the notorious Geronimo, who received most of the popular and official blame for the hostilities, increased the force of this argument. But ironically, it was the needs of the military that brought matters to a head.

Fort Sill, of course, had been a cavalry post during the Indian wars. Following that came a long period of inactivity. Then the War Department, because of the extensive and varied terrain of the reservation, began from 1902 on to recognize its importance for the training of artillery; and in 1910 it was selected as the site of the artillery school of fire. But the Apache prisoners, with their

4 U.S., *Statutes*, XXXII, 467, Act of June 28, 1902; XXXIII, 26, Act of February 18, 1904.

5 National Archives and Records Service, Record Group No. 75, Records of the Carlisle Indian Industrial School, Student Folder No. 72.

villages, their grazing cattle, their hay meadows, and their cultivated fields, were all in the way of the big guns. "These so-called
prisoners of war have more rights than free men," reported the
disgusted officer in charge of drawing up regulations for the
school.[6]

In 1911 their old friend Hugh L. Scott (then Colonel Scott),
was brought to Fort Sill for the special duty of making permanent
provision for them. He and another officer held a council with
them at the post. Naiche was the spokesman. "All we want is to be
freed and be released as prisoners," he said, "and given land and
homes that we can call our own. This is all we think about. We
are thinking the same today as the last time, and that is why we
are here now, to say these things. . . . Half or more than half of these
people talk English. Half or more than half can read and write;
they all know how to work. You have held us long enough. We
want something else now."[7]

A law releasing them was passed by Congress the following
year on August 24, 1912.[8] It made an appropriation of two
hundred thousand dollars for their settlement on lands to be
selected for them by the secretaries of war and the interior, and a
supplemental appropriation of one hundred thousand dollars was
made in 1913. A search for a suitable location indicated that the
Mescalero Reservation was the most desirable. (Arizona was completely out of the question because of the feeling against them
there.) A delegation from the prisoners was taken to visit the
Mescaleros, and they expressed their willingness to accept the band
on equal terms. But some of the prisoners wanted to remain in
Oklahoma, and it was decided to purchase individual farms for
them from the heirs of deceased Comanche, Kiowa, and Kiowa-
Apache allottees. They were allowed to choose between the two
locations, and numerous councils were held with them to deter-

6 Nye, *Carbine and Lance*, pp. 399–405.

7 Chapman, "Notes—Apaches," quoting National Archives and Records Service,
AGO 1808991B, Box 3142, 1912.

8 U.S., *Statutes*, XXXVII, 534.

mine their individual decisions.[9] Wratten, however, did not serve as their interpreter and did not assist in closing out their affairs. He had died on June 23, 1912, after almost twenty-six years of close association with them.

By this time, their number had declined to 261, of whom 183 chose to go to Mescalero and 78 decided to remain in Oklahoma.[10] Their cattle, about six thousand head, said to be the finest herd in the state, were sold, and they were compensated for the fence they had built around the reservation. The proceeds, $165,000, was placed to their credit to assist them in settling.[11]

The personal property of the Mescalero party—horses, mules, wheeled vehicles, household goods—was shipped to the reservation. They themselves were taken there on a special train under the escort of an army officer, arriving on April 4, 1913. Among them was Geronimo's widow with her young grandnephew, Paul Guydelkon, and his father.[12] All the surviving warriors of the last holdout band that surrendered to Miles were in the party with their families. There were Naiche, his wife, Ha-o-zinne, and five of his children; his old mother, Dos-teh-seh, daughter of Mangas Coloradas and widow of Cochise; his two half sisters, daughters of Cochise; and Ha-o-zinne's parents, Beshe and U-go-hun, and her half brother, Calvin Zhonne. The chief left in the Fort Sill cemetery the graves of his wives Nah-de-yole and E-clah-heh and eight of his children; and Dorothy, the wife of James Kaywaykla, remained in Oklahoma. Ahnandia had died of tuberculosis in Alabama. His wife, Tah-das-te, had remarried and went with her husband to Mescalero. Geronimo's "brother" Perico also went there with his stolen wife, Bi-ya-neta, and several of their children. His first wife, Hah-dun-key, had died at Fort Sill, and so had his half brother,

[9] Oklahoma Historical Society, Indian Archives, Kiowa—Apache Prisoners of War, Colonel Hugh L. Scott and Kiowa Superintendent Ernest Stecker to Adjutant General, October 5, 1912.

[10] Secretary of the Interior, *Annual Report*, 1913, p. 36; 1914, p. 58. This number varies slightly in official reports. A few babies born before the final settlement was made were added to the totals, and some who died before receiving land in Oklahoma were dropped from the record (Benedict Jozhe, interview, April 12, 1971).

[11] Benedict Jozhe, interview, July 29, 1959.

[12] Eve Ball to Angie Debo, January 18, 1973.

Burdett Tsisnah. The warrior La-zi-yah also had died at Fort Sill. Geronimo's nephew Jasper Kanseah joined the Mescalero group; and so did his brother-in-law, Yahnozha.

The betrayed scouts, Chatto, Noche, Kayihtah, and Martine, went there with their families, as did Toclanny and Siki with their children. So did Kaahteney, but he had buried Guyan at Fort Sill. Asa Daklugie and his wife, Ramona, and their children were also in the Mescalero party. There, the capable, independent-minded Daklugie became one of the strong leaders of the band. Eugene Chihuahua and his wife were in the group. Two daughters went with them, but they left the graves of six children at Fort Sill. The early Carlisle student Dexter Loco also chose Mescalero.[13]

Two of the missionaries went with the band to their new home. (The Fort Sill Mission, of course, was closed.) On the first Sunday eighty-seven of the band united by letter with the Reformed Church there.[14] They settled down quietly on the reservation in a locality of their own, good workers living in good houses, somewhat apart from the Mescaleros, but joining in reservation activities. The historian Frank C. Lockwood paid them several visits during the 1930's and made a careful study of the ones who had figured in their turbulent past, interviewing those still living, checking records, and questioning the former agency superintendent O. M. Boggess and the Reformed missionary Richard Harper. Then Mrs. Eve Ball came to live in nearby Ruidoso and began the friendly association with members of the band that was to lead to recording their reminiscences.

One glimpses in these experiences the steady character of these once wild people. Lockwood met Chihuahua's "two remarkable children," Eugene, "an industrious and successful farmer," and Ramona Daklugie in her "tidy, well-furnished little home," both proudly showing enlarged, framed photographs of their father. Naiche had died, but the missionary and the agency farmer told of his "earnestness of character," his good influence among his

13 Griswold, "The Fort Sill Apaches," various biographies.
14 Harper, "The Missionary Work of the Reformed (Dutch) Church in America, in Oklahoma," pp. 330–31, 334.

people, and his satisfaction with the life at Mescalero in contrast to the hardships of the warpath. Harper remembered Kaahteney as so mild and cooperative that it was hard for him to credit the army accounts of his rebellious past. Lockwood found Kayihtah and Toclanny genial and friendly, strangely unembittered by their unjust treatment. Martine, old and feeble in mind and body, seemed more resentful.[15]

Chatto had suffered most of all from the official ingratitude. He had greatly admired Crook and had committed himself completely to his new allegiance. No doubt when he found himself in favor he had lorded it over the bellicose members of the band. Then he had been given the same punishment. He brooded over this injustice, and he felt the resentment of the tribal members who regarded him as a turncoat. Boggess, who knew him well, considered him an excellent citizen with a satisfactory home life, and Harper characterized him as a man of striking bearing and dignity of character. But the factional hatred, held in check while the prisoners were under military control, now asserted itself so strongly that he and his family made their home apart from the Fort Sill settlement. In 1934 he and some others had been drinking together up in a canyon, and on their way down their automobile left the road and turned turtle in a creek. Chatto was so badly injured that he died. For many years his medal and his treasured copy of Davis' book were kept in the agency safe.[16] Perhaps they are still there.

Jasper Kanseah, the boy in Geronimo's band, lived until 1959. He could look back to a childhood memory of the great Cochise, retained a vivid impression of events on the warpath, and was the last surviving eyewitness of Geronimo's final surrender. After that came Carlisle, the prison experiences at Fort Sill, and the placid years at Mescalero telling and retelling the turbulent episodes of his people's history.[17]

Charles Istee, the only surviving son of Victorio, also joined the

15 Lockwood, *The Apache Indians*, pp. 325–43.
16 *Ibid.*, p. 326; Eve Ball, interview, July 25, 1971.
17 Ball, *In the Days of Victorio*, pp. 51, 152–53 and n. 3, 185–87. If Charlie Smith was with Geronimo's band until the last, he retained no memory of the surrender.

Mescalero party with his wife. Their son, Evan Istee, born shortly after their arrival, still lives on the reservation with his family.[18] So do the descendants of Geronimo. Lenna died young but left descendants. Robert, the mild son of the fierce raider, lived until 1966.[19] His four children, with their families, were still living on the reservation at the last report.

Meanwhile, as this band was settling into life with the Mescaleros, the government officials were purchasing farms for their relatives who chose to remain in Oklahoma. Most of this land was in a rich agricultural area north of Fort Sill centered around the town of Apache, which still perpetuates their name. They had to adjust to a more difficult life-way than did their kinsmen on the reservation, supporting themselves by farming and trades and establishing social relationships in a predominantly white society. In general it was the more progressive ones of the band, especially the Carlisle graduates, who made this choice.

Several of them were relatives of Geronimo. Among them were Jason Betzinez and his mother, Nah-thle-tla. His sister's family had all died at Fort Sill, the five children one by one, then Ellen herself and her husband, Ambrose Chachu, in 1899. Nah-thle-tla, active and sturdy, lived to the remarkable age, as nearly as it could be determined, of 110 years, dying in 1934. Jason worked at the blacksmith trade he had learned at Carlisle and tended his eighty-acre farm. Late in life he married a Chicago woman who had served the prisoners at the Reformed Church Mission and brought her to his neat little house. Every Sunday he drove his automobile to Lawton, twenty miles away, to attend church. The two lived until 1960, Jason dying at the age of one hundred as the result of an automobile accident. They had no children.

Sam Haozous also remained in Oklahoma and became a successful farmer and good community citizen. He died in 1957, but his wife, the half-Apache daughter of George Wratten, an attractive woman much younger than her husband, continued until

18 I met him and his much younger wife at the Reformed Church service there on July 24, 1971, and was struck by the remarkable beauty of their little boy.
19 *Newsweek*, November 7, 1966.

recently to live at the old home. On the walls of the pleasant farmhouse hung many paintings by their gifted son, Allan Houser, who now teaches in the Institute of American Indian Arts at Santa Fe. Three of their four children who grew to adulthood graduated from college.

The Jozhes also settled on their land, where Jozhe became a successful farmer and Mrs. Jozhe won many prizes at the county fair for her canned fruit and vegetables. Their son, who was to serve more than forty years as tribal chairman, graduated from the American Indian Institute of Wichita, Kansas, a Presbyterian school headed by the well known Indian educator, Henry Roe Cloud. A great-grandson through his mother of Chief Loco, and a descendant through his father of the great Mahko, he is a nephew of Geronimo's "brothers," Perico, Fun, and Tsisnah. Gifted with a keen mind and a reflective disposition, he has become an authority on tribal history, genealogy, and present legal problems.

The Kaywayklas also made their living and reared their children on their farm. Dorothy died in 1946, but James lived until 1963, the last of his people who remembered Victorio and the disaster at Tres Castillos. Their descendants still live in Oklahoma. John Loco, the son of the chief, who had served as the head of Loco's village after the death of his father, also chose to settle in Oklahoma. In his later years he sometimes preached in a Reformed Church near Apache. He died in 1946.[20] His sons still live in the neighborhood.

But the members of the band who remained in Oklahoma have shown more of a tendency than have their Mescalero relatives to "enter the mainstream of American life"—to quote a shibboleth of early-day educators—finding their living elsewhere and even marrying non-Indians. One of John Loco's grandsons, married to a white woman, is a tool designer in Detroit. A granddaughter lives in a suburb of Washington, and her white husband, John A. Shapard, Jr., a historical legislative research analyst in the Indian

20 *Oklahoma City Times*, August 29, 1946.

Bureau, has done extensive independent research and writing in Apache history. Harry Perico, the son of Geronimo's lieutenant, sold his land and used the money for a college education. Then with his Chilocco-taught printer's trade he began working for the *Arkansas City (Kansas) Traveler*, and for many years until his recent retirement he served as foreman of its commercial printing department. For more than fifty years he was a member of the municipal band, and for three years he was the city golf champion. Arthur Guydelkon, whose brother accompanied Geronimo's widow to Mescalero, remained in Oklahoma. He and his young wife, a daughter of Talbot Gooday, lived for a time on their farm. Then they sold it, and he took a position in the civil service. They made their home in Lawton. Throughout his long life—he died in 1967—he was an important source of information regarding the life of Geronimo.[21]

Thus, the released prisoners have found their living in their separate ways. Like all ethnic groups, they range in character from the upright to the profligate. Their numbers have increased since they were freed from captivity. (Perhaps Crook was not far wrong when he cited "the dreary monotony of empty lives" as a contributing factor in their mortality.) No one is living now of the generation that remembered the raids, the hunted existence, and the bloody encounters with the military forces of two nations, but their descendants still have a strong sense of tribal solidarity. The Oklahoma and Mescalero bands maintain their contacts through frequent visits, and even the scattered members of the group cherish the traditions of their elders.

At a recent conference a son of John Loco, born a Fort Sill prisoner, smilingly held up his smooth wrists, saying, "See the scars of the fetters."[22] He was joking, of course. The prisoners were

---

21 Griswold, "The Fort Sill Apaches," various biographies; Benedict Jozhe, James Kaywaykla, and Moses Loco, joint interview, July 29, 1959; Benedict Jozhe, "A Brief History of the Fort Sill Apache Tribe," *Chronicles of Oklahoma*, Vol. XXXIX, No. 4 (Winter, 1961/62); *Arkansas City (Kansas) Traveler*, June 17, 1970.

22 At Anadarko, Oklahoma, August 27, 1973.

never chained, certainly not the small children, and any scars left on the souls of the captives are likewise invisible. But the experience may have given a special character to their descendants. And through their collective memories the story of Geronimo lives on.

BIBLIOGRAPHY

Source Material
I. Manuscript Material

Fort Sill, Okla. United States Army Artillery and Missile Center Museum. Archives.

Fremont, Ohio. Rutherford B. Hayes Library. George Crook Letterbook I.

Gatewood, Charles B. "An Account of the Surrender of Geronimo." Tucson, Arizona Historical Society, Gatewood Collection. Manuscript, 1895.

Huddleson, S. M. "An Interview with Geronimo and His Guardian, Mr. G. M. Wratton." Tucson, Arizona Historical Society, Gatewood Collection.

Norman, Okla. University of Oklahoma Library, Western History Collections; Phillips Collection.

Oklahoma City, Okla. Oklahoma Historical Society. Indian Archives.

Tallahassee, Fla. National Park Service.

Washington, D.C. National Archives and Records Service.

Consolidated File 1066 AGO 1883.

Inspectors File No. 1732.

Record Group No. 75, Bureau of Indian Affairs, Letters Received 1881–1907; Records of the Carlisle Indian Industrial School.

455

Record Group No. 94, AGO 445841.

II. Government Documents

Annual Reports of the Secretary of the Interior, 1858–69, 1881, 1913, 1914.

Annual Reports of the Secretary of War, 1882–87, 1890, 1892, 1894–96.

Kappler, Charles J. *Indian Affairs, Laws and Treaties. S. Doc. No. 452*, Vol. II, 57 Cong., 1 sess., 1904.

Malloy, William M. *Treaties, Conventions, International Acts, Protocols and Agreements between the United States of America and Other Powers. S. Doc. No. 357*, 61 Cong., 2 sess., 1910.

U.S., Congress, *Senate Executive Documents, Nos. 73, 117*, 49 Cong., 2 sess.; *Nos. 35, 83, 88*, 51 Cong., 1 sess.

U.S., *Congressional Record*, Vol. VIII (1879).

U.S., *Statutes at Large*, Vols. 16, 20, 28, 32, 33, 37.

III. Books and Articles

Anderson, Hattie M. "Mining and Indian Fighting in Arizona and New Mexico—Memoirs of Hank Smith," *Panhandle-Plains Historical Review* (Canyon, Texas), Vol. I (1928).

———. "With the Confederates in New Mexico during the Civil War—Memoirs of Hank Smith," *Panhandle-Plains Historical Review*, Vol. II (1929).

Ball, Eve. *In the Days of Victorio: Recollections of a Warm Springs Apache*. Tucson, University of Arizona Press, 1970.

———. "On the Warpath with Geronimo," *The West*, Vol. XV, No. 3 (August, 1971).

Barrett, S [tephen] M[elvil]. *Geronimo's Story of His Life*. New York, Duffield and Company, 1906.

———. *Sociology of the American Indians*. Kansas City, Mo., Burton Publishing Company, 1946.

Bartlett, John Russell. *Personal Narratives of Explorations and Incidents in Texas, New Mexico, California, Sonora, and Chihuahua Connected with the United States and Mexican Boundary Commission during the Years 1850, '51, '52, and '53*, Vol. I. New York, D. Appleton, 1854.

Basso, Keith H. (ed.). *Western Apache Raiding and Warfare: From the Notes of Grenville Goodwin.* Tucson, University of Arizona Press, 1971.

Begay, Alberta, as told to Eve Ball. "Massai—Broncho Apache," *True West,* Vol. VI, No. 6 (July–August, 1959).

Betzinez, Jason. *I Fought with Geronimo.* Ed. and annotated by Wilbur Sturtevant Nye. Harrisburg, Pa., Stackpole, 1959.

Bourke, John G. *An Apache Campaign in the Sierra Madre.* New York, Charles Scribner's Sons, 1958.

———. *On the Border with Crook.* New York, Charles Scribner's Sons, 1891.

Burbank, E[lbridge] A[yer], and Ernest Royce. *Burbank among the Indians.* Caldwell, Idaho, The Caxton Printers, Ltd., 1946.

Catlin, George. *Episodes from Life among the Indians and Last Rambles.* Ed. Marvin C. Ross. Norman, University of Oklahoma Press, 1959.

Clum, John P. "Apache Misrule," *New Mexico Historical Review,* Vol. V, No. 3 (July, 1930).

———. "Geronimo," *New Mexico Historical Review,* Vol. III, No. 1 (part 1, January, 1928), and No. 2 (part 2, April, 1928).

———. "The San Carlos Apache Police," *New Mexico Historical Review,* Vol. IV, No. 3 (part 1, July, 1929), and Vol. V, No. 1 (part 2, January, 1930).

Clum, Woodworth. *Apache Agent: The Story of John P. Clum.* Boston, Houghton, Mifflin, 1936.

Conner, Daniel Ellis. *Joseph Reddeford Walker and the Arizona Adventure.* Ed. and annotated by Donald J. Berthrong and Odessa Davenport. Norman, University of Oklahoma Press, 1956.

Crary, B. F. "Historical Museum Letter," *Pensacola Historical Society Quarterly,* Vol. II, No. 2 (April, 1966).

Cremony, John Carey. *Life among the Apaches.* San Francisco, A. Roman & Company, 1868. Reprinted by Rio Grande Press, Glorieta, N.M., 1969.

Davis, Britton. *The Truth about Geronimo.* New Haven, Yale University Press, 1929.

Edgerton, Joseph K. "A Glimpse of the Sunny South," *Plattsburgh Republican,* Plattsburgh, N.Y., February 25, 1893.

Gage, Lucy. "A Romance of Pioneering," *Chronicles of Oklahoma,* Vol. XXIX, No. 3 (Autumn, 1951).

Goodwin, Grenville. "Experiences of an Indian Scout," *Arizona Historical Review*, Vol. VII, No. 1 (part 1, January, 1936), and No. 2 (part 2, April, 1936).

Hopps, Howard B. "Lawton," *Chronicles of Oklahoma*, Vol. XXIII, No. 3 (Autumn, 1945).

Howard, O[liver] O[tis]. *Famous Indian Chiefs I Have Known*. New York, The Century Company, 1907.

———. *My Life and Experiences among Our Hostile Indians*. Hartford, Conn., A. D. Worthington & Company, 1907.

Institute of the Great Plains. "Lawton." Lawton, Okla., 1971, reprint of early newspaper articles.

Jacobson, O[scar] B[rousse], and Jeanne d'Ucel. "Art in Oklahoma," *Chronicles of Oklahoma*, Vol. XXXII, No. 3 (Autumn, 1954), Jacobson's impressions of Geronimo.

Jordan, Julia A. "Oklahoma's Oral History Collection," *Chronicles of Oklahoma*, Vol. XLIX, No. 2 (Summer, 1971).

Klasner, Lily. *My Girlhood among Outlaws*. Ed. and annotated by Eve Ball. Tucson, University of Arizona Press, 1972.

Miles, Nelson A. *Personal Recollections*. Chicago and New York, The Werner Company, 1897.

———. *Serving the Republic*. Freeport, N.Y., Books for Libraries Press, 1971.

Opler, Morris E[dward]. "A Chiricahua Apache's Account of the Geronimo Campaign of 1886, *New Mexico Historical Review*, Vol. XIII, No. 4 (October, 1938).

Reed, Walter. "Geronimo and His Warriors in Captivity," *The Illustrated American*, Vol. III (August 16, 1890).

Santee, Ross. *Apache Land*. New York, Charles Scribner's Sons, 1947, Chapter 17, Jimmie Stevens' reminiscences.

Schmitt, Martin F. (ed.). *General George Crook: His Autobiography*. Norman, University of Oklahoma Press, 1960.

Scott, Hugh Lenox. *Some Memories of a Soldier*. New York and London, Century Company, 1928.

Thomas, Alfred Barnaby (ed.). *Forgotten Frontiers: A Study of the Spanish Indian Policy of Don Juan Bautista de Anza, Governor of New Mexico, 1777–1787*. Norman, University of Oklahoma Press, 1932.

Wheatley, Richard. "The Caged Tigers of Santa Rosa," *Pensacola Historical Society Quarterly*, Vol. II, No. 2 (April, 1966).

The Women's Missionary Boards of the Reformed Church in America. "The Story of the Apache Prisoners," *Missionary Lesson Leaflet*, Vol. VII, No. 2 (June, 1906).

Wood, Norman B. *Lives of Famous Indian Chiefs.* Aurora, Ill., Indian Historical Publishing Company, 1906.

IV. Interviews

Betzinez, Jason. Apache, Okla., January 26, 1955; August 21, 1959.

Geronimo, Robert. Mescalero, N.M., August 7, 1957.

Hammond, Ruth. Stillwater, Okla., March 11, 1973.

Haozous, Sam. Apache, Okla., January 27, 1955.

Jozhe, Benedict. Marshall, Okla., July 29, 1959; September 16, 1969; April 12, 1971.

Kaywaykla, James. Marshall, Okla., July 29, 1959.

Loco, Moses. Marshall, Okla., July 29, 1959; September 16, 1969.

Naiche, Amelia. Mescalero, N.M., July 23, 1971.

V. Contemporary Newspapers and News Magazines

Arkansas City (Kansas) Traveler. Arkansas City, Kans., June 17, 1970.

Beaver County Democrat. Beaver, Okla., July 18, 1907.

Beaver Herald. Beaver, Okla., August 17, 1911.

Beaver Journal. Beaver, Okla., January 18, 1906.

Lawton Constitution-Democrat (weekly edition). Lawton, Okla., February 18, 25, 1909.

Mangum Star. Mangum, Okla., January 18, 1906.

Muskogee Times-Democrat. Muskogee, Indian Territory, November 8, 1906.

Mobile Daily News. Mobile, Ala., September 12, 1894.

Newsweek. November 7, 1966.

Oklahoma City Times. Oklahoma City, Okla., August 29, 1946.

Oklahoman. Oklahoma City, Okla., September 10, 1902; April 22, 1906; July 26, October 18, 1907; March 1, 1953.

Pensacolian. Pensacola, Fla., September 18, October 23, 30, November 13, 1886; June 11, 1887. Typed articles furnished by National Park Service, Gulf Islands National Seashore, Gulf Breeze, Fla.

Perkins Journal. Perkins, Okla., October 14, 1904.

Vinita Chieftain. Vinita, Indian Territory, July 28, 1904; April 20, 1905.

Secondary Material
I. Manuscript Material

Chapman, Berlin Basil. "Notes—Apaches." In possession of Dr. Chapman, Orlando, Fla.

Goodman, David Michael. "Apaches as Prisoners of War, 1886–1894." Ph.D. dissertation, Texas Christian University, Fort Worth, 1968.

Griswold, Gillett. "The Fort Sill Apaches: Their Vital Statistics, Tribal Origins, Antecedents." U.S. Army Artillery and Missile Center Museum, Archives. Fort Sill, Okla.

Musgrove, Ora E. "A Belated Reward for the Surrender of Geronimo." Unpublished article in possession of Angie Debo.

Pollard, William Grosvenor, III. "Structure and Stress: Social Change among the Fort Sill Apache and Their Ancestors, 1870–1960." M.A. thesis, University of Oklahoma, Norman, 1965.

Siegel, Martha R. "Field Notes." In possession of Martha R. Blaine, Oklahoma City, Okla.

II. Government Publications

Hodge, Frederick Webb (ed.), *Handbook of American Indians North of Mexico. Bureau of American Ethnology, Bulletin No. 30.* Washington, Government Printing Office, 1907–10.

Mooney, James. "The Ghost-Dance Religion and the Sioux Outbreak of 1890," *Bureau of American Ethnology Fourteenth Annual Report.* Washington, Government Printing Office, 1896.

Royce, Charles C. "Indian Land Cessions in the United States," *Bureau of American Ethnology Eighteenth Annual Report*, Part 2. Washington, Government Printing Office, 1899.

III. Books and Articles

Baylor, George Wythe. *John Robert Baylor, Confederate Governor of Arizona.* Ed. and annotated by Odie B. Faulk. Tucson, Arizona Pioneers Historical Society, 1966.

Borden, W. C. "The Vital Statistics of an Apache Indian Community." Boston, Damrell & Upham, 1893. Reprint from *Boston Medical and Surgical Journal*, July 6, 1893.

Debo, Angie. *A History of the Indians of the United States.* Norman, University of Oklahoma Press, 1970.

Faulk, Odie B. *The Geronimo Campaign.* New York, Oxford University Press, 1969.

————. *Too Far North: Too Far South.* Los Angeles, Westernlore Press, 1967.

Federal Writers' Program. *New Mexico: A Guide to the Colorful State.* New York, Hastings House, 1953.

Forbes, Jack D. *Apache, Navaho, and Spaniard.* Norman, University of Oklahoma Press, 1960.

Gipson, Fred. *Fabulous Empire.* Boston, Houghton Mifflin Company, 1946.

Harper, Richard H. "The Missionary Work of the Reformed (Dutch) Church in America, in Oklahoma," *Chronicles of Oklahoma,* Vol. XVIII, No. 4 (December, 1940).

Jozhe, Benedict. "A Brief History of the Fort Sill Apache Tribe," *Chronicles of Oklahoma,* Vol. XXXIX, No. 4 (Winter, 1961/62).

La Farge, Oliver. *A Pictorial History of the American Indian.* New York, Crown Publishing Company, 1956.

Lockwood, Frank C. *The Apache Indians.* New York, The Macmillan Company, 1938.

Nye, W[ilbur] S[turtevant]. *Carbine and Lance.* Norman, University of Oklahoma Press, 1937.

Ogle, Ralph Hedrick. *Federal Control of the Western Apaches, 1848–1886.* Albuquerque, University of New Mexico Press, 1970.

Opler, Morris Edward. *An Apache Life-Way.* Chicago, University of Chicago Press, 1941.

————. *Apache Odyssey: A Journey between Two Worlds.* New York, Holt, Rinehart, and Winston, 1969.

————. "Mountain Spirits of the Chiricahua Apache," *The Masterkey,* Vol. XX, No. 4 (July, 1946).

————. "Some Implications of Culture Theory for Anthropology and Psychology," *American Journal of Orthopsychiatry,* Vol. XVIII (October, 1948).

Page, Elizabeth M. *In Camp and Tepee.* New York. Chicago, Fleming H. Revell Company, 1915.

Peterson, Karen Douglas. *Plains Indian Art from Fort Marion.* Norman, University of Oklahoma Press, 1971.

Sonnichsen, C. L. *The Mescalero Apaches*. Norman, University of Oklahoma Press, 1958.

Thrapp, Dan L. *Al Sieber, Chief of Scouts*. Norman, University of Oklahoma Press, 1964.

———. *The Conquest of Apacheria*. Norman, University of Oklahoma Press, 1967.

———. *General Crook and the Sierra Madre Adventure*. Norman, University of Oklahoma Press, 1972.

———. "Geronimo's Mysterious Surrender," *Brand Book*, Los Angeles Corral, Vol. XIII (1969).

———. *Juh: An Incredible Indian. Southwestern Studies, Monograph No. 39*. El Paso, Texas Western Press, 1973.

———. *Victorio and the Mimbres Apaches*. Norman, University of Oklahoma Press, 1974.

Turner, Katherine C. *Red Men Calling on the Great White Father*. Norman, University of Oklahoma Press, 1951.

IV. Interviews

Ball, Eve. Ruidoso, New Mexico, July 23–28, 1971.

V. Letters

Ball, Eve. December 10, 1957; December 20, 1960; March 8, 1971; February 27, November 13, 1972; February 27, March 10, June 25, 26, July 13, 1973.

Blaine, Garland J. August 21, 1974.

Clark, Elaine. June 5, 1973.

Rudisill, Richard. July 17, 1972; July 8, 1975.

Self, Frank J. February 12, 1973.

Slonaker, John J. July 9, 1973.

Thrapp, Dan L. December 8, 1972.

INDEX

P/B

p H X

5o

p

4748